THEATER
The Lively Art

FOURTH EDITION

THEATER
The Lively Art

Edwin Wilson

The City University of New York

Alvin Goldfarb

Illinois State University

Boston   Burr Ridge, IL   Dubuque, IA   Madison, WI   New York
San Francisco   St. Louis   Bangkok   Bogotá   Caracas   Kuala Lumpur
Lisbon   London   Madrid   Mexico City   Milan   Montreal   New Delhi
Santiago   Seoul   Singapore   Sydney   Taipei   Toronto

Photos by Donald Cooper/PhotoStage

Front cover: Left to right: Alexandra Gilbreath as Rosalind and Nancy Carroll as Celia in AS YOU LIKE IT by William Shakespeare, Royal Shakespeare Company production.

Back cover: Left to right: Ralph Fiennes as King Richard II and Linus Roache as Henry Bolingbroke in RICHARD II by William Shakespeare, Almeida Theatre Company production, Gainsborough Studios, London.

McGraw-Hill Higher Education

*A Division of The **McGraw-Hill** Companies*

THEATER: THE LIVELY ART

Published by McGraw-Hill, an imprint of The McGraw-Hill Companies, Inc. 1221 Avenue of the Americas, New York, NY, 10020. Copyright ©2002, 1999, 1996, 1991, by Edwin Wilson and Alvin Goldfarb. All rights reserved. No part of this publication may be reproduced or distributed in any form or by any means, or stored in a database or retrieval system, without the prior written consent of The McGraw-Hill Companies, Inc., including, but not limited to, in any network or other electronic storage or transmission, or broadcast for distance learning. Some ancillaries, including electronic and print components, may not be available to customers outside the United States.

This book is printed on acid-free paper.

3 4 5 6 7 8 9 0 VNH/VNH 0 9 8 7 6 5 4 3 2

ISBN 0-07-240718-2

Editorial director: *Phillip A. Butcher*
Associate editor: *Allison McNamara*
Senior marketing manager: *David Patterson*
Project manager: *Karen J. Nelson*
Production supervisor: *Rose Hepburn*
Director of design: *Keith J. McPherson*
Senior supplement coordinator: *Rose M. Range*
Photo researcher coordinator: *Judy Kausal*
Photo researcher: *Inge King*
Media technology producer: *Shannon Rider*
Cover Design: *Keith J. McPherson*
Interior Design: *Maureen McCutcheon*
Compositor: *Carlisle Communications, Ltd.*
Typeface: *10/12 Sabon*
Printer: *Von Hoffmann Press Inc.*

Library of Congress Cataloging in Publication Data

Wilson, Edwin
    Theater: The lively art / Edwin Wilson, Alvin Goldfarb, –4th ed.
        p.   cm
    Includes bibliographical references and index.
    ISBN 0-07-240718-2
    1. Theater   2. Theater–History.   I. Goldfarb, Alvin   II. Title.
    PN2037.W57   2002
    792–dc21   2001030494

To Our Wives,
Catherine Wilson & Elaine Goldfarb

Brief Contents

Preface   xxi

Introduction   1

PART 1
Creating Theater

1	Audiences and Critics	19
2	Stage Performers	37
3	The Director and the Producer	59
4	Theater Spaces	77
5	Designers: Scenery and Costumes	97
6	Designers: Lighting and Sound	123
7	The Playwright	143
8	The Text: Dramatic Genres	173
9	Profile of a Production	193

PART 2
Theater Tradition and Theater Today

10	Greek and Roman Theater	209
11	Asian and Medieval Theater	233
12	Renaissance Theater	255
13	Theater from 1660 to 1875	287
14	Modern Theater: 1875 to 1945	317
15	Modern Theater: 1945 to 1990	341
16	Contemporary Trends	369

Glossary   390

Bibliography   399

Index   405

Contents

Preface   **xxi**

Introduction   1

Experiencing Theater   1
Theater as an Art Form   7
   What is Art?   7
   The Art of Theater   10
Summary   14

PART 1

Creating Theater

CHAPTER 1

Audiences and Critics   19

The Theater Audience   20
How the Audience Participates   22
Diversity of Audiences   23
Play Synopsis: *Fences*   26
The Theater Critic   28
What is Criticism?   28
Critics and Reviewers   28
Getting Started in Theater—*Mel Gussow: Critic*   29
Preparing for Criticism   30
Criteria for Criticism   30
Descriptive versus Prescriptive Criticism   34
Summary   35
Theater on the Web   35

CHAPTER 2

Stage Performers   37

A Historical Perspective: Demands of Classical Acting   38

Three Challenges of Acting   40

Getting Started in Theater—*James Earl Jones: Performer*   41

   Mastering the Craft of Acting   42

   Making Characters Believable   46

Play Synopsis: *The Cherry Orchard*   49

   Synthesis and Integration   54

Making Connections: Acting   55

Judging Performances   56

Summary   57

Theater on the Web   57

CHAPTER 3

The Director and the Producer   59

The Director   60

   Evolution of the Director   60

   The Auteur Director   61

   The Director at Work   62

Getting Started in Theater—*Richard Foreman:*
Director, Playwright, and Designer   63

Getting Started in Theater—*Zelda Fichlander:*
Director and Artistic Director   68

   The Director's Collaborators   68

The Producer or Manager   70

   Producers in Commercial Theater   70

   Noncommercial Theaters   71

Summary   73

Theater on the Web   74

CHAPTER 4

Theater Spaces   77

Proscenium or Picture-Frame Stage: History and Characteristics   78

Thrust Stage: History and Characteristics   82

Arena Stage: History and Characteristics   87

Making Connections: Popular Performance Spaces   90

Created or Found Spaces   91

Multifocus Environments   92

All-Purpose and Experimental Spaces   93
Summary   94
Theater on the Web   94

CHAPTER 5

Designers: Scenery and Costumes   97

Scene Design   98
  The Scene Designer's Objectives   98
Getting Started in Theater—*Robin Wagner: Scene Designer*   99
  Elements of Scene Design   104
  The Process of Scene Design: Steps in the Design Process   109
  The Scene Designer's Collaborators   110
  Designing a Total Environment   111
Costume Design   111
  The Costume Designer   112
  The Costume Designer's Objectives   112
Getting Started in Theater—*Jess Goldstein: Costume Designer*   113
  Elements of Costume Design   115
  The Costume Designer's Collaborators   119
Summary   120
Theater on the Web   120

CHAPTER 6

Designers: Lighting and Sound   123

Stage Lighting   124
  Lighting in Theater History   124
Getting Started in Theater—*Peggy Eisenhauer: Lighting Designer*   125
  Objectives of Lighting Design   125
  Elements of Stage Lighting   128
  The Lighting Designer's Resources   131
  The Lighting Designer's Collaborators   134
Sound Design   134
  The Sound Designer   134
  Objectives of Sound Design   134
  Sound Reproduction and Sound Reinforcement   135
  Elements of Sound: Sound Technology   136
  The Sound Designer's Collaborators   138
Special Effects in Lighting and Sound   138
Summary   140
Theater on the Web   140

CHAPTER 7

The Playwright   143

The Playwright's Centrality   144
Getting Started in Theater—*Emily Mann: Playwright–Director*   **145**
The Playwright's Tasks   145
Subject   146
Focus and Emphasis   146
Dramatic Purpose   147
Making Connections: Writers   **148**
Structure in Drama   150
   Essentials of Dramatic Structure   *150*
   Creating a Dramatic Structure   *153*
Getting Started in Theater—*August Wilson: Playwright*   **154**
   Two Basic Structures: Climactic and Episodic   *156*
Play Synopsis: *Mother Courage and Her Children*   **162**
   Other Dramatic Structures   *163*
Creating Dramatic Characters   164
   Types of Dramatic Characters   *165*
   Juxtaposition of Characters   *168*
Summary   169
Theater on the Web   170

CHAPTER 8

The Text: Dramatic Genres   173

What Is Genre?   174
Tragedy   174
   Conditions for Tragedy: Theater and Society   *176*
   Traditional Tragedy   *177*
   Modern Tragedy   *179*
Comedy   180
   Characteristics of Comedy   *180*
   Forms of Comedy   *183*
Play Synopsis: *Tartuffe*   **184**
Heroic Drama   185
Melodrama   187
Domestic or Bourgeois Drama   187
Tragicomedy   188
Shakespearean Tragicomedy   189
Modern Tragicomedy   189
Summary   190
Theater on the Web   191

CHAPTER 9

Profile of a Production — 193

PART 2

Theater Tradition and Theater Today

CHAPTER 10

Greek and Roman Theater — 209

Origins of Theater — 210
Greece — 211
    Background: The Golden Age of Greece — 211
    Theater and Culture: Greek Theater Emerges — 211
Timeline: Greece — 212
Greek Tragedy — 214
Living History: *Antigone* — 215
Play Synopsis: *King Oedipus* — 217
    Greek Comedy — 219
    Theater Production in Greece — 220
    Dramatic Criticism in Greece: Aristotle — 220
    Later Greek Theater — 221
Rome — 221
    Background: Rome and Its Civilization — 221
    Theater and Culture in Rome — 222
    Popular Entertainment in Rome — 222
Timeline: Rome — 223
Roman Comedy: Plautus and Terence — 224
Living History: *The Menaechmi* — 225
    Roman Tragedy: Seneca — 226
    Making Connections: Greek and Roman Popular Arts — 227
    Dramatic Criticism in Rome: Horace — 228
    Theater Production in Rome — 228
    Decline of Roman Theater — 229
Summary — 231
Theater on the Web — 231

CHAPTER 11

Asian and Medieval Theater — 233

Asia — 234
    Background: Asian Theater — 234
    Theater in India — 234
Timeline: Asia — 236

Contents   xiii

Living History: *The Sea Gull*   326
    Realistic Theater between 1915 and 1945   327
Timeline: 1915 to 1945   328
Departures from Realism   330
    Antirealist Playwrights: Ibsen, Strindberg, and Wedekind   330
    Symbolism   331
    Antirealist Designers: Appia and Craig   332
    Russian Theatricalism: Meyerhold   332
    Early Eclectics   334
    Departures from Realism: 1915–1945   334
Totalitarianism, the Second World War, and Theater   337
Summary   338
Theater on the Web   338

CHAPTER 15

Modern Theater: 1945 to 1990   341

Postwar Realistic Theater   342
    Background: The Postwar Era   342
Timeline: 1945 to 2000   343
    American Selective Realism   344
Play Synopsis: *Death of Salesman*   345
    The "Angry Young Men" in England and Documentary
     Drama in Germany   346
Experimentation and Departures from Realism: 1945 to 1980   346
Living History: *Waiting for Godot*   347
    Existentialism and Theater of the Absurd   348
    Experimental Theater   349
Play Synopsis: *Waiting for Godot*   350
    Postwar Eclectics   351
Developments in Postwar American Theater   352
    African American Theater   352
    Musical Theater   356
    Alternatives to Commercial Theater   361
Making Connections: Film and the Other Mass Media   362
Summary   366
Theater on the Web   367

CHAPTER 16

Contemporary Trends   369

The Beginning of a New Century   370
Today's Theater: Diversity and Eclecticism   370
    Asian American Theater   371
    Hispanic Theater   372
    Native American Theater   374
    Feminist Theater   374
Play Synopsis: *Fefu and Her Friends*   376
    Gay and Lesbian Theater   377
    Performance Art   378
    Postmodernism   380
    International Trends   382
    Two African Playwrights   382
Today and Tomorrow: A Look Ahead   384
Making Connections: The Digital Arts   386
Summary   387
Theater on the Web   387

Glossary   390

Bibliography   399

Index   405

Getting Started in Theater

Mel Gussow: *Critic* 29

James Earl Jones: *Performer* 41

Richard Foreman: *Director, Playwright, and Designer* 63

Zelda Fichlander: *Director and Artistic Director* 68

Robin Wagner: *Scene Designer* 99

Jess Goldstein: *Costume Designer* 113

Peggy Eisenhauer: *Lighting Designer* 125

Emily Mann: *Playwright-Director* 145

August Wilson: *Playwright* 154

Synopses of Plays

Fences 26

The Cherry Orchard 49

Mother Courage and Her Children 162

Tartuffe 184

King Oedipus 217

Sotoba Komachi 243

The Way of the World 293

A Doll's House 322

Death of a Salesman 345

Waiting for Godot 350

Fefu and Her Friends 376

Timelines

Greece 212
Rome 223
Asia 236
Middle Ages 247
Italian Renaissance 257
English Renaissance 265
Spanish Golden Age 275
Neoclassical France 281
English Restoration 290
Eighteenth Century 296
Nineteenth Century, 1800 to 1875 306
1875 to 1915 319
1915 to 1945 328
1945 to 2000 343

Living History

Antigone 215
The Menaechmi 225
Sotoba Komachi 241
Noah's Ark 249
Commedia dell'Arte 259
Hamlet 268
The King, The Greatest Alcalde 276
Tartuffe 282
The Country Wife 291
The Marriage of Figaro 301
The Sea Gull 326
Waiting for Godot 347

Making Connections

Acting 55
Popular Performance Spaces 90
Writers 148
Greek and Roman Popular Arts 227
The Popular Arts of Shakespeare's Time 272
Nineteenth-Century Popular Theatrical Arts 310
Film and the Other Mass Media 362
The Digital Arts 386

Preface

Theater is not only an art form, it is one of the performing arts. As such its quality is elusive. Theater exists only at the moment when a performance occurs, and to study it in a book or classroom is to be one step removed from that immediate experience. This fact is uppermost in the minds of those who teach theater in a classroom setting. At the same time, it is also known that an introduction to theater course can immeasurably enhance an audience's comprehension of theater.

The experience of seeing theater can be many times more meaningful if audience members understand a number of things: the component parts of theater; the various creative artists and technicians who make it happen; the tradition and historical background from which theater springs; and the genre or movement of which a particular play is a part. It is our hope that *Theater: The Lively Art* will provide the background to make this possible and that it will encourage and inspire students to become lifelong audience members if not actual participants in theater.

In its fourth edition, *Theater: The Lively Art* remains a comprehensive introductory theater text that incorporates a number of elements in one volume: an introduction to the audience's experience of theater, an investigation of the elements of theater, and a study of the important developments in the history of theater.

Several things set *Theater: The Lively Art* apart from other introductory texts. A particularly important element is our emphasis on the audience. All students reading the book, we assume, are potential theatergoers, not just in their college years but throughout their lives. We have therefore, attempted to make *Theater: The Lively Art* an ideal one-volume text to prepare students as future audience members. It will give them a grasp of how theater functions, of how it should be viewed and judged, and of the tradition behind any performance they may attend.

In addition to serving as an ideal text for nonmajors, *Theater: The Lively Art* will also prepare students who wish to continue studies in theater, as majors, as minors, or as students from other disciplines who take advanced courses. It provides a foundation for further studies in every aspect of theater: acting, directing, design, dramatic literature, history, theory, and criticism.

Organization

Part One: Creating Theater

Part One, Creating Theater, introduces students to the people who make theater possible, to the elements of theater, and to significant concepts of theater. We explore first the role of the audience. Not only do audiences form a vital link in any theater event, but students will find themselves in the role of audience members more frequently than in any other.

We then investigate acting and directing, including various acting techniques and methods of training performers, as well as the major approaches to directing. We study design and technical production, including the nuts-and-bolts aspects of scenery, costumes, lighting, and sound. We look at the work of the playwright, or the person or group creating a script, particularly in the creation of dramatic structure and dramatic characters.

Following that we investigate point of view in a text as expressed in tragedy, comedy, tragicomedy, melodrama, and so forth.

Getting Started in Theater. In separate boxes throughout Part One, autobiographical accounts from playwrights, performers, directors, designers, and others explain how various individuals became attracted to theater, received their training, and were given their first opportunities to work in theater. Students should find these firsthand accounts not only informative but insightful, providing them with a genuine sense of what involvement in theater means.

Plot Summaries. Summaries of plays, set aside in boxes within individual chapters, provide the necessary context for discussion of both the elements and the history of theater (Parts One and Two). All together, eleven important plays, ranging from Greek to modern and including representative works by Asian, African-American, and women playwrights, are included. The summaries, moreover, are comprehensive accounts of the action of these plays. We have added a new feature to the plot synopses in Part One—questions for consideration at the end of each play summary, which link it to chapter topics.

Chapter 9: Profile of a Production

This chapter bridges Part One and Part Two. We trace a production of *The Taming of the Shrew* from its inception to the final production, showing how the elements of Part One

intersect with the historical material in Part Two.

Part Two: Theater Tradition and Theater Today

In Part Two, Theater Tradition and Theater Today, we begin with Greek theater and continue through to the present. This look at the history of theater is not intended to be definitive and in no way should it be viewed as a substitute for advanced courses on theater history. At the same time, we believe that we have covered every important movement, every key figure, and every relevant aspect of the development of theater.

The final three chapters (Chapters 14, 15, 16) are devoted to theater of the past hundred years. The forces that began a century ago—in realism and departures from realism, in acting techniques, in the emergence of the director, in scene and lighting design—defined the theater we have today. As we point out in Chapter 16, ours is a diverse, eclectic theater, rich in variety and innovation. We look at the many crosscurrents and trends making up the theater that students of today and audiences of tomorrow will be attending.

Historical Context. Within the chapters dealing with theater history, each section contains background information on the political, scientific, and cultural milieu in which theater developments unfold.

Time Lines. For each period and country, time lines outline landmark events and accomplishments in the social and political arenas on one side and significant theater events on the other.

Living Histories. Every period includes a narrative of an actual event, taking the readers back in time so that they have a sense of being present in the audience at a performance of, say, *Antigone* in Athens in 441 B.C., or at the premiere of *Hamlet* at the Globe Theater in London.

Writing Style

This same sense of immediacy and personalization has been a goal, as well, in our writing style. We have attempted to write *Theater: The Lively Art* in the most readable language possible. To this end, we have dispensed with dry, pedantic language, and wherever possible we have avoided "laundry lists" of names, dates, and titles. The book contains a wealth of information, but we hope it is presented in a manner that makes it vivid and alive.

New to This Edition

This fourth edition of *Theater: The Lively Art* includes extensive revisions and substantive changes from previous editions. These improvements will be of great benefit, we believe, to both faculty members and students.

Changes in Content

There are a number of significant changes and additions in the fourth edition of *Theater: The Lively Art*. The material on diversity in today's theater has been moved from Chapter 1 to the final chapter, where it more appropriately belongs. As a result, Chapter 1 has become a more streamlined discussion of the theater audience, along with a discussion of the critic. In the section on the critic we have added an important feature: two contrasting reviews of the same production, which demonstrate differences in the opinions of even highly respected and well-known critics.

In Chapter 2 we have taken account of important acting teachers of modern theater such as Sanford Meisner, and in Chapter 4 we have added coverage of multifocus events. In Chapters 5 and 6 we have made all headings consistent throughout so that discussions of designers will unfold according to predictable, understandable logic.

Major changes have been undertaken in Chapter 7 and Chapter 8. We have reversed much of the material in these two chapters to reflect current thinking. Chapter 7 is now devoted to the playwright, or to other artists who prepare a text, including the development of dramatic structure and dramatic characters. Chapter 8 covers the text itself, especially in terms of genre.

Chapter 9 features a new stage production, with more photographs—and especially more color photographs—than appeared in the previous edition.

In Chapter 11, the material on Asia now precedes medieval theater—a plan that is more logical and understandable historically.

Chapter 16 has been considerably updated, and (as noted above) the extensive material on modern diversity and multiculturalism formerly found in Chapter 1 has been placed here, within its historical context.

Production Shots

Another feature of this new edition is more than 200 photographs, most of them in color, which are directly tied to the text. The illustrations—both photographs and line drawings—do not exist in isolation but explain and enhance the material in the text. Moreover, the photographs have been selected to be dynamic and "dramatic" in and of themselves.

Not only are there more photographs, but the entire book has been redesigned to create more visual interest and to make the material easier to understand and assimilate. The new design and the extended photo program make for a bolder and more vibrant text.

Making Connections

A key addition to the fourth edition of *Theater: The Lively Art* is a special feature called "Making Connections." This segment examines the close relationship of theater and other forms of popular entertainment through the ages, from the mimes and jugglers of ancient Rome to the circuses and vaudeville of the nineteenth century to the rock concerts and theme parks of today.

Theater on the Web

In response to the expanding community of theater sites on the World Wide Web, we have added to the conclusion of each chapter a boxed feature: "Theater on the Web." This entirely new section guides students in exploration of chapter topics on the Internet. Links to reliable, up-to-date sites tie the content of each chapter to the World Wide Web and are available on the book's Online Learning Center www.mhhe.com/livelyart.

Support for Instructors

Please note: The supplements listed here and below in Support for Students *may accompany this text. Please contact your local McGraw-Hill representative for details concerning policies, prices, and availability, as some restrictions may apply. If you are not sure who your representative is, you can find him or her by using the Rep Locator at* www.mhhe.com.

Instructor's Manual

McGraw-Hill offers an Instructor's Manual to all instructors who adopt *Theater: The Lively Art* for their courses. Each chapter of the Instructor's Manual includes:

- Overview and outline of the text chapter
- List of significant names and terms found in the chapter
- Questions for student essays or discussions
- Suggestions for demonstrations and exercises for class involvement
- Play recommendations for the chapter

The last section of the Instructor's Manual contains a sample test bank, organized by chapter, for in-class quizzes and testing.

Computerized Test Bank

The test questions from the Instructor's Manual are available on MicroTest CD, a powerful but easy-to-use test-generating program that runs on both Windows and Macintosh personal computers. With MicroTest, you can easily view and select the test item, file questions, and then print a test and answer key. You can customize questions, headings, and instruction; you can add or import questions of your own; and you can print your test in a choice of fonts allowed by your printer.

Online Learning Center: www.mhhe.com/livelyart

The website and online Learning Center is an internet-based resource for students and faculty. Instructor's Resources are password-protected and offer the complete text of the Instructor's Manual, a correlation guide for *Anthology of Living Theater* and *Theater: The Lively Art,* and a link to our customizable database of plays. To receive a password for the site, contact your local sales representative or e-mail us at theater@mcgraw-hill.com.

Additionally, the online Learning Center offers chapter-by-chapter quizzes for testing students. These brief quizzes are separate from those offered in the Instructor's Manual and generate instant grades; the results can be e-mailed directly to the instructor with the click of a button (see Student Resources below). This special quizzing feature is a valuable tool for the instructor who requires a quick way to check reading comprehension and basic understanding without using up valuable class time.

Student Resources

Making the Grade CD-ROM

This CD-ROM, packaged free with the text, provides students with an excellent resource that offers enrichment, review, and self-testing. The following components are included:

- Internet Primer
- Study skills primer
- Guide to electronic research in theater
- Multiple-choice questions for each chapter—graded automatically
- Learning assessment
- Link to the book's website.

McGraw-Hill Theatergoer's Guide

A recently revised *Theatergoer's Guide* is packaged with every copy of the text. The guide is an excellent introduction to the art of attending and critiquing a play, from making theater reservations and knowing when to applaud to evaluating a performance and doing research on the Internet.

Online Learning Center: www.mhhe.com/livelyart

McGraw-Hill offers extensive Web resources for students with Internet access. Students will find the Online Learning Center of particular use with *Theater: The Lively Art*. For each chapter, it offers glossary terms, chapter objectives, discussion questions, and online testing. In addition, the site offers links to promote getting involved in theater and conducting research on the web. Visit www.mhhe.com/livelyart.

McGraw-Hill Guide to Electronic Research in Theater

This brief booklet is designed to assist students in locating theater sites on the Web, evaluating on-site information, and referencing on-line sources. This supplement can be packaged free with the text.

Acknowledgments

There is a long list of colleagues and others who have helped to make this book possible and to whom we are deeply grateful. We thank Prof. J. Thomas Rimer and Prof. James V. Hatch for providing valuable material on Asian theater and African-American theater respectively. In addition, we are particularly grateful to Sam Lieter of Brooklyn College CUNY for reviewing and assisting in the revision of the Asian section. Scott Walters developed the Instructor's Manual. Michael Ricci of Hibbing Community College for his contribution to the Making the Grade CD-ROM. Susan Tenneriello compiled the index. John Sipes of the Oregon Shakespeare Festival and Barbara Acker of Arizona State University, respectively, provided the movement and voice exercises in Chapter 2. At Illinois State University, a number of people provided computer assistance. We would particularly like to thank Georgia Bennett, David Williams, David Kuntz, and Jody DeCremer. Steve Meckstroth, of Illinois State University's Milner Library, was also of great assistance, as were Kymberly Harris, Michelle Sullivan, Robyn Jackson, Mary Ellen O'Hara, and Travis Stern—theater graduate assistants—in research and in a number of other areas. A further expression of thanks to everyone at the ISU Shakespeare Festival who made Chapter 9 possible.

Reviewers

The following people, who read and commented on the manuscript in various stages of development, made important contributions to the final result: B. J. Bray, University of Arkansas at Little Rock; Beverly Byrd, Mesa Community College; Edward Douglas, Glendale Community College; Julia Gagne, Valencia Community College; Michael Gravois, University of Memphis; Lani Johnson, Central Connecticut

State University; Michael Kirkland, Kutztown University; Nina LeNoir, Minnesota State University–Mankato; Donald Lillie, Missouri Western; John Murphy, Youngstown State University; Tina Redd, University of Washington; Susan Reinecke, Guilford Technical Community College; Tom Smith, New Mexico State University.

Questionnaire Respondents

Barbara Alkofer, *Southeastern Oklahoma State University*
David Allen, *Midland College*
John Anglin, *East Central College*
Scott Blanks, *Benedict College*
John Brokaw, *University of Texas at Austin*
Malcolm Callery, *California University of Pennsylvania*
Lou Campbell, *Belhaven College*
Jack Carroll, *Darion College*
Joyce Cavarozzi, *Wichita State University*
Thorne Compton, *University of South Carolina*
Marcia Cook, *Sewanee—The University of the South*
Michael Corriston, *Southeast Community College*
Renee Dobson, *Ohio Northern University*
Kathleen Downs, *Tennessee Wesleyan College*
Charles Falcon, *San Antonio College*
Greg Fiebig, *Southwest Baptist University*
James Filippelli, *Dominican College*

James Fisher, *Wabash College*
Carol Fisher, *Highland Community College*
Steven Folstein, *University of Wisconsin–Mamtowoe*
John Galyean, *Abraham Baldwin Agricultural College*
Joanna Goff, *Blue Mountain Community College*
Judyth Gonzalez, *Delta College*
Kiki Gounaridou, *Smith College*
Albert Harris Jr., *University of Louisvile*
Brad Hellwig, *University of Georgia*
David Hoover, *University of New Orleans*
Clark Hutton, *Volunteer State Community College*
Patrick Immel, *Northwest Missouri State University*
Joe Jeffreys, *SUNY at Stony Brook*
Robin Johnson, *Capital University*
Arnie Johnston, *Western Michigan University*
Jasmin Lambert, *College of William and Mary*
David Magidson, *Wayne State University*
Mark Mallett, *Morehead State University*
Nancy McCoy, *College of the Canyons*
Susan McCully, *Worcester State College*
Bill McPherson, *Nunez Community College*
Michelle Michael-Lippens, *Erie Community College North*
James Moore, *University of Pittsburgh at Johnstown*
Paul Msoczka, *Plymouth State College*

Sara Nalley, *Columbia College*
Harold Nichols, *Georgia Southwestern State University*
Debra Otte, *Long Island University*
John Pereira, *Nassau Community College*
Cindy Peterson, *Mid-American Nazarene University*
Richard Pettengill, *DePaul University*
Tony Piazza, *Allen County Community College*
Rick Plummer, *West Shore Community College*
Anne Pluto, *Lesley College*
Kimberly Poppiti, *Dowling College*
Norman Roberts, *Northampton Community College*
John Rude, *Victor Valley College*
Frances Ruoff, *Kingsborough Community College*
Belinda Russell, *Northeast MS Community College*
Pam Saalfeld, *Northeast Community College*
Albin Sandau, *Black Hills State University*
Jan Savage, *University of West Florida*
Robert Schweitzer, *Edinboro University*
Brian Simmons, *Cascade College*
Mary Jo Sodd, *Central College*
Janet Speer, *Lees-McRae College*
Robin Stone, *St. Louis Community College–Forest Park*
Frank Thornton, *Duquesne University*
Rebecca Thrash, *University of Central Arkansas*

Eric Trumbull, *Northern Virginia Community College*

Patrick Vaughn, *Angelina College*

Daniel Watermeier, *University of Toledo*

Cynthia Watts, *Atlanta Metropolitan College*

Kevin Wetmore, *Denison University*

F. Larry Wheeler, *Hardin-Simmons University*

John Wilk, *City College of San Francisco*

Bob Willenbrink, *University of Central Arkansas*

L. K. Williamson, *University of Texas at Dallas*

Antoinette Winstead, *Our Lady of the Lake University*

Sallie Wolfe, *Arapahoe Community College*

John Woodtin, *University of Missouri*

Robert Yowell, *Northern Arizona University*

Finally—at McGraw-Hill—we are grateful to our extraordinary editor, Allison McNamara, who has been enormously supportive and helpful throughout. We extend our appreciation as well to our project manager, Karen Nelson; designer, Keith McPherson; editorial assistant, Ashaki Charles; and our marketing manager, David Patterson. We also express our deep appreciation to and continued admiration for two longtime associates: Susan Gamer, our unsurpassed copy editor; and Inge King, our inspired and ever resourceful photography editor.

Edwin Wilson

Alvin Goldfarb

Introduction

Experiencing Theater

We have used the term *lively art* in the title of our book on theater because we believe that theater is the liveliest of human activities. Think of how often we use theater as a metaphor to describe an activity in daily life. We say that someone is melodramatic or highly theatrical or acts like a prima donna. When we don't believe children, we say that they are play-acting. We refer to the battleground on which a war is fought as its theater. As we will note in Chapter 2, acting is part of our everyday lives. We describe the role-playing we do in our professional and personal spheres as if we were performers on the stage of life. Children and adults imitate behaviors that they admire, in the same way as actors and actresses mimic behavior.

Clearly, theater is an activity that we use to describe how we live. And theatricality is all around us in many of the popular forms that engage us. The relationship between theater, film, and television, for example, is quite apparent. On television, we can see a wide range of dramatic offerings. Daytime soap operas present a variety of domestic crises in family and other relationships; nighttime situation comedies depict young as well as middle-age characters in farcical and humorous encounters; hospital and police shows present the thrills and suspense of traditional melodrama. On television even news documentaries are framed in dramatic terms: a car crash in which a prom queen dies; a spy caught because of an E-mail message; a high government official or a corporate officer accused of sexual harassment.

As for movies, they provide dramatic material of many kinds: science fiction, romantic comedies, action-packed stories of intrigue, historical epics, and even film versions of such Shakespearean plays as *Hamlet, Othello,* and *Romeo and Juliet.* And then there is a combination of film and video when we watch movies at home on a VCR or DVD player.

When we turn from electronic media to live performance, we see that theater has informed and influenced a popular musical form with which we are all familiar: rock and roll. Throughout its history, rock has appropriated theatrical elements. In addition, when they have come under attack for being too controversial in terms of subject matter or performance style, many rock stars have used theatrical comparisons to defend their work. When Madonna undertook the

THEATRICALITY IN THE
POPULAR ARTS
*Good examples of the
cross-over of theatrical
elements between popular
art and traditional theater
are the elaborate
presentations by a number
of rock groups, which
employ stunning lighting,
sound, and scenic effects. A
case in point is the concert
seen here of the group N'
Sync. Note the cloud
effects, the striking lighting,
and the fact that the
members of the group are
suspended above the stage
like giant puppets. (Chris
Pizzello/AP/Wide World
Photos)*

controversial tour that was documented in the film *Truth or Dare*, she justified the performance as follows:

> *My show is not a conventional rock show, but a theatrical presentation of my music. And like theater, it asks questions, provokes thought, and takes you on an emotional journey—portraying good and bad, light and dark, joy and sorrow, redemption and salvation.*[1]

Like Madonna, numerous rock stars have created theatrical characters for their performances. In the 1950s, Little Richard developed a highly theatrical identity, as did Elvis Presley. In the 1960s, the Beatles adopted theatrical personae for themselves which translated well into two films: *A Hard Day's Night* and *Help*. In the 1970s and 1980s, David Bowie, Alice Cooper, Kiss, and The Village People used costumes, props, and makeup to create theatrical characterizations. The actual performers were often less recognizable than their stage personae.

An extremely controversial contemporary performer is Marilyn Manson, who argues that his concerts, which contain simulated acts of violence and sexu-

---

[1]Madonna, from the documentary film, *Truth or Dare*, Dir. by Alex Keshishian, Miramax Films.

ality, are pieces of theater. The connection between rock performance and theater is also illustrated by the many rock stars who have acted, including Elvis Presley, the Beatles, Madonna, Ice T, Tupac Shakur, and Prince, to name just a few.

Current rock concerts are also highly theatrical events, using live performers, lights, sound, and properties in ways that are like multimedia stage presentations. For example, the extremely popular group N' Sync employs all these elements as well as highly theatrical choreography, including a number in which the members appear as dancing puppets attached to strings, in an attempt to bombard their audiences' senses. The teenage phenomenon Britney Spears also stages her concerts like pieces of theater performance, employing spectacular lighting effects and dance routines. Without such theatrical elements, audiences would not be so emotionally engaged in these events.

Rock illustrates that we have come to expect theatrical elements as part of our popular entertainments and that theater is around us in many unexpected venues. Amusement parks like Disneyworld, Sea World, and Universal studios incorporate theatrical material; most, for example, present staged productions based on films, which attract huge audiences.

In cities such as Orlando, Florida, dinner theaters present theatrical entertainments based on Roman gladiators, medieval knights, and gangsters of the 1930s. Las Vegas is a highly theatricalized environment. Hotels, such as New York, New York and Treasure Island, are constructed almost like huge theatrical sets for their patrons. Lavish stage shows, such as *Mystere* and *O* by Cirque du Soleil and *F/X* by Tommy Tune (who is a Broadway director, choreographer, and performer), use all the elements of theater to entertain audiences daily.

With such an abundance of dramatic material available in movie houses and on television, and with musicians appropriating theatrical material so extensively, is there any place left for traditional theater? To put it another way, why should people today go to the theater or study theater?

Before answering these questions, we should speak briefly about the word *theater* itself. To begin with, there is the matter of the way the word is spelled. The British, and many people in the United States and Canada, spell it *theatre*. There is no right or wrong about this; how the word is spelled is a matter of personal choice, and we have chosen the less formal spelling *theater*. Then there is the word's meaning—or rather its meanings, since there are several. *Theater* denotes, first of all, a building in which theatrical performances take place, and in this sense the term refers to a physical space. But the word also refers to an art form, and to a discipline. In the same way that we speak of other art forms—opera, dance and music—we speak of theater: *theater* encompasses the history, practices, and institutions of the art form.

We can now return to our questions: Why do we go to the theater and study theater? The first answer is historical. Theater is the foundation of all drama—in films, on television, on computer screens, in theme parks, and in fact in every medium. The ancient Greeks, 2,500 years ago, established the categories of tragedy and comedy that are still used today. They also developed dramatic structure, acting, and theater architecture. Roman domestic comedies are the prototype of every situation comedy we see in the movies or on television.

In other words, though we may not be aware of it, each time we see a performance we are taking part in theater history. When audiences watch a performance of a Shakespearean play in an outdoor theater—for example, at the Shakespeare festival in Ashland, Oregon, or at the Old Globe in San Diego, California—they are not only watching a play by a dramatist who lived 400 years ago; they are also sharing in an environment, a configuration of audience and stage space, that goes back much further, to the ancient Greeks.

When an audience is in a theater with a picture-frame stage, seeing a play by the French playwright Molière, the spectators are not only partaking of a theatrical tradition that traces its roots to seventeenth-century France. They are also partaking of a tradition that goes back to Italian commedia dell'arte, which came to prominence a century earlier. And the theater space goes back to the proscenium stage, which originated during the Italian Renaissance in the early seventeenth century.

Similarly, at a college production of Bertolt Brecht's *The Good Person of Setzuan,* the audience members are not only seeing a play by one of the most inno-

TAKING PART IN THEATER HISTORY

When we attend a theater performance each one of us is participating in theater history: either seeing a new play or the revival of an older one. A good example is the audience shown here at a production of Shakespeare's The Merry Wives of Windsor *by the Ashland, Oregon, Shakespeare Festival where the spectators are part of a tradition that dates back to England four hundred years ago.* (© Gregory Ventana/ Oregon Shakespeare Festival)

vative playwrights of the twentieth century; they are seeing a play that was strongly influenced by techniques of ancient Asian theater.

Along with its historical impact, there is a second, more immediate reason to attend and study theater. It has to do with the word *live*. We call theater the *lively art* not only because it is exciting, suspenseful, and amusing but also because it is alive in a way that makes it different from every other form of dramatic presentation.

The special nature of theater becomes more apparent when we contrast the experience of seeing a drama in a theater with seeing a drama on film or television. In many ways the dramas presented are alike. Both offer a story told in dramatic form—an enactment of scenes by performers who speak and act as if they were the people they represent—and film and television can give us many of the same feelings and experiences that we have when watching a theater performance. One can learn a great deal about theater from watching a play on film or television, and the accessibility of film and television means that they play a crucial role in our overall exposure to the depiction of dramatic events and dramatic characters.

Characteristics of Art.

Art can be divided into three categories: *literary, visual,* and *performing.* The literary arts include novels, short stories, and poetry. The visual arts include painting, sculpture, architecture, and photography. The performing arts are theater, dance, opera, and music. (Film, another art form, partakes of both the visual and the performing arts.)

One characteristic of all art—visual, literary, or performing—is that it is selective. As the three categories suggest, different art forms focus on certain elements and eliminate others. The visual arts, for example, deal solely with sight and touch—what we can see and feel—and they exclude sound. When we visit an art gallery, there is a hush in the air because the concentration is purely on what the eye observes. Moreover, in the visual arts, a composition is frozen and constant. We value the visual arts partly because they capture subjects—faces, landscapes, a series of colors or shapes—and hold them fast in a painting or a sculpture. We can look at a statue of a Roman soldier from 2,000 years ago, or a madonna and child painted 500 years ago, and see exactly the same artifact that its first viewer observed.

THE PERMANENCE OF THE VISUAL ARTS
If they are preserved, painting and sculpture—unlike performing arts such as theater, dance, or music—are permanent and unchanging. An example is this sculpture of the biblical figure Moses by the Italian artist Michelangelo. This artifact is virtually the same today as when it was created over four centuries ago.
(Bettmann/Corbis)

Music, to take another example, concentrates on sound. Although we may watch a violinist playing with a symphony orchestra or observe a soprano singing at a recital, the essence of music is sound. We prove this whenever we close our eyes at a concert, and whenever we listen to recorded music. In both cases, the emphasis is totally on sound. By concentrating on sound, we block out distractions and give our full attention to the music itself. This kind of selectivity is one quality that makes any art form effective.

Another characteristic of art is its relationship to time or space, and thus a second way to differentiate the arts is in temporal and spatial terms. The visual arts exist in space; space is their primary mode of existence. They occupy a canvas, for instance, or—in the case of architecture—a building. By contrast, music moves through time. It does not occupy space; musicians performing a symphony exist in space, of course, but the music they perform does not. The music is an unfold-

THE PERFORMING ARTS
Like theater, opera, and music, dance is one of the performing arts, which share a number of common characteristics. Among them are the fact that they move through time, that they require interpreters as well as creators, and that they must be seen live by an audience. In this photo we see the New York City Ballet and students from the American Ballet Theatre performing Balanchine's "Harlequinade". (Marty Lederhandler/AP/Wide World Photos)

ing series of sounds, and the duration of the notes and the pauses between notes create a rhythm that is an essential part of music. This, in turn, becomes a time continuum as we move from one note to the next.

Unlike painting or sculpture on the one hand or music on the other, theater, dance, and opera occupy both time and space. Let's now consider the special characteristics of the performing arts.

Characteristics of the Performing Arts.   The performing arts, of which music, theater and dance are a part, have several characteristics in common. One is the movement through time described above. Another is that they require interpreters as well as creators. A playwright writes a play, but actors and actresses perform it; a composer writes a piece of music which singers and instrumentalists will perform; a choreographer develops a ballet which dancers will interpret.

Another quality shared by the performing arts is that they require an audience. A performance can be recorded on film or tape, but the event itself must be "live," that is, it must occur in one place at one time with both performers and audience present. If a theater performance is recorded on film or tape without the presence of an audience, it becomes a movie or a television show rather than a theater experience. To put this distinction another way, when an audience watches a film in a movie theater, there are no performers onstage; there are only images on a screen; hence there is no interaction between performers and audience. Such interaction is absolutely essential to the performing arts. In Chapter 1, we will talk more about the special nature of "live" performance and the crucial role of the audience.

In addition to the general qualities we have been discussing, each art form has unique qualities and principles that set it apart from other art forms and help us to understand it better. When we know how shapes and designs relate to overall composition, for instance, and how colors contrast with one another and complement one another, we are in a better position to judge and understand painting. In the same way, we can appreciate theater much more if we understand how it is created and what elements it consists of. We'll now consider theater as an art form, and the creation and elements of theater will be the focus of Part One of this book.

The Art of Theater

Elements of Theater.   When we begin to examine theater as an art form, we discover that there are certain elements common to all theater. These elements are present whenever a theater event takes place; without them, an event ceases to be theater and becomes a different art form and a different experience.

Performers.   The first element essential to theater is performance: people onstage presenting characters in dramatic action.

Acting is at the heart of all theater. One person stands in front of other people and begins to portray a character—to speak and move in ways that convey an image of the character. At this point the magic of theater has begun: the transformation through which an audience accepts, for a time, that a performer is actually someone else. The character portrayed can be a historical figure, an imaginary figure, or even a self-presentation; still, everyone accepts the notion that it is the character, not the actor or actress, who is speaking.

Acting is a demanding profession. In addition to native talent—the poise and authority needed to appear onstage before others, and the innate ability to create a character convincingly—acting requires considerable craft and skill. Performers must learn to use both voice and body with flexibility and control; they must be able, for example, to make themselves heard in a large theater even when speaking in a whisper. (This takes extensive physical and vocal training, which we will discuss in more detail in Chapter 2.) Performers must also be able to create believability, or the emotional truth of the characters they portray; that is, the audi-

PERFORMANCE: THE HEART OF THEATER

At the center of a theatrical event and a theatrical experience is the performance of actors and actresses viewed by an audience. This personal interaction separates theater from film and television as well as the other arts. Here we see a performance of The Green Bird *by Carlo Gozzi, directed by Julie Taymor, who also designed the masks.* (© Joan Marcus)

ence must be convinced that the actor or actress is thinking and feeling what the character would think and feel. (This, too, is a difficult task requiring a special kind of training—which we will also discuss in Chapter 2.)

Audience.   Although this may not be readily apparent, another element necessary for theater is the audience. In fact, the essence of theater is the interaction between performer and audience. A theater, dance, or musical event is not complete—one could almost say it does not occur—unless there are people to see and hear it. When we read a play in book form, or listen to recorded music, what we experience is similar to looking at a painting or reading a poem: it is a private event, not a public one, and the live performance is re-created and imagined rather than experienced firsthand.

   Later, we will explain this in more detail, but now we can note simply that in the performing arts a performance occurs when the event takes place, not before and not after. All the performing arts, including theater, are like an electrical connection: the connection is not made until positive and negative wires touch

Introduction

and complete the circuit. Performers are half of that connection, and audiences are the other half.

One audience member who is not essential to the theater experience, but who can enhance it for other audience members, is the critic. He or she can provide criteria by which audiences can judge productions and can offer helpful information about the playwright, the play, theater history, and other important subjects. The critic's contributions make attendance at the theater more meaningful.

Director. A key element of a theater production is the work of the director: the person who rehearses the performers and coordinates their actions to make certain that they interpret the text appropriately, intelligently, and excitingly. As we will see in Chapter 3, the separate role of the director became prominent for the first time in modern theater, but many of the functions of the director have always been present.

Theater Space. Another necessary element of theater is the space in which performers and audiences come together. It is essential to have a stage, or some equivalent area, where actors and actresses can perform. It is also essential to have a place for audience members to sit or stand. We will discover that there have been several basic configurations of stage spaces and audience seating. Whatever the configuration, however, a stage and a space for the audience must be a part of it. Also, there must be a place for the actors and actresses to change costumes, as well as a way for them to enter and exit from the stage.

Design Elements. Closely related to the physical stage is another important element: the design aspects of a production. Design includes visual aspects—costumes, lighting, and some form of scenic background—and a nonvisual aspect, sound.

A play can be produced on a bare stage with minimal lighting, and with the performers wearing everyday street clothes. Even in these conditions, however, some attention must be paid to visual elements; there must, for instance, be sufficient illumination for us to see the performers, and clothes worn onstage will take on a special meaning even if they are quite ordinary.

Usually, visual elements are prominent in theater productions. Costumes, especially, have been a hallmark of theater from the beginning; and scenery has sometimes become more prominent than the performers. In certain arrangements, visual aspects come to the forefront; in others—such as the arena stage, where the audience surrounds the action—elaborate scenery is impractical or even impossible.

The visual aspects of theater are particularly interesting to trace through history because their place in theater production has shifted markedly from time to time. For example, stage lighting changed dramatically when the electric lightbulb came into use at the end of the nineteenth century.

As we noted above, a design element that is not visual is sound. This, too, is a modern element that has come into its own with modern technology. Of course, there were always sound effects, such as thunder and wind created by offstage machines; and there was frequently music, especially during certain periods, when every intermission was accompanied by orchestral performances. In modern times, though, with electronic inventions, there are far more elaborate sound effects; and frequently there are also microphones, sometimes in the general stage area and sometimes actually worn by the performers.

Dramatic Action Embodied in a Text.   A final element essential to theater is the text that is performed. This is a story, an incident, or an event that has been put into dramatic form by a playwright, or perhaps by performers or a director. It might be a true story about other people, such as an incident reported in newspapers or on television. It might be an autobiographical story, something that happened to the author. It might be a historical event, such as the American Civil War; or the story of someone involved in the event, such as Abraham Lincoln. It might be a fantasy, a made-up story with the quality of a dream. It might be a myth, such as the legends on which Greek dramatists of the fifth century B.C. based their plays.

Whatever the source of the dramatic story, it must be present for theater to occur. In its written form, a dramatic story is called a *text,* and it most commonly takes the form of a *script.* The person who creates the text is usually the playwright. He or she transforms the raw material—the incident, the biographical event, the myth—into a drama which features characters talking and interacting with one another. Making this transformation is not easy. It requires intimate knowledge of stage practices, of how to breathe life into characters, of how to build action so that it will hold the interest of the audience and arouse anticipation for what is coming next. In other words, the playwright must create characters and develop a dramatic structure. (There are times when a script is created not by a playwright but by a director or collectively by performers. In such cases, the function of the playwright does not cease to exist; it is a matter of other artists assuming the role of the playwright.)

Along with structure, a text must have a focus and a point of view. Who is the play about? What is it about? Are we supposed to regard the characters and the story as sad or funny? The person who creates the text has the power as well as the responsibility to direct our attention toward certain characters and away from others—and to slant the story so that we look on it as tragic or comic. We will discover more about how these tasks are accomplished when we look at the nature of a dramatic text in Chapters 7 and 8.

To sum up, the following are the major elements of theater:

Performers
Audience
Director
Theater space
Design aspects: scenery, costume, lighting, and sound
Text, which includes focus, purpose, point of view, dramatic structure, and
    dramatic characters

Theater as a Collaborative Art. It is important to stress that theater is a collaborative art. For theater to occur, its elements must be brought together and coordinated.

The director must stage the play written by the playwright and must share with the playwright an understanding of structure, theme, and style. At the same time, the director must work closely with the performers in rehearsing the play, and with the designers of scenery, lights, costumes, and sound, to bring the production to fruition. During performances many elements must be coordinated: the work of actors and actresses along with technical aspects—scene changes, lighting shifts, and sound cues. The people working on these elements are joined, in turn, by a number of collaborators: the stage manager, stage carpenters, makeup experts, those who make costumes , and computer lighting experts.

Another essential component in this collaborative enterprise is the business and administrative side of a production or theater organization. This includes producers and managers, and their staffs—the people who organize and administer press and public relations, advertising, scheduling, fund-raising, and all the details of keeping the theater running smoothly, including ticket sales, ticket taking, and ushering.

Ultimately, the many elements integrated in a production—text, direction, design, and acting, assisted by the technical side and the business side—must be presented to an audience. At that point occurs the final collaboration in any theater enterprise: the performance itself before spectators.

We will understand both the collaborative process and the individual elements of theater when we examine these elements in detail in Chapters 1 through 8, beginning with the work of the performers and the director. Following that, in Chapter 9, we will see how these elements are brought together.

SUMMARY

The theater experience has been created many thousands of times over the centuries and continues to be created every day throughout the world. A great variety of theater experiences can be found in the United States today.

To have a full and rewarding appreciation of theater, it is important to understand that theater is an art form, and that theater has a long and fascinating history.

Art forms can be categorized as literary, visual, and performing; theater is one of the performing arts. All art is selective, and selectivity is one way of distinguishing one art form from another. Art forms may also be distinguished in terms of time and space: the visual arts exist primarily in space; music exists in time rather than space; and theater (along with dance and opera) exists in both time and space.

Important characteristics of the performing arts include the need for interpreters and the need for an audience.

Understanding theater involves understanding its history, its elements, and how it is created.

The major elements of theater are performers, audience, theater space, director, design elements, and text. Because these elements must be coordinated, theater is a collaborative art.

Creating Theater

PART 1

OUTLINE

1. Audiences and Critics

2. Stage Performers

3. The Director and the Producer

4. Theater Spaces

5. Designers: Scenery and Costumes

6. Designers: Lighting and Sound

7. The Playwright

8. The Dramatic Genres

9. Profile of a Production

In Part I we look at the wide range of people who create a theater event: performers, directors, playwrights, designers, and audience. We examine how various artists go about their tasks singly and in conjunction with others leading to a production and performance.

The scene shown here is a play-within- a-play from the *The Seagull* by Anton Chekhov. On a country estate in Russia, a stage has been set up where viewers can watch a play written by Constantine, the son of the owner of the estate, the actress Arkadina. Director: Ron Daniels; set: Antony MacDonald; lighting: James Ingalls; costumes: Catherine Zuber; in center: Stephanie Roth as Nina. (© Richard Feldman/ American Repertory Theatre)

Chapter 1

Audiences and Critics

◀ THE KEY ROLE OF THE AUDIENCE

Theater is an encounter, a collaborative art; playwright, director, performers, designers, and technicians combine their efforts to create a theater production. One of the most important collaborations of all is that between performers and audience. It is only when a production takes place in front of an audience that a theater event can be said to occur. Here we see a performance of Shakespeare's The Tempest *before an audience in the reconstructed Shakespeare's Globe Theatre in London, the recently opened replica of the theater for which Shakespeare wrote. (© Donald Cooper/ PhotoStage, England)*

The Theater Audience

How the Audience Participates

Diversity of Audiences

Play Synopsis: *Fences*

The Theater Critic

What is Criticism?

Critics and Reviewers

Getting Started in Theater— Mel Gussow: Critic

Preparing for Criticism

Criteria for Criticism

Different Critics, Different Views

Descriptive versus Prescriptive Criticism

Summary

The Theater Audience

If you asked someone to list the essential components of a theater experience, the chances are the person might say the actors, the script, and the stage; he or she might in addition mention the scenery and costumes. If you pressed for further elements, however, the list would still probably not include a crucial ingredient—the audience.

This is understandable, particularly today in light of the pervasiveness of film and television. In these two media, which are so much like theater in many ways, the "product," as it is sometimes called, stands alone as a finished production. When you go to a video store to rent a film, it has been completed in its absolutely final form. The same is true of a film in a movie theater; when released it might be shown in 1,000 theaters simultaneously across the United States, and it will be exactly the same in each location, night after night. The audience watches but plays no part in what appears on the screen.

Theater is different. It is not just a matter of film or television being more flexible and having a wider range, though that is the case. In film, computer-generated effects can take us to the land of the dinosaurs in the past or to some interplanetary war in the future; and helicopter shots can let us climb Mount Everest or swoop into the Grand Canyon.

Clearly this is one difference between theater and film, but there is another. Even when the story and the characters presented in the two are identical—in a film and stage presentation of Shakespeare's *Romeo and Juliet,* for instance—there is a less obvious, but equally important difference: the fact that each theater performance is unique and occurs in the presence of an *audience*. The ramifications of the audience are far-reaching. To begin with, the performers have no opportunity to play a scene over or to correct mistakes. Most people are aware that in creating a film most scenes are filmed a number of times. These repetitions are called "takes" and there may be four, five, or even twenty takes before the director feels that a scene is "right." Moreover, once scenes are filmed, the director decides in the editing room where each scene begins and ends and how scenes are joined together.

In theater, there is no repeating and no editing. The performers onstage move through a production from beginning to end, and if there is a mishap—if an actor forgets a line, or an unexpected noise occurs offstage—the performers must recover and carry on. The result of all this is that each theater event is live and immediate.

The dynamics and the excitement of being in the presence of a living person are as old as time and have not changed despite the many technological advances of the past hundred years. People still wait for hours or stand in the rain to see a rock star or a hip-hop performer in person, although the same performer is readily available on a CD, video, or DVD. The same is true of film personalities and charismatic political figures—people eagerly throng to see someone "in person." This same chemistry is possible at every stage performance when the actors and actresses and the members of the audience are in the same place at the same time.

RICH AUDIENCE DIVERSITY

As a reflection of contemporary society, today's theater is diversified, with offerings appealing to a wide variety of audience members. Shown here is the audience at a performance of Two Gentlemen of Verona *at Shakespeare's Globe Theatre in London. The audiences which attended Elizabethan plays in Shakespeare's day were widely diverse, including people from all walks of life. The same can be said of the many types of audiences that attend theater today.* (Stefan Rousseau/AP/Wide World Photos)

There is another aspect in which the audience plays a significant part: the effect the audience has on performers. The drama critic Walter Kerr (1913–1996) explained the special relationship between audience and performers at a theater event:

> *It doesn't just mean that we are in the personal presence of performers. It means that they are in our presence, conscious of us, speaking to us, working for and with us until a circuit that is not mechanical becomes established between us, a circuit that is fluid, unpredictable, ever-changing in its impulses, crackling, intimate. Our presence, the way we respond, flows back to the performer and alters what he does, to some degree and sometimes astonishingly so, every single night. We are contenders, making the play and the evening and the emotion together. We are playmates, building a structure.*[1]

---

[1]Source: Walter Kerr, "We Call It 'Live' Theater, But Is It?" *The New York Times*, January 2, 1972. Copyright 1972 by The New York Times Company. Reprinted by permission.

In other words, the audience has an enormous effect on actors and actresses. They are buoyed up by a responsive audience and discouraged by an unresponsive one. Sometimes, if an audience is not reacting, they might try harder than ever to make contact. This is the case not only with comedy, where laughter is a clear gauge of the audience's response, but also with serious drama. Performers know whether or not spectators are caught up in the action. When audience members are involved in a serious play, they become very quiet; you can sense their fierce concentration. When an audience is not engaged there may be noticeable coughing or rustling of programs. Reacting to this, actors and actresses will change their performances in subtle but very real ways.

How the Audience Participates

At the heart of the theater experience, then, is the performer-audience relationship: the immediate, personal exchange; the chemistry and magic which give theater its special quality. We might ask how the audience becomes involved in a theater event, aside from sending the performers such obvious signals as laughter, silence, and tension. How can a group of people, in seats separated from the performers, be an integral part of the experience? The answer lies in the power of the imagination.

Audience members do not participate physically in a theater performance, the way they would if they were riding a bicycle, working at a computer, or singing in a chorus. Rather, they participate *vicariously,* through the mind and the heart. The astonishing thing is how powerful these aspects of the human psyche are. Through our imagination, we come to believe in the reality of what we see onstage and to identify with the characters. We feel deep sympathy for those we sense are being treated unjustly, and we suffer with them; we feel hatred for those we consider mean or despicable; we laugh at those we consider foolish.

So real become the events onstage that we often forget who we are and where we are and enter the imaginary world we see before us. We can be transported to a foreign country, to another century, to an imaginary place—or to the kitchen of people who might be our own neighbors. Some situations in theater are so vivid and so engrossing that we cry real tears, even though a part of us knows that the events onstage are not actually happening and that the people are only actors and actresses. This experience comes about because of a phenomenon which the English poet and critic Samuel Taylor Coleridge (1772–1834) called *willing suspension of disbelief.* In other words, we want so much to believe in the reality of what is happening onstage that we put aside all literal and practical considerations in order to enter into the world of the drama.

Another factor which allows us to enter into an imaginative world—even though we are aware that it is separate from everyday reality—is referred to as *aesthetic distance.* Aesthetic distance is a requirement of virtually all involvement with the arts. It means that the viewer, spectator, or audience member must be in some sense separated from the performance or object—and must be aware that it is a work of art—in order to experience its aesthetic qualities. Paradoxically, once the proper distance is established, the observer can enter into the experience fully and completely.

Throughout theater history, the power of the audience's mental and emotional participation has manifested itself in both positive and negative ways. Negatively, it has taken the form of censorship—which indicates that those in authority fear the effect theater can have on audiences. The Greeks of ancient Athens considered certain subjects unfit for drama and banned them. In fourth-century Rome, in the early days of Christianity, the church had a great deal to do with stopping theatrical activity. In 1642, the Puritans closed all the theaters in England. In modern times, there have been many examples of censorship, especially in places like China and the former Soviet Union, where only drama that was approved of by the political authorities could be presented.

Positively, the power of audience participation can be seen in many ways. To take just one example, many political groups and other groups use theater as a means of educating people or furthering a cause. In recent times, we have seen theater representing various groups: feminist theater, gay theater, and radical political theater, for instance. The people who present such productions feel that the imaginative and symbolic power of theater will affect their audiences.

In sum, the ability of the audience to enter into the world presented onstage is one reason why it is always a key factor in any theater event.

Diversity of Audiences

Makeup of Audiences: Past and Present.   As we trace the history of theater, one thing we will note is that the makeup of audiences has varied from time to time and from place to place. In ancient Greece, for example, a large percentage of an entire city, such as Athens or Epidaurus, would attend the theater. The same was true of medieval theater in western Europe and England. When we come to Restoration theater in late-seventeenth-century England, however, we find that the audience was sometimes rarefied, consisting of only the upper classes. This affected the kind of writing and acting seen onstage; as a result, Restoration plays still remain less accessible to the general population. In Europe in the nineteenth century, theater once again came to be a form of art popular with a wide range of people.

In today's theater there is a great diversity in both the size and the makeup of those who are present at a theater event. As to size, in a small, intimate theater, there may be no more than 100 or 200 people attending. On the other hand, at a large city auditorium, there may be upward of 2,000 or 3,000 people watching a large-scale musical. This factor will make a difference, both to audience members and to performers. In an intimate space there is more awareness, on the part of everyone, of the interaction between actors and spectators. In a large amphitheater, a different, less personal relationship exits. In a theater somewhere in between—a house that seats 800 or 900 people—the relationship will be a mixture of the two. (We will consider the actor-audience relationship in the context of theater spaces in more detail in Chapter 4.)

THE PHYSICAL THEATER
HELPS SHAPE THE
EXPERIENCE
*The size, the shape, and
the configuration of a
theater affect the audience
experience. The theater may
be small and intimate, it
may be indoors or outdoors,
it might be large and expansive: all of these factors will
have an impact on the
experience of attending the
performance, even though
we usually think that the
only important aspect is
what occurs on stage. Here
we see a performance of*
Twelfth Night *by the Utah
Shakespearean Festival at
the Adams Memorial
theater. (*Courtesy of the
Utah Shakespearean Festival)

Aside from the question of size, today there is often a wide variety in the makeup among theater audiences. Some audiences are homogeneous: the audience members come mostly from similar backgrounds and experience. A good example would be a college or university theater production in which the audience consists primarily of students, faculty members, and their friends. Another example would be a performance presented to a group of senior citizens in a retirement village. Other audiences are heterogeneous, such as the spectators at free performances of Shakespeare in New York's Central Park or at any of the other outdoor summer festivals. Here you would find people of many ethnic and social backgrounds and of all ages. A third audience mix would be found at a Broadway theater or in a similar downtown theater in any large city. The members of the audience would be mostly middle- and upper-class but might include children, students, or foreign visitors. Even among traditional audience groups such as these, however, the chemistry of the audience will change from night to night for no apparent reason. At a comedy, for instance, on some nights the audience will laugh at everything; on other nights, audience members may enjoy the show just as much, but they will barely chuckle and seem never to indulge in a hearty laugh.

American Audiences Today: Multicultural and Diverse. Along with the variety among audiences described above, there is a further factor which has affected the makeup of contemporary audiences. Increasingly, people in the United States are becoming aware of the multiracial and multicultural aspects of our society. In the late nineteenth century and the early twentieth century, the United States was known as a "melting pot," a term which implied that the aim of many foreign-born people who came here was to become assimilated and integrated into the prevailing white, male, European culture. (Women during this era had to fight for some very basic rights, such as voting.) In recent decades, however, many people in our society have come to believe that such a homogeneous culture has at its core many biases; as a result, they urge us to recognize, maintain, and celebrate our differences. This trend toward diversity has been reflected in theater; many organizations have emerged which present productions by and for groups with special interests. They represent a number of political, ethnic, gender, and racial entities. These theater groups, which will be discussed in detail in Chapters 15 and 16, include the following:

African-American

Asian-American

Hispanic

Native American/American Indian

Feminist

Gay and Lesbian

Political Theater. The theaters just mentioned sometimes have a strong political component, but there are also theaters that exist specifically to espouse political causes and address political issues of many kinds. These theaters usually appeal to audiences which believe that art must have a social conscience and must be used to change social conditions. Among such groups, the San Francisco Mime Troupe has been prominent for many years.

Avant-Garde and Experimental Theater. Theater that breaks away from the mainstream was part of the landscape for most of the twentieth century and is continuing in the twenty-first. This type of theater has frequently appealed to a small audience, often young people who question prevalent theatrical traditions and practices. Movements such as expressionism, surrealism, theater of cruelty, and absurdism appeared during the first seventy-five years of the twentieth century. Their descendants continue into the present. Among theater movements of this kind are multimedia theater, which incorporates theater, dance, painting, and video into a single art form; and performance art, in which a highly individual theater piece is created by one person, or at most only a few people.

In summary, the role of the audience is crucial to a theater event, because of the importance of the performer-audience relationship. The audience completes the

FENCES (1987)

By August Wilson, (1945–   )

(AP/Wide World Photos)

Characters:

Troy Maxon—53, *a sanitation worker*
Jim Bono—*a fellow worker*
Rose—43, *Troy's wife of 18 years*
Cory—17, *their son*
Lyons—*Troy's son by his first wife*
Gabriel—*Troy's younger brother*
Raynell—*Troy's daughter by another woman*

Setting:

The backyard of Troy Maxon's house in a northern industrial city.

Act I, Scene 1: A Friday evening, fall 1957. Troy, a large, self-confident man, and Bono, his sidekick, enter. Rose tells Troy that their son Cory is being recruited by a college football team. Troy objects because he himself was a talented baseball player, but African Americans could not play in the major leagues at that time. Troy describes a past encounter with Death, whom he "wrassled" and beat.

Lyons, Troy's older son, who wants to be a jazz musician, comes to borrow money, which Troy refuses to give him.

Scene 2: The next morning. Troy's younger brother Gabriel enters. Gabriel has a metal plate in his head—a result of a wound in World War II. He carries a trumpet because he thinks he is the angel Gabriel. Soon, Troy disappears, claiming that he is going to listen to a ball game on the radio.

Scene 3: A few hours later. Cory enters and then Troy arrives. Troy is building a fence around the backyard and wants Cory to help him. Troy again expresses strong disapproval of Cory's taking a football scholarship. Cory asks why Troy doesn't like him. Troy says that he puts food on the table for Cory and a roof over his head. That's enough: "What law is there say I got to like you?"

Scene 4: The following Friday. Troy and Bono enter. Troy tells about his past: his family in the south lived in poverty; he left home at 14 and had to steal to live; he was thrown in jail for 15 years. When he got out of jail, it was too late for him to star in baseball. Then he met Rose and settled down. Cory arrives, and there is another confrontation between him and Troy.

Act II, Scene 1: Saturday. Bono warns Troy that he shouldn't mess around with Alberta, another woman—Rose is a good woman and doesn't deserve such treatment. Troy starts to work on his fence as Rose arrives. Troy, with great difficulty, tells Rose that he has made another woman pregnant. Rose denounces him, explaining all that she has sacrificed for him.

Scene 2: Friday, spring 1958. Troy, who has stayed away from the house, returns to get his clothes. Rose accuses him of committing Gabriel to an institution, so that he himself can take part of the money that will come as a result. Troy angrily denies this, but it becomes clear that it is true. The phone rings, and Rose learns that Alberta has had a baby girl but has died in childbirth. Left alone, Troy once more challenges Death to come get him.

Scene 3: Three days later. Troy shows up at the house with Alberta's baby daughter, Raynell. He wants Rose to raise her. Rose says no, but later she agrees.

Scene 4: Two months later. Cory has graduated from high school, and he and Troy have another confrontation. Troy orders Cory out of the house; Cory says that the house was built partly with money that Troy took from Gabriel's disability payments. The two fight with a baseball bat. Troy finally gets the bat but does not hit Cory.

Scene 5: Summer 1965. Troy has died, and it is the morning of his funeral. Cory, now a Marine, is home, but he refuses to go to the funeral. Rose says that staying away is not the way to become his own man. Rose explains how much she sacrificed to be Troy's wife, but life has given her as compensation little Raynell, whom she loves like her own daughter. Cory decides that he will go to the funeral. Gabriel attempts to blow his trumpet, unsuccessfully, but instead does a dance that announces Troy's arrival at heaven's gate.

DISCUSSION QUESTIONS

- How would the experience of seeing *Fences* differ for different ethnic and racial groups?

- What themes in *Fences* have universal audience appeal?

- Could a reviewer or critic who is not African American do justice to *Fences*? Explain your answer.

electrical circuit that provides the immediacy and excitement of a live theater performance. In addition, the makeup of the audience is a key factor, and one that audience members themselves should be aware of. The following are questions for you, as an individual audience member, to consider. Is the audience a homogeneous group—similar in background and attitude—or a diverse one? Do you, as a member of the audience, relate to other audience members or not? Is the event being presented primarily by and for a particular group—cultural, social, gender, or political? If so, are you a member of the group, or outside it? During the performance, is the audience involved in the production or not? If it is a serious event, is the audience concentrating and empathizing? If the event is comic, is the audience caught up in the amusement and laughter?

THE CRUCIAL ROLE OF THE AUDIENCE
In any theater event, the audience plays an essential part. A performance is a two-way street with impulses passing back and forth between members of the audience and the actors and actresses on stage. An electrical circuit is established to which each contributes, making the experience a joint, communal one. Acknowledging this in a curtain call after a performance of Seven Guitars *by August Wilson are the performers appearing before the audience. (Hakim Mutlag/AP/Wide World Photos)*

The Theater Critic

A person who can be considered a special type of audience member is the critic. A simple definition of a *critic* is someone who observes theater and then analyzes and comments on it. In a sense the critic stands between the theater event and the audience, serving in ideal circumstances as a knowledgeable and highly sensitive audience member. At the same time, most theatergoers are amateur critics. When a person says about a performance, "It started off great, but it fizzled," or "The star was terrific, just like someone in real life," or "The woman was OK, but the man overacted," he or she is making a critical judgment. The difference between a critic and an ordinary spectator is that the critic presumably is better informed about the event and has developed a set of standards by which to judge it.

The reason audiences can learn from critics is not only that critics impart information and judgments but, as suggested above, that the critic shares with audience members the point of view of the spectator. Unlike those who create theater—writers, performers, designers—critics sit out front and watch a performance just as other members of the audience do. By understanding how the critic goes about his or her task, audience members can increase their knowledge of how theater works and make their own theater experiences more meaningful.

What Is Criticism?

The popular image of the theater critic is a caustic writer who makes sharp, rapier-like thrusts at performers and playwrights. Some epithets of critics have become legendary. John Mason Brown (1900–1969) described an actress's performance in a production of Shakespeare's *Antony and Cleopatra* by saying, "Tallulah Bankhead barged down the Nile last night as Cleopatra and sank." When Katherine Hepburn (1907–   ), who was a stage actress before she went into films, appeared in the play *The Lake,* the critic Dorothy Parker (1893–1967) wrote that Hepburn "runs the gamut of emotions from A to B." Before he became a playwright, George Bernard Shaw was a critic, and he had harsh things to say about a number of people, including Shakespeare: "With the single exception of Homer, there is no eminent writer, not even Sir Walter Scott, whom I can despise so entirely as I despise Shakespeare when I measure my mind against his."

But criticism is much more than this sort of thing. The word *criticize* has at least two meanings. Perhaps the most familiar meaning is "to find fault," and that is what we see in the comments above. But *criticize* also means "to understand and appraise," and this meaning is much more important for a theater critic.

Critics and Reviewers

In theater, a distinction is often made between the critic and the reviewer. A *reviewer* usually works for a newspaper, a magazine, or a television station and reports on what has occurred at a theater event. He or she will explain briefly what the theater event is about, describing the plot and stating whether it is a musical, a comedy, or a serious play. The reviewer will generally add an opinion on whether

Mel Gussow: Critic

Mel Gussow is a critic and theater writer for the New York Times *and has been a recipient of the George Jean Nathan Award in dramatic criticism. He has published books on his interviews with the playwrights Samuel Beckett, Harold Pinter, and Tom Stoppard. In the spring of 2000, he received numerous awards for his book* Edward Albee: A Singular Journey.

I have been with the *New York Times* serving as theater critic and writer about theater since 1969, but my interest in theater began when I was still in school. It came into particular focus while I was undertaking graduate studies.

While studying at Columbia University's Graduate School of Journalism, I spent my evenings in the theater. It was the 1955–1956 season, an astonishingly diverse year, with *My Fair Lady, A View from the Bridge, The Diary of Anne Frank, The Most Happy Fella,* Jason Robards in *The Iceman Cometh,* Orson Welles in *King Lear* (he was in a wheelchair at the performance I attended) and, most important of all, the Broadway premiere of *Waiting for Godot.*

I saw everything on Broadway and many plays off-Broadway, which had become a burgeoning theatrical movement, led by the New York Shakespeare Festival, the Phoenix Theater, and David Ross's productions of Chekhov. More than anything else, that season encouraged my enthusiasm for theater—for the idea of becoming a drama critic. Earlier, at Middlebury College, I had reviewed plays for the student newspaper and had taken courses in playwriting, theater history, and Shakespeare. But that year was at the core of my theatrical education.

My professional critical life did not actually begin until the early 1960s at *Newsweek* magazine, where I wrote feature stories about the arts, movie reviews, and occasional reviews of off-Broadway shows. When T. H. Wenning, the magazine's distinguished theater critic, suddenly became ill and incapacitated soon after the Broadway opening of Edward Albee's *Who's Afraid of Virginia Woolf?* I acted as that magazine's critic. I began my regular theater reviewing at the top, with the Albee play, and then during the rest of the season covered plays and musicals across the board, from Harold Pinter one-acts to *Beyond the Fringe.* Since this was the time before bylines in news magazines, few people knew that I was a critic. But I knew I was a critic.

or not the event was done well and is worth seeing. In most instances, the reviewer is restricted by time or space. A reviewer on a television news program, for instance, will have only a minute or two on the air to describe a play and offer a reaction. A newspaper reviewer, similarly, is restricted by space and by the need to submit his or her article quickly to meet a deadline.

Many reviewers have limited experience and training in their specialty. They may have taken college courses in theater and the other arts, but frequently they come from other positions in television or print journalism, such as general or investigative reporting. Once they are assigned to theater, however, the most conscientious reviewers make it their job to become as knowledgeable as possible. This type of review is important to the general audience, which turns to reviewers for information about arts events and guidance in deciding whether or not to attend, especially when an event is expensive.

In contrast to a reviewer, a *critic* goes into greater detail in describing and analyzing theater events, and has the time and space to do so. Critics generally publish their analyses in magazines and scholarly journals. At times they go beyond articles and essays to write books about playwrights, plays, or theatrical movements. Critics also attempt to put a playwright or a group of plays into the larger context of theater history and into the broad framework of the arts and society.

Ideally, a critic should have a thorough grounding in the history of theater, in the elements that make up theater, and in the nature of acting and production. He or she should be able to analyze a script for structure and meaning, should understand various styles of acting, and should be aware of the visual aesthetics of theater. The critic should then use this knowledge to discuss—both for audiences and for the theater community—just what is right and wrong about a production. Generally speaking, the critic's audience is more specialized and demanding than the reviewer's audience. The critic's readers or viewers have a right to expect informed judgments and helpful background information.

Preparing for Criticism

How do critics and reviewers prepare for their work? We said above that, ideally, a critic should have a complete and thorough knowledge of all aspects of theater. A reviewer's knowledge is not expected to be as extensive as that of a critic, but it should be as comprehensive as possible.

Background information for a critic or reviewer should include a solid grounding in theater history—the periods covered in Part Two of this book. It should also include thorough knowledge of dramatic literature—major plays from all important eras—and familiarity with theater production. Production aspects include acting, directing, theater architecture, and the design elements: scenery, costumes, and lighting.

Reviewers or critics have individual preferences with regard to reading a play before seeing a performance. Because acting and directorial interpretation are crucial in a theater experience, some prefer to see a performance without specific preparation. Others, especially when they are seeing a classic such as a Shakespearean play, prefer to refresh their memory of the text by reading the play beforehand.

Criteria for Criticism

It has been suggested that there are three criteria which the critic should use in assessing a theater event:

1. What is the playwright or production attempting to do?
2. How well has it been done?
3. Is it worth doing?

In looking at these three criteria, it must be remembered that in theater both the play and the production are under consideration. Critics, therefore, must make it clear whether they are assessing a script, a production, or both.

Criterion 1: What Is Being Attempted?   Applying the first criterion, the critic must explain exactly what is being attempted, both by the playwright and by the director. Sometimes this is clear—in a comedy or farce, for example—but sometimes it is not.

A playwright, for instance, may be attempting to criticize excessive behavior with satire, but this might not be obvious from what the audience sees onstage. Perhaps a playwright is parodying the work of another writer—that is, deliberately imitating and making fun of the other writer. If the audience understands this, it will make the play clearer.

Regarding the work of the director, the critic again must determine what is being attempted. Is the director trying to present a play exactly as the playwright intended, or is he or she trying something different? An *auteur director* (discussed in Chapter 3) usually attempts to present his or her own version of a dramatic work, not necessarily that of the playwright. The critic should make this clear to the reader, to help audiences understand what is happening onstage.

Criterion 2: How Well Has the Attempt Succeeded?   Applying the second criterion, the critic makes a personal evaluation. How well has the playwright realized his or her goals, and how well have the performers and the director brought the play to life? Generally a reviewer or critic makes personal evaluations in arriving at a conclusion and does not take into account the reactions of the audience. At times, however, the reviewer might comment on the response of the audience, especially if audience members reacted favorably to a play that the reviewer did not regard as well written or well acted.

Criterion 3: Was the Attempt Worth Making?   Applying the third criterion, the critic evaluates the overall undertaking. Is this kind of play or production valid? Does it fulfill a legitimate purpose? Is it meaningful or significant? Is the play or production itself a worthwhile undertaking?

A critic should clearly state the context in which he or she is making this value judgment. It may be in terms of other plays in the same historical period; it may be in terms of great plays from all periods; it may be in terms of plays of the same genre, such as tragedies, comedies, or melodramas; or it may be in terms of the arts generally, setting this work in the context of other performing arts and even the visual arts. The important thing is not simply to evaluate but also to explain the basis for judgment.

Theater encompasses a broad range of activities, from low farce to high tragedy, and so value is not merely a question of depth or profundity but often a question of comparing the goal with the achievement. If the purpose of a play is clearly understood to be entertainment, for example, then the question becomes how well this intention is carried out in the production. On the other hand, a play can be pretentious, claiming to have depth when it actually does not, and a critic should point that out.

It is important to remember, with regard to evaluative criticism, that reactions to theater—as to all art—are highly subjective. In theater, unlike geometry or

Different Critics, Different Views

Critics often have divergent views about the same production. An example is found in two reviews of a production of Eugene O'Neill's *The Iceman Cometh* when it opened in New York in April, 1999. The star was the actor Kevin Spacey. On the right is an excerpt from the review of Ben Brantley of the *New York Times.* On the next page, an excerpt from the review of Michael Feingold in the *Village Voice.* The two men agree on the importance of the play but disagree about other elements, including the work of the director, Howard Davies.

Ben Brantley *The New York Times*

The silence is so taut that it hurts. It descends around 11 P.M. at the Brooks Atkinson Theater, the resounding soundlessness of a crowd of hundreds scarcely daring to breathe, much less cough or whisper or unwrap one of those notorious lozenges.

A question has been asked on the stage, the home of the new revival of *The Iceman Cometh,* and Kevin Spacey, playing the man who must answer, breaks off in mid-response to pause. The

A production of *The Iceman Cometh* featuring Kevin Spacey and James Hazeldine. (© Joan Marcus)

pause keeps growing; it becomes an ocean. And Mr. Spacey, for those wide, penetrating seconds, seems like the most powerful man on earth.

When was the last time you heard that kind of hush in a theater? That this one occurs four hours into the performance of *Iceman,* which officially opened last night, is a testament to the abiding potency of Eugene O'Neill's great, lumbering barroom metaphysics lesson of a play and to the hypnotic pull of this production, which arrives by way of the Almeida Theater in London and is directed by Howard Davies. In the land of the puny attention span, here is an American audience, still wide awake after prime time and hanging on to an actor's pause as though it were the edge of a cliff.

The question that inspires this moment is one of many asked in the course of *Iceman,* O'Neill's down-in-the-depths masterwork from 1946. By the time it is posed, the play's plot-driving mysteries, never that impenetrable to begin with, have already been uncovered, and its philosophical queries remain what they were in the first act.

But when Harry Hope (James Hazeldine), the owner of the grimy saloon where the work is set, eagerly asks Theodore Hickman (Mr. Spacey), the charismatic salesman known as Hickey, to confirm that he, Hickey, has lost his mind, it is the highest-stakes question of all. What hangs in the balance is nothing less than the ability of Hope and his cronies to go on living, not happily, mind you, but with some degree of serenity, in the state of mind that O'Neill famously summed up as a "pipe dream."

Ben Brantley for *The New York Times,* April 9, 1999.

Michael Feingold *Village Voice*

I should, I suppose, be grateful for small favors. The Broadway system that can make the tourists line up for a four-and-a-half-hour play, at $100 a pop, must be doing something right. *The Iceman Cometh,* being a great play, deserves sold-out houses, even if its greatness is no more visible here than in earlier Broadway revivals. It was established as a masterpiece, of course, by the late José Quintero's 1956 Off-Broadway revival, with the young Jason Robards at the peak of his youthful form. I saw the reduced version shown on NET, and the image of Robards is still stuck in my memory, smiling his salesmanlike way through Hickey's marathon last speech, his haunted eyes seeming to sink deeper and deeper into his skull.

No image so intense is likely to remain with me from Howard Davies's current revival. The gist of O'Neill's play is big and simple, as tragedy should be, and Davies hasn't violated it by imposing any topsy-turvy interpretations or grotesque visions of the kind that have maimed his earlier productions. His *Iceman Cometh* is perfectly competent work, with a number of good performances.

Yet there's something wrong. The feel of the play, as opposed to its sense, is caught for a minute or two, then drifts away into inconse-quence, like an alcoholic's conversation. The fierce kick of the play's negative beauty is gone; we're deprived of it as efficiently as Hickey, forcing the onstage drunks to see their own pretenses, deprives their booze of its old kick. Just as life, for O'Neill, isn't livable without the illusion that keeps you besotted, the play, without its beauty, might not be worth experiencing. . . .

Davies does away with both claustrophobic realism and religiosity, starting with an eccentric set, by Bob Crowley. . . . This dissipates the close atmosphere, while Davies reverses the play's pattern of emphasis: Casual remarks are inflated by yells, pauses, and poses into heavily italicized sermonettes; the more-significant scenes tend to be raced through at power-saw tempo.

Michael Feingold for *The Village Voice,* April 20, 1999.

physics, there is no right or wrong answer. Nor are there absolutes in theater, like the mathematical formulation that 8 times 9 equals 72. Sincere, intelligent people often disagree on whether or not a play is profound, moving, or skillfully written. There are principles of dramatic structure, as we will discover in Chapter 8, and there are aesthetic criteria that we can apply to scenery and costumes. However, the ultimate test is whether or not one is affected by a performance, and whether one thinks a play is exceptional or merely routine—and this is up to the individual spectator.

At the same time, there is no doubt that critics can be helpful in answering such questions. Critics can provide valuable information and incisive opinions that help us arrive at our own independent judgment. Perhaps one way to view critics is to say that while we should not slavishly follow their ideas, we should at the same time learn from them everything we can.

Descriptive versus Prescriptive Criticism

From a historical perspective, it is helpful to be aware that critics have generally taken one of two different approaches. The first approach, which can be called *descriptive criticism,* is an attempt to describe as clearly and accurately as possible what is happening in a performance. The second approach can be called *prescriptive criticism,* meaning that the critic not only describes what has been done but offers advice and sometimes even insists on what should be done.

Two theater critics from ancient times established these different approaches. In the fourth century B.C., the Greek philosopher Aristotle undertook to analyze the tragedies of playwrights like Aeschylus, Sophocles, and Euripides. Aristotle was also a scientist, and his method was chiefly to describe tragedy: to break it down into its component parts and to note how it worked and what effect it had on spectators.

On the other hand, in the first century B.C. the Roman writer Horace attempted not just to describe theater but to prescribe what it should be. In other words, he wanted to establish rules. He said, for example, that tragedy and comedy should never be mixed in the same play and that dramatic poetry should instruct as well as please the audience.

Since the time of Aristotle and Horace, critics have tended to fall into one category or the other: either analyzing and describing, or setting down rules. The prescriptive approach, it should be noted, entails the danger of becoming overly rigid and moralistic in judging what theater should be, and of excluding drama that audiences find both meaningful and pleasurable.

Having looked at the audience and the critic, we turn next—in Chapter 2—to the other essential element of theater, the performers. In Chapter 3 we will turn to the person who coordinates all the production elements, the director.

SUMMARY

The presence of an audience is an essential element in a live theater performance. Just as no two performances of the same production are ever exactly alike, no two audiences are identical. Each audience is composed of a different mix of people, with varied ages, educational backgrounds, and occupations. Among the diverse groups toward which productions are aimed and whose members constitute specific audience groups are African Americans, Asian Americans, Hispanics, Native Americans, feminists, gays and lesbians, and other political and experimental groups. Also, the particular response of each audience affects the acting of the performers.

A special member of the audience is the critic or reviewer, who is assumed to be a knowledgeable observer of the theater event. A reviewer is usually a reporter for a newspaper, magazine, or television station. After viewing a theater event, the reviewer describes it and gives his or her own opinion as to whether it was well done and is worth seeing.

A critic, usually writing for a magazine or scholarly journal, describes and analyzes a theater event in greater detail than the reviewer does. The critic should have a solid education in theater history, dramatic literature, and theatrical production so that he or she can offer readers an informed judgment along with useful background information.

Theater criticism may be either descriptive, explaining what actually happens onstage; or prescriptive, offering advice and prescribing what should take place.

THEATER ON THE WEB

The Internet is an excellent place to find amateur reviews as well as professional criticism of current theatrical productions.

New York Times on the Web   http://www.nytimes.com
Reviews and listings for Broadway are found in the Arts section. You will have to register for this service, but registration is free.

Aisle Say   http://www.aislesay.com
An Internet magazine of stage reviews and opinions written by theatergoers.

Playbill On-Line   http://www.playbill.com
A magazine for theater buffs.

What's Good and What Ain't   http://www.geocities.com/Broadway/1835/html/core.html
This Web site lets you publish and read your own theatrical reviews.

After looking through these sites and reading some of the posted reviews, did you find any more or less credible than others? Why? How do reviews written by audience members differ from those written by professional critics? Find an example of a review that fully addresses the questions that should be answered by a critic.

Chapter 2

Stage Performers

A Historical Perspective: Demands of Classical Acting

Three Challenges of Acting

Getting Started in Theater— James Earl Jones: Performer

Mastering the Craft of Acting

Making Characters Believable

Play Synopsis: *The Cherry Orchard*

Synthesis and Integration

Making Connections: *Acting*

Judging Performances

Summary

◀ THE ART OF ACTING

Acting is a demanding profession, requiring extensive training in vocal work, physical movement, character development, and a host of other skills. Along with the craft are certain indefinable qualities such as being able to connect with the audience and project the personality and complexity of the character being portrayed. Seen here are two skilled English actors, Liam Neeson in the role of Oscar Wilde and Tom Hollander as Lord Alfred Douglas in the play The Judas Kiss. *(© Donald Cooper/ PhotoStage, England)*

Acting is almost as old as the human race. From the earliest days of civilization, people have mimicked other people and have told stories, imitating the voices and gestures of the characters in those stories. There have also been rituals and ceremonies in which the celebrants wore costumes and performed assigned roles—one example is a priest in a church service.

Today, in schools, on street corners, and at parties we often see people performing or imitating others in some way. When telling a story, a person often adopts the voices and attitudes of the characters; some people seem to be particularly adept at doing this and are referred to as "natural" actors or actresses. The desire to imitate others, or to take on the personality of an imaginary character, seems irresistible; and the pleasure we take in watching others do this is universal. In this process of enactment and impersonation is the origin of stage acting. A closely connected type of "acting" in daily life is role-playing. The current term *role model* refers to a person whose life, or "role," serves as a model or guide for others to emulate or imitate.

In theater, this practice of imitation becomes conscious and deliberate. *Acting* can be defined as assuming a role onstage; to put it another way, acting is impersonating a character in a dramatic presentation before an audience. Actors and actresses develop their craft and then carefully rehearse a play in order to bring the text to life. In the process, they speak words and perform actions that give flesh and blood to the characters on the page.

A Historical Perspective: Demands of Classical Acting

Before the twentieth century, the challenges facing performers were dictated by the very specific demands of the type of theater in which performers appeared. Both classic Greek theater and traditional Asian theater stressed formal movement and stylized gestures similar to classical ballet. The chorus in Greek drama both sang and danced its odes, and Asian theater has always had a significant component of singing and dancing. In addition, Greek performers wore masks and Asian performers often wore richly textured makeup.

In western theater, from the time of the Renaissance through the nineteenth century, actions onstage were not intended to replicate the movements or gestures of everyday life. For example, performers would often speak not to the character they were addressing but directly to the audience.

In England during the eighteenth and nineteenth centuries, acting alternated between exaggerated and more natural styles. Throughout this period, every generation or so an actor or actress would emerge who was praised for performing in a less grandiose, more down-to-earth way. But exaggerated or not, performance before the twentieth century was more formal and stylized than what we are accustomed to onstage, and especially in films and on television.

No one would expect an actress or actor today to perform a classical play in the manner in which it was originally presented; such a performance would seem ludicrous. Besides, we do not know exactly how classical acting looked or sounded.

At the same time, it should be clear that any performer today who is appearing in a play from the past must develop a special set of skills and be able to respond successfully to a number of challenges.

As an example, let us consider an actor undertaking the role of Hamlet. He must convince the audience that he is experiencing numerous and often contradictory emotions: that he is aware of lies and treachery taking place around him; that he is saddened by the recent death of his father and the hasty marriage of his mother to his uncle; that he believes his uncle has murdered his father; that he wants to murder his uncle but cannot bring himself to do so; that he berates himself for not being more decisive; that he loves Ophelia but is repelled by the web of circumstances in which he is caught and of which she is an unwitting part.

For an actor, one aspect of conveying these emotions lies in developing the inner feelings that Hamlet has from moment to moment. How does it feel to have such conflicting emotions about your mother or about your duty? An actor playing Hamlet must answer such questions; he must understand in his own innermost depths what Hamlet's emotions are like and then communicate them to the audience.

At the same time, the actor must have a sense of the physical and vocal qualities that a man like Hamlet would have. How would Hamlet walk? How would he handle a sword? How would he greet a friend like Horatio? What movements and gestures would he use? How would he speak? What vocal range and speech patterns would he use?

Along with these personal characteristics, moreover, the actor playing Hamlet must be able to speak Shakespeare's lines distinctly and intelligently. This is particularly true of Hamlet's soliloquies—the speeches he delivers while alone on-stage. Because much of the language of Shakespeare's plays is poetry, and because there are many extended phrases which must be spoken without interruption, the speeches call for tremendous breath control. To achieve beauty of sound, the performer must, in addition, have a resonant voice; and to achieve clarity, he must have an accurate understanding of the words.

In portraying Hamlet, an actor must also have athletic ability and control of his body. If the stage setting has ramps and platforms, he must be able to navigate them with ease; and since he must engage in a sword fight with Laertes in a scene near the end of the play, he must have mastered many of the techniques of fencing.

Similarly, an actress playing Ophelia must have a wide range of accomplishments. She must be able to portray the interior emotions of the character convincingly, speak clearly and intelligently, move with poise and authority, and interact with the other performers. In addition, the role calls for the actress to sing and to play a scene in which she must convince us that Ophelia has lost her sanity, although of course the actress herself is perfectly sane.

We should note that in addition to roles like Ophelia or Juliet in Shakespeare, an actress—like an actor—might be called on to perform many different kinds of roles, using a variety of techniques and approaches. For instance, she will probably be called on to play characters in modern realistic plays: Nina in Chekhov's *The Sea Gull*, for example, or Laura in Tennessee Williams's *The Glass Menagerie*, or the young woman leaving prison in Marsha Norman's *Getting Out*. She will also be asked to undertake roles in the classics: female characters in Shakespeare,

STAGE ACTING

Acting is a difficult artistic endeavor, requiring not only arduous training in vocal and movement techniques but also the ability to create believable characters. In addition, it is necessary to project physical qualities and characterization to the audience. Shown here are two performers, Greg Naughton and Pamela Payton-Wright, in a scene from Ibsen's Ghosts *directed by Irene Lewis at Baltimore's Center Stage.* (© Richard Anderson)

Antigone or Electra in Sophocles, or one of the ingenues in a play by Molière. If she wants to appear in musical theater, she will have to master singing and dancing as well as acting. And there are also experimental and avant-garde theater events, which often call for special skills such as mime and acrobatics.

Three Challenges of Acting

Throughout theater history it can be said that three main challenges face an actor or actress:

1. To acquire the many skills—both physical and vocal—that stage performances demand; in other words, to master the craft of acting
2. To make characters believable
3. To integrate these two, that is, to combine skills with credibility

To understand the first two aspects of acting, we will examine them separately. We begin with the craft of acting—specific techniques required in performance—and then turn to the believability of characters.

James Earl Jones: Performer

James Earl Jones is one of the most prominent American actors of the last half century. He has played prominent roles year after year on stage and in films, appearing in productions from the play The Great White Hope *to the* Star Wars *film series.*

My whole career, starting off-off-Broadway in the late 1950s, has grown in small, incremental steps. I can remember the summer of 1960, when I did my first work for the New York Shakespeare Festival. Alan Schneider was going to direct *Measure for Measure* in the park, and when I went backstage after seeing another play he had directed, I approached him and said, "Mr. Schneider, I'm an actor, and in reading the plays you'll be directing this summer for Joe Papp, I noticed there's a character called Abhorson in *Measure for Measure.* It appears that he wears a mask. It shouldn't matter whether he's Caucasian, African, or Asian skin color. I want to play that character." He said, "OK, OK"—without reading me. One doesn't think of Alan Schneider being intimidated at all, but he later told me, "You were pretty large. I saw you, and you meant it." . . .

I also had the chance to do a Shakespeare Festival play with Mitchell Ryan. Mitchell was going to play Leontes, the king in *The Winter's Tale,* and I could play his majordomo, Camillo. It was not a great role, but it meant working with Mitchell and playing a mature, responsible, stable, human Shakespearean character. In the back of my mind, I was working towards a shot at playing Othello someday. . . . The next season, I was asked to play Othello to Mitchell Ryan's Iago. That casting, I think, is the best choice ever made, in terms of an American production of the play—to have Othello and Iago the same age, the same size, the same temperament, the same zodiac sign even. . . .

Those were wonderful years off-Broadway. The spring after I played my first roles at the Shakespeare Festival, I was in the United States premiere of Jean Genet's *The Blacks,* which ran for several seasons. That company included many of the African American actors you know of now—Roscoe Lee Browne, Cicely Tyson, Godfrey Cambridge, Louis Gossett. . . .

My father gave me a sense of the reality of the business. . . . I geared my standard of living to the real income. I didn't live in plush or drive plush. In my early days, the best domicile I had was a cold-water flat in that hub between Little Italy and Chinatown. It cost nineteen dollars a month. . . . I did not raise my standard of living until *The Great White Hope* in 1968. . . . Not-for-profit theater is like subsistence farming. You're not there to make a killing. You're there hopefully to have a good, a fruitful, a productive season. . . .

Coming right off the service in the American Theatre Wing, I knew physical training. At the Wing it was called body movement . . . and we did a lot of fencing. That training continued through all the years at the Shakespeare Festival. . . . My voice is both a gift and something I worked for. The genetic gift was a vocal timbre that has to do with resonating cavities, size of body, and so on, and I inherited that from my father, who is six feet four. . . . I've concluded, by the way, that speech is not natural to human beings. Sound is, music perhaps . . . but speech is an intellectual exercise that's acquired. I had no trouble speaking *Fences* because August Wilson is a great poet. I'm from the south, and he was writing his characters from the south, so a lot of things fell right into place.

Source: *Actors' Lives: On and Off the American Stage* by Holly Hill, copyright 1993 by Holly Hill. By permission of Theatre Communications Group.

Mastering the Craft of Acting

Many techniques of acting are the equivalent of technical skills required in the other performing arts, such as learning the movements of ballet and developing the physical agility to carry them out, or mastering a musical instrument and learning to play it successfully in public.

The Performer's Body.   Traditional theater makes strong demands on the performer's body. In Shakespeare, for instance, performers must frequently run up and down steps or ramps, meet other characters in sword fights, and enact prolonged death scenes. Anyone who has seen an impressive sword fight onstage senses how difficult it must be. A duel, in which the combatants strike quickly at one another—clashing swords continually without hitting each other—resembles a ballet in its precision and grace, and it entails a great deal of physical exertion.

Adept physical movement is also required in modern realistic acting. For example, an activity in a modern play analogous to a sword fight would be a headlong fall down a flight of stairs or two people engaged in a knife fight, like the one in Arthur Miller's A *View from the Bridge*.

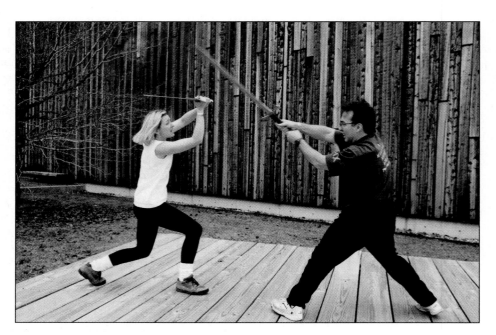

PHYSICAL DEMANDS OF PERFORMING
Acting requires physical as well as emotional and vocal resources. This is especially true in performing the classics which require physical agility and extensive vocal ability. Musicals, too, call for the skills of dancing, singing and other specialties. Here we see two experts practicing hand to hand combat. On the left is fight teacher Corinna May and on the right, fight master Tony Simotes of Shakespeare & Company. (© Richard Feldman)

The following are typical examples of exercises for body movement:[1]

1. Lie on your back. Beginning with the feet, tense and relax each part of the body—knees, thighs, abdomen, chest, neck—moving up to the face. Note the difference in the relaxation of various muscles and of the body generally after the exercise is completed.

2. Stand with feet parallel, about as far apart as the shoulders. Lift one foot off the ground and loosen all the joints in the foot, ankle, and knee. Repeat with the other foot off the ground. Place the feet down and move hip, spine, arms, neck, etc., loosening all joints.

3. Stand with feet parallel. Allow all tension to drain out of the body through the feet. In the process, bend the knees, straighten the pelvis, and release the lower back.

4. Begin walking in a circle; walk on the outside of the feet, then on the inside, then on the toes, and then on the heels. Notice what this does to the rest of the body. Try changing other parts of the body in a similar fashion and observe the effect on your feelings and reactions.

5. Imagine the body filled with either helium or lead. Notice the effect of each of these sensations, both while standing in place and while walking. Do the same with one body part at a time—each arm, each leg, the head, etc.

It should be emphasized that these physical exercises are mainly for warm-up. There are more specific advanced exercises for such things as fencing, dancing, and rapid movement up and down stairs or platforms. Physical training also includes developing the skills necessary to deal with the peculiarities of specific historical periods, such as the curtsy and bow for plays involving kings and queens.

The Performer's Voice. A primary requirement for performers is to make certain that the lines they speak are heard clearly by the audience. To be heard throughout a theater seating a thousand people, a performer must *project*—throw his or her voice into the audience so that it penetrates to the uttermost reaches of the theater. In modern realistic plays this task is made more difficult by the necessity of maintaining believability. For example, in real life the words of a man and a woman involved in a love scene would be barely audible even to people only a few feet away; in a theater, however, every word of such a scene must be heard by the entire audience. A performer needs to strike a balance, therefore, between credibility and the necessity of being heard.

In western theater before the modern period, from the fifth century B.C. in Greece to the middle of the nineteenth century, vocal demands on actors and actresses were even greater than they are today. The language of plays was most often poetry; and poetry—with its demanding rhythms, sustained phrases, and exacting meters—required intensive training in order for the performer to speak the

---

[1]These physical exercises have been provided by John Sipes of the Oregon Shakespeare Festival.

lines intelligently and distinctly. There were problems of projection, too. A Greek amphitheater was an acoustical marvel, but it seated as many as 15,000 spectators in the open air, and throwing the voice to every part of the theater was no small task.

In Elizabethan England, Christopher Marlowe, a contemporary of Shakespeare, wrote superb blank verse which made severe demands on performers' vocal abilities. One example is found in Marlowe's *Doctor Faustus;* this is a speech by Faustus to Helen of Troy, who has been called back from the dead to be with him:

> O' thou art fairer than the evening's air
> Clad in the beauty of a thousand stars;
> Brighter art thou than flaming Jupiter
> When he appear'd to hapless Semele;
> More lovely than the monarch of the sky
> In wanton Arethusa's azured arms;
> And none but thou shalt be my paramour!

These seven lines of verse are a single sentence and, spoken properly, will be delivered as one overall unit, with the meaning carried from one line to the next. How many of us could manage that? A fine classical actor can speak the entire passage as a whole, giving it the necessary resonance and inflection as well. Beyond that, he can stand onstage for 2 or 3 hours delivering such lines.

Today, because of microphones and sound amplification, we have increasingly lost our appreciation of the power of the human voice. But in the past, public speakers from Cicero to Abraham Lincoln stirred men and women with their oratory; and throughout its history, the stage has provided a natural platform for stirring speeches. Beginning with the Greeks and continuing through the Eliza-

THE PERFORMER'S VOICE: PROJECTION
Among the skills which actors and actresses must develop is the ability to use the voice: to project it to the far reaches of an auditorium, to modulate it, to articulate poetry properly, and in some cases, to master accents. The scene here shows Derrick Lee and Helmar Augustus Cooper, with Caroline Stefanie Clay (in the background) in August Wilson's Joe Turner's Come and Gone *in a Powerhouse Theater production at the Milwaukee Repertory Theatre. (© Mark Avery)*

bethans, the French and Spanish theaters of the seventeenth century, and other European theaters at the close of the nineteenth century, playwrights wrote magnificent lines which performers, having honed their vocal skills to a fine point, delivered with zest. Any performer today who intends to act in a revival of a traditional play must learn to speak and project stage verse, which requires much the same kind of vocal power and breath control as opera.

In order to develop projection and balance it with credibility, a performer must train and rehearse extensively. For example, an actor or actress might use breathing exercises, controlling the breath from the diaphragm rather than the throat so that vocal reproduction will have power and can be sustained. Many of these exercises are similar to those used by opera singers. Also, head, neck, and shoulder exercises can be used to relax the muscles in those areas, thus freeing the throat for ease of projection.

To give an indication of the types of exercises performers must undertake during their years of training—and during their careers as professionals—it is interesting to look at some samples of vocal exercises that free the throat and vocal cords:[2]

1. Standing, begin a lazy, unhurried stretch. Reach with your arms toward the ceiling, meanwhile lengthening and widening the whole of your back. Yawn in a deep breath and hum on an exhalation. Release your torso so that it rests down toward your legs. Yawn in another deep breath and hum on an exhalation. On an inhalation, roll up the spine until you are standing with your arms at your sides. Look at something on the ceiling and then at something on the floor; then let your head return to a balance point, so that the neck and shoulder muscles are relaxed.

2. Put your hands on your ribs, take in a deep breath, and hum a short tune. Repeat several times. Hum an *m* or *n* up and down the scale. Drop your arms; lift the shoulders an inch and drop them, releasing all tension.

3. Take in a deep breath and with the palm of your hand push gently down on your stomach as you exhale. Do this several times. Exhale on sighs and then on vowels.

4. Standing, yawn with your throat and mouth open and be aware of vibrations in the front of your mouth, just behind your front teeth, as you vocalize on the vowels *ee, ei,* and *o*. Take these up and down the scales. Sing a simple song and then say it, and see if you have just as much vibration in your mouth when you are speaking as when you are singing.

5. Using a light, quick tempo, shift to a tongue twister (such as *Peter Piper picked a peck of pickled peppers*). Feel a lively touch of the tongue on the gum ridge on the *t*'s and *d*'s, and a bounce of the back of the tongue on the *k*'s and *g*'s. Feel the bouncing action on the lips on the *p*'s and *b*'s.

Centering. As a part of body and voice training, many acting teachers emphasize *centering*. This is a way of pulling everything together and allowing the performer to eliminate any blocks that impede either the body or the voice. Centering involves locating the place, which is roughly in the middle of the torso, where all the lines of force of the body come together. It is the "point of convergence of the muscular, emotional and intellectual impulses within our bodies."[3] When performers are able to "center" themselves, they achieve a balance, a freedom, and a flexibility they could rarely find otherwise.

---

[2]These vocal exercises have been provided by Professor Barbara Acker of Arizona State University.

[3]Mira Felner, *Free to Act: An Integrated Approach to Acting*, Harcourt, Brace, Fort Worth, Tex., 1990, p. 14.

All this should make it clear that to master the many techniques required to play a variety of roles and to be at ease onstage—moving and speaking with authority, purpose, and conviction—performers must undergo arduous training and be genuinely dedicated to their profession.

Making Characters Believable

Along with developing the craft of acting, a performer's second major task is credibility. If the audience is to believe in the characters that appear onstage, performers must be convincing.

The Development of Realistic Acting.

From the mid-seventeenth century on, serious attempts were made to define the craft or technique of credible, natural acting. Such an approach became more important than ever at the end of the nineteenth century, when drama began to depict characters and situations close to everyday life. Three playwrights—Henrik Ibsen of Norway, August Strindberg of Sweden, and Anton Chekhov of Russia—perfected a type of drama which came to be known as *realism*. This drama was called realistic because it closely resembled what people could identify with and verify from their own experience. In performing plays by these dramatists, not only the spirit of the individual dramatic

PORTRAYING A BELIEVABLE CHARACTER
Since the advent of realistic theater, at the end of the 19th century, a primary challenge for performers is making the characters they portray convincing and credible. Many techniques and exercises have been developed for this, but it also calls for total sincerity on the part of the performer. Shown here is Cherry Jones, on the left, in Tina Howe's Pride's Crossing, *in which she portrays a woman in many stages of her life, from adolescence to old age. On the right is actress Kandis Chappell. (© Ken Howard)*

characters but also the details of their behavior had to conform to what people saw of life around them. This placed great demands on actors and actresses to avoid any hint of fakery or superficiality.

The Stanislavski System: A Technique for Realistic Acting. Before the realistic drama of the late 1800s, individual actresses and actors, through their own talent and genius, had achieved believability onstage, but no one had developed a system whereby it could be taught to others and passed on to future generations. The person who eventually did this most successfully was the Russian actor and director Constantin Stanislavski.

A cofounder of the Moscow Art Theater in Russia and the director of Anton Chekhov's most important plays, Stanislavski was also an actor. By closely observing the work of great performers of his day, and by drawing on his own acting experience, Stanislavski identified and described what these gifted performers did naturally and intuitively. From his observations he compiled and then codified a series of principles and techniques.

We might assume that believable acting is simply a matter of being natural; but Stanislavski discovered first of all that acting realistically onstage is extremely artificial and difficult. He wrote:

> All of our acts, even the simplest, which are so familiar to us in everyday life, become strained when we appear behind the footlights before a public of a thousand people. That is why it is necessary to correct ourselves and learn again how to walk, sit, or lie down. It is essential to reeducate ourselves to look and see, on the stage, to listen and to hear.[4]

To achieve this "reeducation," Stanislavski said, "the actor must first of all believe in everything that takes place onstage, and most of all, he must believe what he himself is doing. And one can only believe in the truth." To give substance to his ideas, Stanislavski developed a series of exercises and techniques for the performer which had the following broad aims:

1. To make the outward behavior of the performer—gestures, voice, and rhythm of movements—natural and convincing.
2. To have the actor or actress convey the goals and objectives—the inner needs—of a character. Even if all the visible manifestations of a character are mastered, a performance will appear superficial and mechanical without a deep sense of conviction and belief.
3. To make the life of the character onstage not only dynamic but continuous. Some performers tend to emphasize only the high points of a part; in between, the life of the character stops. In real life, however, people do not stop living.
4. To develop a strong sense of ensemble playing with other performers in a scene.

Let us now look in some detail at Stanislavski's techniques.

---

[4]Constantin Stanislavski, *An Actor Prepares,* Theater Arts, New York, 1948, p. 73.

Relaxation. When he observed the great actors and actresses of his day, Stanislavski noticed how fluid and lifelike their movements were. They seemed to be in a state of complete freedom and relaxation, letting the behavior of the character come through effortlessly. He concluded that unwanted tension has to be eliminated and that the performer must at all times attain a state of physical and vocal relaxation.

Concentration and observation. Stanislavski also discovered that gifted performers always appeared fully concentrated on some object, person, or event while onstage. Stanislavski referred to the extent or range of concentration as a *circle of attention.* This circle of attention can be compared to a circle of light on a darkened stage. The performer should begin with the idea that it is a small, tight circle including only himself or herself and perhaps one other person or one piece of furniture. When the performer has established a strong circle of attention, he or she can enlarge the circle outward to include the entire stage area. In this way performers will stop worrying about the audience and lose their self-consciousness.

Importance of specifics. One of Stanislavski's techniques was an emphasis on concrete details. A performer should never try to act in general, he said, and should never try to convey a feeling such as fear or love in some vague, amorphous way. In life, Stanislavski said, we express emotions in terms of specifics: an anxious woman twists a handkerchief, an angry boy throws a rock at a trash can, a nervous businessman jangles his keys. Performers must find similar concrete activities. Stanislavski points out how Shakespeare has Lady Macbeth in her sleepwalking scene—at the height of her guilt and emotional upheaval—try to rub blood off her hands.

The performer must also conceive of the situation in which a character exists—what Stanislavski referred to as the *given circumstances*—in terms of specifics. In what kind of space does an event take place: formal, informal, public, domestic? How does it feel? What is the temperature? The lighting? What has gone on just before? What is expected in the moments ahead? Again, these questions must be answered in concrete terms.

Inner truth. An innovative aspect of Stanislavski's work has to do with inner truth, which deals with the internal or subjective world of characters—that is, their thoughts and emotions. The early phases of Stanislavski's research took place while he was also directing the major dramas of Anton Chekhov. Plays like *The Sea Gull* and *The Cherry Orchard* have less to do with external action or what the characters say than with what the characters are feeling and thinking but often do not

THE IMPORTANCE OF SPECIFICS IN CREATING A CHARACTER
One of the techniques for acting emphasized by Stanislavski is concentrating on specific actions and details. An example, in a performance of Shakespeare's Macbeth, *is having Lady Macbeth (Seana McKenna) attempt to burn an incriminating document. The production was at the Stratford Festival in Stratford, Ontario. (Cylla von Tiedemann)*

(Bettmann/Corbis)

THE CHERRY ORCHARD (1904)

By Anton Chekhov, (1860–1904)

Chief Characters

Lyubov Andreyevna, *owner of the estate*
Anya, her daughter, *age 17*
Varya, *her adopted daughter, age 24*
Gaev, *her brother*
Lopahin, *a merchant*
Trofimov, *a student*
Charlotta, *a governess*
Firs, *an old servant*
Yasha, *a young servant*

Act I:

The nursery in the country estate of Lyubov Andreyevna, who has returned to Russia from a self-imposed exile in Paris to seek peace in her girlhood home. With her are her brother Gaev, an ineffectual aristocrat, and her daughter, Anya, age 17, who had gone to Paris to make the return trip with her. Lyubov's estate, with its famous cherry orchard, is heavily mortgaged and about to be foreclosed, leaving the family virtually penniless. Lyubov, absent since the death of her husband seven years before, laments her past. Among those who have come to greet her is Lopahin, a merchant who recalls her as a splendid, kindhearted woman. Lopahin's father had been a serf on the estate.

Varya, Lyubov's adopted daughter, is the housekeeper of the estate. Anya tells Varya that her mother cannot comprehend the change in their fortunes. Although they had only enough money for the trip from Paris, Lyubov brought her young valet Yasha with her, as well as Anya's governess Charlotta. The merchant, Lopahin, is supposed to marry Varya, but Varya tells Anya that Lopahin has still failed to propose to her.

Act II:

A meadow near an old chapel near the house. Lopahin tells Madam Lyubov that he will always be grateful to her for her kindness to him when he was a boy. He tells her that she can avert the forced sale of the estate, if she will tear down the house and cherry orchard and develop the land for summer villas. He offers a loan to help, but Lyubov and Gaev cannot bear the thought of destroying the beautiful old orchard. Trofimov, a student, makes a speech, saying that the lazy intelligentsia of Russia should work; he himself, however, does not work.

Later, Lopahin persists in his attempts to get Lyubov to act to save the estate but she talks of summoning an orchestra for a dance and laments the drabness of the peasants' lives. She dis-courages Gaev's plan to work in a bank. In other words, she does nothing to save the estate. Although the servants and family have only soup to eat, she gives a beggar a gold piece and asks for another loan from Lopahin.

Act III:

The drawing room of the house on an evening in August. Lyubov has engaged an orchestra for a dance, although it is the evening of the sale of the estate. Her daughter Varya comforts her with the assurance that Gaev has probably bought the estate with money to be sent by a wealthy great-aunt, but Lyubov knows that the sum is not enough. She tells Trofimov, the penniless student who has won Anya's heart, that he should experience more of life, perhaps even have a mistress. He stamps angrily out of the room. Gaev and Lopahin, the latter giddy with joy, return. Lyubov demands to know if the home is lost. Lopahin cries, "I have bought it! . . . Now the cherry orchard's mine! Mine! . . . I have bought the estate where my father and grandfather were slaves." Lyubov sits down, crushed and weeping.

Act IV:

The same scene as Act I. The nursery is now stripped bare, and the time for leave-taking has come. Lyubov is going to Paris to live as long as possible on the money sent by the great-aunt. Gaev is to work in a bank; Varya is to be a house-keeper in a distant town; Anya is to remain in school while Trofimov, her be-trothed, completes his studies in Moscow. An ax is heard in the distance, and Anya pleads for the workers chopping down the cherry trees to wait until Lyubov has gone. Lyubov speaks of two cares: the health of the old butler Firs, and Varya's future. She is assured that Firs has been sent to the hospital and Lopahin promises to marry Varya; but left alone with Varya, he again fails to propose.

Lyubov and Gaev, the last to go, fall into each others arms. Lyubov weeps: "Oh, my sweet, beautiful orchard! My life, my youth, my happiness, good-bye!" They leave, and Firs, who is quite ill, totters in; he has not been sent to the hospital but left behind. We hear an ax cutting down the cherry orchard—and the symbolic sound of a broken string.

DISCUSSION QUESTIONS

- Suggest performers from theater, film, or television who might success-fully play the roles of Lyubov Andre-yevna, Anya, Lopahin, and Trofimov.

- What acting technique seems most appropriate for a production of *The Cherry Orchard*? Explain your choice.

- If you were an actress performing Anya, what type of research would you undertake, and what questions would you ask about your character?

verbalize. It becomes apparent that Stanislavski's approach would be very beneficial in realizing the inner life of such characters.

Stanislavski had several ideas about how to achieve a sense of inner truth, one being the **magic if**. *If* is a word which can transform our thoughts; through it we can imagine ourselves in virtually any situation. "*If* I suddenly became wealthy . . . " "*If* I were vacationing on a Caribbean island . . . " "*If* I had great talent . . . " "*If* that person who insulted me comes near me again . . . " The word *if* becomes a powerful lever for the mind; it can lift us out of ourselves and give us a sense of absolute certainty about imaginary circumstances.

Action onstage: What? Why? How? Another important principle of Stanislavski's system is that all action onstage must have a purpose. This means that the performer's attention must always be focused on a series of physical actions (also called *psychophysical actions*), linked together by the circumstances of the play. Stanislavski determined these actions by asking three essential questions: What? Why? How? An action is performed, such as opening a letter (the *what*). The letter is opened because someone has said that it contains extremely damaging information about the character (the *why*). The letter is opened anxiously, fearfully (the *how*), because of the calamitous effect it might have on the character.

Through line of a role. According to Stanislavski, in order to develop continuity in a part, the actor or actress should find the *superobjective* of a character. What is it, above all else, that the character wants during the course of the play? What is the character's driving force? If a goal can be established toward which the character strives, it will give the performer an overall objective. From this objective can be developed a *through line* which can be grasped, as a skier on a ski lift grabs a towline and is carried to the top. Another term for through line is *spine*.

To help develop the through line, Stanislavski urged performers to divide scenes into units (sometimes called *beats*). In each unit there is an objective, and the intermediate objectives running through a play lead ultimately to the overall objective.

Ensemble playing. Except in one-person shows, performers do not act alone; they interact with other people. Stanislavski was aware that many performers tend to "stop acting," or lose their concentration, when they are not the main characters in a scene or when someone else is talking. This tendency destroys the through line and causes the performer to move into and out of a role. That, in turn, weakens the sense of ensemble—the playing together of all the performers.

Stanislavski and Psychophysical Action. Stanislavski began to develop his technique in the early part of the twentieth century, and at first he emphasized the inner aspects of training: for example, various ways of getting in touch with the performer's unconscious. Beginning around 1917, however, he began to look more and more at purposeful action, or what he called *psychophysical action*. A student at one of his lectures that year took note of the change: "Whereas action previously had been taught as the expression of a previously-established 'emotional state,' it is now action itself which predominates and is the key to the psychological."[5] Rather than seeing emotions as leading to action, Stanislavski came to believe that it was the other way around: purposeful action undertaken to fulfill a character's goals was the most direct route to the emotions.

Modern Approaches to Realistic Acting.   In the second half of the twentieth century, there were three broad approaches to actor training in the United States. Two of these derived from the methods of Stanislavski.

In the 1930s and 1940s a number of performers and directors in the United States became greatly interested in the ideas of Stanislavski. One of these, Lee Strasberg, a founder of the Actors Studio in New York City, focused on the inner aspects of Stanislavskian theory. Strasberg emphasized a technique called *emotional recall*, a tool intended to help performers achieve a sense of emotional truth onstage. It consists of remembering a past experience in the performer's life that is similar to one in a play. By recalling sensory impressions of an experience in the past (such as what a room looked like, and the temperature and any prevalent odors in the room) emotions associated with that experience are aroused and can be used as the basis of feelings called for in a role in a play.

Though the teachings of Strasberg and his followers were successful with certain performers, other acting teachers, such as Stella Adler (1902–1992), Sanford

---

[5] Jean Benedetti, *Stanislavski*, Routledge, New York, 1988, p. 217.

Meisner (1905–1997), and Uta Hagen (1919–   ), felt that Strasberg emphasized the inner aspects of acting to the exclusion of everything else. Following the lead of Stanislavski in his later approach with psychophysical action, they balanced the emphasis on inner resources with the inclusion of given circumstances and purposeful action.

A third approach was really an update of older methods that stressed classical training. The idea was that the methods of American disciples of Stanislavski might work well for realistic drama, but not so well for the works of writers such as Shakespeare and Molière. Thus, institutions like the Juilliard School in New York City included a strong curriculum of classical training in vocal techniques and body movement, as well as special techniques such as fencing.

Ideally, given the diversity of today's theater, many feel that the best modern training for actors should be well-rounded and include aspects of various approaches.

Additional Training Techniques.   An approach to actors' training, as well as to directing, that is gaining acceptance and wider use in our contemporary theater is known as "viewpoints" theory. Based on ideas from the avant-garde choreographer Merce Cunningham (born 1919) and the experimental director Jerzy Grotowski, viewpoints was originally incorporated into performance training at the Experimental Theatre Wing of NYU/Tisch School of the Arts. It combines elements of dance and stage movement with concepts of time and space. Initially viewpoints had six components: space, time, shape, movement, story, and emotion. The director Anne Bogart (1951–   ), one of the chief proponents of viewpoints, has further broken the element of time into four segments and space into five segments. The viewpoints theory provides a new vocabulary for certain elements that have always been significant in performance and directing: spatial relationships onstage, movement, the notion of time, and so forth.

In modern training of actors and actresses, teachers borrow from other disciplines. A good example is Asian theater. Stylization and symbolism characterize the acting of the classical theaters of India, China, and Japan. To achieve the absolute control, the concentration, and the mastery of the body and nerves necessary to carry out the stylized movements, performers in the various classical Asian theaters train for years under the supervision of master teachers. Every movement of these performers is prescribed and carefully controlled, combining elements of formal ballet, pantomime, and sign language. Each gesture tells a story and means something quite specific—a true symbolism of physical movement.

One Asian discipline, not from theater but from martial arts, which modern acting teachers have found helpful is tai chi chuan, commonly called *tai chi*. Unlike some martial arts, tai chi is not aggressive: it is a graceful, gentle exercise regimen performed widely by men, women, and children in China. It has spread to other countries, where it is sometimes practiced in conjunction with meditation

Chapter 3

The Director and the Producer

The Director
   Evolution of the Director
   The Auteur Director
   The Director at Work

Getting Started in Theater:
Richard Foreman: Director,
Playwright, and Designer

Getting Started in Theater:
Zelda Fichlander: Director and
Artistic Director

   The Director's Collaborators

The Producer or Manager
   Producers in Commercial
   Theater

   Noncommercial Theaters

Summary

◄ THE DIRECTOR: A KEY FIGURE IN THEATER

The director coordinates the activities of performers and designers in bringing to life the playwright's script. She or he confers with the dramatist (in the case of a living playwright), rehearses the actors, and guides the work of the designers. Shown here is director/choreographer Susan Stroman working with Sean Martin Hingston and Stephanie Michels in a scene from Contact. (© Paul Kolnik)

The Director

The person most closely associated with the performers in preparing a production is the director, who not only guides the performers but coordinates the entire artistic side of a production. More than any other person, the director is responsible for the overall style, pace, and visual appearance of a production. The entire process requires organizational skills as well as aesthetic sensibility—qualities the director must have in abundance. In modern theater the director is indispensable, but this role was not always so comprehensive.

Evolution of the Director

It is sometimes argued that the theater director did not exist before 1874, when George II, duke of Saxe-Meiningen determined to make the productions of his court theater in Germany as effective as possible. He supervised every element, paid great attention to details, and strove for historical accuracy in order to create an integrated whole. It is true that beginning with Saxe-Meiningen, the director emerged as a full-fledged, indispensable member of the theatrical team, taking a place alongside the playwright, the performers, and the designers. Though the title may have been new, however, the function of the director has always been present in one way or another.

We know, for example, that the Greek playwright Aeschylus directed his own plays and that the chorus in a Greek play rehearsed under the supervision of a leader for many weeks before a performance. At various times in theater history, the leading performer or playwright of a company served as a director, though without the name. Molière, for instance, not only was the playwright and the chief actor of his company but functioned as its director also. We know from Molière's short play *The Impromptu of Versailles* that he had definite ideas about how actors and actresses should perform; no doubt the same advice he offered in that play was frequently given to his performers in rehearsal. When Hamlet gives instructions and advice to the players who are about to perform the "play within the play," we could say that he is functioning as a director of this visiting theatrical troupe. In fact, in England after the time of Shakespeare, from the seventeenth through the nineteenth century, there was a long line of performer-managers who gave strong leadership to their theater companies and performed many of the functions of the director, although they still were not called by that name.

The actual term *director* came into common usage at the end of the nineteenth century. It is perhaps significant that the emergence of the director as a separate creative functionary coincides with important social changes which began to take place during the nineteenth century. First, with Sigmund Freud, Charles Darwin, and Karl Marx there came a breakdown in established social, religious, and political concepts. Second, there was a marked increase in communication. With the advent of the telegraph, the telephone, photography, motion pictures, and eventually television, various cultures which had remained remote from or even unknown to one another suddenly became linked. The effect of these two changes was to alter the monolithic, ordered view of the world which individual societies had maintained. There is a close relationship between theater and society: when a society has an ordered, unified view of the world, its drama reflects this; and when a society views the world as a changing, heterogeneous, global culture, its drama will reflect that outlook.

Before the changes of the late nineteenth century and the early twentieth century, individual countries had a more unified view of society, and therefore consistency of style in theater was easier to achieve. Within a given society, writers, performers, and audiences stood on common ground. For example, the comedies of the English playwrights William Wycherley and William Congreve, written at the end of the seventeenth century, were aimed at an elite, upper-class audience which relished gossip, acid remarks, and well-turned phrases. The society's code of behavior was well understood by performers and audiences alike. Questions of style in a production hardly arose, because a common approach to style was already present in the very fabric of society. The way a man took a pinch of snuff, or a nobleman flirted with a maid, or a lady flung open her fan was so clearly delineated in daily behavior that performers had only to refine and perfect these actions for the stage. In such a society, the task of the manager or leader of a theatrical company was not really to impose a style on a production but simply to prevent the performers from overacting, to see that they spoke their lines properly, and to ensure that the cast worked together as a unit.

Today, however, because style, unity, and a cohesive view of society are so elusive, the director's task is more important. The director must draw disparate elements together to create a unified whole. Today's directors get their training in a variety of ways. Many of them begin as actors and actresses and find that they have a talent for working with other people and for coordinating the work of designers as well as performers. Others train in the many academic institutions that have specific programs for directors. These institutions include large universities that offer theater as part of a liberal arts program, as well as conservatories and other specialized schools.

The Auteur Director

An important development during the twentieth century is the emergence of the *auteur director.*

Auteur is a French word meaning "author." Just after World War II, French critics began using this term to refer to certain film directors, who, they said, were really the authors of the films they made. In these films, point of view—and the implementation of a point of view—came almost entirely from the director rather than from a writer. Since then, the term *auteur* has also been applied to a type of stage director.

Once the director came to the forefront as a full-fledged member of the creative theatrical team, most directors worked closely with a text. Almost from the start, however, there was a breed of director who took a different approach. Interestingly enough, one of the first and most important of these began his work

THE AUTEUR DIRECTOR

There is a twentieth-century tradition of directors who have imposed their own vision and ideas on a theatrical production. Sometimes they take an older text and place it in a different time period; sometimes they create a new theater piece out of older plays; sometimes they add other elements to a drama, such as acrobatics, film, and dance. Shown here is the work of one of the best-known contemporary auteur directors, Richard Foreman. The production is Foreman's Pearls for Pigs, *featuring actor David Patrick Kelley at the Hartford Stage. (© T. Charles Erickson)*

with Stanislavski and then went out on his own: this was Vsevolod Meyerhold in the early twentieth century. Meyerhold, a Russian like Stanislavski, developed a type of theater in which he controlled all the elements. He would rewrite or eliminate text in order to present his own vision of the material, but the text was only one of many elements that he used for his own purposes. Performers, too, were subject to his overall ideas; often, for example, they were called on to perform like circus acrobats or robots. The finished product was frequently exciting and almost always innovative, but it represented Meyerhold's point of view, strongly imposed on all the elements, not that of a writer or anyone else.

Many avant-garde directors of the twentieth century followed in Meyerhold's footsteps. They could also be classified as auteur directors because they did not see themselves as serving the purposes of a text; rather, they demanded that the text serve their purposes. For some of them—such as the director Robert Wilson, who produced visual tableaux and called for ritualistic, repetitive movements by his performers—the text is only fragmentary and is one of the least important elements. Auteur directors do not hesitate to alter texts drastically; to combine texts from different sources; to introduce other elements such as film, video, dance, and the visual arts; or to rearrange times and places in which the action of a dramatic piece occurs. In such cases, the director is actually serving not only as director but also as author; and it is the director's vision, not that of the playwright, which controls what the audience sees onstage.

The Director at Work

As we consider directors at work, however, we return to the approach of the more traditional director rather than the auteur director. Such a director begins with a close examination of the text. This is true whether the play is from the past—a work by Shakespeare or Molière, for instance—or is a new work that has not been produced before.

The director must first of all understand dramatic purpose and dramatic structure (which will be covered in Chapters 7 and 8). What is the playwright's in-

Richard Foreman: Director, Playwright, and Designer

Richard Foreman, a director-designer-playwright, founded the Ontological-Hysteric Theatre in New York City in 1968. He has also coproduced his work with the New York Shakespeare Festival and the Wooster Group. Foreman has directed for the Hartford Stage Company and the New York Shakespeare Festival.

How does a young man born in Staten Island, removed to Scarsdale, who goes to Brown and Yale in the 1950s, and then goes to New York to write Broadway comedies, become a unique revolutionary artist in the theatre? For some reason, from the time that I was very young, I had an attraction for the strangest material. I read *The Skin of Our Teeth* for the first time at about twelve and thought, "It's like a dream, it's so weird, it's wonderful." I remember seeing Elia Kazan's production of *Camino Real,* which I dragged my Scarsdale parents to, and they said, "What's this all about?"

I have always gravitated to things that try to talk to some more spiritually oriented level, rather than realistic discussions and manipulations of the real, practical, empirical world in which we live.

Then the big revelation was discovering Brecht—and especially his saying that you could have a theatre that was not based on empathy. For some reason, even at an early age what I hated in the theatre was a kind of asking for love that I saw manifested on the stage, getting a unified reaction from everybody in the audience. Brecht said it didn't have to be like that, and until I was in my middle twenties, he was the beginning, middle, and end of everything for me. That only changed when I came to New York and encountered the beginnings of the underground film movement, and that reoriented me, because up to that point I had thought of America as being rather unsophisticated, naive and simplistic as compared with the complexities and aggressiveness of European art and thought. Then in America, in the middle 1960s, I discovered people my age were making their own movies, operating on a level that was akin to poetry rather than storytelling. And I thought, "Aha! Why can't the techniques of poetry that operate in film, operate in theatre?" I came to terms with trying to make an American kind of art that exploited and put onstage everything that up till then I had wanted to reject about myself. I gravitated to theatre even though I was opened up by filmmakers.

Source: Richard Foreman, from *The Director's Voice: Twenty-One Interviews* by Arthur Bartow, copyright 1988 by Arthur Bartow. By permission of Theatre Communications Group.

tention: to entertain, to educate, or to arouse strong feelings in the audience? What is the playwright's point of view toward the characters and events of the play: does he or she see them as tragic or comic? How has the playwright developed the action in the play: in other words, how is the play constructed? Such considerations are crucial because the director is the one person who must have an overall grasp of the text, in order to guide the performers in making it come alive. If an actor or actress has a question about a character or about the meaning of a scene, the director must be able to provide an answer.

In preparing a production, one of the director's first steps is to discover the *spine* of the play. The American director and critic Harold Clurman says in his

THE DIRECTORIAL CONCEPT OR IDEA

At times, directors create an overall image or metaphor for interpreting a play. This serves both to illuminate the text and give unity and cohesion to the production. Frequently the director develops an approach that throws new light on the text. A good example was a production of True West *by Sam Shepard in which director Matthew Warchus on certain nights had actor Philip Seymour Hoffman portray one of the two brothers and John C. Reilly play the other brother, and on other nights, had the two actors switch roles. This, of course, gave two different perspectives to the play.* (© Joan Marcus)

book *On Directing* that a director's first task is to find in the text the general action which "motivates the play." The director must determine the "fundamental drama or conflict" of which "the script's plot and people are the instruments."[1] Clurman calls this fundamental action or conflict the "spine"; it could also be called the *main action* of the play.

As they seek an approach to a text—a way to translate it from page to stage—directors sometimes develop a *directorial concept*. The directorial concept is an overall image or metaphor of a play. For example, a director might develop a concept of Shakespeare's *Macbeth* in terms of "blind ambition." In their insatiable desire for power, both Macbeth and Lady Macbeth are blind to the immorality, the dangers, and the consequences of their actions. Following this notion, the concept of blindness—of what people can and cannot see—would permeate the play.

At the same time that the director becomes thoroughly familiar with all aspects of the text, he or she begins casting the play. The term **casting** comes from sculpture—from casting a mold. In theater, it refers to finding an actor or actress for each role. In the past—in Shakespeare's day, for example—a company of performers worked together regularly, and it was understood who would play the hero, who the clown, who the young female lead, and so forth. In modern times, when very few theaters have a repertory company of regular performers, directors hold **auditions** at which actors and actresses try out for var-

---

[1]Harold Clurman, *On Directing*, Macmillan, New York, 1992, p. 27.

ious roles. Sometimes performers will be interviewed, and sometimes they will be asked to read scenes from the play being produced or from another play. Sometimes, too, a director is already familiar with the work of a performer, having seen or worked with the person before. From a combination of auditions and previous knowledge, the director casts the play, deciding which actor or actress will play each of the parts.

While the director is preparing the script and choosing the performers, he or she is also working closely with the scene, costume, and lighting designers to develop the visual aspects of the production. This is the point at which questions of style and genre become important. The director and the designers must work closely together to be certain that the acting style will be reinforced by the visual elements, and vice versa. Performers who will be speaking high-flown language, as in an Elizabethan play, would seem out of place in a setting that looked like a suburban backyard. In the same way, if a play is set in a modern living room, one would not want the performers to act as if they were the chorus in a Greek tragedy. The director also makes certain that the physical appearance of the production is itself consistent and unified.

A few weeks before the play is to be performed for the public, the director begins rehearsals. This is the period when he or she works most intensively with the performers. The director explains the text—not only the meaning of the play but the style in which it will be presented—and then begins to work with the actors and actresses. At first they may read through the text while simply sitting around a table; next they "get the play on its feet," beginning to sketch in the details of the setting and the characters' interaction.

Initially, the performers work with the text still in their hands. Gradually, they memorize their lines and flesh out their characters. Each performer begins to discover emotional depth in his or her character and becomes aware of the dynamics of scenes where the character confronts others. In the beginning, individual scenes are prepared separately; later, a whole act is put together. After that, the entire play is rehearsed so that the performers get a sense of its overall shape.

THE DIRECTOR AT WORK
The modern director works closely with the playwright on a new script or develops an understanding and interpretation of a well-known script, casts and rehearses the play, and works closely with the designers and others to bring the play to fruition. Here, preparing for a production of Henrik Ibsen's Hedda Gabler, *we see director Daniel Sullivan (left) conferring with playwright Jon Robin Baitz, who adapted the script, and actress Annette Bening who played the title role.* (Monica Almeida/ NYT Pictures)

In preparing the action onstage, the director keeps in mind what the production will look like to the audience. In a sense, the director is the eye of the audience—a person who sits out front and sees the performance before the public does. To ensure a smooth, clear flow of stage action, the director develops the blocking with the performers. *Blocking* means the arrangement and movements of performers relative to each other as well as to furniture and to the places where they enter and leave the stage. If two performers are playing a scene together, they must both be seen clearly by the audience, and they must be in positions that allow them to play the scene to maximum effect. The director also coordinates stage business. In contrast to blocking, which has to do with movements and physical arrangements onstage, *business* is the term for activities of performers such as opening an umbrella, writing a letter at a desk, arranging pillows on a sofa, and the like.

In all this, the director is aware of the *stage picture* or *visual composition,* that is, how the entire scene onstage will appear to the audience. Is the placement of performers balanced? Is it aesthetically pleasing? One goal of the director is to make the visual images onstage striking and effective. Also, the director underscores the meaning of specific scenes through visual composition. The spatial relationships of performers convey information about characters. For example, important characters are frequently placed on a level above other characters—on a platform, say, or a flight of stairs.

Another spatial device is to place an important character alone in one area of the stage while grouping other characters in another area; this draws the spectator's eye to the character standing alone. In addition, if two characters are opposed to each other they should be placed in positions of physical confrontation on the stage. Visual composition is more crucial in plays with large casts, such as Shakespearean productions, than in plays with only two or three characters.

The director gives shape and structure to a play in two dimensions: in *space,* as was just described, and in *time.* Since a production occurs through time, it is important for the director to see that the *movement,* the *pace,* and the *rhythm* of the play are appropriate. If the play moves too quickly, if we miss words and do not understand what is going on, it is the director's fault. The director must determine whether there is too little or too much time between speeches or whether a performer moves too slowly or too quickly across the stage. The director must attempt to control the pace and rhythm within a scene—the dynamics and the manner in which the actors and actresses move from moment to moment—and the rhythm between scenes.

The director must see to it that the movement from moment to moment and scene to scene has enough thrust and drive to maintain our interest. However, variety is also important. If a play moves ahead at only one pace, the audience will become fatigued simply by the monotony of that pace.

Before rehearsals, the director has met with the scene, costume, lighting, and sound designers to develop the approach to the play in each of these areas. While rehearsals with the performers are proceeding, other activities which will eventu-

GUIDING THE PERFORMERS' MOVEMENTS

In a musical, the person who directs the dancers is the choreographer. Even in a nonmusical, however, there is movement which is the responsibility of the director. Shown here is Bill Rauch, at the right, rehearsing a group of performers for a production of The Good Person of New Haven *at the Long Wharf Theatre. (© T. Charles Erickson)*

ally be under the director's control are also going forward: the people building the scenery and costumes and the technicians preparing the lights are doing their work.

Just before the play is to be shown to the public, these elements are brought together, under the supervision of the director, in a ***technical rehearsal.*** At this point, production elements are integrated for the first time in a ***run-through:*** the performers wear their costumes to get accustomed to them, and the lighting "cues" are set with the performers onstage. Scene changes are rehearsed and coordinated. Following this comes the ***dress rehearsal,*** when the play is performed as it will be for the public. This is when last-minute problems are discovered and dealt with.

Then the play is performed for the first time before audiences. These first performances are often called *previews,* or dress rehearsals for an invited audience. We have seen in Chapter 1 how vital the audience is to a production. In previews, the audience's reaction first becomes part of the production process. The response from the audience lets the director and performers know whether a comedy is as funny as they thought, or whether a serious play holds people's attention. The audience lets everyone know which scenes are successful and which are not, so that adjustments can be made if there are problems.

Zelda Fichlander: Director and Artistic Director

Zelda Fichlander was a cofounder of the Arena Stage in Washington, D.C., one of the leading American regional theaters. She was its producing director from 1951 to 1990. She also served as head of the graduate acting program at New York University and artistic director of the Actors Company.

What would you say to a young director striving to get into the profession? It's very hard to get into this field. You have to make your own opportunities at the very beginning. You have to do something somewhere; get some people in a room, just to see whether *you* like it. There's too much concentration on getting other people to like your work. Young directors have to find out whether *they* really like their work, or if they want to change it before they start showing it. You have to find out whether you have a work method and whether you have something that's ready for you to feel good about. These are practical considerations. "If I show this work, will it be seen as good?" Directors can work in any city. You don't have to work in New York.

Anyplace there are people, there is an audience. You simply have to start anywhere you can, under any circumstances. It becomes a matter of persisting until you find a play that reveals your work as special—defined by your personality, your insights, and your personal set of images. The price of being a director is high. It's a life of enormous concentration, but of great rewards. . . .

Source: Zelda Fichlander from *The Director's Voice: Twenty-One Interviews* by Arthur Bartow, copyright 1988 by Arthur Bartow. By permission of Theatre Communications Group.

The Director's Collaborators

The director is the person who works most closely with the performers; for a new text the director collaborates with the playwright; in developing a production, the director consults closely with the design team to make certain that all aspects are coordinated. In addition to these collaborators, there are others with whom the director works and who are essential to the production.

In musical theater, these others would include the composer, lyricist, choreographer, and music director. In a nonmusical play, various technicians and artists may be indispensable to the director. For example, a fencing or fight consultant may be needed for a classic play, such as a play by Shakespeare. If a play calls for regional accents—as in a Tennessee Williams play set in the south—a vocal coach would be helpful.

Another significant collaborator with the director is the ***stage manager,*** the person who coordinates all the rehearsals and the actual running of a performance. The stage manager calls rehearsals; lets the performers know their rehearsal schedule; makes all important announcements concerning technical rehearsals and other events involving performers; coordinates all the elements of light, sound, and scene changes during the technical rehearsals and previews; and is in charge of all the same elements, as well as the entrances and exits of performers, during each performance. Clearly, the stage manager is an essential member of any

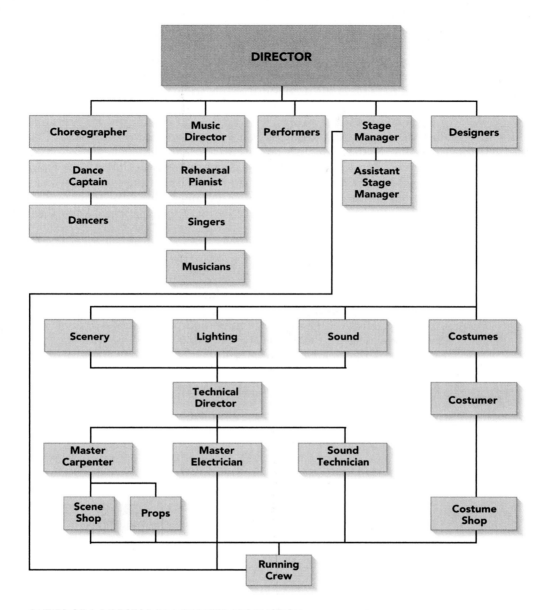

DUTIES OF A DIRECTOR IN A THEATER PRODUCTION
Once a director has decided on a script (and worked with the playwright, if it is a new play), he or she must organize the entire artistic side of the production. This chart indicates the many people the director must work with and the many elements that must be coordinated.

production team: he or she has the immense responsibility of seeing to it that a performance comes off satisfactorily.

In Europe, there is a long-standing practice of having a *dramaturg*—a literary manager or dramatic adviser—collaborate with the director. In the United States, the role of the dramaturg or literary manager is relatively new; but in recent years many regional professional groups and nonprofit theaters have engaged full-time dramaturgs. In a number of the directorial decisions outlined above, a dramaturg can be extremely helpful. Among the duties frequently undertaken by the dramaturg are discovering and reading new plays, working with playwrights to develop new scripts, identifying overlooked plays from the past; preparing information on the history of classical works, researching past productions and criticism, and writing program articles. The dramaturg can also aid the director in making decisions regarding style, approach, and concept.

The Producer or Manager

Audiences frequently confuse directors with producers, perhaps because both the director and the producer function behind the scenes. Actually, the *producer,* or *manager,* is the director's counterpart in the business and management side of a theater production. Here too, coordination of elements is crucial, and the producer or manager is the person chiefly responsible. As the term itself suggests, the producer is a key figure in a production.

Producers in Commercial Theater

In commercial theater, a producer has many responsibilities. In general, the producer oversees the entire business side of a production, including publicity. His or her duties include the following:

1. Raising money to finance the production
2. Securing rights to the script
3. Dealing with the agents for the playwright, director, and performers
4. Hiring the director, performers, designers, and stage crews
5. Dealing with theatrical unions
6. Renting the theater space
7. Supervising the work of those running the theater: in the box office, auditorium, and business office
8. Supervising the advertising
9. Overseeing the budget and the week-to-week financial management of the production

If a production is to succeed, the producer must have the artistic sensibility to choose the right text and hire the right director. Aside from raising capital and having the final say in hiring and firing, the producer oversees all financial and business operations in a production.

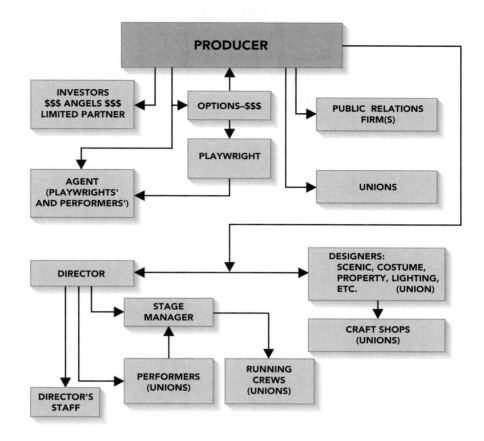

Noncommercial Theaters

Administrative Organization of a Nonprofit Theater.

Most nonprofit theaters—including those in smaller urban centers as well as large noncommercial theaters in major cities like New York, Chicago, and Los Angeles—are organized with a board of directors, an artistic director, and an executive or managing director.

The board is responsible for selecting both the artistic and the managing directors. The board is also responsible for overseeing the financial affairs of the theater, for fund-raising, for long-range planning, and the like. To carry out some of these tasks, the board frequently delegates authority to an executive committee.

The *artistic director* is responsible for all creative and artistic activities. He or she selects the plays that will constitute the season and chooses directors, designers, and other creative personnel. Frequently the artistic director also directs one or more plays during the season.

Responsibilities of the Noncommercial Producer or Manager.

The managing director in a noncommercial theater is, in many respects, the counterpart of a producer in commercial theater. In both a commercial production and the running

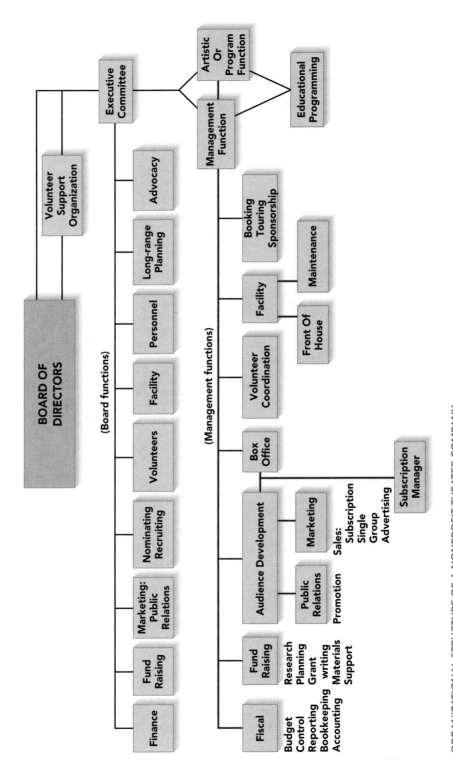

ORGANIZATIONAL STRUCTURE OF A NONPROFIT THEATER COMPANY

A nonprofit theater is a complex institution with many facets. This chart shows the various activities that must be organized for the successful management of such a theater.

of a nonprofit theater organization, the tasks of the person in charge of administration are many and complex.

The producer or manager is responsible for the maintenance of the theater building, as well as for the budget, making certain that the production stays within established limits. The budget includes salaries for the director, designers, performers, and stage crews, and expenditures for scenery, costumes, and music. Again, an artistic element enters the picture; some artistic decisions—such as whether a costume needs to be replaced or scenery needs to be altered—affect costs. The producer or manager must work very closely with the director and the designers in balancing artistic and financial needs.

The producer or manager is also responsible for publicity. The audience would never get to the theater if it did not know when and where a play was being presented. A host of other tasks come under the supervision of the producer or manager: tickets must be ordered, the box office must be maintained, and plans must be made ahead of time for how tickets are to be sold. The securing of ushers, the printing of programs, and the maintenance of the auditorium—usually called the *front of the house*—are also the responsibility of the producer or manager.

Once again, plans must be made well in advance. In many theater organizations, an entire season—the plays that will be produced, the personnel who will be in charge, and the supplies that will be required—is planned a year ahead of time. Coordination and cooperation are as important in this area as they are for the production onstage. (For the organization of a nonprofit theater company, see the chart.)

In Chapter 4 we will turn our attention to the places where audiences interact with performers and where directors stage their productions, as we examine the variety of theater spaces available to contemporary audiences.

SUMMARY

The special function of the director emerged during modern times, when the great diversity of styles in modern theater and the international nature of theater required someone to provide an overall vision for a production and to coordinate all the elements. The director begins by analyzing the text, whether it is a classic or a new play. The director discovers the meaning and the intention of the playwright in order to translate these into stage terms. To do this organically and effectively, the director frequently develops a concept, an overall image or point of view, that will guide and inform the work of everyone connected with the production. An auteur director usually substitutes his or her own vision for that of the playwright, choosing texts to be used and rearranging time periods and other elements.

The director works with the actors and actresses, supervising rehearsals and guiding their performances. The director has many other duties as well. He or she casts the play, selecting an actor or actress for each role. Also, the director works closely with scene, costume, and lighting designers, coordinating the visual elements of the production. The overall artistic quality of the production—its style, pace, and visual appearance—is also the responsibility of the director.

The director may have many collaborators, such as a choreographer, a stage manager, and a dramaturg. Behind the scenes, the producer or manager works to coordinate the business and management elements.

THEATER ON THE WEB

Directors and producers have found a new sense of community on the Web. The following links serve directors, producers, dramaturgs, and choreographers.

Stage Directors and Choreographers Foundation   http://www.ssdc.org/foundation
Provides forums and services for stage directors and choreographers.

Stage Directions Magazine   http://www.stage-directions.com
Web site of magazine *Stage Directions*, which provides industry news for the theater
    community.

What kinds of services are available to directors and choreographers on these sites? How do directors get work? What are some similarities between this community and the performing community? What are some differences?

TheatreForum   http://www-theatre.ucsd.edu/TF
An international theater magazine, published by the University of California–San
    Diego, focusing on new and innovative performance works.

Project Muse   http://muse.jhu.edu/journals
A searchable database of journals found online.

TheatreWorld Internet Magazine   http://members.aol.com/mouseuk/stage
An online journal with articles about the British theater scene.

Of what use would these sites be to a director or producer? Why do you think it is important for producers to stay abreast of national theater news? What could a director learn by reading an article about a new production? What kinds of topics in theater articles pertain to a director? A producer? A dramaturg?

Theater Spaces

Proscenium or Picture-Frame Stage: History and Characteristics

Thrust Stage: History and Characteristics

Arena Stage: History and Characteristics

Making Connections: *Popular Performance Spaces*

Created or Found Spaces

Multifocus Environments

All–Purpose and Experimental Spaces

Summary

◀ WHERE THEATER TAKES PLACE

Western theater began in ancient Greece. To present their plays, Greeks created amphitheaters by placing seats on a hillside surrounding a circle and a stage space at the base of the hill. Through the years, performance spaces have been developed in many sizes and shapes: large and small, indoors and outdoors, and with important variations in the physical relationship of the stage to the spectators. The ancient Greek theater seen here is at Kas, Turkey. (© Adam Woolfitt/Woodfin Camp & Associates)

A theater event occurs in a *theater space:* a place where the audience and performers come together. Since theater is a live experience—an event that occurs only when performers and audience are in the presence of one another—the physical environment where it happens becomes a necessary ingredient.

In addition to a stage—the area where the actors and actresses perform—and an adjoining space where the spectators sit or stand, a theater space also includes a place adjacent to the stage where performers can change costumes and from which they can make entrances and exits. For the audience, provision is usually made for a lobby and other public spaces.

A theater space can be indoors or outdoors, permanent or temporary, large or small. However, it is interesting to note that throughout theater history four fundamental stage arrangements have been predominant. Each of these has its own advantages and disadvantages, each is suited to certain types of plays and certain types of productions, and each provides the audience with a somewhat different experience.

The four basic arrangements are: (1) the proscenium, or picture-frame, stage; (2) the thrust stage with three-quarters seating; (3) the arena, or circle, stage; and (4) created and found stage spaces. We will learn their features and characteristics as we look at each more closely, beginning with the proscenium stage. (In contemporary theater, there are also spaces which combine characteristics of these four types.)

Proscenium or Picture-Frame Stage: History and Characteristics

PROSCENIUM THEATER
The audience faces in one direction, toward an enclosed stage encased by a picture-frame opening. Scene changes and performers' entrances and exits are made behind the proscenium opening, out of sight of the audience.

For many people, the most familiar type of stage is the **proscenium,** or *picture-frame,* stage. Broadway theaters, which were models for other theaters throughout the United States, have proscenium stages.

The term *proscenium* comes from the *proscenium arch,* the frame which separates the stage from the auditorium and forms an outline for the stage. This frame was first introduced in Italy during the Renaissance in the early seventeenth century. Although in the past it was an actual arch, today it is usually a rectangle. As the term *picture-frame stage* indicates, the proscenium arch resembles a large picture frame through which the audience looks at the stage. Before the 1950s, there was usually a curtain just behind the proscenium opening; when the curtain rose, it revealed the "picture." Another term for this type of stage is *fourth wall,* from the idea of the proscenium opening as an invisible or transparent wall through which the audience looks at the other three walls of a room.

Because most of the action on a proscenium stage takes place behind the opening or frame, the seats in the auditorium—or *house,* as it is often called—all face in the same direction, toward the stage, just as seats in a movie theater face the screen. The auditorium itself is slanted downward from the back of the auditorium to the stage. (In theater usage, the slant of an auditorium or stage floor is called a *rake.*) The stage itself is raised several feet above the auditorium floor, to increase visibility.

The main floor where the audience sits is called the *orchestra.* (This is the modern usage of the term *orchestra;* in ancient Greek theater, the orchestra was the circular acting area at the base of a hillside amphitheater.) There is usually a

THE MODERN PROSCENIUM-STAGE THEATER
In this cutaway drawing we see the audience seating at the left, all facing in the one direction toward the stage. Behind the orchestra pit in the center is the apron on the stage; and then the proscenium frame, behind which are the flats and other scenic elements and—at the far right—a cyclorama. Overhead, scenery can be raised into the fly loft above the stage area.

THE PROSCENIUM STAGE

In a proscenium theater, the audience faces in one direction—toward the stage—and the stage itself is enclosed in a giant picture frame through which scenery and action are viewed. This arrangement is perfect for the box set as well as for spectacular scenic effects. Seen here is a typical proscenium space, the Broadhurst Theater in New York. (© Peter Aaron/Esto)

balcony (sometimes there are two balconies), protruding about halfway over the main floor, to provide additional seating. In certain theaters, as well as proscenium-stage concert halls and opera houses, there are horseshoe-shaped tiers or boxes ringing the auditorium for several floors above the orchestra.

Beginning in the late seventeenth century, the proscenium theater was adopted in virtually every European country. The popularity of this type of stage spread throughout the United States in the nineteenth and early twentieth centuries.

The stage area of all these proscenium theaters was usually deep, allowing for elaborate scenery and scene shifts; and there was a tall *fly loft* above the stage to hold scenery. The loft had to be more than twice as high as the proscenium opening so that scenery could be concealed when it was raised, or *flown,* above the stage. Scenery was usually hung by ropes or cables on a series of parallel pipes, one behind the other, running from side to side across the stage. With this arrangement, many pieces of scenery could be raised and lowered. Ingenious mechanisms for raising and lowering scenery were developed during the Italian Renaissance, when the proscenium stage was being refined.

Throughout the seventeenth and eighteenth centuries, there were times when everyone—audiences, scene designers, and technicians—seemed so carried away with spectacle that it was emphasized above everything else, sometimes even above the text and the acting. In Paris, for example, there was a theater called the

THE PROSCENIUM: IDEAL FOR SPECTACLE

One of the advantages of a proscenium theater is that it allows elaborate scenery and effects to be created behind the proscenium opening. Machinery for changing scenery can be hidden, and impressive visual pictures can appear as if by magic. Here is a scene from the recent revival of The Music Man *with colorful sets and costumes and numerous scene changes, all made to seem magical because they occur behind the proscenium opening. (© Joan Marcus)*

Salle des Machines—"Hall of Machines"—its name indicating that visual effects were its chief attraction. At times there was nothing onstage but visual display: cloud machines brought angels or deities from up high; rocks opened to reveal wood nymphs; the scene onstage was changed from a banquet hall to a forest; smoke, fire, twinkling lights, and every imaginable effect appeared as if by magic. Later, such heavy concentration on spectacle went out of favor for many years; but fascination with this type of theater returned in the latter part of the twentieth century, in Broadway musicals such as *The Phantom of the Opera, Les Misérables,* and *Miss Saigon.* The proscenium stage is ideal for such spectacles because the machinery and the workings of the scene changes can be concealed behind the proscenium opening.

In addition to providing an opportunity for spectacle, the proscenium stage offers other advantages. Realistic settings—a living room, an office, a kitchen— are particularly effective in a proscenium theater. A scene designer can create the illusion of a genuine, complete room more easily with a proscenium stage than with any other kind. Also, the strong central focus provided by the frame rivets the attention of the audience. There are times, too, when the audience wants the detachment—the distancing—which a proscenium provides.

There are also disadvantages, however. As we have seen, the proscenium stage creates a temptation to get carried away with visual pyrotechnics. In addition, a proscenium stage tends to be remote and formal. Some spectators prefer the intimacy and informality—the experience of being close to the action—found in the thrust and arena theaters.

Thrust Stage: History and Characteristics

In one form or another, the *thrust stage* has been the most widely used of all theater spaces. In the basic thrust arrangement, the audience sits on three sides, or in a semicircle, enclosing a stage which projects into the center. At the back of the playing area is some form of stage house providing for the performers' entrances and exits, and for scene changes. The thrust stage offers a sense of intimacy, giving the "wraparound" audience a feeling of surrounding the action. Also, the rear wall of the thrust stage—the facade of the stage house—provides a focused background for the action in the playing area.

The thrust stage was developed by the Greeks for their tragedies and comedies. Before they had formal theaters, the Greeks had areas for religious ceremonies and tribal rituals. It is believed that these areas sometimes took the form of a circle in a field, with an altar at the center. In forming their theaters, the Greeks modified this arrangement by placing the circle, which they called the *orchestra*, at the base of a curving hillside. The slope of the hill formed a natural amphitheater for the spectators, and the level circle at the foot formed the stage. At the back of the circle, facing the hillside, there was a stage house which had formal doors for the performers' entrances and exits, created a background for the action, and provided a place for changing costumes. The stage house and the audience seating in Greek theaters began as wooden structures in the fifth century B.C., but during the next two centuries they came to be made of stone. The largest Greek theaters seated 15,000 or more spectators. This design was duplicated all over Greece, particularly in the years following the conquests of Alexander the Great during the early part of the fourth century B.C. Remnants of these theaters remain today throughout that part of the world, in such places as Epidaurus, Priene, Ephesus, Delphi, and Corinth.

A MODERN THRUST STAGE

The thrust stage, with a stage area extending into audience seating that surrounds it on three sides, is one of the oldest arrangements, having been used by the Greeks and by the Elizabethans in the time of Shakespeare. It has been revived successfully in the modern period and is widely used in Europe and the United States. A good example is the thrust stage of the Tom Patterson Theatre at the Stratford Festival in Ontario, Canada. (Courtesy of Stratford Festival, Ontario)

AN EARLY THRUST STAGE

One of the earliest arrangements in Western theater was the thrust stage of the Greek theater of the 5th century, B.C. An outdoor theater cut into a hillside to form an amphitheater, it had audience seating on three sides of a circle—called the orchestra—which stood in front of a stage house. The background was usually an impressive landscape. Shown here is the 4th century, B.C. theater at Epidaurus in Greece as it looks today. (© Jean Pragen/Tony Stone Images)

THRUST STAGE WITH THREE-QUARTERS SEATING

The stage is surrounded on three sides by the audience. Sometimes seating is a semicircle. Entrances and exits are made from the sides and backstage. Spectators surround the action, but scene changes and other stage effects are still possible.

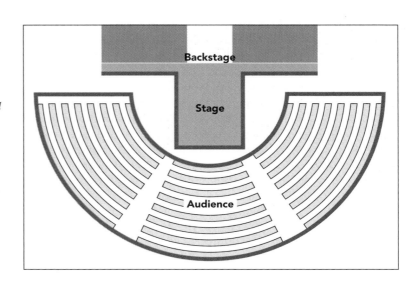

Chapter 4   Theater Spaces

83

The Romans adapted the Greek form, making it a complete structure and developing a theater that was not strictly a thrust but a forerunner of the proscenium. Instead of using the natural amphitheater of a hillside, they created a free-standing stone structure in which the stage house was joined to the seating area and the orchestra was a semicircle. In front of the stage house, which was decorated with arches and statues, they erected a long platform stage where most of the action occurred.

In the medieval period, formal theater, which had disappeared for several hundred years, was revived. Short religious plays in Latin began to be presented in churches and cathedrals in England and parts of continental Europe. Around A.D. 1300, religious plays written in the common language were presented outdoors. One popular space for these outdoor performances was another form of the thrust, known as a *platform stage*. A simple platform was set on wooden supports called *trestles* (hence, this arrangement is sometimes also called a *trestle stage*), with a curtain at the back which the performers used for entrances and costume changes. The area underneath the stage was closed off and provided a space from which devils and other characters could appear, sometimes in a cloud of smoke. In some places the platform was mounted on wheels (a *wagon stage*) and moved from place to place through a town. The audience stood on three sides of the platform, making it an improvised thrust stage. This type of performance space was widely used between the thirteenth and fifteenth centuries in England and various parts of continental Europe.

In the sixteenth century, just before Shakespeare began writing for the theater, a particular type of thrust stage took shape in England. A platform stage was set up at one end of the open inner courtyard of an inn. Such a courtyard was surrounded on four sides by the interior walls of the inn, three or four stories high. The rooms facing the courtyard served as boxes for some of the spectators; on the ground level, other spectators stood on three sides of the stage. The fourth side of the courtyard, behind the platform, served as the stage house. Interestingly, an almost identical theater took shape in Spain at the same time. Spanish inns were called *corrales,* and this name was given to the courtyard theaters which developed there.

Formal English theaters of Shakespeare's day, such as the Globe and the Fortune, were similar to the inn theaters: some of the spectators stood in an open area around a platform stage while others sat in three levels of closed galleries at the back and sides. A roof covered part of the stage; at the back, some form of raised area served for balcony scenes, such as the one in *Romeo and Juliet*. On each side at the rear were doors used for entrances and exits. (In the spring of 1997, a reproduction of the Globe Theater was opened on the South Bank of the Thames River in London, only a short distance from the site of the original Globe. Built to the same dimensions as the original and using authentic materials, it re-creates the feeling of the thrust theater used in Shakespeare's day.)

English theaters like the Globe and the Fortune were a fascinating combination of diverse elements: they were both indoors and outdoors, and some spectators stood while others sat; also, the audience was made up of almost all levels of

THE RESTORED GLOBE THEATER
On the South Bank of the Thames River in London, a theater has been constructed quite near the site of the original Globe, built in 1599. It was for this theater that Shakespeare and several of his contemporaries wrote their most masterful dramas. The reconstruction has attempted to duplicate the original dimensions, use the same materials and in general create for audiences an experience similar to the one for audience's in Shakespeare's time. Shown here is the reproduction during the process of construction. (Max Nash/AP/Wide World Photos)

society. The physical environment must have been stimulating, since performers standing at the front of the thrust stage were in the center of a hemisphere of spectators—on three sides around them as well as above and below. Although such a theater held 2,000 spectators or more, no one in the audience was more than 60 feet or so from the stage, and most people were much closer. Being in the midst of so many people, enclosed on all sides, but with the open sky above, must have instilled a feeling of great communion among the spectators and the performers.

Shortly after Shakespeare's day, in the latter part of the seventeenth century, two things occurred, not only in England and Spain but throughout Europe: theater moved completely indoors, and the stage began a slow but steady retreat behind a frame—the proscenium opening—which enclosed the stage action. For the next two centuries the thrust theater was in eclipse, and it was not to reappear

A MODERN THRUST-STAGE THEATER

This cutaway drawing of a thrust stage shows how the playing area juts into the sudience, which surrounds the stage on threes sides. This configuration affords intimacy, but at the back (shown here at the right) is an area that furnishes a natural backdrop for the action.

until around 1900, when a few theaters in England began using a version of the thrust stage to produce Shakespeare.

The return of the thrust stage in Great Britain and the United States during the past hundred years has resulted from a growing realization that certain plays—not only Shakespearean works but those of his fellow Elizabethans and the playwrights of the Spanish golden age—can be done best on a stage similar to the one for which they were written. In the United States and Canada, the thrust stage was not revived until after World War II; since then, however, a number of fine thrust-stage theaters have been built, including the Tyrone Guthrie in Minneapolis; the Shakespeare Theater in Stratford, Ontario; the Mark Taper Forum in Los Angeles; and the Long Wharf in New Haven.

The basic stage of traditional Chinese and Japanese drama (including nōh theater in Japan) is a form of thrust stage: a raised, open platform, frequently covered by a roof, with the audience sitting on two or three sides around the stage. Entrances and exits are made from doors or ramps at the rear of the stage.

The obvious advantages of the thrust stage—the intimacy of the three-quarters seating, the close audience-performer relationship, and the fact that so many of the world's great dramatic works were written for it—give it a significant place in theater.

THE JAPANESE NŌH STAGE
An ancient Asian form of the thrust stage is the nōh stage in Japan. As shown here, it is a platform stage with the audience sitting on one side and in front. (Billy Rose Theatre Collection, New York Public Library for the Performing Arts; Astor, Lenox, and Tilden Foundations)

Arena Stage: History and Characteristics

The *arena stage,* also called *circle theater* or *theater-in-the-round,* has a playing space in the center of a square or circle, with seats for spectators surrounding it. This arrangement is similar to that in sports arenas which feature boxing or basketball. The stage may be raised a few feet off the main floor, with seats rising from the floor level; or it may be on the floor itself, with seats raised on levels around it. When the seating is close to the stage, there is usually some kind of demarcation indicating the boundaries of the playing area.

One advantage of the arena theater is that it offers the most intimacy, particularly in comparison with the picture-frame stage. With the performers in the center, even in a large theater, the audience can be closer to the action because seating is on all four sides instead of only one side. If the same number of people attend a performance in an arena theater and a picture-frame theater, at least half of those in the arena theater will be nearer the stage. Moreover, in an arena theater there is no frame or barrier to separate the performers from the audience.

An arena arrangement also allows for the unconscious communion which is created when people form a circle. The configuration of a circle seems to come naturally to human beings: we embrace with encircling arms, form circles to play children's games, and make human enclosures around fires and altars. An unusual

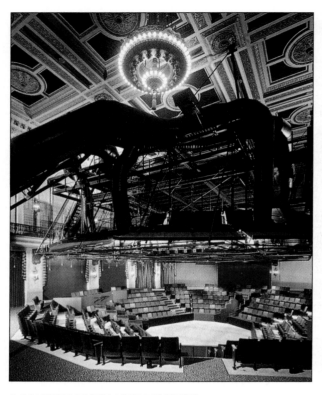

A CONTEMPORARY ARENA THEATER
Arena theaters attempt to capture the intimacy and immediacy of primitive theater. They use only the barest essentials of stage scenery but the full resources of contemporary stage lighting. Seen here is the arena stage space at A Contemporary Theatre in Seattle, Washington. (Steve Keating for Callison Architecture/Courtesy of A Contemporary Theatre, Seattle, WA)

event will automatically draw people into a circle to watch; during a street fight, for instance, notice how the onlookers form a circle, to take a close look without getting so near that they would become involved. In view of this universal instinct to form circles, it is not surprising that virtually all primitive forms of theater were "in the round."

There is also a practical, economic advantage to the arena stage: any large room can be converted into this arrangement. You simply designate a playing space, arrange rows of seats around the sides, and hang lights on pipes above, and you have a theater. Elaborate scenery is unnecessary; in fact, it is impossible because it would block the view of large parts of the audience. A few pieces of furniture, with perhaps a lamp or sign hung from the ceiling, are all you need to indicate where a scene takes place. Many low-budget groups have found that they can build a workable and even attractive theater-in-the round when a picture-frame theater would be out of the question.

These two factors—intimacy and economy—no doubt explain why the arena theater is one of the oldest stage spaces. As we have mentioned, ceremonies in ancient Greece were held in a circular space which was the forerunner of the Greek thrust stage. From as far back as we have records, we know that religious observances and tribal rituals in all parts of the world have been held in some form of circle theater. One example is the war dance of the Apache; another is the festival plays of Tibet, which portray the struggle of Buddhism to supplant an earlier religion. In the medieval period, several of the religious plays in England and France were performed in arena-type spaces. In the modern period in the United States, there was a proliferation of arena stages after World War II.

In spite of its long history and its recent resurgence, however, the arena stage has often been eclipsed by other forms. One reason is that its design, while allowing for intimacy, also dictates a certain austerity: as we have noted, elaborate scenery is impossible because it would block the view of many spectators. Also, performers must make all their entrances and exits along aisles that run through the audience, and so they can sometimes be seen before and after they are supposed to appear onstage.

These problems may explain why some of the circle theaters which opened in the United States 30 or 40 years ago have since closed. A number survive, however, and continue to do well, one of the best-known being the Arena Stage in

PLAN OF AN ARENA STAGE
The audience sits on four sides or in a circle surrounding the stage. Entrances and exits are made through the aisles or through tunnels underneath the aisles. A feeling of intimacy is achieved because the audience is close to the action and encloses it.

Washington, D.C. In addition, throughout the country there are a number of tent theaters in arena form, where concerts and revivals of musicals are given.

Before we leave the three major types of theater arrangements—proscenium, thrust, and arena—we should point out that with each of them, there is customarily space just outside the main seating and stage areas where the audience assembles and tickets are sold and taken. Also, backstage or offstage, there must be dressing rooms for performers and facilities for the stage manager, stage crews, and anyone else concerned with mounting and running a show. (**Running** is the term used to describe the unfolding of a performance. When actors, actresses, and stage crew move through a performance, they are said to be *running* the show.)

A CONTEMPORARY ARENA THEATER
Arena theaters attempt to capture the intimacy and immediacy of primitive theater. It uses only the barest essentials of stage scenery but the full resources of contemporary stage lighting.

Making Connections:

Popular Performance Spaces

A POLITICAL SPECTACLE
A Democratic National Convention at Madison Square Garden in New York City. (AP/Wide World Photos)
(© Joe Sohm/Visions of America)

Many spaces used for live popular entertainments are reminiscent of theater environments. Arenas used for sports, circuses, and rock concerts are configured much like the theatrical spaces discussed in this chapter. Madison Square Garden in New York, Soldier Field in Chicago, and the Rose Bowl in Pasadena, California are all large spaces that primarily house sporting events but are also used for rock concerts and other popular spectacles.

Madison Square Garden, for example, has housed the Ringling Brothers and Barnum and Bailey Circus, an extravagant staging of *The Wizard of Oz*, Frank Sinatra, Barbara Streisand, Bruce Springsteen, the Grammys, and the VH1 Awards, to name just a few events. This means that an arena like the Garden is often equipped with the most innovative technology for lighting, stage, and sound effects.

Spectacular performance spaces for magicians, circuses, and concerts are also found in all of the extravagant hotels in Las Vegas. There is live entertainment presented in spaces at fairgrounds and amusement parks as well. To explore the variety of popular spaces and entertainments in the United States you might want to visit the website *www.amusementbusiness.com*.

These spaces for popular performance are most often configured in the round, with spectators surrounding the events. (Some are configured three-quarter-round.) The reason is to maximize the number of audience members as well as to create an electrifying, interactive environment. With these configurations, the spectators are also able to watch and possibly influence each other's reactions.

Such popular performance spaces are usually extremely large, much

larger than environments created exclusively for theater. For example, the Rose Bowl accommodates 92,542 for football games. Even a comparatively small collegiate basketball complex, Redbird Arena on the campus of Illinois State University, seats approximately 11,000 spectators.

The relationship between spaces for popular entertainment and theatrical environments is complex. In later chapters, we will see that often in theater history, spaces were used for popular arts and for theatrical performances. Modern theater artists have experimented with staging dramatic performances within spaces created for circuses and concerts.

For that matter, the performance qualities of sports, the circus, and rock concerts underscore their shared heritage with the theatrical arts. It is not surprising, then, that their spaces for performance are also similar.

Created or Found Spaces

A fourth type of stage is called *created* or *found space.* This term means that a theater is set up in a space not ordinarily used for performance. All early theaters probably began in some type of created or found space. Tribal ceremonies, for example, were performed in outdoor spaces such as a circle with an altar at the center. In the Middle Ages, theater performances were originally held in churches or cathedrals. When these performances became longer and more secular in nature, they were presented outside; but even then, there were no permanent theaters—only temporary stages erected in the "found" space of town squares.

In the twentieth century, there was renewed interest in the concept of theater performed in unusual places: street corners, public parks, and the like. This was meant partly to bring theater closer to people, and partly to put theater into a new and different context so that people would think about its purpose and impact. Nontheater spaces are often of special interest to experimental, avant-garde, or political theater practitioners. In the 1960s, the Polish director Jerzy Grotowski made novel use of space, an important part of his productions, rearranging an open area in different configurations for different plays. In his production of a play about Doctor Faustus, for example, Faustus gives a banquet; for this, Grotowski filled the open theater space with two long tables at which audience members sat, as if they were guests at a dinner party, while the actors and actresses performed on the tabletops. For another play, which took place in a mental hospital, the action was set inside a simulated hospital ward, with the performers on beds and the spectators moving around the beds.

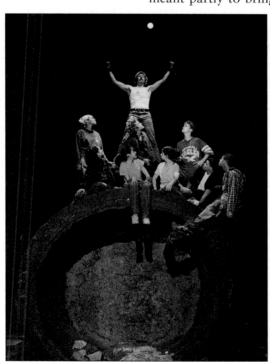

CREATED OR FOUND THEATER SPACE
Frequently in modern theater, directors or groups have worked in nontraditional spaces: either putting a theater production in space ordinarily used for another purpose or creating a space in an empty area. A good example was the production of the Touchstone Theatre of Steelbound *dealing with the closing of a Bethlehem Steel mill that threw many people out of work and impacted a number of families. The production took place in the windows and other locations of an abandoned Bethlehem Steel iron foundry.* (© Edward A. Leskin)

One manifestation of found or created space has been *street theater,* which takes place—as the name suggests—in the streets. One purpose of street theater is to bring performances to neighborhoods, especially in inner cities, where people do not normally attend traditional theater. Street theater can also serve a political purpose: it is sometimes used to make a moral or political point, by people who feel that being in the streets will bring their message home to audiences more forcefully.

By now, every conceivable type of space has been used for theater: lofts, warehouses, fire stations, basements, churches, breweries, gymnasiums, jails, parks, subway stations. Of course, such sites present problems for any kind of long-range theater. They are, obviously, impermanent, and matters such as how to handle tickets raise difficult questions. Also, there is usually only a minimum of scenery, and the accommodations for spectators can be less than ideal. Nevertheless, created and found spaces have been important at various times in theater history and take their place as one of the four major theater arrangements or environments.

Multifocus Environments

An approach that sometimes accompanies unusual theater arrangements is *multifocus theater.* Put simply, this means that there is more than one playing area (such as the four corners of a room), and that something is going on simultaneously in several areas. Multifocus theater is somewhat like a three-ring circus, where we see an activity in each ring and must either concentrate on one ring or divide our attention.

There are several theories behind the idea of multifocus theater. One theory is that a multifocus event is more like everyday life; if you stand on a street corner, for instance, there is activity all around you—in the four directions of the streets and in the buildings above—not just in one spot. You select which area you will observe, or perhaps you watch several areas at once. The argument is that you should have the same choice in theater.

THE MULTIPURPOSE OR "BLACK BOX" THEATER
A popular type of modern theater is the multi-purpose space, sometimes called a "black box." It consists of an open space with perhaps a pipe grid on the ceiling from which lighting and sound instruments can be suspended. A stage platform can be positioned at any place in the space and movable chairs for spectators can be placed around the playing area. The diagram at the right suggests some of the possibilities of stage arrangements in a multipurpose theater.

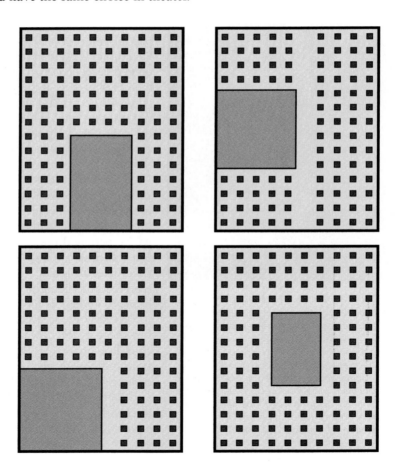

Designers: Scenery and Costumes

Scene Design

The Scene Designer's Objectives

Getting Started in Theater—Robin Wagner: Scene Designer

Elements of Scene Design

The Process of Scene Design: Steps in the Design Process

The Scene Designer's Collaborators

Designing a Total Environment

Costume Design

The Costume Designer

The Costume Designer's Objectives

Getting Started in Theater—Jess Goldstein: Costume Designer

Elements of Costume Design

The Costume Designer's Collaborators

Summary

◀ THE VISUAL ELEMENTS: SCENERY AND COSTUMES

Designers determine the look of a production, especially in scenery and costumes. They emphasize whether a production is realistic or nonrealistic, whether it is modern or historical. They add color and visual excitement. Seen here are costumes designed by Jenny Tiramani for a production of Shakespeare's Antony and Cleopatra *at London's Old Globe Theatre. Mark Rylance plays Cleopatra (left) and Paul Shelley is Antony. (© Donald Cooper/ PhotoStage, England)*

97

As spectators sit in a theater, watching what unfolds before them, they naturally focus most keenly on the performers. But audiences also notice the visual images created by scenery, costumes, and lighting—and they may also hear music underscoring the action, and sound effects such as rain, thunder, or traffic. These visual and aural elements, which add a significant ingredient to the total mixture of theater, are created and organized by designers.

The *scene designer* is responsible for the stage set, which can run the gamut from a bare stage furnished only with stools or orange crates to the most elaborate large-scale production. No matter how simple, however, every set has a design. Even the absence of scenery constitutes a stage set and can benefit from the ideas of a scene designer. The *costume designer* is responsible for selecting, and in many cases creating, the outfits and accessories worn by performers.

Designers must deal with practical as well as aesthetic considerations. A scene designer must know in which direction a door should open onstage, how high each riser should be on a flight of stairs, what materials work best in building scenery, and what kinds of paint to use for painting it. A costume designer must know how much material it takes to make a certain kind of dress and how to "build" clothes so that performers can wear them with confidence and have freedom of movement.

In this chapter, we will deal with scene and costume design. Chapter 6 will take up lighting and sound design.

Scene Design

The Scene Designer's Objectives

In preparing scenery for a stage production, a scene designer has the following objectives:

1. Help set the tone and style of the production
2. Establish the locale and period in which the play takes place
3. Develop a design concept consistent with the director's concept
4. Provide a central image or metaphor, where appropriate
5. Ensure that scenery is coordinated with other production elements
6. Solve practical design problems

Establishing Tone and Style.   A stage setting can help establish the mood, style, and meaning of a play. In the arts, *style* refers to the *manner* in which a work is done: how scenery looks, how a playwright uses language or exaggerates dramatic elements, how performers portray characters. (A realistic acting style, for example, resembles the way people behave in everyday life; in contrast, the lofty quality of traditional tragedy calls for formal, larger-than-life movements and gestures.)

A slapstick farce might call for a design style involving comic, exaggerated scenery, like a cartoon; and perhaps for outrageous colors, such as bright reds and

Robin Wagner: Scene Designer

Robin Wagner has been designing sets in New York for more than two decades. His work includes the Broadway shows A Chorus Line; 42nd Street; The Great White Hope; Kiss Me, Kate; Saturday Night Fever; Crazy for You; *and* Angels in America. *He was recently inducted into The Theatre Hall of Fame.*

Robin, tell us about how you began your career. I'm from San Francisco originally. I had a regular high school education and then two years of art school at the California School of Fine Arts. Aside from little projects in high school, I didn't have any particular theater instruction. I'd never really given much thought to what goes on behind the scenes—as far as I was concerned, theater was just a group of actors who showed up onstage and put on a play. In fact, I was out of high school and an art student before I was exposed to theater. And then when I took a closer look, I discovered that the accumulation of all the work that goes on behind the scenes was even more interesting to me than what was going on in the performance. I realized that it requires so many people to produce a play that I knew there was room for me.

I worked at a number of so-called weekend theaters in San Francisco—the equivalent of off-off-Broadway in New York—where there was no pay but plenty of variety. I started painting scenery and working backstage, but I also had a little design experience. I was fortunate in starting in a city like San Francisco, where at that time there were very few professional designers. Even though I was only an art student just out of high school, I got experience designing that I would never have had if I had had any competition. I first came to New York in 1958, when the Actor's Workshop production of *Waiting for Godot* that I designed was selected to go to the World's Fair in Brussels. My first real training was in New York, working for three years as an assistant to Oliver Smith, who designed *Hello, Dolly* and *110 in the Shade*. After I worked around the country at a number of regional theaters, I returned to New York and worked off-Broadway until I was asked to design *Hair*. It was 1968, and *Hair* was a breakthrough musical—it had a completely different kind of sound.

oranges. Such scenery would match the acting, which would also be exaggerated, with lots of physical comedy—people tripping over carpets, opening the wrong doors, and so forth. A satire would call for a comment in the design, like the twist in the lines of a caricature in a political cartoon. A serious play would call for less exaggerated or comic scenery.

As an illustration of what is called for in scene design, let us consider two plays by the Spanish playwright Federico García Lorca. His *Blood Wedding* is the story of a young bride-to-be who runs away with a former lover on the day she is to be married. The two flee to a forest. In the forest, allegorical figures of the Moon and a Beggar Woman, who represents Death, seem to echo the fierce emotional struggle taking place within the characters, who are torn between duty to their families and passion for each other. For this part of the play, the scenery and costumes must have the same sense of mystery, of the unreal, which rules the characters. The forest must not have real trees but must represent the thicket of emotions in which the man and woman are entangled; the costumes of the Moon

Chapter 5 Designers: Scenery and Costumes

REALISM AND
NONREALISM IN
SCENERY
Scene design helps indicate whether a production is realistic or nonrealistic. Shown here are good examples of the two approaches. Above is a contemporary, down-to-earth setting for the play Dinner with Friends *by Donald Margulies. The scenic design is by Neil Patel, and the lighting by Rui Rita, and the costume designer is Jess Goldstein. The performers are (left to right) Lisa Emery, Matthew Arkin, Julie White, and Kevin Kilner. The other scene is from* The Green Bird, *a fantasy by Carlo Gozzi. Here, neither sets nor costumes is realistic, but rather symbolic and fantastic. The scenic designer is Christine Jones, and the actress is Kristine Nielsen. (© Joan Marcus)*

and the Beggar Woman must not be realistic but must suggest the forces which endanger the lovers.

Another play by García Lorca, *The House of Bernarda Alba,* is a contrast in style: it has no fantasy or symbolic characters. This play concerns a woman and her five daughters. The mother has grown to hate and distrust men, and so she locks up her house, like a closed convent, preventing her daughters from going out. From a design point of view, it is important to convey the closed-in, cloistered feeling of the house in which the daughters are held as virtual prisoners. The walls of the house and its furniture should all have solid reality, creating an atmosphere that will convey a sense of entrapment.

Scene design is especially important in indicating to the audience whether a play is realistic or departs from realism. **Realism** in theater means that everything connected with a production conforms to our observation of the world around us. This includes the way characters speak and behave, the clothes they wear, the events that occur in the play, and the physical environment. Characters presented in a living room or a bar, for example, will look and act as we expect people in those settings to look and act.

On the other hand, *nonrealism* (or *departures from realism*), means all types of theater that depart from observable reality. A musical in which characters sing and dance is nonrealistic because people do not ordinarily go around singing and dancing in public places. A play like Shakespeare's *Macbeth* is unrealistic because it has witches and ghosts—two types of creatures not encountered in everyday existence. Also, the language of the play is poetry, and there are soliloquies in which characters speak thoughts out loud—again, these are elements that depart from the reality we see in our daily lives. Nonrealistic elements are, of course, highly theatrical and can increase our pleasure and excitement. Moreover, they often indicate a deeper reality than we see on the surface. Thus the term *nonrealism* does not imply that something is not genuine or not true; it simply means that something is a departure from what we see around us.

The terms *realistic* and *nonrealistic*, then, are simply ways of categorizing aspects of theater; and they are particularly important in scene design, because scenery can quickly signal to an audience which type of theater we are viewing.

Establishing Locale and Period.   Whether realistic or nonrealistic, a stage set should tell the audience where and when the play takes place. Is the locale a saloon? A bedroom? A courtroom? A palace? A forest? The set should also indicate the time period. A kitchen with old-fashioned utensils and no electric appliances sets the play in the past. An early radio and an icebox might tell us that the period is the 1920s. A spaceship or the landscape of a faraway planet would suggest that the play is set in the future.

In addition to indicating time and place, the setting can also tell us what kinds of characters a play is about. For example, the characters may be neat and formal or lazy and sloppy. They may be kings and queens or members of an ordinary suburban family. The scenery should suggest these things immediately.

Developing a Design Concept.   In order to convey information, the scene designer frequently develops a *design concept*. Such a concept should be arrived at in consultation with the director and should complement the directorial concept (discussed in Chapter 3). The design concept is a unifying idea carried out visually. For García Lorca's *The House of Bernarda Alba,* for example, such a concept would be a claustrophobic setting which sets the tone for the entire play.

A POWERFUL DESIGN IMAGE OR METAPHOR

In certain productions, the scene designer creates a strong visual image or metaphor which gives unity and focus to the whole. Shown here are two excellent examples. Above is the circular playing area which designer Peter J. Davison created for the play Copenhagen *by Michael Frayn. Surrounded by a low wall, the circle defines the action and contains the area within which furniture is rearranged and the characters interact in this intellectual battle between the scientists Niels Bohr (Philip Bosco) in the center and Werner Heisenberg (Michael Cumsty), right. At the rear is Bohr's wife (Blair Brown). The other setting shows an ascending circular spiral which, again, defines and gives focus to the action of the play. This is a design by Ferdinand Wogerbauer and Stefan Mayer for Peter Stein's production of* Faust *by the German writer Goethe. Stein wanted to emphasize the circularity of Goethe's thought and also the notion of a spiral to represent the approach to heaven. (© Joan Marcus) (© Ruth Walz)*

A strong design concept is particularly important when the time and place of a play have been shifted. Modern stage designs for Shakespeare's *A Midsummer Night's Dream* illustrate this point. In most productions, this play is performed in a palace and a forest, as suggested by the text. But for a production done in the early 1970s, the director Peter Brook wanted to give it a modern, clean, spare look so that the audience would see its contemporary implications. Accordingly, the scene designer, Sally Jacobs (1932–), fashioned a single set consisting of three bare white walls, rather like the walls of a gymnasium. This single set was used as the background for all the scenes in the play, giving visual unity to the production and also creating a modern, somewhat abstract atmosphere. As part of the action, trapezes were lowered onto the stage at various times, and in some scenes the performers actually played their parts suspended in midair.

Providing a Central Image or Metaphor.   The design concept is closely related to the idea of a *central image* or *metaphor*. Stage design not only must be consistent with the play; it should have its own integrity. The elements of the design—lines, shapes, and colors—should add up to a complete visual universe for the play. Often, therefore, the designer tries to develop a central image or metaphor.

For the original production of *The Royal Hunt of the Sun* (1964), a play by Peter Shaffer (1926–) about Pizarro and the conquest of Peru, the designer, Michael Annals (1938–1990), set a huge sunburst, resembling a gold medallion, in midair at the back of the stage. Twelve feet in diameter and symbolizing both gold and the sun, the sunburst dominated the stage, providing a vivid focal point for the production.

In his design for the original Broadway production of *Death of a Salesman*, Jo Mielziner (1901–1976) created a set that combined various elements inherent in the play. On the one hand, there was the real home of Willy Loman, including a kitchen with a refrigerator, a table, and chairs. At the same time, surrounding the house was a skyline consisting of apartment houses closing in on Willy's world. When Willy moved from the present to his memory of the past, the lights would shift so that the audience could see through transparent walls of his house to the world around him. From the real world, Willy moved, as if by magic, through the walls of his home into the past. In these scenes, the hope and promise of Willy's youth, when his world was full of fresh, growing things, was symbolized by projections of green leaves thrown over the entire set, hiding the surrounding apartments. Mielziner's set provided a central metaphor for the play, with Willy's home as the constant, and the green plants—depicting youthful hope—ultimately blocked out by the encroaching skyline.

Coordinating Scenery with the Whole.   Because scenic elements have such strong symbolic value and are so important to the overall effect of a production, the designer needs to provide scenery consistent with the playwright's intent and the director's concept. If the text and acting are highly stylized, the setting should be stylized too. If the text and acting are realistic, the setting should also be realistic, rather than some kind of fantastic or overpowering spectacle. As with other elements, the setting should contribute to the overall effect of a production.

Solving Practical Design Problems.   Finally, the scene designer must deal with practical problems of design. Many of these involve physical elements of stage design, to which we'll now turn.

Elements of Scene Design

Five Elements of Scene Design.   As the scene designer proceeds, he or she makes use of the following elements:

1.   *Line,* the outline or silhouette of elements onstage; for example, predominantly curved lines versus sharply angular lines
2.   *Mass,* the overall bulk or weight of scenic elements; for example, a series of high, heavy platforms or fortress walls versus a bare stage or a stage with only a single tree on it
3.   *Composition,* the balance and arrangement of elements; the way elements are arranged: for example, mostly to one side of the stage, in a vertical or horizontal configuration, or equally distributed onstage
4.   *Texture,* the "feel" projected by surfaces and fabrics; for example, the slickness of chrome or glass versus the roughness of brick or burlap
5.   *Color,* the shadings and contrasts of color combinations

The designer will use these elements to affect audiences, in conjunction with the action and other aspects of the production.

Physical Layout: The Playing Area.   A playing area must, obviously, fit into a certain stage space and accommodate the performers. A designer cannot plan a gigantic stage setting for a theater where the proscenium opening is only 20 feet wide and the stage is no more than 15 feet deep. By the same token, to design a small room in the midst of a 40-foot stage opening might be ludicrous.

The designer must also take into account the physical layout of the stage space. If a performer must leave by a door on the right side of the stage and return a few moments later by a door on the left, the designer must obviously provide space for crossing behind the scenery. If performers need to change costumes quickly offstage, the scene designer must make certain that there is room offstage for changing. If there is to be a sword fight, the actors must have space in which to make their turns, to advance and retreat.

Any type of physical movement requires a certain amount of space, and the scene designer must allow for this in his or her ground plan. A ***ground plan*** is a blueprint, or floor plan, outlining the various levels on the stage and indicating the placement of all scenery, furniture, doors, windows, and so on. The designer, working in conjunction with the director, is chiefly responsible for ensuring a practical ground plan.

How doors open and close, where a sofa is placed, at what angle steps will lead to a second floor—all these are important. Performers must be able to execute stairs easily and to sit in such a way that the audience can readily see them, and they must have enough space to interact with each other naturally and convincingly. If a performer opens a door onstage and is immediately blocked from the view of the audience, this is obviously an error on the part of the scene designer.

To designate areas of the stage, scene designers, directors, performers, and technicians use terminology peculiar to theater. *Stage right* and *stage left* mean the right side and the left side of the stage, respectively, as seen from the position of a performer facing the audience. (In other words, when spectators in the auditorium look at the stage, the area to their left is known as **right stage** and the area to their right as **left stage.**) The stage area nearest the audience is known as **downstage;** the area farthest away from the audience is *upstage.* The designations *downstage* and *upstage* come from the eighteenth and nineteenth centuries, when the stage was raked—that is, it sloped downward from back to front. As a result of this downward slope, the performer farthest away from the audience was higher, or "up," and could be seen better. Also, performers downstage from—below—an upstage performer would be forced to turn their backs on the audience when addressing him or her. This is the origin of the expression *to upstage someone.* Today the term is used whenever one performer grabs the spotlight from everyone else or calls attention to himself or herself by any means whatever. At first, however, it meant simply that one performer was in a better position than the others because he or she was standing farther back on the raked stage and hence was higher.

Materials and Devices of Scene Design. In creating a stage set, a designer begins with the stage floor. At times, trapdoors are set into the floor; through them, performers can enter or leave the stage. For some productions, tracks or

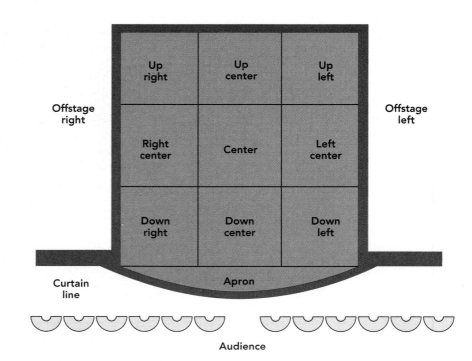

STAGE AREA
Various parts of the stage are given specific designations. Near the audience is downstage; away from the audience is upstage. Right and left are from the performers' point of view, not the audience's. Everything out of sight of the audience is offstage. Using this scheme, everyone working in the theater can carefully pinpoint stage areas.

Offstage
right

Offstage
left

Up right	Up center	Up left
Right center	Center	Left center
Down right	Down center	Down left

Curtain
line

Apron

Audience

slots are set into the stage floor, and set pieces or wagons are brought onstage in these tracks. A *wagon* is a low platform set on wheels. Wagon stages are brought onstage mechanically or by stagehands hidden behind them. This type of scene change is frequently used in musical comedy. Another device used along the stage floor is a *treadmill,* which can carry performers, furniture, or props from one side of the stage to the other. Sometimes the stage floor includes a *turntable*—a circle, set into the floor, which is rotated mechanically to bring one set into view as another disappears.

Formerly, equipment such as turntables, wagons, and treadmills would be moved mechanically or by hand. In recent years, however, these operations have been computerized. Complicated scene changes can be controlled by computer so that they take place efficiently and simultaneously. Computers can also control the turning and shifting of scenic elements. For instance, panels, screens, and scenic flats (discussed below) can not only be moved on- and offstage but can also be shifted or rotated while onstage. In addition, safety features are built into the new computerized equipment. When performers are on a moving treadmill, for example, light beams or pressure-sensitive plates can detect a malfunction and shut the system down before anyone is hurt.

Instead of coming from the sides, scenery can be dropped from the *fly loft; to fly* is the term used when scenery is raised into the area above the stage, out of sight of the audience.

From floor level, ramps and platforms can be built to any height desired. To create walls or divisions of other kinds, for many years the most commonly used element was the *flat,* so named because it is a single flat unit. A traditional flat consisted of canvas stretched on wood; the side of the flat facing the audience was painted to look like a solid wall, and flats used in conjunction were made to look like a complete room.

Today scene designers and shop technicians are turning more and more to the *hard flat,* sometimes called a *movie* or *Hollywood* flat; it consists of a thin, solid material, called *luan,* mounted on a wooden or hollow metal frame. A hard flat can be painted, and three-dimensional plastic moldings can be attached to it, creating cornices, chair rails, and other interesting features. A hard flat also has the advantage of not vibrating or shaking when it is touched. Other vertical units are *cutouts*—small pieces made like flats or cut out of plywood. These too can be painted.

SPECIAL SCENIC EFFECTS: THE SCRIM
Scene designers use various materials and devices to achieve their effects. One popular scenic element is the scrim, which can be transparent when light comes from behind it and opaque when light comes from the front. It is especially effective for scenes of memory and fantasy. In this scene from a production of Marie Antoinette *at the Jean Cocteau Repertory Theatre, we see Elizabeth Fuller as Marie with a shadow puppet, representing one of her relatives, projected on a scrim behind her.* (© Gerry Goodstein/The Independent Eye)

A special type of scenery is the *scrim*—a gauze or cloth screen. A scrim can be painted like a regular flat; however, the wide mesh of the cloth allows light to pass through. When light shines on a scrim from the front— that is, from the audience's point of view—it is reflected off the painted surface, and the scrim appears to be a solid wall. When light comes from behind, the scrim becomes transparent and the audience can see performers and scenery behind it. Scrims are particularly effective in scenes where ghosts appear or when eerie effects are desired. Scrims are also useful in memory plays or plays with flashbacks: the audience sees the scene in the present in front of the scrim; then, as the lights in front fade and the lights behind come up, a scene with a

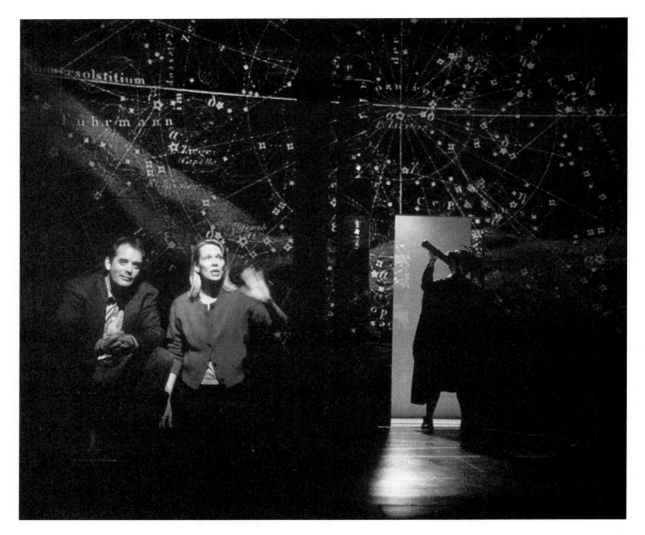

SCREEN PROJECTIONS

Effective scenic supplements to traditional scenery are video and screen projections—either still images or moving images. Visual effects can be superimposed or used in the background of stage action. Shown here are large projections of stars and constellations that formed the backdrop of the production Space *written and directed by Tina Landau and presented at the Joseph Papp Public Theater. The projections were designed by Jan Hartley. (© Michal Daniel/Joseph Papp Public Theater/New York Shakespeare Festival)*

cloudy, translucent quality appears through the gauzelike scrim, indicating a scene taking place in someone's memory or in the past.

Another scenic device is *screen projection.* A picture or drawing is projected on a screen either from in front—as in an ordinary movie theater—or from behind. The advantage of projection from behind is that the performers will not be in the beam of light, and thus there will be no shadows or silhouettes. Obviously, projections offer many advantages: pictures can change with the rapidity of cinema, and vast scenes can be presented onstage in a way which would otherwise require tremendously elaborate scene painting.

In recent years, many avant-garde artists have also incorporated video screens and video projections into production design, frequently to draw stark parallels or contrasts between the live performance and something captured on video.

Special Effects.   Scrims and projections bring us to a consideration of *special effects*. These are effects of scenery, lighting, sound, and props that seem unusual or even miraculous. (The term **prop** comes from the word *property;* it refers to any object that will be used onstage but is not a permanent part of the scenery or costumes. Props are such things as lamps, mirrors, computers, walking sticks, umbrellas, and fans.) Special effects include fog, ghosts, knives or swords that appear to stab victims, walls and windows that fall apart, and so on. Today, films and television—because of their technical capabilities—have very realistic special effects, like burning buildings and exploding cars. Also, computers can create the world of dinosaurs or storms at sea. Special effects onstage, however, are almost as old as theater itself. From the Greeks on, theater has tried to create the illusion of the miraculous or extraordinary.

See-through scrims and projections are used to create a number of special effects, such as dream sequences. Fog machines create a cloudy vapor that can be blown across the stage by fans, giving an impression of clouds or fog. In *The Phantom of the Opera*, a huge chandelier falls from the top of the auditorium onto the stage; and in *Miss Saigon*, a helicopter lands on top of the American embassy in Saigon to rescue fleeing soldiers and civilians. In Chapter 6, we will see that there are also many special effects of lighting and sound.

The Process of Scene Design: Steps in the Design Process

In meeting the objectives described above, how does the scene designer proceed? Although every designer has his or her own method, usually the same general pattern is followed.

The designer reads the script and develops his or her ideas about scene designs and a design concept. He or she may even make a few rough sketches to illustrate thoughts about the designs. Meanwhile, the director also has ideas about the scenery. These ideas may vary considerably, depending on the director: they may be vague, or they may be an exact picture of what the scenery should look like.

Director and designer meet for a preliminary conference to exchange ideas about the design. During these discussions, they will develop and discuss questions of style, a visual concept for the production, the needs of the performers, and so on.

Next, the designer develops preliminary sketches, called *thumbnail sketches,* and rough plans to provide a basis for further discussions about the scenic elements.

As the designer proceeds, he or she attempts to fill out the visual concept with sketches, drawings, models, and the like. Sometimes the designer will bring the director sketches showing several possible ideas, each emphasizing different elements to achieve different results.

When the director and the designer have decided on an idea and a rough design, the designer will make a more complete sketch, usually in color, called a *rendering*. If the director approves of the rendering, the designer will make a small-scale three-dimensional *model* which the director can use to help stage the show. There are two types of models. One shows only the location of the platform and walls, with perhaps some light detail drawn in; it is usually all white. The other is a complete, finished model: everything is duplicated as fully as possible, including color and perhaps moldings and texture.

Today, more and more designers are using computers and computer graphics to develop not only ground plans but also three-dimensional models of sets. Because computer design is so flexible, a designer can make instantaneous changes in what appears on the screen. The director can be shown easily and quickly alternative plans and features of a stage set.

The Scene Designer's Collaborators

As with every element of theater, the visual elements of a production are created collaboratively. A number of important people, in addition to the scene designer, are required to develop scenic effects.

First, there may be people who help the scene designer draw the architectural plans for platforms, ramps, flats, and other scenery. These plans require exact measurements that conform to the stage space, and to the proscenium opening if there is one. They must be drawn precisely to scale, like the blueprints used by architects and engineers in constructing buildings. Today, computers can assist in this drafting.

Once a rendering, model, or computer design is complete and has been approved, it is turned over to the **technical director** of the production, who is also given all the necessary ground plans. Together with building and painting crews, the technical director sees that the necessary elements are built, painted, and installed onstage.

Stage carpenters—people who understand materials and methods of construction—build the platforms, set pieces, flats, and other scenic elements; then scene painters paint them. Scene painting often requires both talent and technique—to create, for instance, the feeling of rare old wood in a library, or of bricks, or of a glossy wall in an expensive living room. There are also people who find fabric for draperies, slipcovers for furniture, and other items that "dress" the stage set.

When the time comes for technical rehearsals, dress rehearsals, and actual performances, a production requires stagehands and a stage manager to coordinate scene changes, to remove and replace scenery and furniture, and to see that each setting is correct and is put into place quickly.

It is clear from all this that a scene designer works closely with others: first with the director—to develop a concept and a visual approach consistent with the overall production—and then with the many people who build, paint, and dress the set and "run" the show after it opens. (To *dress a set* means to add all the furniture and details: draperies, rugs, cushions, and the like.

Designing a Total Environment

Sometimes, in addition to all these duties, a designer goes further, designing not only scenery and special effects but the entire theater space. For example, a designer might decide to rearrange the position of the stage and the audience seating area around it. Seats might be removed to make way for additional stage space; or, in a flexible area without fixed seating, the stage might be put in one corner rather than in a central position.

Costume Design

Of all the visual elements in theater, costumes are the most personal because they are actually worn by the performers. Visually, performer and costume are perceived as one; they merge into a single image onstage. At the same time, costumes have a value of their own, adding color, shape, texture, and symbolism to the overall effect. Closely related to costumes are makeup, hairstyles, and masks.

Outside of the theater, most people think of costumes in terms of a holiday parade, a masquerade ball, or a historical pageant with figures such as Queen Elizabeth and George Washington. Costumes, however, also play a significant role in daily life. People wear clothes not only for comfort but to convey information about themselves. If we look around us, we are actually surrounded by costumes: the formal, subdued uniform of a police officer; the sparkling outfits of a marching band at a football game; sports gear, such as hockey and baseball uniforms; caps and gowns at a graduation; a priest's cassock; brightly colored bathing suits at a swimming pool.

Clothes have always suggested a number of things about the wearer:

Position and status
Gender
Occupation
Flamboyance or modesty
Independence or regimentation
Occasion—work or leisure, a routine event or a special event

As soon as we see what people are wearing, we receive a great many messages and impressions about them; we instantaneously relate those messages to our own experiences and preconceptions; and we form judgments, including value judgments. Even if we have never before laid eyes on people, we feel we know a great deal about them when we first see the clothing they wear.

In theater, clothing also sends us signals; but, as with other elements of theater, there are significant differences between theatrical costumes and costumes in everyday life. Although stage costumes, like ordinary clothes, communicate information about gender, status, and occupation, this information is magnified onstage because it is in the spotlight. Also, of course, stage costumes must meet other requirements, not normally imposed on everyday clothing.

The Costume Designer

The person responsible for creating costumes for performers is the *costume designer.* Every production requires someone who takes responsibility for the costumes. Like a scene designer, a costume designer must develop visual ideas with the director and communicate those ideas through drawings. Drawings by a costume designer are frequently accompanied by swatches of material. It is the costume designer's responsibility to determine how costumes will actually look on performers in front of an audience. Obviously, all this requires both training and talent.

The costume designer should begin with a thorough knowledge of the play—its subject matter, period, style, and point of view—and with an intimate understanding of the characters. The costume designer must also be aware of the physical demands of the text—what is called for in terms of sitting, moving, dancing, fighting, and so on. Finally, the designer must be acquainted with the physical characteristics of the performers themselves in order to create costumes accommodating their individual physiques and patterns of movement.

Additionally, the costume designer must decide whether the costumes are to be *pulled* or *built.* *Pulling* costumes means renting them from a costume warehouse or choosing them from an inventory owned by a theater company. *Building* costumes means creating them in a costume shop under the supervision of the designer. Built costumes must be sewn, fitted, and completed with accessories and ornamentation. Sometimes, a designer will pull some costumes for a production but build the more unusual ones.

THE COSTUME DESIGNER AT WORK
The costume designer is responsible for the look of each performer on stage: the shape, color, and style of what the performer wears, the accessories which accompany the clothes, and the way the costumes of various characters blend together and offset one another. Shown here is an award-winning costume designer, Jane Greenwood, in a design studio working on a costume for the musical High Society. *(Jack Manning/NYT Pictures)*

The Costume Designer's Objectives

Stage costumes should meet six requirements:

1. Help establish the tone and style of a production
2. Indicate the historical period of a play and the locale in which it is set
3. Indicate the nature of individual characters or groups in a play: their stations in life, their occupations, their personalities
4. Show relationships among characters: separate major characters from minor ones, contrast one group with another

Jess Goldstein: Costume Designer

Jess Goldstein has designed costumes for Broadway (The Most Happy Fella, A Streetcar Named Desire, and Love! Valour! Compassion!); for off-Broadway (The Substance of Fire, Other People's Money, Proof, and Dinner with Friends); for many major regional theaters; and for the New York City Opera. He teaches costume design at the Yale Drama School.

Growing up in the New Jersey suburbs right outside New York City, I began seeing Broadway theater at a relatively early age. I think I was always most impressed with the costume and set design, possibly because I had no talent for performing yet seemed to show some aptitude for drawing and painting. But the world of theatrical design, from my naive perspective, seemed far too exotic and unattainable, so I enrolled as a commercial art major at Boston University. But I continued to see a lot of theater in Boston, which in the early 1970s was still an important tryout stopover for Broadway shows.

At B.U. I met students who were majoring in design in the theater school. Somehow, the fact that one could earn a degree in theater design seemed to endow it as a career choice with some validity and security. Well, talk about "naive"! Nevertheless, I switched majors, and really found school and classwork exciting for the first time in my life.

But it was going to the theater and seeing those Hal Prince, Bob Fosse, Gower Champion, and Michael Bennett musicals that really inspired me. The stars of those shows were terrific, but my heroes were Irene Sharaff, Raoul Pene duBois, Patricia Zipprodt, and Florence Klotz. Watching the way colors and shapes might be manipulated in a scene or the way a skirt would move to the choreography was a significant part of my early training.

I soon began seeking out other kinds of theater: plays off-Broadway, the Shakespeare festivals in New York and Stratford, Connecticut, as well as opera and ballet; and by the time the off-off-Broadway theater movement was in full swing in New York in the late 1970s, I had just completed my M.F.A. at the Yale School of Drama and was ready as a designer to be a part of it.

5. Meet the needs of individual performers: make it possible for an actor or actress to move freely in a costume; allow a performer to dance or engage in a sword fight, for instance; when necessary, allow performers to change quickly from one costume to another

6. Be consistent with the production as a whole, especially with other visual elements

Let us look at these objectives one at a time.

Setting Tone and Style.   Along with scenery and lighting, costumes should inform the audience about the style of a play. For a production taking place in outer space, for instance, the costumes would be futuristic. For a Restoration comedy, the costumes would be elegant, with lace at the men's collars and cuffs, and elaborate gowns for the women. For a tragedy, the clothes would be somber and dignified; seeing them, the audience would know immediately that the play itself was somber and its tone serious.

Indicating Time and Place.   Costumes indicate the period and location of a play: whether it is historical or modern, set in a foreign country or the United States, and so on. A play might take place in ancient Egypt, for instance, in seventeenth-century Spain, or in modern Africa. Costumes should tell us when and where the action occurs. In some productions, the director and designers want to indicate timelessness, in which case the costumes should not suggest any one period.

Sometimes, as we have already seen, a costume designer and a director decide to shift the period of a play. Such a shift may come as a shock to the audience, and it is up to the costume designer to help the audience adjust to it. For example, if *Hamlet* is to be performed in modern dress, the costume designer in certain scenes might have Hamlet wear a tuxedo and Gertrude an evening gown.

For most historical plays, the director and the costume designer actually have a range of choices. For example, depending on the directorial concept, costumes for Shakespeare's *Julius Caesar* could indicate the time and place in which Caesar lived—ancient Rome—and thus would include togas and soldiers' helmets. Or the costumes could be Elizabethan, since we know that in Shakespeare's day stage costumes were simply a heightened version of contemporary English clothes, regardless of the period in which a play was set. Or the designer could use costumes from an entirely different period, including the present. Whatever the choice, though, the historical period should be clearly indicated by the costumes.

Indicating Characterization.   Just as everyday clothes often do, costumes tell us whether their wearers are aristocrats or ordinary people, blue-collar workers or professionals. In the theater, such signals must be clear and unmistakable. For example, a person in a long white coat could be a doctor, a laboratory technician, or a hairdresser. A stage costume must indicate the exact occupation, and so it may be necessary to add accessories, such as a stethoscope for a doctor.

Costumes also tell us about characters' personalities: a flamboyant person will be dressed in flashy colors; a shy, retiring person will wear subdued clothes.

Costumes can also be used to create symbolic or nonhuman characters. Many plays call for special costumes, denoting abstract ideas or giving shape to fantastic creatures. Here the costume designer must develop an outfit which has the appropriate imaginative and symbolic qualities. A good example would be the Moon and Beggar Woman in *Blood Wedding*.

Indicating Relationships among Characters.   Characters can be set apart by the way they are costumed. Major characters, for example, will be dressed differently from minor characters. Frequently, a costume designer will point up the major characters in

COSTUMES INDICATE RELATIONSHIPS

Along with their many other properties, costumes can signal the relationships and contrasts among characters in a production. The lead character may be dressed more vividly than those surrounding her or him; opposing forces such as the two families in Romeo and Juliet *will be dressed in different colors. A good example is shown in this scene from a modern production of Shakespeare's* As You Like It *by The Acting Company. The two cousins Rosalind (Felicity Jones, left) and Celia (Heather Robison, right) are dressed in strikingly contrasting costumes. (© T. Charles Erickson)* a play by dressing them in distinctive colors, in sharp contrast to the colors worn by other characters. Consider, for instance, Shaw's *Saint Joan,* a play about Joan of Arc. Obviously, Joan should stand out from the soldiers surrounding her. Therefore, her costume might be bright-blue while theirs are steel-gray. In another play of Shaw's, *Caesar and Cleopatra,* Cleopatra should stand out from her servants and soldiers. Though she will be dressed like them in an Egyptian costume, she should wear a more elegant outfit, in brighter colors.

Costumes also underline important differences between groups. In *Romeo and Juliet,* the Montagues wear costumes of one color; the Capulets wear another color. In a modern counterpart of *Romeo and Juliet,* the musical *West Side Story,* the two street gangs are dressed in contrasting colors: the Jets might wear various shades of pink, purple, and lavender; the Sharks might wear green, yellow, and chartreuse.

Meeting Performers' Needs.   Virtually every aspect of theater has practical as well as aesthetic requirements, and costume design is no exception. No matter how attractive or how symbolic a costume may be, it must work for the performer. A long flowing gown may look beautiful; but if it is too long and the actress wearing it trips every time she walks down a flight of steps, the designer has overlooked an important practical consideration. If an actor is called on to engage in hand-to-hand combat or fight a duel, his costume must stand up to this wear and tear; and his arms and legs must be free to move, not constrained by the costumes. If performers are to dance, they must be able to turn and leap freely.

Ensuring Consistency with the Whole.   Finally, costumes must be consistent with the entire production, especially with the other visual elements. A realistic production set in the home of everyday people calls for down-to-earth costumes. A highly stylized production requires costumes designed with flair and imagination.

Elements of Costume Design

Resources of the Costume Designer.   Among the resources a costume designer works with are:

Line, shape, and silhouette
Color
Fabric
Accessories

Line.   Of prime importance is the cut or line of a costume. Do the lines of the outfit flow, or are they sharp and jagged? Does the clothing follow the lines of the body, or is there some element of exaggeration, such as shoulder pads in a man's jacket or a bustle at the back of a woman's dress? The outline or silhouette of a costume has always been significant.

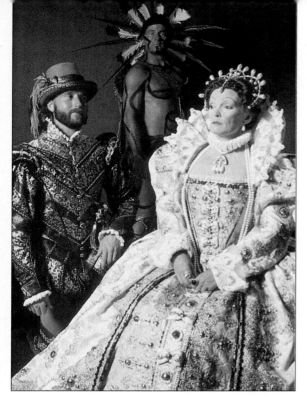

STYLE, FABRIC AND CUT IN COSTUMES

The type of fabric employed, the line and shape of the outfit, the ornateness of the trim and finishing: these tell us a great deal about the characters in a play. Shown here are the costumes of William Ivey Long for Queen Elizabeth, a Native American chief, and one of her courtiers in the outdoor drama The Lost Colony. *Note how regal and how formal the queen's outfit is; we know immediately that this is historical, and that it involves royalty.* (Walter V. Gresham, III)

Color. A second important resource for costume designers is color. Earlier, we saw that major characters can be dressed in a color which contrasts with the colors worn by minor characters, and that the characters in one family can be dressed in a different color from those in a rival family. Color also suggests mood: bright, warm colors for a happy mood; dark, somber colors for a more serious mood.

Fabric. Fabric is a third resource of the costume designer. In one sense, fabric is the medium of the costume designer, for it is in fabric that silhouette and color are displayed. Texture and bulk of a fabric are also important. Does a fabric have a smoothness or sheen that reflects light? Or is it rough, so that it absorbs light? How does it drape on the wearer? Does it fall lightly to the floor, outlining the body, or does it hide the body? Does it wrinkle naturally, or is it smooth? Beyond its inherent qualities, fabric has symbolic values. Burlap or other rough-textured cloth, for example, suggests peasants or earthy people, or people of modest means. Silks and satins, on the other hand, suggest elegance, refinement, and perhaps even royalty.

In terms of fabric, a number of improvements have been made in recent years, just as they have in other fields of design. William Ivey Long (1947–   ) is an award-winning designer who designs for Broadway, off-Broadway, and the long-running outdoor drama *The Lost Colony* in North Carolina. In an interview, Long explained the improvements in fabric: "We're actually using more accurate fabrics. When I was growing up, polyester was what was available, and blends. Flax is now available—wool, silk, cotton, linen, flax. We are able to use more plastics (to support the costumes), and we have better products for maintaining the costumes that are fabric-, people- and environment-friendly."

Accessories. Ornamentation and accessories are another resource for costume designers. Fringe, lace, ruffles, feathers, belts, and beads can add to the attractiveness and individuality of a costume. Walking sticks, parasols, purses, and other items that are carried or worn can give distinction and definition.

Using the combined resources of line, color, fabric, and accessories, the costume designer arrives at individual outfits which tell us a great deal about the characters who wear them and convey important visual signals about the style and meaning of the play as a whole.

Related Elements. Three elements that are closely related to costumes are makeup, hairstyles, and masks.

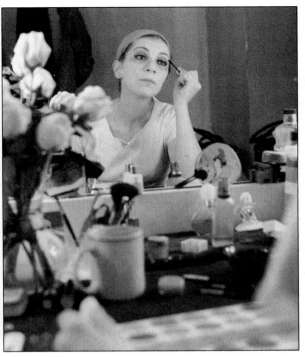

ORNAMENTATION IN COSTUMING
Those who create costumes, wigs, and hairstyles often use a wide variety of objects and accessories: feathers, fabrics, jewelry, and the like. A vivid example are the costume, wig and hairpiece for the actress Pamela Payton-Wright in a production of She Stoops to Conquer at the Long Wharf Theatre in New Haven. The costume is by Linda Fischer and the wig by Paul Huntley. (© T. Charles Erickson)

MAKEUP
The application of makeup is frequently employed so that facial features will not be washed out by bright theater lights, or to change the appearance of a performer—to make a younger person look older, for example. Shown here is actress Shelley Williams applying makeup for a role in Brecht's In the Jungle of the Cities produced by the Alley Theatre in Houston. (© T. Charles Erickson)

Makeup.   Makeup—the application of cosmetics such as paints, powders, and rouges to the face and body—helps a performer personify and embody a character. Makeup can be particularly useful if there are age or ethnic differences between the performer and the character.

Makeup used to be more popular in the theater than it is today. In a modern small theater, performers playing realistic parts will often simply go without makeup of any consequence. But makeup has a long and important history in theater, and sometimes it is still a necessity—a good example being makeup to highlight facial features which would not otherwise be visible in a large theater. Even in a smaller theater, bright lights tend to wash out cheekbones, eyebrows, and so on. Makeup is often essential because the age of a character differs from that of the performer. If a 19-year-old performer is playing the part of a 60-year-old, the appropriate age can be suggested with makeup, such as a little gray in the hair or simulated wrinkles. Makeup is also necessary in creating fantastic or other non-realistic creatures.

Asian theater frequently relies on heavy makeup. For instance, Japanese kabuki, a highly stylized theater, uses completely nonrealistic makeup. The main characters must apply a base of white covering the entire face; over this base, bold patterns of red, blue, black, and brown are painted. These colors and patterns symbolize the character. In Chinese theater, too, the colors of makeup are symbolic: all white means treachery; black means integrity; red means loyalty; green indicates demons; yellow stands for hidden cunning; and so forth.

Hairstyles. Closely related to makeup are hairstyles. Outside the theater, hairstyles have varied a great deal in different historical periods and among differ-

WIGS AND HAIRSTYLES

Hairstyle and wigs indicate social status and other facts about a character; it also provides crucial information about the period in which a play is taking place. The scene here shows the highly stylized and elaborate costumes designed by Howard Crabtree for his play When Pigs Fly. *The production was a gay musical revue that featured outrageous, over-the-top costumes and wigs which added humor as well as flamboyance to the look of the presentation. (© Gerry Goodstein)* ent social classes. In certain periods, for example, men have worn wigs: the time of the American Revolution is a good example, and judges in England still wear wigs today. In the theater, such styles can be used to indicate a historical era or social status.

In the middle of the nineteenth century, women often wore ringlets like Scarlett O'Hara's in the film *Gone with the Wind*. A few decades later, near the turn of the century, women piled their hair on top of the head in a pompadour; this was referred to as the "Gibson girl" look. In the 1920s, women wore their hair in waves, sometimes slicked down close to the head.

Today, women tend to wear their hair in more natural styles, but actually there is tremendous variety. Some women have short curly hair; some have short straight hair; some have frizzy hair; others have long hair, perhaps even down to the waist, and again, this can be straight or quite curly.

Masks.   Masks seem to be as old as theater. They were used in ancient Greek theater and in the drama developed by primitive tribes. In one sense, a mask is an extension of a performer: a face on top of a face. There are several ways to interpret masks. They remind us, first, that we are in the theater, that the act going on before our eyes is not real in a literal sense but is rather symbolic or artistic. Second, masks allow a face to be frozen in one expression—a look of horror, perhaps—which we see throughout a production.

The Costume Designer's Collaborators

Like the scene designer, the costume designer works closely with a number of other people. There are, for example, experts at making wigs and masks, and people who specialize in makeup. The actual costumes must be sewn and fitted to the performers by professionals. Sometimes the making and sewing of a costume can be an extremely complicated affair, especially if sequins, feathers, a special corset, or other items are required. Accessories and other personal properties such as hats, umbrellas, and walking canes must be made or found. A costume designer must work closely with these specialists at the same time that he or she is realizing the overall concept developed with the director.

MASKS

Almost from the beginning of theater, both in the West and the East, masks have been an integral part of presentations. Masks can change the appearance of a performer, make the face and head larger than life, and freeze the face into a fixed expression. They can also be fanciful and imaginative, suggesting animals or other-worldly creatures. Shown here are masks created by Dionysis Fotopoulos for Peter Hall's production of Tantalus, *a version of the events of the Trojan war written by John Barton and first presented at the Denver Theatre Center. In this scene we see Mia Yoo, above, as Iphigenia and Greg Hicks as Agamemnon wearing masks.* (© P. Switzer/ Denver Center for the Performing Arts)

In Chapter 6 we turn to two other important contributors to the visual and aural elements of theater productions: the light and sound designers.

SUMMARY

Two important visual elements of theater are scenery and costumes. These elements are used both to convey information and for aesthetic effect. Scene and costume designers create and organize these visual aspects of theater production.

The scene designer's goals are to help set the tone and style of the production, establish locale and period, develop a design concept, coordinate scenery with other production elements, and solve any practical design problems. Basic elements used by the scene designer are line, mass and composition, texture, and color.

The costume designer also helps establish tone, style, historical period, and locale. In addition, the costume designer helps indicate the personality and social status of individual characters and shows relationships between characters. Costumes—like settings—must be designed so that performers can use them safely and easily. Related to costume are hairstyles and masks, which must also be appropriate and functional.

Scene and costume designers work closely with people who construct sets, props, and costumes and see that they function properly during productions.

THEATER ON THE WEB

The Internet has a wealth of resources for costume and scene designers.

International Costumers' Guild, Inc., ICG   http://www.costume.org
A worldwide organization of costume professionals and hobbyists. Links to costume resources, events, and area chapters.

U.S. Institute for Theater Technology   http://www.ffa.ucalgary.ca/usitt
USITT is an association of theater technology professionals.

IATSE http://www.iatse.lm.com
The labor union representing technicians, artisans, and craftspersons in the entertainment industry.

Glossary of Technical Theatre Terms   http://www.ex.ac.uk/drama/tech/glossary.html
This is a list of technical theater terms, based on usage in the United Kingdom.

Costumers Manifesto   http://www.costumes.org
Includes photos, renderings, history, and information on costuming. Extensive links to other costuming collections.

After looking at these resources, what sort of picture do you have of the theatrical design and technical community? How are these professionals different from performers? How are they similar? What are their concerns? How do designers find work? How are design resources different from the resources a producer or director would need? How are they similar? Looking at the professional organizations, answer the following: What are the differences between IATSE and ICG? How is IATSE similar to Actors' Equity Association?

Chapter 6

Designers: Lighting and Sound

Stage Lighting
Lighting in Theater History

Getting Started in Theater:
Peggy Eisenhauer: Lighting Designer

Objectives of Lighting Design

Elements of Stage Lighting

The Lighting Designer's Resources

The Lighting Designer's Collaborators

Sound Design
The Sound Designer

Objectives of Sound Design

Sound Reproduction and Sound Reinforcement

Elements of Sound: Sound Technology

The Sound Designer's Collaborators

Special Effects in Lighting and Sound

Summary

◀ THE MAGIC OF STAGE LIGHTING

Lighting can define a stage area, create mood, indicate changes of scene and contribute a host of other accomplishments to a theater production. Note in this scene from a production of Edward Albee's Tiny Alice, *a circle of light in the foreground, and the lights in the model of a building in the rear. Actor Richard Thomas lies prone in the center of the circle in an attitude of crucifixion. The circle of light illuminates him, but also provides a powerful focus for the figure. The lighting designer is Donald Holder. (© Jennifer Lester/Hartford Stage)*

123

In Chapter 5, we explored the work of scene and costume designers. In this chapter, we turn to two other important aspects of theatrical design: lighting and sound. We begin with lighting, which must be coordinated closely with scene design. We'll consider how lighting has been used in earlier periods of theater history, what its aesthetic functions and qualities are, and how a lighting designer works. Next, we discuss sound design and its use. Finally, we'll look at special effects in lighting and sound design.

Stage Lighting

Lighting in Theater History

For the first 2,000 years of its recorded history, theater took place mostly outdoors during the day, one important reason being the need for illumination—the sun, after all, is an excellent source of light.

Since artificial lighting was unavailable, playwrights used the imagination to suggest nighttime, or shifts in lighting. Performers would bring on torches—or a candle, as Lady Macbeth does—to indicate night. Playwrights also used language in place of lighting. When Shakespeare has Lorenzo say, in *The Merchant of Venice* (1596–1597), "How sweet the moonlight sleeps upon this bank," this is not just a pretty line of poetry but also serves to remind us that it is nighttime. The same is true of the eloquent passage in which Romeo tells Juliet that he must leave because dawn is breaking:

> Look, love, what envious streaks
> Do lace the severing clouds in yonder East:
> Night's candles are burnt out, and jocund day
> Stands tiptoe on the misty mountain tops.

Around A.D. 1600, theater began to move indoors. Candles and oil lamps were used for illumination until 1803, when a theater in London installed gaslights. With gas, lighting became more manageable, allowing some control of intensity and color, but it remained crude, primitive, and limited in its effectiveness. In addition, gas and other lighting systems of the time involved open flames and thus posed a constant threat of fire. During this period, there were several tragic and costly fires in theaters, in both Europe and the United States.

In 1879, Thomas Edison invented the incandescent lamp—the electric lightbulb—and the era of technological theater lighting began. Not only are incandescent lamps safe, but their intensity can be controlled by means of rheostats and other devices. Brightness can be increased or decreased, so that the same lighting instrument can produce the full light of noonday or the dim light of dusk. Also, the color of the light can be controlled by putting a colored film over the source.

Beyond the power and versatility of electric light, there have been numerous other advances in controls and equipment over the past 50 years. Lighting instruments have been constantly refined to become more powerful, as well as more subtle, and to throw a more concentrated, more sharply defined beam. Moreover, miniaturization and computerization have been incorporated into lighting more

Peggy Eisenhauer: Lighting Designer

Peggy Eisenhauer is a lighting designer whose credits include concert designs for David Bowie's and Linda Ronstadt's tours, and the Broadway shows Will Rogers Follies; Angels in America; Grand Hotel; Twilight: Los Angeles; Bring in 'da Noise, Bring in 'da Funk; *and many others.*

I grew up in the New York Metropolitan area, the lucky child of parents who exposed me to the thrill and excitement of live performance. By the time I was 10, I had seen the New York City Ballet, Bill Baird, Ringling Brothers, and Broadway shows, as well as local concerts and theater. By working in community theater in my high school years, I became familiar with all theatrical crafts and became especially interested in lighting design.

The Broadway production of *Pippin*, with direction by Bob Fosse and lighting by Jules Fisher, was the deciding factor in my choice of career. Jules's unique musicality expressed through lighting design spoke to me, and I tried to see as much of his work as I could. I went on to study lighting design at his alma mater, Carnegie-Mellon University, and met Jules there.

After graduation, and after gaining working experience with other designers on and off Broadway, I saw my dream come true: I assisted Jules on a Broadway project, and we've been working together ever since. Our second production together was Bob Fosse's final musical, *Big Deal,* which opened nearly 10 years to the day after I saw *Pippin.* Our recent joint designs include *Tommy Tune Tonight; Twilight: Los Angeles, 1992;* the *Whitney Houston Bodyguard Tour;* and *A Christmas Carol.*

successfully than into any other elements of theater. After all, costumes must still be sewn individually, and scenes on flats must still be painted by hand. Lighting, however, is controlled by electricity and therefore offers a perfect opportunity to take advantage of innovations in electronics and technology. First came resistance systems, then thyratron vacuum tubes, and after that a series of technologies with names such as *magnetic amplifiers* and *silicon-controlled rectifiers.*

Applied to lighting, these innovations allowed for increasingly complex and sophisticated controls. For a large college theater production, 100 to 200 lighting instruments may be hung around and above the stage; for a large Broadway musical, there may be up to 800 or more depending on the type of show and the technology being used. Each of these instruments can be connected to a central computer board, and light settings—the level, direction, and color of the lighting instruments—can be stored in the computer. By pushing a single button, an operator can bring about a shift in literally dozens of instruments in a split second. The resulting flexibility and control are a remarkable tool for achieving stage effects.

Objectives of Lighting Design

The following are the functions and objectives of stage lighting:

1. Provide visibility
2. Help establish time and place
3. Help create mood

4. Reinforce the style of the production
5. Provide focus onstage and create visual compositions
6. Establish rhythm of visual movement

Providing Visibility.   The chief practical function of lighting is, of course, illumination or visibility. First and foremost, we must be able to see the performers' faces and actions. Occasionally, lighting designers, carried away with the atmospheric possibilities of light, will make a scene so dark that we can hardly see what is happening. Mood is important, of course, but seeing the performers is obviously more important. At times, a script does call for the lights to dim; in a suspense play, for instance, the lights in a haunted house might go out. But these are exceptions. Ordinarily, if you cannot see the performers, the lighting designer has not carried out his or her assignment.

Establishing Time and Place.   The color, shade, and intensity of lighting can suggest time of day, giving us the pale light of dawn, the bright light of midday, the vivid colors of sunset, or the muted light of evening. Lighting can also indicate the season of the year, because the sun strikes objects at very different angles in winter and summer. Lighting can also suggest place—indoor or outdoor light, for instance.

LIGHTING ESTABLISHES TIME AND PLACE
By the use of color, direction, and intensity, lighting can help establish the time and place in which a theater event takes place. Pale light can be dawn or dusk, bright light, midday, and muted light, evening. In the scene here from a production of Shakespeare's Romeo and Juliet *at the Trinity Repertory Theatre of Providence, R. I., nighttime is created through the use of lighting. Playing Romeo is Mark H. Dold and Juliet, Tori Signor. The set was by Mark Wendland and lighting by Mimi Jordan Sherin.* (© T. Charles Erickson/ Trinity Repertory Company)

Creating Mood.   Light together with scenery and costumes can help create a certain mood. Rarely, however, can lighting alone create mood. For example, if a stage is filled with blue light, it might be inviting, romantic moonlight, but it could also be a cold, dark, evil setting. When action, scenery, and words are combined with light, they tell us exactly what the mood is. In general, a happy, carefree play calls for bright, warm colors, such as yellows, oranges, and pinks. A more somber piece will lean toward blues, blue-greens, and muted tones.

LIGHTING CREATES FOCUS

Lighting helps create focus and powerful visual arrangements onstage. An example is this scene from a production of Life is a Dream *by Calderón at the Yale School of Drama. The faces of the characters in the center are brightly lit, at the same time that backlighting on the characters casts shadows in front. This is a striking use of lighting effects by designer Matthew Richards. (© T. Charles Erickson)*

Reinforcing Style. With regard to style, lighting can indicate whether a play is realistic or nonrealistic. In a realistic play, the lighting will simulate the effect of ordinary sources, such as table lamps and sunlight. In a nonrealistic production, the designer can be more imaginative: shafts of light can cut through the dark, sculpturing performers onstage; a glowing red light can envelop a scene of damnation; a ghostly green light can cast a spell over a nightmare scene.

Providing Focus and Composition. In photography, the focus has to do with adjusting the lens of a camera so that the picture recorded on the film is sharp and clear. In theater lighting, *focus* means that beams of light are aimed at, or "focused on," a particular area.

Focus in lighting directs our attention to one part of the stage—generally the part where the important action is occurring—and away from other areas. Lights should illuminate the playing area, not the scenery. If more light is on the scenery than on the performers, the audience's attention will be drawn to the scenery and away from the actors and actresses. Therefore, the first objective of focus is to aim the light at the right place. A good example of the use of focus occurs when there is a split stage, with half the action on one side and half on the other side. The lights can direct our attention from side to side as they go down in one area and come up in another.

Composition is the way lighted areas are arranged onstage in relationship to one another—which areas are dimmed, which are brightly lit, and what the overall stage effect is with regard to light. By means of focus, light can create a series of visual compositions onstage. The effects can vary from turning the stage into one large area to creating small, isolated areas.

Establishing Rhythm. Since changes in light occur over a time continuum, they establish a rhythm running through a production. Abrupt, staccato changes with stark blackouts will convey one rhythm; languid, slow fades and gradual crossfades will convey another.

Lighting changes are timed in coordination with scene changes. The importance of this coordination is recognized by directors and designers, who take great care to "choreograph" shifts in light and scenery, like the movements of dancers.

Elements of Stage Lighting

A *lighting designer* knows which elements or qualities of light will achieve the objectives we have just been discussing. Let's consider these qualities.

Intensity. First of all, light has brightness, or *intensity*. Intensity is controlled by an electronic device called a *dimmer,* which can make a scene brighter or darker.

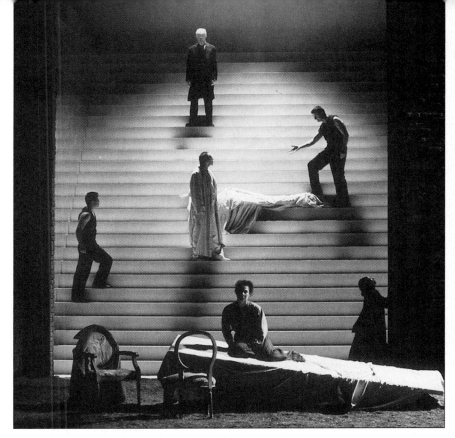

Dimmers allow a scene at night to take place in very little light and a daylight scene to take place in bright light.

Color. Another quality, a very powerful aspect of light, is *color*. Theater lights can be changed very easily to any one of several hundred colors simply by putting colored material in slots at the front of the lighting instruments. This material is usually called *gel*—short for *gelatin*, the cellophane of which it was originally made. Today, however, these color mediums are generally made of plastic mylars and acetates. With modern technology, color can even be changed electronically without gels (the special equipment is described below, in the section on the lighting designer's resources).

LIGHTING AIDS COMPOSITION
Lighting can create arrangements on stage that in themselves are striking visual pictures. These can serve the play by emphasizing certain characters and they can also be aesthetically pleasing and exciting. An example is this scene from a production of Electra *at the McCarter Theatre in Princeton. Note the white lighting on the steps, which isolates the figures standing there, and the figure down stage on a slanted white slab. The lighting designer is Paul Pyant.* (© T. Charles Erickson)

Color is mixed so that the strong tones of one shade will not dominate, creating an unnatural appearance. Warm lights (amber, straw, gold) are mixed with cool (blue, blue-green, lavender) to produce depth, texture, and naturalness. One exception to the usual mixing of angles and colors of light, however, would be a scene calling for special effects: for example, we would expect stark shadows and strange colors—such as an eerie blue—when Hamlet confronts the ghost of his father.

Direction. A third quality of light is direction, that is, the way lights are placed on or near the stage so that illumination comes from a particular angle. In earlier days, footlights—a row of lights across the front of the stage floor—were popular. However, because the light source was below the performers, footlights had the disadvantage of casting ghostly shadows on their faces. Footlights also created a barrier between performers and audience. With the development of more powerful, versatile lights, footlights have been eliminated.

Today, most lighting hits the stage from above, coming from instruments in front of the stage and at the sides. The vertical angle of the light beams is close to 45 degrees, to approximate the average angle of sunlight. The lights converge from different sides to avoid the harsh shadows which result when light hits only one side of a performer's face.

COLOR IN LIGHTING
One key quality of stage lighting is color. By the use of gels and other electronic means, an almost infinite variety of colors can be created and combined. Two examples are shown here: a production of the musical Aida *which shows figures silhouetted against a red background by lighting designer Natasha Katz, and the Broadway production of* The Lion King, *again with figures, human and animals, featured against a red-orange background created by lighting designer Donald Holder.* (© Joan Marcus/Walt Disney Theatrical Productions)

Once performers are properly illuminated by lights from the front and sides and from above, other lighting is added—*downlighting* from directly overhead and *backlighting* from behind—to give further dimension and depths to figures onstage.

Form.   The *form* or *shape* of light is a fourth quality. It can be a single shaft of light, like a nightclub spotlight, a single beam of moonlight through trees, or general lighting. Light can also create a pattern, such as dappled sunlight through the leaves of trees in a forest. The edges of the light can be sharp and clearly defined, or soft and diffused. To accomplish either kind of definition, light can be shaped by special shutters that close in at the edges and give it an outline as it hits the stage area.

Movement.   A fifth quality of light is movement. With various types of dimmers, light can shift its focus from location to location and can also change from color to color. In addition, light can move to suggest changing time of day, sunsets, and so on, providing more information for the audience.

For an example of how these qualities function, consider the lighting for a production of *Hamlet*. To emphasize the eerie, tragic quality of this play, with its murders and graveyard scene, the lighting would be generally cool rather than warm. In addition to lighting from the front of the stage, there might be lighting angled down from above and backlighting to give a sculptured, occasionally unreal quality to the characters. In terms of movement, the lights would change each time there was a shift in locale. This would create a rhythm of movement through the play and would also serve to focus the audience's attention on particular areas of the stage.

The Lighting Designer's Resources

Types of Stage Lights.   Among the resources of the lighting designer are various kinds of lighting instruments and technical and electronic equipment. The different types of stage lights include:

1. *Soft-edged spotlights.* The most popular soft-edged spotlight is the *fresnel* (pronounced "fruh-NEL"). The lens of a fresnel spotlight produces a soft-edged beam and allows for a variable beam spread. It is especially useful for area lighting where a feathered or undefined edge is desirable. Many lighting designers use this instrument for top- and backlighting.

2. *Sharp, concentrated spotlights.* The best-known sharp spotlight is the ellipsoidal reflector spotlight, which most lighting designers consider the "workhorse of contemporary practice." It affords greater control of light than the fresnel and allows for shaping the edges of the beam with shutters. This instrument can also project patterns of light by means of templates. In recent years, the standard ellipsoidal spotlight has undergone revisions that have resulted in a brighter unit using only about half as much energy; there is also a new lens system. A mobile spotlight, which an operator can shift to follow a performer across the stage, is called a *follow spot.*

3. *Floodlights, "scoops," strip lights, and border lights.* These lights bathe a section of the stage or scenery in a smooth, diffused wash of light.

Lighting Controls.   Among the visual elements of theater, lighting is by far the most technologically developed. Lighting instruments can be hung all over a theater and beamed at every part of the stage; and all these instruments can be controlled by one person sitting at an electronic panel, or computer board.

Lighting changes—or *cues,* as they are called—can be arranged ahead of time. In a complicated production (a musical, say, or a Shakespearean play), there may be several hundred light cues. A cue can range from a *blackout* (all the lights are shut off at once); to a *fade* (the lights dim slowly, changing the scene from brighter to darker, or, with a *fade-in,* from dark to light); to a *cross-fade* (one set of lights comes down while another comes up). Moreover, with today's modern equipment, such changes can be timed automatically so that a cross-fade will take exactly the number of seconds called for and all guesswork is eliminated.

Using contemporary technology, all cues can be prearranged by computer so that during a performance, the operator at the console pushes a button and an entire change occurs automatically.

New Technology in Lighting.   Stage lighting has benefited from technological advances that were originally developed for rock musicians and others who perform before vast audiences and for whom light and sound are essential elements. Huge banks of lights are focused on the stage; sometimes there are banks of lights behind the performers, forming part of the stage picture.

To achieve maximum flexibility and control, new instruments have been devised. These instruments, known variously as *automated lights* or *moving lights,* are amazingly versatile, allowing a degree of control that was previously impossible for a single instrument. Moreover, not just one element can be controlled, but three: color, direction, and movement. Without a follow-spot operator, these lighting instruments can *pan* (move from side to side) and *tilt* (move up and down) to create movement and change the angle of the beam and therefore the focus onstage. And it is no longer necessary to change color by putting a gel over a beam by hand; instead, by means of dichoric filters these instruments can change to any one of hundreds of colors, shades, and hues.

The sharpness and width of the beam, as well as the pattern it projects, can be changed instantaneously in each instrument because both the *iris* (which controls the size of the pool of light) and the *gobo* or template (which determines patterns of light) are variable and changeable. All these adjustments are made not manually but remotely, from a central computer panel by an operator pushing a switch or button. Everything is preset on the computer: each movement of the light, each change in color, each alteration in direction or size of the beam. This is done for what are sometimes hundreds of instruments. At a given moment, at the touch of a button by an operator at the central lighting computer, dozens of lights go off, dozens more come on as they swivel in a different direction and change color—and all of this occurs simultaneously.

DIFFERENT LIGHTING INSTRUMENTS SERVE DIFFERENT PURPOSES

Most lights have three key elements: a lamp that is the source of light, a reflector, and a lens through which the beams of light pass. Shown here are four types of instruments used to light the stage. Upper left is a flood light. Flood lights are employed, singly or in groups, to provide general illumination for the stage or scenery. The light from floods can be blended in acting areas, or used to "tone" setting and costumes. They are also employed to illuminate cycloramas or ground rows. (Selecon) Upper right is a small spotlight known as a fresnel (pronounced "fruh-NEL"). All spotlights illuminate limited areas of the stage with a concentrated beam of light. They precisely define an area that is to be lighted and leave other areas in darkness. The fresnel spotlight has a spherical reflector and a special flat lens on one side and ridges of concentric circles on the other, an arrangement that allows for a thinner, lighter lens that softens the edges of the beam. The fresnel is generally used in positions near the stage. (Selecon) Lower left is a zoom spotlight. Generally this is an ellipsoidal reflector lighting instrument that is more efficient than the fresnel because it can throw a stronger beam of light much farther. Most spotlights of this type have an ellipsoidal reflector that partially surrounds the lamp and sends a strong beam through two plano-convex lenses. It is used when the distance between instrument and stage area is greatest—for example, from positions outside the proscenium opening in the auditorium. (Selecon) The fourth light (lower right) is the newest and most versatile instrument of the group. Sometimes known as an automated light or a moving light, it can do the work that in the past would have to be carried out by several lighting instruments. Rather than having to change the angle of the beam, or its color, or its shape, this light can carry out all these alterations automatically when commanded from a computer. It can change colors (to any one of nearly 1,000 hues and shades), change focus by swiveling in place, and shift beams. All of this is done remotely and has been made possible by advances in the technology of computers, electronics, and other elements. This instrument is particularly useful in elaborate musical productions and is widely used in rock concerts. (Vari *Lite)

The Lighting Designer's Collaborators

A number of people work closely with the lighting designer. When the lighting designer has determined what instruments, colors, and so on will be used, he or she develops a *light plot*—a detailed outline or diagram showing where each instrument is placed in relation to the stage. The designer may have experts assist in drawing up light plots.

When the time comes to put the lights in place, they are *hung,* which means that they are attached to pipes—or *battens,* as these pipes are sometimes called—backstage and in various other places throughout the theater. This requires technicians who are familiar with the instruments and the pipes. These same technicians will assist the designer in focusing the lights. (To *focus* lights, as we have seen, means to aim them at a certain area onstage.)

During a performance, experts are required to *run* the lights—that is, to operate the computer or whatever device executes light changes and light cues. These experts take cues from the stage manager and coordinate their work with the other technical aspects of the production. The *follow spot* (a moving spotlight) requires an operator who aims the beam at the proper person or area of the stage.

Sound Design

Sound—which has become an increasingly important element in theater productions—may be said to include all sound effects, recordings, and electronic enhancement. Audiences have become increasingly aware of sound as such, partly because of concerts by groups who attach microphones to themselves and their instruments and use huge banks of speakers to project their music to the audience.

In recent years, sound, in addition to having its own *sound designer,* has developed its own artistry and technology.

The Sound Designer

A counterpart to designers for visual aspects of theater is the sound designer. Like other designers, he or she reads the script to see what the sound requirements will be. Understandably, the needs of a musical theater production will be different from those of a nonmusical drama. In the former, the orchestra and all singing voices must be heard and carefully blended.

After reading the script and noting all requirements, the sound designer meets with the director to discuss those requirements and to take note of special requests which the director might have. Following this, the sound designer plans how he or she will go about meeting the needs of the production with regard to sound.

Objectives of Sound Design

Basically, the objectives of sound design are twofold: (1) to provide all background or other aural effects called for in the production, and (2) to reinforce spoken and musical sounds.

Sound Reproduction and Sound Reinforcement

Reproduction is the use of motivated or environmental sounds. *Motivated sounds* would be, for instance, a car crunching on gravel, a car motor turning off, and a door slamming—a sequence that could announce the arrival of a character at a house where a scene is taking place. Motivated sounds, then, are those called for by a script. *Environmental sounds* are noises of everyday life that help create verisimilitude in a production: street traffic in a city, crickets in the country, loud music coming from a college dormitory. Such sounds are usually heard as background.

One form of sound reproduction is *sound effects,* which can be defined as any sounds produced by electronic or human means to create for the audience a noise associated with the play.

In earlier years—for several centuries, in fact—various devices were developed to create such sounds. A noise sounding like wind, for example, can be produced by a wooden drum made from slats: when the drum is turned, by means of a handle, it makes a noise like howling wind. For a slamming door, a miniature door or even a full door in a frame can be placed just offstage and opened and shut. Two pieces of wood slammed shut can also simulate the sound of a closing door, and in some cases this device can sound like a gunshot. A gunshot can also be created by firing a gun using blank cartridges. (Real guns—that is, those which fire ammunition—should never be used onstage; and in some states there are also

SOUND REPRODUCTION AND REINFORCEMENT
In the play Side Man, *the entire mood is created and carried forward by sound, and the reactions of the actors to sound. The play is about a group of musicians from the swing and jazz eras who have been left behind. In the scene here, the characters reminisce about the past while listening to a recording of a particularly poignant trumpet solo. The performers are Michael Mastro, Frank Wood, and Joseph Lyle Taylor.* (© Carol Rosegg)

laws forbidding the purchase of blank guns.) Thunder can be simulated by hanging a large, thick metal sheet backstage and gently shaking it.

In recent years, however, most sound effects are reproduced on audiotape or disks. Virtually every sound imaginable—from birds singing to dogs barking to jet planes flying—can be found on recordings. These are available not only to expensive professional productions but to college, university, and community theaters.

Reinforcement is amplification of sounds produced by a performer or a musical instrument. In recent decades, with the growth of electronics in music, more and more instruments are amplified. In today's theater, this is also true of the voices of actors and singers. We turn now to various types of technology for sound reproduction and reinforcement.

Elements of Sound: Sound Technology

Microphones and Loudspeakers. Speech reinforcement involves using microphones to pick up dialogue and songs. Several types of microphones are used for this. A *shotgun mike* is highly directional and is aimed from a distance at a specific area. A *general mike* picks up sounds in the general area toward which it is aimed. A *body mike* is popular today in musicals. At first, body mikes were small microphones attached in some way to performers' clothing; a wire ran from the mike to a small transmitter concealed on the performer, and from the transmitter the sound was sent to an offstage listening device that fed it into a central sound-control system.

SOUND TECHNOLOGY
The audio side of theater has made great advances in recent years. It has also become pervasive, especially in musical theater. In the musical Rent, *for example, each of the principal characters wears a personal microphone—shaped like a telephone instrument—which is connected by a remote arrangement with a central sound control system. The microphones worn by the actors are similar to those worn by rock performers and reflect the influence of that popular form. (© Joan Marcus and Carol Rosegg)*

In today's lavish musical productions, the microphone worn by a performer is often a small instrument—hardly larger than a piece of wire—worn, perhaps, over one ear alongside the temple, or under a wig. In some musicals, such as *Rent*, performers wear microphones that resemble a telephone operator's headset.

Microphones not worn by performers are placed in various locations. One position is alongside the downstage edge of the stage, where the footlights used to be located. Another position is in the air, with microphones placed near the overhead lights.

Any type of microphone must be hooked up to an amplifier that increases the electronic energy of the sound and sends it through speakers. Placing loudspeakers is both an art and a science. It is necessary to determine the correct speakers for the size and shape of the theater, and to position them so that they carry sound clearly and evenly into the auditorium—to the upper levels of the balcony, to the side seats, and to the areas underneath the balcony as well as the first few rows of the orchestra. Also, sound must reach the sides and back of the theater at the same time that it reaches the front. One problem in this regard is that sound travels much more slowly than light. The speed of sound is only 1,100 feet per second—which means that for a spectator seated at the back of a large theater, sound from a speaker at the rear of the auditorium will be heard before the human voice from the stage. Developments in digital electronics have led to devices that process, sample, and synthesize sound for various effects; and one useful device addresses this problem, delaying the electronic sound so that it arrives through a loudspeaker at the same time as the much slower live sound.

Placing microphones and speakers in a theater and on the stage is a complicated process. The goal is clear but unobtrusive sound. When electronic sound is not properly modulated, it can become an artificial barrier between performers and audience and can seriously interfere with the actor-audience relationship.

Sound Recordings. The process of assembling sound recordings is similar for professional and nonprofessional productions. First, a list is made of all nonmusical sound effects required. This list is usually developed by the sound designer in consultation with the director, and possibly with a composer: for a show with a great deal of sound or music, there may be both a sound designer and a music composer. Once the list is drawn up, a master recording is made and the sounds are arranged in their order of appearance in the script. This process is called *editing*. When the production moves into the theater, there is a technical rehearsal without performers, during which each sound cue is listened to and the volume is set. When rehearsals with the performers start in the theater, more changes will be made. Depending on the action and the timing of scenes, some cues will be too loud and others too soft; some will have to be made shorter and others made longer.

During an actual performance of a production using sound reinforcement, an operator must sit at a complex console "mixing" sound—that is, combining all elements from the many microphones and from the master sound recording—so that there is a smooth, seamless blend of sound. Also, the operator must make certain not only that all sound is in balance but that sound does not intrude on the performance or call attention to itself, away from the stage and the performers.

New Technologies in Sound.   As with lighting, in recent years we have seen frequent advances and breakthroughs in sound equipment and technology. The new body microphones and a device that delays the delivery of electronic sound have already been mentioned. But there are other developments as well.

Analog reel-to-reel tape decks, which were standard only a few years ago, are now giving way to digital technology such as digital audiotape (DAT), recordable compact disks, minidisks, and direct playback from a computer's hard drive. Sound is now recorded and edited at digital audio workstations, based on personal computers. Such stations allow easier editing of sound, more complex effects, and higher-quality sound. Digital playback systems allow very easy and precise cueing of shows, as well as greatly improved sound quality.

It should be clear that sound is rapidly taking its place alongside other design aspects as a key feature of theater productions.

The Sound Designer's Collaborators

Like all designers, the sound designer has a number of people with whom she or he collaborates. There are technicians who understand the intricacies of sound equipment; there are specialists in the art of hanging and coordinating speakers around the stage and in the auditorium; there are experts at *running* sound in a production. This list includes managing the sound console at the back of the auditorium or in the sound booth. Among other things, this involves handling the complexities of the many microphones required in a large musical presentation; some of these microphones are on the performers and others are in the orchestra pit or offstage. It would detract enormously from a performance if a body microphone were turned on when it was supposed to be off, or if the reverse occurred.

Special Effects in Lighting and Sound

As in scene design, some effects of lighting and sound can seem unusual or even miraculous.

There are several special lighting effects that can be used to create interesting visual pictures. One simple effect is to position a source of light near the stage floor and shine the light on the performers from below. This creates shadows under the eyes and chin and gives performers a ghostly or horrifying quality. Another common special effect is ultraviolet light, a very dark blue light that causes phosphorus to glow; when the stage is very dark, or completely dark, costumes or scenery that have been painted with a special phosphorus paint will "light up."

An effect of slow motion or of silent movies—where the performers seem to be moving in jerks—is created by a *strobe light,* a very powerful, bright gas-discharge light which flashes at rapid intervals. As we saw earlier, technological advances in lighting have made it possible to create even more spectacular effects.

SPECIAL LIGHTING EFFECTS
Both lighting and sound can be employed to create unusual effects. In the scene here, from a production of Shakespeare's Cymbeline, *effects of clouds and perhaps the smoke of battle, are added to silhouettes for the characters in the back, and strong focus and composition in the front. The lighting designer is Marcia Madeira and the production was by the Huntington Theatre Company of Boston.* (© Richard Feldman)

There are also a number of special sound effects. Sometimes speakers are placed completely around the audience so that the sound can move from side to side. Echoes can be created by a machine that causes reverberations in sound waves. Expanding audio technology also allows for more complex sound effects. Computerized noises and electronic music can be used to create special sounds for various situations, and compact disks give instantaneous access to any element of the sound design. Also, with computerized synthesizers, a few musicians can replace a large orchestra.

Finally, we should add that lighting and sound, like scenery and costumes, are means to an end: they add to and complement the artistic and aesthetic aspects of a production, thereby contributing to the overall experience.

In Chapters 5 and 6, we have looked at the design of scenery, costumes, lighting, and sound. To create theater, these must be coordinated and integrated with acting and directing—and with the text, which we will discuss in Chapters 7 and 8.

SUMMARY

Lighting—historically the last of the visual elements of theater to be fully developed—is today the most technically sophisticated of all. Once the incandescent electric lamp was introduced, it was possible to achieve almost total control of the color, intensity, and timing of lights. Lighting controls have also benefited from computerization; extensive light shifts can now be hooked up to computer boards and controlled by an operator at a console.

Lighting design is intended to provide illumination onstage, to establish time and place, to help set the mood and style of a production, to focus the action, and to establish a rhythm of visual movement. Lighting should be consistent with all other elements. The lighting designer uses a variety of lighting instruments and controls to achieve effects and works closely with a group of collaborators to place lighting instruments in the theater and to see that lighting changes are carried out effectively during a performance.

Another design element in theater is sound. In today's theater, sound is reproduced and reinforced by various means, many of them technologically advanced. For example, sound effects can be created by primitive mechanical means—such as pieces of wood slapped together to simulate a closing door—or by sophisticated computer and digital technology. These techniques are constantly improving and effect the way sound is created, reproduced, and conveyed throughout a theater auditorium.

Special effects in lighting and sound include such things as ultraviolet light, strobe lights, echo effects and computerized synthesizers.

THEATER ON THE WEB

Since the lighting and sound industry is, by nature, extremely technical and tied into the world of electronics and computing, there are many online links to sites that pertain to lighting and sound. Here are just a few.

IATSE   www.iatse.lm.com

The labor union representing technicians, artisans, and craftspersons in the entertainment industry.

Lighting Links   http://waapa.cowan.edu.au/lx

This site has extensive links to lighting resources including professional lighting organizations, designers, and retailers.

Lighting and Electronics   http://www.le-us.com

This equipment manufacturer maintains links to safety guides, mathematical formulas for lighting designers and electricians, and a page on which solutions to lighting problems are discussed.

BackstageWorld   http://www.stagelight.se/backstage/010_SweB_eng.html
This is a website for people working in the entertainment industry who want
   information on the latest sound and lighting equipment.
Theater Sound Design Directory and Resource   http://www.show-
   control.com/tsindex.html
A comprehensive list of links aimed at sound designers and technicians.

How are the lighting and sound design community and the costume and scenic design
community similar? How are they different? Take a look at the IATSE link and compare
it with the United Scenic Artists link listed in Chapter 5. At what community is each
union aimed? Where are sound designers and technicians mostly represented? Why?

Chapter 7

The Playwright

The Playwright's Centrality

Getting Started in Theater:
Emily Mann: Playwright-Director

The Playwright's Tasks

Subject

Focus and Emphasis

Dramatic Purpose

Making Connections: *Writers*

Structure in Drama

   Essentials of Dramatic Structure

   Creating a Dramatic Structure

Getting Started in Theater:
August Wilson—Playwright

   Two Basic Structures: Climactic and Episodic

Play Synopsis: *Mother Courage and Her Children*

   Other Dramatic Structures

Creating Dramatic Characters

   Types of Dramatic Characters

   Juxtaposition of Characters

Summary

◀ THE PLAYWRIGHT AND THE THEATER

Playwright Arthur Miller stands on the stage of Town Hall in New York City. The playwright, or the person or persons, involved in fashioning a drama must work with many others: performers, a director, designers, technicians, and so forth. But ultimately the play comes to life on a stage before an audience. In this scene, Miller seems to be contemplating what it means to bring a production to fruition and then have it performed before the audience.
(Adam Nadel/AP/Wide World Photos)

We turn now to a person who through most of theater history has been considered as essential to creating theater as the performers and the audience: the *playwright,* also known as the *dramatist.*

Without a script, there would be no characters for performers to impersonate, no words for them to speak, no actions for them to take, no story for them to re-create. The importance of the script in western theater is reflected in the simple phrase used by many people before attending a production: "I'm going to see a play."

The Playwright's Centrality

We should note, however, that some contemporary commentators have questioned the centrality of the playwright and the play. These critics point out that there have been companies whose performers or directors, sometimes with the assistance of audiences, improvise presentations: they create a presentation while actually performing it. There have also been times when texts were developed by performers or by a director who assembled material from various sources. Some critics argue, therefore, that an "authorless" theater exists: theater in which performers create their own works, sometimes using a traditional text only as a jumping-off point. An example of this concept of authorless theater might be performance art (which is discussed in Chapter 16); some contemporary performance artists create pieces in which they narrate details from their own lives.

Critics who question the centrality of the text also argue that the playwright's importance has been overstated—that a play is simply something to be produced and that the artists who create a stage presentation are its true "authors." In addition, they hold that each audience member may create his or her own "reading" of a production; in this sense, the spectator is the "author," and any discussion of a play's theme or meaning is inappropriate.

While certain critics have adopted this concept, many others continue to take a more traditional approach. Also, the argument seems to be in some instances a question of semantics. If a theater piece is created by a group of performers or by a director, then these people are in effect operating as playwrights. The playwright's function has not been eliminated; it is simply being carried out by someone else.

This consideration does not answer the question of the playwright's centrality, of course, but our purpose in this book is not to try to settle such arguments. Although many contemporary theories challenge us to rethink the place of the playwright in theater, the fact remains that throughout the history of both western and eastern theater the crucial role of the playwright has been widely accepted.

Whether it is a dramatist like Sophocles, Shakespeare, or Ibsen in the west, or Chikamatsu—an eighteenth-century Japanese dramatist—in the east, both their own contemporaries and later generations have seen their dramatic texts as blueprints on which productions are based. Whether it is the work of one playwright or others performing the task of the playwright, it is this aspect of theater which we discuss in Chapters 7 and 8.

Emily Mann: Playwright-Director

Emily Mann is currently artistic director of the McCarter Theatre in New Jersey. She has also directed at the Guthrie Theatre, the Brooklyn Academy of Music, and the Actors Theatre of Louisville. She received Obie awards in 1981 for distinguished playwriting and directing for her play Still Life. *Her play* Execution of Justice *won a 1986 Drama Desk Award. In 1994, she adapted and directed* Having Our Say.

How did you get interested in theatre? I was in high school, at the University of Chicago Laboratory School, in 1966 and things in my neighborhood were heating up. The Hyde Park area was a seat of political ferment: the Weathermen and SDS, the Panthers ten blocks away. Elijah Muhammad lived three doors down, drugs were coming in, people were getting heavily politicized. When we arrived in 1966 the neighborhood was integrated and absolutely for integration. By '68, with Black Power, the separatist movement had taken hold and there was a lot of heartbreak for everyone.

I was always interested in music, writing, art, and literature, and the theatre became a place where these came together in a very exciting way. You worked in a collaborative fashion and made something beautiful, something positive or critical—but still in a positive way—to say to a community. It felt much better to me than being one in a mass of people marching—not that I didn't march, but I have always distrusted crowds. I don't like that anonymity, being part of a group that can get whipped up. I'm sure it's all my training about Nazi Germany. This rather brilliant guy at the Labora-tory high school, Robert Keil, took a lot of emotionally churned up, smart, excited and excitable young people and turned all that energy into an artistic endeavor, making theatre.

I hadn't really had much interest in theatre before that. I remember my first Broadway show was *Fiorello!* about the mayor of New York. We were invited to go because my father, who's a historian, had just written the biography of LaGuardia. I was very excited—I was seven, I think—and I got to go backstage and meet Tom Bosley. But theatre never occurred to me as something you actually did, as a serious person in the world.

Source: Emily Mann from *In Their Own Words: Contemporary American Playwrights* by David Savran, copyright 1988 David Savran. By permission of Theatre Communications Group.

The Playwright's Tasks

The playwright, or whoever creates a dramatic text, has a number of questions to answer and many choices to make, involving at least six aspects of a drama:

1. Selecting the specific subject of the play
2. Determining focus and emphasis
3. Establishing purpose
4. Developing dramatic structure
5. Creating dramatic characters
6. Establishing point of view

In this chapter, we will examine the first five of these aspects. In Chapter 8, we will look at point of view.

Subject

The subject matter of drama is always human beings. In theater, unlike certain other art forms—music, for instance, or abstract painting—people are invariably at the center. At the same time, a play cannot simply be about "human beings" or "people" in general, or even about "people's concerns," and the first task of the person or persons creating a dramatic text is therefore to decide what aspect of human existence to write about.

Will the drama be based on history—for example, an episode or incident from the Civil War, from World War II, or from the Vietnamese War? Or will it be based on biography—on the life of Abraham Lincoln, Eleanor Roosevelt, or Martin Luther King Jr.? Another possibility is the dramatization of someone's personal life: confronting some problem of growing up, or facing a personal crisis as an adult. A different possibility would be an imaginary story, resembling everyday life or based on a fantasy or nightmare.

Focus and Emphasis

Along with selecting a subject to be dramatized, a decision must be made as to who and what to focus on. For example, the same playwright can emphasize a particular character trait in one play and a very different trait in another play.

THE PLAYWRIGHT PROVIDES EMPHASIS AND POINT OF VIEW
In Peer Gynt, *Henrik Ibsen makes it clear that his play is about the title character, who is in virtually every scene. The play itself—which is serious but has numerous comic and tragicomic episodes—ranges over many years and many locations. The character of Peer is always compromising, always running away, and Ibsen shows the consequences of that. The scene here, from a production at the Shakespeare Theatre in Washington, D.C., shows Peer (Wallace Acton) riding on a pig with his mate (Kate Skinner). (© Carol Rosegg)*

This is what the Norwegian playwright Henrik Ibsen often did. In his *Brand,* the leading character is a stark, uncompromising religious man who will sacrifice everything—family, friends, love—for his principles. On the other hand, in Ibsen's *Peer Gynt,* the central character is just the opposite: a man with no principles who is always compromising, always running away.

In determining focus, a playwright may need to decide how to interpret the characters and events of an existing story; in doing this, the playwright may even change the order of events. A good example is the way three tragic dramatists of ancient Greece dealt with the myth of Electra. This myth concerns Electra's revenge on her mother, Clytemnestra, who has murdered Electra's father, Agamemnon, and then married a lover, Aegisthus. In wreaking revenge on Clytemnestra, Electra enlists the help of her brother, Orestes, who has just returned from exile. In *The Libation Bearers* (458 B.C.) by Aeschylus, and also in *Electra* (c. 412 B.C.) by Euripides, Electra and Orestes first murder Clytemnestra's lover, Aegisthus, and then murder Clytemnestra herself—their mother. This puts emphasis on the horror and aberration of killing one's own mother. But Sophocles saw the story differently. He wanted to emphasize that Electra and Orestes are acting honorably and obeying an order from the gods. He therefore needed to play down the murder of the mother, and so in his version of *Electra* (c. 410 B.C.) he reversed the order of the murders: Clytemnestra is killed first, and then the action builds to the righteous murder of Aegisthus.

By means of focus, then, whoever creates a text lets us know whom the play is about—the main character or characters—and how we are to view the characters: whether we are to look at them favorably or unfavorably.

Dramatic Purpose

Another challenge in creating a text is to determine the purpose of a play. A purpose may be casual or unconscious, or conscious and deliberate, but every theater event is intended to serve some purpose.

Throughout theater history, plays have been written to serve different purposes: to entertain, to probe the human condition, to provide an escape, to impart information. Various types of contemporary theater are frequently presented for a specific purpose: these include feminist theater, Hispanic theater, and African American theater. In theater of this kind, those who create the event are addressing the concerns of a particular constituency.

There is a long tradition of theater as a source of entertainment—similar to modern situation comedies on television and comic films that offer us pleasure and an escape from the cares of everyday life. The comedies of the Roman playwrights Plautus and Terence, written 2,000 years ago, were designed for this sort of entertainment. In the United States, for many years Broadway provided comedies that were written purely for fun.

Making Connections:

Writers

Playwright David Mamet
(© Gerry Goodstein)

How do we compare writing for the stage and writing for films or television? Obviously many writers engage in both, moving from the theater to films or television and back again. Some writers, however, seem to have a natural affinity for one field or the other. There are playwrights who have never attempted to write screenplays and never want to. By the same token, there are people who write for films or television who have never been interested in writing plays or musicals for the stage.

David Mamet is a good example of a writer who frequently moves back and forth between the theater and film. Others who write primarily for the theater at times write films as well; they include Wendy Wasserstein, John Guare, and Marcia Norman. Many playwrights write almost exclusively for the theater, dramatists such as Edward Albee, Paula Vogel, Terence McNally, A. R. Gurney, and Lanford Wilson.

Whatever path a writer takes, he or she must meet the requirements we discuss in the chapters on the playwright and the text: decide on the subject, develop a plot, create the characters, compose the dialogue, and undertake all other necessary steps in creating a completed script. In undertaking these tasks, the writer for film or television must follow a path similar to that of the playwright for the stage, but there are important differences. The requirements of film, for instance, are not the same as those for the stage. Many scenes in film are action scenes: shots from a helicopter, shots of car crashes, a villain stalking his prey. Such scenes may be described by the writer, but their realization is mostly in the hands of the director and cinematographer. They contain almost no dialogue. As a rule, whatever the story line, there is far less dialogue in a film than in a play.

Because of the nature of theater, as opposed to film or television, the role of the writer is different in other ways. The Dramatists Guild contract, under which most dramas are produced, states unequivocally that no dialogue in a production may be deleted or changed without the permission of the author. By contrast, in films and television two things happen. First, there are usually a number of writers on a script. There may be two, three, or more. This means that no one writer has the authority to maintain his or her vision over the material. Second, the writer is unable to prevent changes in the script made by directors, producers, performers, or other writers. Thus in films and television, unlike theater, the writer has less control over what happens to his or her words.

Another crossover area for dramatic writers would be the fields of opera and musical theater, where the playwright would provide the libretto, and perhaps the lyrics as well. When working on an opera or musical piece, the dramatist must collaborate with a composer as well as with a director and others.

There have been times when plays were intended primarily to teach. In the medieval period, from the mid-fourteenth century to the mid-sixteenth century, very few people could read or write. In order to teach people about the Bible, the church encouraged plays that presented religious stories and precepts. Today, political dramatists often write plays specifically to put forward their own opinions and ideas.

At times, the purpose of drama has been to raise philosophical questions or to probe timeless themes, such as why the innocent suffer or why there is so much hatred and violence in the world.

Sometimes a play is intended simply to thrill or frighten us. A horror story or a melodrama is not supposed to make us think or meditate; it is intended to draw us into the action so that we will experience the same fears and apprehensions as the characters.

At times a play serves more than one purpose. Satirical comedies may be intended not only to make us laugh, but also to take stabs at hypocrites or charlatans. The works of the French playwright Molière are frequently of this kind: comical, but also revealing human folly. His *Tartuffe,* for instance—about a man who moves into a household falsely posing as a pious cleric—is an indictment of hypocrisy but is also amusing.

Whatever their approach, those creating a text should make the purpose of a theater event clear. Sometimes a playwright may begin working without an exact purpose—the purpose may emerge only as the script goes through several revisions. Before a play goes into production, however, the playwright should know where it is headed. Once the purpose is clear, the director, performers, and designers join the playwright in working to achieve it.

Once subject, focus, and purpose have been decided, two crucial steps in writing a play are developing dramatic structure and creating dramatic characters.

Before we discuss these in detail, however, a word about the writing process is in order. In choosing a subject, developing a structure, or creating characters, the playwright often works intuitively, sometimes even subconsciously. When the imagination of the playwright is captured by a certain episode or attracted to certain characters, he or she begins to create a drama. Usually a play evolves, rather than being put together in a mechanical fashion.

In past eras, the type of structure used and the characters chosen by a playwright were in some measure the traditionally accepted practices of a given period and society. Playwrights in ancient Greece, for example, based both their plots and their characters on well-known myths. In modern times, however, playwrights often begin without a clear plan and only later discover the type of structure and the nature of the characters they have chosen to create. Having said this, we must emphasize that although a playwright's decisions are sometimes subconscious, the playwright does make *choices* of the kind described above and in the sections to follow.

Structure in Drama

Though it may not be readily apparent, every work of art has some type of structure. When does the action of a play begin? How are the scenes put together? How does the action unfold? What is the high point of the action? Questions like these are related to dramatic structure, but we should note that structure is significant in all art.

In a sense, the structure of a play is analogous to that of a building. In designing a building, an architect plans a skeleton or substructure which will provide inner strength; the architect determines the depth of the foundation, the weight of the support beams, and the stress on the side walls. Similarly, a playwright develops a dramatic structure. The playwright introduces various stresses and strains in the form of conflicts; sets boundaries and outer limits, such as how many characters participate, how long the action lasts, and where it takes place; and calculates dynamics—when tension increases and slackens. Some feminist critics argue that the playwright's gender might also influence structure and that feminist dramas are less linear and less traditional in building dramatic tension. In any case, though, the playwright "constructs" a play.

Buildings vary enormously in size and shape: they can be as diverse as a skyscraper, a cathedral, and a cottage. Engineering requirements vary according to the needs of individual structures: a gymnasium roof must span a vast open area, and this calls for a construction different from that of a sixty-story skyscraper. Plays, too, vary; they can be tightly or loosely constructed, for instance. The important point is that each play, like each piece of architecture, has its own internal laws and its own framework, which give it shape, strength, and meaning. Without structure, a building will collapse, and a play will fall apart.

Naturally, structure is manifested differently in theater and architecture. A play is not a building; it unfolds through time, developing like a living organism. As we experience this development, we become aware of a play's structure because we sense its underlying pattern and rhythm. The repeated impulses of two characters in conflict, the quickening pace and mounting tension of a heated argument—these elements insinuate themselves into our subconscious like a drumbeat. Moment by moment we see what is happening onstage; but below the surface we sense the structure, the framework of the dramatic action.

Essentials of Dramatic Structure

There are several essentials of dramatic structure. First, the story on which a drama is based must be turned into a plot. Second, the plot involves action. Third, the plot includes conflict. Fourth, there are strongly opposed forces. Fifth, a reasonable balance is struck between the opposed forces.

Plot Our first essential of dramatic structure, *plot,* is the arrangement of events or the selection and order of scenes in a play. The term *plot,* can mean a secret scheme or plan. The word is also used to describe the sequence of scenes or events in a novel, but we are speaking here specifically of plot in drama.

A dramatic plot is usually based on a story. Stories are as old as the human race, and today stories form much of the substance of our daily conversation, of newspapers and television, of novels and films. Every medium presents a story in a different form. In theater, the story must be presented by living actors and actresses on a stage in a limited period of time, and this requires selectivity. Thus the plot of a play differs from a story. A *story* is a full account of an event or series of events, usually in chronological order; a *plot* is a selection and arrangement of scenes from a story for presentation onstage. The plot is what actually happens onstage, not what is talked about.

For example, the story of Abraham Lincoln begins with his birth in a log cabin and continues to the day he is shot at Ford's Theater in Washington. In developing a plot for a play about Lincoln, however, the playwright must make choices. Will the play include scenes in Springfield, Illinois, where Lincoln served as a lawyer and held his famous debates with Stephen A. Douglas? Or will the entire play take place in Washington after Lincoln has become president? Will there be scenes with Lincoln's wife, Mary Todd; or will all the scenes involve government and military officials? Decisions like these must be made even when a play is based on a fictional story: the plot must be more restricted and structured than the story itself.

Action　A second essential of dramatic structure is *action.* If we were to construct a "grammar of theater," the subject would always be human beings—dramatic characters who represent human concerns. In linguistic grammar, every subject needs a verb; similarly, in the grammar of theater, dramatic characters need a verb—some form of action that defines them. The word *drama* actually derives from a Greek root, the verb *dran,* meaning "to do" or "to act." At its heart, theater involves action.

Conflict   A third essential of dramatic structure is *conflict,* the collision or opposition of persons or forces in a drama that gives rise to dramatic action. We can perhaps best understand dramatic conflict in terms of everyday experience. People often define themselves by the way they respond to challenges, such as marriage, a job, sudden good fortune, or a serious illness. If they cannot face up to a challenge, that tells us one thing; if they meet it with dignity, even though defeated, that tells us another; if they triumph, that tells us something else. We come to know our family, our friends, and our enemies by being with them over a period of time. We see how they respond to us and to other people, and how they meet crises in their own lives and in ours.

In life, this process can take years—in fact, it continues to unfold for as long as we know a person—but in theater we have only a few hours. The playwright, therefore, must devise means by which characters will face challenges and be tested in a short time. The American playwright Arthur Miller called one of his plays *The Crucible* (1953). Literally, a crucible is a vessel in which metal is tested by being exposed to extreme heat. Figuratively, a crucible has come to stand for any severe test of human worth and endurance—a trial by fire. Every play provides a crucible of a sort: a test devised by the playwright to show how the characters behave under stress. Such a test, and the characters' reaction to it, is one way that the meaning of a play is brought out.

STRONGLY OPPOSED FORCES
In developing a dramatic structure, a playwright sets powerful forces and characters against one another to provide conflict and dramatic confrontations. A good example is the opposition between the two chief characters in A Streetcar Named Desire *by Tennessee Williams: Stanley Kowalski and Blanche DuBois. Here—in a production at the Steppenwolf Theatre Company in Chicago—Gary Sinise as Stanley and Laila Robins as Blanche are locked in a life-and-death struggle. The production was directed by Terry Kinney, a co-founder of Steppenwolf.* (Michael Brosilow)

Opposed Forces   A fourth essential of dramatic structure, closely related to conflict, is strongly *opposed forces.* By this we mean that the people in conflict in a play are fiercely determined to achieve their goals; moreover, they are powerful adversaries for one another. The conflicting characters have clear, strong goals or objectives; that is, they have goals they want desperately to achieve, and they will go to any length to achieve them. For example, Macbeth, in the play by Shakespeare, wants to become king; Jean, the servant in August Strindberg's *Miss Julie,* wants to achieve independence; Blanche DuBois, in Tennessee Williams's *A Streetcar Named Desire,* wants to find a haven in the home of her sister. In fighting for their goals, two or more characters find themselves in opposition; and the strength of both sides must be formidable.

A perfect example of two characters bound to clash is found in *A Streetcar Named Desire*. Blanche DuBois is a faded southern belle trying desperately to hold on to her gentility; the crude, aggressive Stanley Kowalski is the chief threat to her stability and her survival. On his side, Stanley, who is insecure about his lack of education and refinement, is provoked almost to the breaking point by Blanche and her superior airs.

One device often used by dramatists to establish friction or tension between forces is restricting the characters to members of a single family. Relatives have built-in rivalries and affinities: parents versus children, sisters versus brothers. As members of the same family, moreover, they have no avenue of escape.

Mythology, on which so much drama is based, abounds with familial relationships. Shakespeare also frequently set members of one family against each other: Hamlet opposes his mother; King Lear is opposed by his daughters. In modern drama, virtually every writer of note has dealt with close family situations. The American dramatist Eugene O'Neill wrote what many consider his finest play, *Long Day's Journey into Night,* about the four members of his own family.

In plays not directly involving families, the characters are usually still in close proximity. They are fighting for the same turf, the same throne, the same woman or man.

Balance of Forces   A fifth essential of dramatic structure is some sort of *balance* between the opposed forces: that is, the people or forces in conflict must be evenly matched. In almost every case, one side eventually wins, but before this final outcome the opposing forces must be roughly equal in strength and determination.

In most sporting events, there are rules ensuring that the contest will be as equal as possible without coming to a draw, and this notion is equally important in theater. In sports, fans want their team to win, but they would prefer a close, exciting contest to a one-sided runaway. The struggle, as much as the outcome, is a source of pleasure; and so rules are set up, with handicaps or other devices for equalizing forces. In basketball or football, when one team scores, the other team gets the ball so that it will have a chance to even the score. In theater, too, a hard-fought and relatively equal contest is usually set up between opposing forces: the vulnerable, artistic Blanche, for example, faces the brutish Stanley.

Creating a Dramatic Structure

Working with these essential elements, a playwright develops a dramatic structure for each play. This development begins with the all-important opening scene.

Opening Scene   The first scene of a drama starts the action and sets the tone and style for everything that follows. It tells us whether we are going to see a serious or a comic play, and whether the play will deal with affairs of everyday life or with fantasy. The opening scene also sets the action in motion, giving the characters a shove and hurtling them toward their destination.

August Wilson: Playwright

August Wilson is currently the best-known African American playwright. He won Pulitzer Prizes for Fences *in 1987 and* The Piano Lesson *in 1990. His other well-known works include* Ma Rainey's Black Bottom, Joe Turner's Come and Gone, Two Trains Running, Seven Guitars, *and* Jitney.

What were your early experiences in theatre? I was a participant in the Black Power movement in the early sixties and I wrote poetry and short fiction. I was interested in art and literature and I felt that I could alter the relationship between blacks and society through the arts. There was an explosion of black theatre in the late sixties—theatre was a way of politicizing the community and raising the consciousness of the people. So with my friend, Rob Penny, I started the Black Horizons Theatre of Pittsburgh in 1968.

I knew nothing about theatre. I had never seen a play before. I started directing but I didn't have any idea how to do this stuff, although I did find great information in the library. We started doing Baraka's plays and virtually anything else out there. I remember the *Drama Review* printed a black issue, somewhere around '69, and we did every play in the book. I tried to write a play but it was disastrous. I couldn't write dialogue. Doing community theatre was very difficult—rehearsing two hours a night after people got off work, not knowing if the actors were going to show up. In '71, because of having to rely so much on other people, I said "I don't need this," and I concentrated on writing poetry and short stories.

Then in 1976 a friend of mine from Pittsburgh, Claude Purdy, was living in L.A. He came back to Pittsburgh and came to a reading of a series of poems I'd written about a character, Black Bart, a kind of Western satire. He said, "You should turn this into a play." He kept after me and eventually I sat down and wrote a play and gave it to him. He went to St. Paul to direct a show and said, "Why don't you come out and rewrite the play?" He sent me a ticket and I thought, "A free trip to St. Paul, what the hell?" So I went out and did a quick rewrite of the play. That was in November '77. In January '78, the Inner City Theatre in Los Angeles did a staged reading of it.

Source: August Wilson from *In Their Own Words: Contemporary American Playwrights* by David Savran, copyright 1988 David Savran. By permission of Theatre Communications Group.

A playwright provides this initial shove by presenting the characters with a problem or establishing an imbalance of forces which compels the characters to respond. Generally, the problem or imbalance has occurred just before the play begins, or it arises immediately after the play opens. In *King Oedipus*, for example, a plague has struck the city just before the opening of the play. In *Hamlet*, "something is rotten in the state of Denmark" before the play opens; and early in the play the ghost of Hamlet's father appears to tell Hamlet that he must seek revenge. At the beginning of *Romeo and Juliet*, the Capulets and the Montagues are at one another's throats in a street fight.

As these examples suggest, in the opening scene the characters are thrust into a situation which provides the starting point for the play.

Obstacles and Complications Having confronted the initial challenge of the play, the characters then move through a series of steps alternating between achievement and defeat, between hope and despair. The moment they accomplish one goal, something cuts across the play; a new hurdle or challenge is thrown up that they must overcome. These hurdles blocking a character's path—or outside forces which are introduced at an inopportune moment—are known as *obstacles* and *complications.*

Shakespeare's *Hamlet* provides numerous examples of obstacles and complications. Hamlet, suspecting that his uncle, Claudius, has killed his father, seeks revenge; but Claudius, as king, controls the army and other instruments of power. Thus the authority of the throne is one obstacle standing in Hamlet's way.

When Hamlet stages the "play within a play," Claudius's reaction confirms his guilt, and Hamlet's path to revenge seems clear. But when Hamlet first tries to kill Claudius, he discovers him at prayer. A complication has been introduced: if Claudius dies while praying, he may go to heaven rather than to hell, and so Hamlet does not kill him.

Later, Hamlet is in his mother's bedroom when he hears a noise behind a curtain. Surely Claudius is lurking there, and Hamlet can kill him instantly. But when Hamlet thrusts his sword through the curtain, he finds that he has killed Polonius, who is the father of Ophelia, the

OBSTACLES AND COMPLICATIONS

In developing a dramatic plot, the playwright often incorporates obstacles and complications which impede the movement of the main characters in attempting to reach their goals. It also adds interest, suspense, and complexity to the dramatic action. A good example are the many twists and turns in the plot of Shakespeare's Hamlet. *Shown here is Hamlet (Mark Rylance) trying to decide whether or not to kill King Claudius (Tim Woodward) when he is at prayer. The production was at the Old Globe in London. (© Donald Cooper/ PhotoStage, England)*

young woman Hamlet is supposed to marry. This is another complication: the murder of Polonius gives Claudius a pretext for sending Hamlet to England with Rosencrantz and Guildenstern, who carry a letter instructing the king of England to put Hamlet to death.

Hamlet gets out of this trap and returns to Denmark. Now, at last, it seems that he can carry out his revenge. But he discovers that Ophelia has killed herself while he was away; and her brother, Laertes, is seeking revenge on Hamlet. This is still another complication: Hamlet is prevented from killing Claudius because he must also deal with Laertes. In the end, Hamlet does carry out his mission—but only after many interruptions.

Crises and Climaxes   As a result of conflicts, obstacles, and complications, dramatic characters become involved in a series of *crises*. Some crises are less complicated than those in *Hamlet*, some even more complicated. A play like *Hamlet* builds from one crisis to another; when the first crisis is resolved, the action leads to a second crisis, and so on. The final and most significant crisis is referred to as the *climax*. Sometimes there is a minor climax earlier in a play and a major climax near the conclusion. In the final climax, the issues of the play are resolved—either happily or tragically, depending on the genre.

Two Basic Structures: Climactic and Episodic

Over the long history of western theater, playwrights have usually adopted one or the other of two basic dramatic structures: *climactic,* or *intensive,* **structure;** and *episodic,* or *extensive,* **structure.** In certain periods, playwrights have combined the two. There are other forms of structure, which we will discuss, but let us consider climactic and episodic structure first.

Climactic Plot Construction   A dramatic form first used in Greece in the fifth century B.C. reemerged, somewhat altered, in France in the seventeenth century; in the late nineteenth century and the twentieth century, this same form was adopted in Norway, Sweden, France, and (somewhat later) the United States. This is the form we will call *climactic* or *intensive.* We use these terms because in this kind of dramatic construction, all aspects of a play—duration, locale, action, and number of characters—are severely restricted; this results in a contained, or intense, structure, in which little time passes until the climax occurs.

A good example of climactic structure is found in *'Night, Mother,* by the modern American playwright Marsha Norman. The play takes place in one space, the kitchen and living room of a home; it involves only two people, a mother and daughter; and it occurs over a brief period, 1½ hours. Also, it has a single action: the daughter is determined to commit suicide and the mother to prevent her.

Climactic plots have several distinctive characteristics, which we'll consider one by one.

CLIMACTIC STRUCTURE

In climactic structure, everything is restricted: the action occurs in a brief time, in limited locations, and with very few characters involved. Climactic structure was first developed in western theater by the Greek dramatists of the fifth century B.C. *in Athens. For example, Sophocles' play* Electra *occurs over a short time in front of the palace of Agamemnon, Electra's father, whose murder she wants to avenge. This scene (with Zoë Wanamaker as Electra) is from a production of* Electra *by Sophocles at the McCarter Theatre in Princeton. (© T. Charles Erickson)*

The Plot Begins Late in the Story   The first hallmark of climactic drama is that the plot begins quite late in the story. The action occurs at a point where the story has reached a climax: within a day, or a few hours, following a series of events. Climactic drama focuses on a moment when everything comes to a head, when lives fall apart, when fate closes in, when there is a final showdown between characters. Because the plot deals with a culmination of events, climactic form is sometimes called *crisis drama,* or *drama of catastrophe.*

King Oedipus by Sophocles offers a good example. When Oedipus is born, it is predicted that he will kill his father and marry his mother; and so his parents, the king and queen of Thebes, order that he be left in the wilderness to die. He is saved, however, and then taken to another country and raised there by the king and queen as their own son. As he grows up, he hears the prophecy about himself; and, assuming that his adoptive parents are his real ones, he leaves home. He goes to Thebes, where he does kill his natural father and marry his mother, not knowing who they are. He becomes king of Thebes; and when a plague strikes the kingdom, he sets out to find the person who has murdered the former king—not knowing that he himself is the murderer. All this happens *before* the play begins. The drama itself focuses on the single day when the full story emerges.

Whether it is *King Oedipus,* or Ibsen's *Ghosts,* or Tennessee Williams's *Cat on a Hot Tin Roof,* any play in climactic form concentrates on the final hours of a long sequence of events. Because so much has happened before the play begins, details about the past must be provided during the course of the play. In drama, the term for this information is ***exposition.***

The effect of beginning the action near the climax of events is to give a play a very sharp focus and a strong sense of immediacy. In climactic form, everything is concentrated on the showdown, the payoff, the final confrontation.

Scenes, Locales, and Characters Are Restricted   Climactic structure is restricted not only in time but also in other ways. For example, it has a limited number of long scenes or acts. *King Oedipus* has only a prologue, four scenes, and a closing episode, separated by choral interludes. Critics in the Renaissance said that a play must have five acts, the form invariably followed by the French neoclassic playwrights. For much of the nineteenth and twentieth centuries, three acts were standard. Today, the norm is two acts, though the long one-act play, performed without intermission, is also common.

Limited scenes in a play usually entail a restricted locale. All the action in *King Oedipus* takes place in front of the royal palace. *No Exit,* a modern climactic play by the French writer Jean-Paul Sartre, confines its three characters to one room from which, as the title suggests, there is no escape. Writers like Ibsen and Strindberg also frequently confined their plays to one room, and contemporary plays provide numerous instances of this device.

Climactic dramatic structure also has a limited number of characters. Aside from the chorus, Greek drama generally has four or five principal characters. *King Oedipus* has four: Oedipus, Jocasta, Creon, and Teiresias. French neoclassical drama and many modern plays have the same number of principal characters: four or five.

Construction Is Tight   Construction is tight in a climactic play: events are arranged in an orderly, compact way, with no loose ends. It is like a chain linked by cause and effect. As in a detective story, A leads to B, B to C, which causes D, leading in turn to E, and so on. Just as time and space are restricted, this chain of events is unbreakable: once the action begins, there is no stopping it.

The French playwright Jean Anouilh (1910–1987), in his *Antigone* (1943), compares tragedy to the workings of a machine.

> The spring is wound up tight. It will uncoil itself. That is what is so convenient in tragedy. The least little turn of the wrist will do the job. . . . The rest is automatic. You don't need to lift a finger. The machine is in perfect order; it has been oiled ever since time began and it runs without friction.[1]

This applies to every play in climactic form. The aim is always to make events so inevitable that there is no escape—at least, not until the very last moment, when a **deus ex machina** may intervene to untangle the knot. *Deus ex machina* is Latin for "god from a machine" and comes from ancient Greece and Rome, when a mechanical contraption on the roof of the stage house was used to bring the gods onstage to resolve the action at the end of a play. The term *deus ex machina* has come to stand for any plot contrivance used to resolve a play at the end.

Episodic Plot Construction   When we turn from climactic structure to *episodic* structure, we find a very clear contrast. As we've seen, in climactic structure there is a tight compression of people, places, and events. Episodic drama contrasts with this in almost every respect.

Episodic structure emerged during the Renaissance in England—Shakespeare's plays offer a prime example—and in Spain, in the plays of Lope de Vega and his contemporaries. Later, episodic form was adopted by the German playwrights Goethe and Schiller during the romantic period, in the late eighteenth century and the early nineteenth century. It was also used in the late nineteenth century by the Norwegian playwright Henrik Ibsen and in the twentieth century by the German playwright Bertolt Brecht. The following are the characteristics of episodic structure.

People, Places, and Events Proliferate   A typical episodic play covers an extended period of time, sometimes many years, and ranges over a number of locations. In one play, we can go anywhere: to a small antechamber, a large banquet hall, the open countryside, a mountaintop.

Short scenes, some only a half-page or so in print, alternate with longer scenes. The large number of characters and scenes in three plays will serve to indicate the expansive nature of episodic drama: Shakespeare's *Antony and Cleopatra* (1607–1608) has thirty-four characters and more than forty scenes; his *Julius Caesar* has thirty-four characters and eighteen scenes; *The Sheep Well* by his Spanish contemporary Lope de Vega has twenty-six characters and seventeen scenes.

There May Be a Parallel Plot or a Subplot   One technique of episodic drama is the *parallel plot,* or **subplot.** In Shakespeare's *King Lear,* for example, Lear has three daughters, two evil and one good. The two evil daughters have convinced their father that they are good and that their sister is wicked. In the subplot—a counterpart of the main plot—the Earl of Gloucester has two sons, one loyal and

---

[1]Jean Anouilh, *Antigone,* Lewis Galantière (trans. and adaptor), Random House, New York, 1946, p. 36. Copyright 1946 by Random House.

Other Dramatic Structures

During the twentieth century, new types of dramatic structure appeared. In some cases, such as ritual structure, the form amounted to adaptation of an ancient structure for modern use. We will now look briefly at these variations in dramatic structure, returning to many of them, in Part 2, when we study the historical periods in which they first appeared.

Ritual as Structure.   Like acting, ritual is a part of everyday life, though we are generally unaware of it. Basically, *ritual* is a repetition or reenactment of some proceeding or transaction which has acquired special meaning. It may be a simple ritual like singing the national anthem before a ball game or a deeply religious ritual like the Catholic mass. We all develop ritualistic patterns of behavior in our personal lives, such as following the same routine when we get up in the morning or taking a day off on Sunday. As we shall see, some historians have theorized that theater grew out of rituals and ritualistic enactments of ancient peoples.

In contemporary theater, some avant-garde groups have made a conscious attempt to return theater to ritual and to focus on ritualistic, repetitive actions which are not necessarily realistic but symbolic.

Patterns as Structure.   Related to ritual are *patterns* of events. In Samuel Beckett's *Waiting for Godot,* the characters have no personal history, and the play does not build to a climax in the ordinary way. But if Beckett has abandoned many techniques of traditional structure, he has replaced them with something else—a repeated sequence of events containing its own order and logic. The play has two acts, and in each act a series of incidents is duplicated. There are differences between the two acts, but the identical sequences of events achieve a pattern which takes on a ritualistic quality.

Serial Structure.   Another kind of structure is a *series* of acts or episodes—individual theater events—offered as a single presentation. In this case, individual segments are strung together like beads on a necklace. Sometimes a central theme or common thread holds the various parts together; sometimes there is little or no connection between the parts.

One example of serial structure is the musical revue, which has a series of short scenes, songs, and dance numbers. An evening of one-act plays is another example.

Avant-Garde and Experimental Structures.   In the second half of the twentieth century, several groups in Europe and the United States experimented with theatrical forms such as ritual; these included the Polish Laboratory Theatre, the Living Theatre, the Performance Group, and the Wooster Group. Such groups questioned long-held beliefs about traditional theater and dramatic structure, and one purpose of their experiments was to return to the ritualistic, religious roots of theater.

From their experiments, these groups developed several significant departures from traditional theater practice. Among them were (1) emphasis on *nonverbal theater*, that is, theater stressing gestures, body movements, and wordless sounds rather than logical or intelligible language; (2) reliance on *improvisation*, or scenarios developed by performers and directors; (3) interest in *ritual* and *ceremony*; (4) stress on the physical *environment* of theater, including a restructuring of the spatial relationship between performers and audience; and (5) stress on each audience member's developing his or her own interpretation of the work being presented.

We should note that there were many historical forerunners of these avant-garde techniques, which we shall review when we discuss modern theater.

Segments and Tableaux as Structure.   Robert Wilson and Richard Foreman, who will be discussed in Chapter 16, organize their avant-garde productions into units analogous to the frames of film and television, or to the still-life tableaux of painting or the moving tableaux of dance. Frequently, directors like Foreman and Wilson will use rapid movements—as in silent films—or slow motion. At times, several actions will occur simultaneously. All of these, however, relate both to an image and to a tableaux or frame.

Creating Dramatic Characters

Along with developing dramatic structure, another major challenge for the playwright is creating the characters who will carry out the action. In drama, as opposed to a novel or a short story, everything must be transformed into conversation between characters—called *dialogue*—or into action. Literature can rely on passages describing what characters are thinking and how they react to each other; in theater, however, everything must be enacted by the characters.

Though they often seem like real people, dramatic characters are actually created in the imagination of the playwright. By carefully emphasizing certain features of a character's personality and eliminating others, the dramatist can show us in 2 hours the entire history of a person whom we might need a lifetime to know in the real world. In *A Streetcar Named Desire,* for example, we come to know Blanche DuBois, in all her emotional complexity, better than we know people we see every day. As we become intimately acquainted with Blanche, the dramatist reveals to us not only her biography but her mind and soul.

In deciding what to emphasize about a character and how to present the character, a playwright has wide latitude. A stage character can be created in many different ways: the character can be drawn with a few quick strokes, as a caricaturist sketches a political figure; given the surface detail and reality of a photograph; or fleshed out with the more interpretive, fully rounded quality of an oil portrait.

Types of Dramatic Characters

Extraordinary Characters Heroes and heroines of most important dramatic works before the modern period are *extraordinary* in some way—"larger than life." Historically, major characters have been kings, queens, generals, members of the nobility, or other figures clearly marked as holding a special place in society.

In addition to filling prestigious roles, extraordinary characters generally represent some extreme of human behavior—men and women at their worst or best. Lady Macbeth is not only a noblewoman; she is one of the most ambitious women ever depicted. In virtually every instance, extraordinary characters are men and women at the breaking point, at the outer limits of human capability and endurance.

For example, the young Greek heroine Antigone and the medieval religious figure Joan of Arc are the epitome of the independent, courageous female, willing to stand up to male authority with strength and dignity. Two heroes from ancient Greece, Prometheus and Oedipus, are men willing to face the worst the gods can throw at them and accept the consequences. Among those qualifying as human beings at their worst is the Greek heroine Medea, who murders her own children.

Comic characters can also be extremes. For instance, the chief character in *Volpone*, by Shakespeare's contemporary, the English comic dramatist Ben Jonson, is an avaricious miser who gets people to present him with expensive gifts because they think he will remember them in his will.

EXTRAORDINARY CHARACTERS
The heroes and heroines of traditional theater usually stand apart from ordinary people and are "larger than life." They are frequently figures of privilege and authority who represent human beings at their best or worst: such people as kings, queens, generals, and members of the nobility. A good example is the title character in Shakespeare's King Lear, *played here by Hal Holbrook in a production at the Old Globe Theatre in San Diego. (© Ken Howard)*

Kings, queens, and other extraordinary figures have continued to be treated in drama of the last hundred years, but beginning in the eighteenth century, ordinary people took over more and more from royalty and the nobility as the heroes and heroines of drama—a reflection of what was occurring in real life as monarchies became less powerful and democracy took hold. Nevertheless, the leading figures of drama continued to be exceptional men and women at their best and worst. The heroine of August Strindberg's *Miss Julie* is a neurotic, obsessive woman at the end of her rope. In *Mother Courage* by Bertolt Brecht, we see a woman who will sacrifice almost anything to survive; she even loses a son by haggling over the price of his release from detention. *The Emperor Jones*, by Eugene O'Neill, shows the downfall of a powerful black man who has made himself the ruler of a Caribbean island.

Representative or Quintessential Characters

Though many characters of modern drama are extraordinary, a new type of main character has emerged—one who is three-dimensional and highly individual, but at the same time ordinary. He or she stands apart not by being exceptional, but by being typical of a large, important sector of the population. Rather than being "worst," "best," or some other extreme, such characters are notable because they embody the characteristics of an entire group. We can call these characters *representative* or *quintessential*.

A good example of a representative character is Nora Helmer, the heroine of Henrik Ibsen's *A Doll's House*. Though Nora has secretly forged a signature to get money for her husband when he was very ill, he regards her as spoiled and flighty. All her life, in fact—first by her father and now by her husband—she has been treated as a doll or a plaything, never as a mature, responsible woman. In the last act of the play, Nora rebels: she makes a declaration of independence to her husband, slams the door on him, and walks out. It has been said that Nora's slamming of the door marked the beginning not only of modern drama but of the emancipation of modern women. Nora's demand that she be treated as an equal has made her typical of all housewives who refuse to be regarded as pets. *A Doll's House* was written in 1879, but today—well over 100 years later—Nora still symbolizes the often inferior position of women.

Another example of a representative character

REPRESENTATIVE CHARACTERS

In much of modern realistic theater, the main characters are distinguished not by being extraordinary or larger than life, but because they are "representative" of a whole group or type. The heroine of Ibsen's A Doll's House, for instance, stands for all women who, through the ages, have been treated as children or "dolls" by their parents and husbands. In a recent production, Janet McTeer was Nora, the heroine, and Owen Teale was Torvald, her husband. (© Joan Marcus)

is Willy Loman, in Arthur Miller's *Death of a Salesman*. Willy stands for all salesmen, traveling on "a smile and a shoeshine." He has accepted a false dream: the idea that he can be successful and rich by putting up a good front and being "well liked."

Nora Helmer and Willy Loman are both examples of characters who stand apart from the crowd, not by standing above it but by embodying the attributes of a certain type of ordinary person.

Stock Characters Many characters in drama are not "complete," not "three-dimensional." Rather, they symbolize and throw into bold relief a particular type of person or one outstanding characteristic of human behavior, to the exclusion of virtually everything else. They are called **stock characters,** and although they can be found in almost all kinds of drama, they appear particularly in comedy and melodrama.

Among the most famous examples of stock characters are those in *commedia dell'arte,* a form of comic improvisational theater which thrived in Italy from the late sixteenth century to the eighteenth century. In commedia dell'arte, there were no scripts; there was only an outline of the action, and the performers supplied the words. There was a set group of stereotypical characters, each one invariably wearing the same costume and displaying the same personality traits. The bragging soldier, called Capitano, always boasted of his courage in a series of fictitious military victories. Pantalone, an elderly merchant, spoke in clichés and chased young women; and a pompous character, Dottore, spouted Latin phrases to impress others with his learning. Among the servant characters, Harlequin was the most popular; both cunning and stupid, he was at the heart of every plot complication.

The familiar figures in situation comedies on television are good examples of stock characters in our own day. The conceited high school boy, the prejudiced father, the harried mother, the dumb blond waitress, the efficient career person, the tough private detective—we can see such stereotypical characters every day on television. We recognize their familiar traits, and their attitudes and actions are always predictable.

Characters with a Dominant Trait   Closely related to stock characters are characters with a ***dominant trait,*** or *humor.* One aspect of such a character dominates all others, making for an unbalanced, often comic, personality. Ben Jonson titled two of his plays *Every Man in His Humour* (1616) and *Every Man Out of His*

A DOMINANT TRAIT
A favorite character of many comic writers through the ages has been one with a clear, strong trait that overrides all others: jealousy, avarice, miserliness, pomposity, and so forth. The French playwright Molière employed this technique frequently, a good example being his play The Miser. *Here we see John Peakes as the title character (right) with Carmen Decker in a scene from a production by the Michigan Public Theater in Boarshead. (© Chris Czopek)*

Humour (1616); and he usually named his characters for their single trait or humor. In his play *The Alchemist* (1610), the characters have names like Subtle, Face, Dapper, Surly, Wholesome, and Dame Pliant.

Playwrights of the English Restoration also gave characters names that described their personalities. In *The Way of the World*, by William Congreve, one character is called Fainall, meaning "feign all"—that is, he constantly pretends. Other characters are Petulant, Sir Wilful Witwoud, Waitwell, and Lady Wishfort, the last being a contraction of "wish for it." Molière frequently emphasized the dominant trait of the main character in his titles: *The Miser, The Misanthrope, The Would-Be Gentleman* (1670), *The Imaginary Invalid*.

Minor Characters.   Characters who play a small part in the overall action are called *minor characters*. Generally, they appear briefly and serve chiefly to further the story or to support more important characters.

Narrator or Chorus.   Generally, a *narrator* speaks directly to the audience, frequently commenting on the action. The narrator may or may not have a dramatic persona in the same sense as the other characters. In Tennessee Williams's *The Glass Menagerie*, the narrator is also a character in the play; in Thornton Wilder's *Our Town*, the narrator becomes several characters during the course of the action. Greek drama used a *chorus* that commented, in song and dance, on the action of the main plot and reacted to it.

Nonhuman Characters.   In many primitive cultures, performers portrayed birds and animals, and this practice has continued to the present. Aristophanes, the Greek comic playwright, used a chorus to play the title parts in his plays *The Birds* (414 B.C.) and *The Frogs* (405 B.C.). In the modern era, the absurdist playwright Eugène Ionesco has people turn into animals in *Rhinoceros* (1959). The contemporary American playwright Edward Albee has performers play lizards in *Seascape* (1974).

Occasionally, playwrights use other kinds of nonhuman roles. For example, as we shall see, medieval dramatists who wrote morality plays created characters representing ideas or concepts.

While authors may create nonhuman characters, however, we should note that their focus is always on drawing parallels with the human experience.

Juxtaposition of Characters

In creating characters, a playwright can use them in combinations that will bring out certain qualities.

One such combination consists of a *protagonist* and an *antagonist*. These terms come from Greek theater. A *protagonist* is the leading character in a play, the chief or outstanding figure in the action. An *antagonist* is the character who opposes the protagonist. In Shakespeare's *Othello*, for example, the protagonist is Othello and the antagonist is Iago, his chief opponent. Through the interaction and conflict between protagonist and antagonist, the individual qualities of both characters emerge.

Another way to contrast characters is to set them side by side rather than in opposition. Frequently, a dramatist will introduce secondary characters to serve as *foils* or *counterparts* to the main characters. In *Hedda Gabler,* by Henrik Ibsen, the main character, Hedda, is destructive and willful, bent on having her own way. Mrs. Elvsted, another character in the play, is Hedda's opposite in almost every regard.

Thus the playwright has a great responsibility, but also a great deal of leeway, in developing dramatic characters. Not only does it require skill and imagination to create convincing individual characters; these characters must interact in a way that will carry the play forward.

In this chapter, we have examined the work of the person or persons creating a dramatic text. We have looked at the development of subject, focus, and purpose and the creation of dramatic structure and dramatic characters. In Chapter 8 we turn to another aspect of the text: point of view as it manifests itself in dramatic genres.

SUMMARY

The person or persons creating a dramatic text have a number of tasks and responsibilities: to develop the subject, focus, and purpose of the text. Beyond that, those creating a text must develop a dramatic structure and dramatic characters.

Like an architect planning a building, those who create a text must develop a structure for a play. Essentials of dramatic structure include plot, conflict, strongly opposed forces, and a reasonable balance between those forces. Working with these essentials, the playwright creates the structure. An opening scene starts the action and sets the tone and style. Then the characters, motivated by objectives or goals, encounter a series of obstacles and complications. The result is a succession of crises leading to the most important crisis, the climax.

In the past, playwrights generally used either climactic or episodic structure. In climactic form, all aspects of a play—such as action, duration, and number of characters and locales—are restricted; in episodic form, these aspects are all expanded. At certain times in theater history, climactic and episodic form have been combined.

A playwright or the equivalent must also create characters, using dialogue and action. Playwrights of the past usually presented extraordinary, "larger than life" characters. A modern dramatist is less likely to present elevated characters such as kings and queens, but present-day playwrights still often give us exceptional characters—people at their best or their worst. Today's playwrights might also choose to present ordinary but representative characters, typical of a large portion of the population. A playwright may also use stock characters, easily recognizable stereotypes.

The playwright or whoever creates a text juxtaposes characters to highlight their individual traits—for example, opposing the main character or protagonist with an antagonist or a contrasting character.

Playwriting links on the Web.

Dramatic Exchange   http://www.dramex.org

This site is dedicated to the public distribution of dramatic works by amateur and professional playwrights.

Playwrights on the Web   http://www.stageplays.com/writers.htm

International database of playwrights and their websites, offering production and publishing opportunities.

Dramatists Play Service Inc.   http://www.dramatists.com

This service represents American theater by publishing and licensing the work of new and established playwrights.

Dramaturgy Pages   http://dramaturgy.net/dramaturgy

This site hosts resources for and about dramaturgs, including plays, seminars, and advice for the aspiring writer.

Artslynx Dramaturgy Resources   http://www.artslynx.org/theatre/drama.htm

Directories of playwrights, theater libraries, and publications to assist the aspiring dramaturg.

Browse through these links and see what the playwriting community looks like. How are these resources similar to the links found in Chapter 4, Theater Spaces? Would these resources be useful to directors? To producers? How do playwrights market themselves? Where do they go for resources? How are playwrights represented professionally?

Chapter 8

The Text: Dramatic Genres

What Is Genre?

Tragedy

    Conditions for Tragedy: Theater and Society

    Traditional Tragedy

    Modern Tragedy

Comedy

    Characteristics of Comedy

    Forms of Comedy

Play Synopsis: *Tartuffe*

Heroic Drama

Melodrama

Domestic or Bourgeois Drama

Tragicomedy

    Shakespearean Tragicomedy

    Modern Tragicomedy

Summary

◀ COMEDY OR TRAGEDY?

Drama is often put into categories: tragedy, comedy, tragicomedy, melodrama, and so forth. Sometimes these categories overlap, but ever since the ancient Greeks separated tragedy and comedy and provided a mask for each, the practice of dividing drama into various types or genres has proved helpful to practitioners and audiences alike. A classic drama which fulfills all the requirements of comedy is Tartuffe *by the French playwright Molière. The performers in this production by The Acting Company are Kristen Gass as the Maid (standing) and Anna Bates as Marianne. (© T. Charles Erickson)*

Before we look at viewpoint in dramatic writing, we should note that not only playwrights but all of us adopt different points of view toward events and toward life in general. Depending on our perspective, we can see the same subject as funny or sad, take it seriously or laugh at it, make it an object of pity or of ridicule. Just why we look at events from different points of view is difficult to say, but there is no question that we do. The English author Horace Walpole (1717–1797) wrote: "This world is a comedy to those that think, a tragedy to those that feel." Whether or not Walpole's formulation is entirely accurate, people undeniably see the world from different perspectives.

In theater, this question of viewpoint—looking at people or events from a particular perspective—becomes crucial. Viewpoint is not taken for granted, as it is in everyday life; rather, it is a conscious act on the part of whoever creates the text. To take an example from modern theater, in most cases death is considered a grave matter, but in his play *Arsenic and Old Lace* (1941) the dramatist Joseph Kesselring (1902–1967) makes it clear that we are to regard death as comic. Kesselring presents two elderly women who kill no fewer than twelve old men by serving them arsenic in glasses of wine. But because the dramatist makes a joke of the way the women prepare the poison and because he removes from the play any feeling that the deaths are to be taken seriously, he engenders in the audience the notion that it is all in fun.

What Is Genre?

In theater, viewpoint is incorporated in what is known as *genre*—a French word meaning "category" or "type." Before examining genre, we should note that often a play does not fit neatly into any category. Those who create a text do not write categories or types of plays; they write individual, unique works—and preoccupation with genre may distract us from the individuality of a play or a production. Still, if we keep these reservations in mind, we will find that it is helpful to understand the traditional genres into which western dramatic literature has fallen.

The oldest and best-known genres in theater are *tragedy* and *comedy.* The Greeks, who first made a clear distinction between the two approaches, created a mask for tragedy and a mask for comedy, and these masks have become the symbol for theater. Before we look specifically at tragedy and comedy, we should note that point of view in drama is strongly influenced by the way a society regards human life.

Tragedy

Tragedy is serious drama involving important personages caught in calamitous circumstances; it evokes in the audience fear and apprehension for the characters who are suffering, and admiration for the courage they display. Many people consider tragedy the loftiest and most profound form of theater—in fact, one of the

IN A FARCE, EVEN DEATH IS COMIC

Point of view determines whether a play is tragic, comic, or some variation of these genres. Even events that ordinarily would be serious become comic when treated humorously. One example is the play Arsenic and Old Lace, *in which two elderly women poison a series of old men. Because the play is a farce, and actions are not looked on as they would be in real life, we laugh rather than become upset when the poisonings occur. This scene is from a production at the Long Wharf Theatre in New Haven, Connecticut. Joanne Woodward (second from right) and Joyce Ebert (far left) are the two ladies; Jack Gilpin (pointing) is a relative of theirs; Richard Spore (right) is a victim.* (© T. Charles Erickson)

most meaningful forms of expression in any of the arts. Why is this so? For one thing, tragedy probes very basic questions about human existence. Why are people sometimes extremely cruel? Why is the world so unjust? Why are men and women called on to endure suffering? What are the limits of human suffering and endurance? In the midst of cruelty and despair, what are the possibilities of human achievement? To what heights of courage, strength, generosity, and integrity can human beings rise?

Tragedy assumes that the universe is indifferent to human concerns, and often cruel or malevolent. Sometimes the innocent suffer while the evil prosper. Some human beings are capable of despicable deeds; others confront and overcome adversity, attaining a nobility which places them, in the words of the psalmist in the Bible, "a little lower than the angels."

A CLIMATE FOR TRAGEDY
Two historical periods particularly suited for the creation of dramatic tragedies were ancient Greece and the Renaissance. Shown here is a product of the Greek period: Euripides's Medea *with British actress Diana Rigg portraying the title character, a woman who murders her own children to get revenge on the husband who betrayed her.* (© Joan Marcus)

Conditions for Tragedy: Theater and Society

When we study theater history, we recognize that theater, like any art form, does not occur in a vacuum. It is created by artists who live in a given culture at a given time. They are shaped by their culture, even though they may question it or rebel against it.

For example, in western civilization, the eighteenth century was known as the age of enlightenment and the nineteenth century as the century of progress. Over the course of these two centuries, there were political revolutions in France and America, the industrial revolution, and many scientific advances. As a result, the eighteenth and nineteenth centuries were optimistic periods, when it was felt that our worst problems—poverty, disease, injustice—could be solved, a point of view that is hardly conducive to tragedy.

By contrast, other periods of western civilization were characterized by a point of view receptive to tragedy. The outlook of these societies created what might be called the *conditions* or *climate* for tragedy. In general, there seem to be two such conditions—which at first appear mutually contradictory but are actually two sides of the same coin. One side of this tragic coin is the idea that human beings are capable of extraordinary accomplishments; the other is the idea that the world is potentially cruel and unjust. Both conditions are evidently necessary; for example, the eighteenth and nineteenth centuries in Europe reflected the concept of humanity as capable of vast accomplishments, but not the concept of the world as cruel and unjust.

Two periods in which both ideas were prominent, and which did prove conducive to tragedy, were the golden age of Greece in the fifth century B.C. and the Renaissance (the fourteenth through seventeenth centuries) in Europe. In both eras, human beings were exalted above all else; the gods and nature were given much less prominence. A look at the history of the two periods shows that the horizons of human achievement were considered unlimited. In the fifth century B.C., Greece was truly enjoying its golden age, in commerce, politics, science, and art: Pythagoras had recently formulated his theories of mathematics; Socrates was holding his philosophical discourses; and the Parthenon was being built atop the Acropolis in Athens. Nothing seemed impossible in the way of architecture, mathematics, trade, or philosophy. The same was true in Europe and England during the Renaissance. Columbus had reached the new world in 1492; the possibilities for trade and exploration appeared infinite; science and the arts were on the threshold of a new day.

In both periods, celebration of the individual was apparent in all the arts, including drama. The Greek dramatist Sophocles exclaimed:

> Numberless are the wonders of the world.
> but none
> More wonderful than man.

And in the Renaissance, Shakespeare has Hamlet say:

> What a piece of work is man! How noble in reason! How infinite in faculty! In form, in moving, how express and admirable! In action how like an angel! In apprehension how like a god!

The credo of both ages was expressed by Protagoras, a Greek philosopher of the fifth century B.C.:

> Man is the measure of all things.

But both periods also reflect the other side of the tragic coin. Along with exalted humanism, there was a simultaneous awareness of what life can do to men and women: an unflinching admission that life can be, and in fact frequently is, cruel, unjust, and even meaningless. Shakespeare, writing in 1606, put it this way in *King Lear:*

> As flies to wanton boys, are we to the gods;
> They kill us for their sport.

In *Macbeth,* he expressed it in these words:

> Out, out brief candle!
> Life's but a walking shadow, a poor player
> That struts and frets his hour upon the stage
> And then is heard no more; it is a tale
> Told by an idiot, full of sound and fury,
> Signifying nothing.

The Greek golden age and the Renaissance, then, encompassed both attitudes toward existence: the greatness of human beings on the one hand, and the cruelty of life on the other. These two sides of the tragic coin are the indispensable conditions for the creation of tragedy.

We must note, however, that—important as it is—the outlook of a society serves only as a background in creating theater. The foreground is the highly personal point of view of the individual artist. This is proved by the fact that playwrights within the same era vary greatly. At the same time that Euripides was writing tragedies in ancient Greece, Aristophanes was writing satirical farces. In France in the seventeenth century, Molière was writing comedies while Jean Racine was writing tragedies. In the modern period particularly, drama expresses a multiplicity of individual viewpoints.

Traditional Tragedy

Tragedy can be divided into two basic kinds: traditional and modern. Let's begin by looking at traditional tragedy. We have noted that Greece in the fifth century

THE TRAGIC HERO
In classic or traditional tragedy, the hero or heroine is caught in circumstances from which there is no escape and which lead inevitably to a fateful end. A good example is the title character in Shakespeare's Othello. *In the scene here, from the Royal Shakespeare Company production, Ray Fearon is Othello (right) and Richard McCabe is Iago, the man who betrays him and sends him to his ruin.* (© Donald Cooper/PhotoStage, England)

B.C. and certain European countries in the Renaissance were conducive to tragedy. What characteristics do the traditional tragedies of these periods have in common?

Tragic Heroes and Heroines. Generally, the hero or heroine of a traditional tragedy is an extraordinary person: a king, a queen, a general, a member of the nobility—in other words, a person of stature. Because these heroes and heroines are important, they stand not only as individuals but as symbols of an entire culture or society.

Tragic Circumstances. The central figure of a traditional tragedy is caught in a set of tragic circumstances. In traditional tragedy, the universe seems to trap the hero or heroine in a fateful web.

Tragic Irretrievability. The tragic situation becomes irretrievable: there is no turning back, no way out. Tragic heroes and heroines suffer a cumulative series of reversals. The figures of traditional tragedy find themselves in situations from which there is no honorable avenue of escape; they must go forward to meet their tragic fate.

Acceptance of Responsibility. A tragic hero or heroine accepts responsibility for his or her actions and also shows a willingness to suffer and an immense capacity for suffering. In many traditional tragedies, the hero or heroine recognizes the flaw or fault of character which leads to the tragic downfall.

Tragic Verse. The language of traditional tragedy is *verse*. Because it deals with lofty and profound ideas, tragedy soars to the heights and descends to the depths of human experience; and many people feel that such thoughts and emotions can be best expressed in poetry.

The Effect of Tragedy. When the elements of traditional tragedy are combined, they appear to produce two contradictory reactions simultaneously. One reaction is pessimistic: the heroes or heroines are "damned if they do and damned if they don't," and the world is a cruel, uncompromising place. And yet, in even the bleakest tragedy, there is affirmation. One source of this positive reaction is the drama itself. Traditional tragic playwrights, although telling us that the world is in chaos, at the same time strike a note of affirmation by the very act of creating such carefully shaped and brilliant works of art.

When we come to the theaters of fifth-century Greece (in Chapter 10), the English Renaissance (in Chapter 12), and neoclassical France (also in Chapter 12), we will look at specific examples of traditional tragedy and their unique characteristics.

Modern Tragedy

Tragedies of the modern period—that is, beginning in the late nineteenth century —do not have queens or kings as central figures, and they are written in prose rather than poetry. For these reasons, as well as more philosophical reasons, debate has raged for some time over whether modern tragedies are true tragedies.

According to one idea, modern tragedy is not true tragedy because modern heroes and heroines—such as the traveling salesman in Arthur Miller's *Death of a Salesman*—lack the grandeur of royal or noble characters. Also, it is argued, in the worldview of our industrialized, computerized age, the individual is a helpless victim of society. If people are not free to act on their own but are controlled by social, political, or industrial forces, how can a modern hero or heroine defy the gods?

The American playwright Arthur Miller wrote an articulate response to this argument in 1949, in an essay entitled "Tragedy and the Common Man." Miller argued that a character who is willing to "lay down his life . . . to secure one thing—his sense of personal dignity"[1] is indeed a person of stature. Miller also argued that modern characters do have some degree or element of choice in shaping

---

[1]Arthur Miller, *The Theater Essays of Arthur Miller,* Viking, New York, 1978, pp. 3–5.

their lives. Furthermore, since it is clear that there are no longer figures of royal or political stature who can symbolize a group or a culture, we must turn to common men and women for such symbolism.

Another argument against modern tragedy is that the lofty ideas of the tragic form cannot be expressed in the language of ordinary conversation; however, we might argue that some prose approaches the level of poetry and uses many poetic devices. As to the question of whether our age allows for a tragic view on its own terms, those who say yes argue that modern dramatists probe the same depths and ask the same questions as their predecessors: Why do men and women suffer? Why is there violence and injustice in the world? And perhaps most fundamental of all: What is the meaning of life?

When we turn to theater of the late nineteenth century and the twentieth century, we will examine specific examples of plays which have been called "modern tragedies."

Comedy

Comedy is humorous drama whose characters, actions, and events are intended to provoke amusement and laughter. People who create comedy are not necessarily frivolous or unconcerned with important matters; they may be extremely serious in their own way. Consider three comic dramatists from different periods—Aristophanes in classical Greece, Molière in seventeenth-century France, and George Bernard Shaw in modern Britain. All three cared passionately about human affairs and human problems. But they—and others like them—took a comic view of life; they saw the world differently from someone whose outlook is somber; they made their points with a smile, an arched eyebrow, a deep laugh. As they observed human follies and excesses, they developed a keen sense of the ridiculous, showing us things which make us laugh.

Laughter is one of the most elusive of human reactions; no one—from philosophers to psychoanalysts—has provided a fully satisfactory explanation of it. Most people do agree, however, that laughter is quintessentially human. Other creatures express pain and sorrow—emotions we associate with tragedy—but apparently only human beings laugh.

It should also be noted that there are many kinds of laughter, ranging all the way from mild amusement at a witty saying or a humorous situation to a belly laugh at wild physical comedy, to cruel derisive laughter at someone who is different. (An example of derisive laughter would be a group of children mocking a newcomer to their school or neighborhood who seems "different"—perhaps a child with a physical disability or a speech impediment.) Theater, which reflects society, includes a similar range of comedy, from light comedies to outrageous farces.

Characteristics of Comedy

If we cannot fully explain comedy, we can at least understand some of the principles that make it possible. Let's look at some important characteristics of comedy.

SUSPENSION OF NATURAL LAWS IN COMEDY

One of the devices that makes comedy possible and that adds greatly to the pleasure of comedy is the suspension of natural laws. Events and characters can be juxtaposed in a way they never could in real life. An example is Steve Martin's play Picasso at the Lapin Agile *in which the painter Picasso, Albert Einstein and Elvis Presley all find themselves at a Paris cafe at the same time—an event that would never happen in actual fact. The scene here is from a production at the American Repertory Theatre in Cambridge, Massachusetts.* (© Richard Feldman)

Suspension of Natural Laws.   One feature of most comedy is a temporary suspension of the natural laws of probability and logic. Actions in a comic play do not have the same consequences as in real life.

In comedy, when a haughty man walking down a street steps on a child's skateboard and goes sprawling on the sidewalk, we do not fear for his safety or wonder if he has been hurt. In comedy, the focus is on the man's being tripped up and getting his comeuppance. We have in some sense suspended our belief in injury. In burlesque, a comic character can be hit on the backside with a fierce thwack, and we laugh, because we know that only his or her pride is hurt. In fact, at one point in stage history a special stick, made of two flat wooden slats fastened closely together, was developed to make the sound of hitting even more fearsome: when this stick was used to hit someone, the two slats would slap together, making the whack much louder. The device was known as a *slapstick,* and its name came to describe all kinds of raucous, knockabout comedy.

Prime examples of the suspension of natural laws in comedy are silent movies and film cartoons. In animated cartoons, characters are hurled through the air like missiles, shot full of holes, and flattened on the sidewalk after falling from buildings; but they always get up, with little more than a shake of the head. The audience has no thought of real injury, of cuts or bruises, because the real-life chain of cause and effect does not apply.

Under such conditions, murder itself can be viewed as comic. The American playwright Arthur Kopit (1937–) titled one of his plays *Oh, Dad, Poor Dad, Mama's Hung You in the Closet and I'm Feeling So Sad* (1960). In Kopit's play, as in *Arsenic and Old Lace*, the serious aspects of murder have been eliminated. We do not dwell on the fact that people are being killed, and we have none of the feelings we would usually have for victims; as a result, we are free to enjoy the irony and incongruity of the situation.

Contrast between Individuals and the Social Order.   Generally, the comic viewpoint stems from a basic assumption about society, against which the writer places other factors, such as unusual events or the characters' behavior. Comedy develops when these two elements—the basic assumption about society and the events of the play—cut against each other like the blades of a pair of scissors. In most instances, comic writers accept the notion of a clear social and moral order in their society; it is not the social order which is at fault when something goes wrong but the defiance of that order by individuals. Human excess, fraud, hypocrisy, and folly are laughed at against a background of normality and moderation. This view, we should note, is in contrast to the view of many serious plays, particularly tragedies, which assume that society itself is upside down, or that, in Hamlet's words, "the time is out of joint."

In Molière's comedy *Tartuffe*, for example, the chief character is a charlatan and hypocrite who pretends to be pious and holy, going so far as to wear clerical garb. He lives in the house of Orgon, a foolish man who trusts him implicitly. The truth is that Tartuffe is trying to possess Orgon's wife as well as his money; but Orgon, blind to Tartuffe's real nature, is completely taken in by him. The audience and Orgon's family are aware of what is going on; they can see how ludicrous these two characters are, and in the end both Tartuffe's hypocrisy and Orgon's gullibility are exposed. But it is the individual—not religion or marriage—that is ridiculed. What Molière criticizes is the *abuse* of religion and marriage.

Many modern comedies reverse the scissors blades; their basic assumption is that the world is not orderly but absurd or ridiculous. Society, rather than providing a moral or social framework, offers only chaos. Against this background, ordinary people are set at odds with the world around them, and the comedy results from thrusting normal people into an abnormal world. This condition—a normal person in an upside-down world—is found especially in tragicomedy and theater of the absurd, both of which will be discussed later in this chapter.

The Comic Premise.   Suspension of natural laws (together with the scissors effect of setting a ridiculous person in a normal world or vice versa) makes possible the development of a comic premise. A *comic premise* is an idea or concept which turns the accepted notion of things upside down. This idea becomes the basis of a play: it provides thematic and structural unity and serves as a springboard for comic dialogue, comic characters, and comic situations.

The Greek satiric dramatist Aristophanes was a master at developing a comic premise. In *The Clouds* (423 B.C.), Aristophanes pictures the philosopher Socrates as a man who can think only when perched in a basket suspended in midair. In *The Birds*, two ordinary men persuade a chorus of birds to build a city between heaven and earth. The birds comply, calling the place Cloudcuckoo Land, and the two men sprout wings to join them. In *Lysistrata*, Aristophanes has the women of Greece go on a sex strike; they will not make love to their husbands until the husbands stop fighting a prolonged war and sign a peace treaty with their opponents.

The comic premise—along with the suspension of natural laws—leads to exaggeration and incongruity in several areas of comedy: verbal humor, characterization, and comic situations. These will be explored in detail when we discuss individual comedies in Part Two.

Forms of Comedy

Depending on the dramatist's intent and comic techniques, comedy takes various forms, including farce, burlesque, satire, domestic comedy, comedy of manners, and comedy of ideas.

Farce. *Farce* thrives on all forms of exaggeration—broad physical humor, plot complications, stereotyped characters. It has no intellectual pretensions but aims simply at entertainment and laughter. One hallmark of farce is excessive plot complications, and its humor usually results from ridiculous situations as well as pratfalls and horseplay. It relies less on verbal wit than the more intellectual forms of comedy do, though puns are used frequently in farce.

In modern times, the Marx brothers' films of the 1930s are examples of farce, as are the films of the actor Jim Carrey (1962–   ), such as *Ace Ventura, Pet Detective; Cable Guy;* and *Liar, Liar.* Mistaken identity, chase scenes, mock violence, rapid movement, and accelerating pace—as in a slapstick scene in a hotel room or a restaurant—are typical of farce. In bedroom farce, marriage and sex are objects of fun; in other types of farce, medicine, law, and business can serve as the butt of jokes.

Burlesque. *Burlesque* also relies on knockabout physical humor, gross exaggerations, and occasional vulgarity. Historically, burlesque was a ludicrous imitation of other forms of drama or of individual plays. The *Naked Gun* series as well as the recent film *Scary Movie,* are contemporary examples. In the United States, the term *burlesque* came to describe a type of variety show featuring low comedy skits and attractive women.

Satire. *Satire* uses wit—especially sophisticated language—irony, and exaggeration to expose or attack evil and foolishness. Satire can attack one specific figure, or it can be more inclusive, as in Molière's *Tartuffe,* which ridicules religious hypocrisy generally.

THE FUN OF FARCE

In farce everything is in fun, and events do not have the serious consequences they do in real life. Exaggeration—in language, in characters, in plot developments—is one of the main ingredients of farce. Shown here is a scene from a classic modern farce about backstage life in the theater, Noises Off! *by Michael Frayn. The production at the Royal National Theatre in London features Arden Gillett (left) as Garry Lejeune and Jeff Rawle as Frederick Fellowes. (© Donald Cooper/PhotoStage, England)*

TARTUFFE (1664)

By Molière, (1622–1673)

(Bibliothèque Nationale, Paris)

Chief Characters

Tartuffe, *a hypocrite*
Mme. Pernelle, *Orgon's mother*
Orgon, *Elmire's husband*
Elmire, *Orgon's wife*
Damis, *Orgon's son*
Mariane, *Orgon's daughter, in love with Valère*
Valère, *in love with Marianne*
Cléante, *Orgon's brother-in-law*
Dorine, *Mariane's maid*

Setting

Orgon's house in Paris in the 1600s.

Background

Tartuffe, a hypocrite who pretends to be a holy man and dresses in a religious habit, is staying at Orgon's home. He has completely fooled Orgon by feigning a virtuous lifestyle.

Act I: When Orgon's mother, Mme. Pernelle, tells the family that they should be virtuous like Tartuffe, they try to persuade her that he is a fraud. The maid, Dorine, tells Orgon's brother-in-law Cléante that Tartuffe has bewitched Orgon, who shows more affection toward Tartuffe than toward his own family. Orgon opposes the wedding of his daughter Mariane to Valère, the young man she loves. This is distressing to her brother Damis, because he wants to marry Valère's sister. When the maid Dorine tells Orgon that his wife was sick while he was away, Orgon, instead of pitying his wife, commiserates with Tartuffe, who is perfectly healthy. Cléante tells Orgon that he is being deceived by Tartuffe, but Orgon continues to believe in Tartuffe's virtue.

Act II: Orgon tells his daughter Mariane that she should marry Tartuffe. Mariane is outraged. When Dorine tries to persuade Orgon that Tartuffe and Mariane are ill-suited, Orgon defends the hypocrite. After Orgon leaves, Dorine tries to persuade Mariane to stand up to her father, but Mariane is weak-willed. Mariane's fiancé Valère confronts her with a rumor that she is planning to marry Tartuffe. The two quarrel until Dorine gets them to make up.

Act III: Dorine tells Damis that his stepmother Elmire—Orgon's wife—might persuade Tartuffe not to marry Mariane. As Damis hides in a closet, Tartuffe, alone with Elmire tries to seduce her. Elmire says she will not tell Orgon of Tartuffe's advances if he agrees not to marry Mariane. Damis appears and tells Tartuffe that he will reveal all. When Damis tells Orgon of Tartuffe's adulterous offer, Tartuffe begs Orgon to drive him out. Orgon, however, disbelieves Damis. When Tartuffe says that he should leave the house, Orgon insists that he stay and, furthermore, he disinherits his children and makes Tartuffe his sole heir.

Act IV: Damis has left. Cléante accuses Tartuffe of exerting influence on Orgon in order to get Damis's inheritance. Dorine tries to enlist Cléante's aid in helping Mariane get out of marrying Tartuffe, but Orgon enters with a marriage contract. Elmire develops a plan to expose Tartuffe. She decides that Orgon should hide in the room while she is alone with Tartuffe. When Tartuffe enters, Elmire expresses her passion for him. Tartuffe wants "palpable assurance" of her favor, meaning that she must let him make love to her. Elmire expresses concern that her husband might be around, but Tartuffe says, "Why worry about that man?" Upon hearing this, Orgon jumps out from under the table and confronts Tartuffe, who boldly replies that he now owns everything in the house. In desperation Orgon goes to find his strongbox.

Act V: Orgon tells Cléante that he had libelous papers in the strongbox and he fears they are now in Tartuffe's possession. M. Loyal, a bailiff, enters with an eviction notice ordering the family to leave. Orgon expects to be arrested because of the libelous papers, but when an officer and Tartuffe enter, Tartuffe is arrested instead. The prince of the realm has realized the sham, invalidated the deed, and pardoned Orgon. All ends happily as Orgon gives his blessing to the marriage of Valère and Mariane.

DISCUSSION QUESTIONS

- Discuss the genre and structure of *Tartuffe*.

- In *Tartuffe*, how might the audience's perception of the playwright's point of view be affected by the director's casting choices? For example, casting the role of Tartuffe with a younger rather than older actor?

- What themes in *Tartuffe* are relevant to contemporary audiences?

Domestic Comedy. *Domestic comedy* usually deals with family situations and is found most frequently today in television situation comedies—sitcoms—which feature members of a family or a neighborhood caught up in a series of complicated but amusing situations. A television show like *Everybody Loves Raymond* or *Friends* would be a good example. This form of comedy was once a staple of theater and can still be found onstage in plays by writers like Neil Simon (1927–   ).

Comedy of Manners.   Concerned with pointing up the foibles and peculiarities of the upper class, **comedy of manners** uses verbal wit to depict the charm of its characters and expose their social pretensions. Rather than relying on horseplay, it stresses witty phrases and clever barbs. In England, a line of comedies of manners runs from William Wycherley, William Congreve, and Oliver Goldsmith in the seventeenth and eighteenth centuries to Oscar Wilde (1854–1900) in the nineteenth century and Nöel Coward (1899–1973) in the twentieth.

Comedy of Ideas.   Many plays of the British writer George Bernard Shaw could be put under a special heading: *comedy of ideas.* In plays like *Arms and the Man* (1894), Shaw used comic techniques to debate intellectual propositions such as the nature of war, cowardice, and romance.

Clearly, comedy comes in many forms, from the most basic type, designed only to provide a laugh; to the more intellectual type, designed to make us think while we are being entertained. In between are many combinations of these two types. Underlying them all, though, is an emphasis on humor. Whatever its form, comedy focuses on the follies and foolishness of men and women, sometimes with a rueful shrug, sometimes with a wry smile, and sometimes with an uproarious laugh.

Heroic Drama

We have begun with the two fundamental genres: tragedy and comedy. However, other genres have also been important in theater history, including heroic drama, melodrama, domestic drama, and tragicomedy.

The term **heroic drama** refers to serious drama which has heroic or noble characters and certain other traits of classic tragedy—such as dialogue in verse, elevated language, or extreme situations—but differs from tragedy in important respects. One way is in having a happy ending; another is in assuming a basically optimistic worldview, even when the ending is sad.

If heroic drama has a happy ending, the chief characters go through many trials and tribulations but finally emerge victorious. We agonize with the hero or heroine, but we are aware all the time that the play will end well. Several Greek plays that are ordinarily classified as tragedies are actually closer to what we are calling heroic drama. In Sophocles' *Electra*, for instance, Electra suffers grievously, but at the end of the play she and her brother Orestes triumph. *The Cid,* written by Pierre Corneille in France in the seventeenth century, has a hero who

HEROIC DRAMA
Though having many of the characteristics of tragedy, heroic drama differs usually in having a happy ending, or an ending in which the dead hero or heroine is exalted in some way. A Greek play usually called a tragedy, but which can qualify as heroic drama is Electra *shown here in a production by the Royal Shakespeare Company of Britain, with Fiona Shaw in the title role.* (© Donald Cooper/PhotoStage, England)

leads his men to victory in battle and in the end wins a duel over his rival, Don Sanche. In the late seventeenth century in England, a form of drama called heroic drama or *heroic tragedy* was precisely the type of which we are speaking—a serious play with a happy ending for the hero or heroine. Although many Asian dramas—from India, China, and Japan—resist the usual classifications and involve much dance and music, they often bear a close resemblance to heroic drama. Frequently, for example, a hero goes through a series of dangerous adventures, emerging victorious at the end. The vast majority of Asian dramas end happily.

A second type of heroic drama involves the death of the hero or heroine, but neither the events along the way nor the conclusion can be thought of as tragic. *Cyrano de Bergerac,* written in 1897 by Edmond Rostand, is a good example. The title character, Cyrano, dies at the end, but only after his love for Roxanne, hidden for 15 years, has been revealed. He dies a happy man, declaring his opposition to oppression and secure in the knowledge that he did not love in vain. *Saint Joan* (1923), by George Bernard Shaw, is another example: Joan is burned at the stake, but her death is actually a form of triumph; moreover, Shaw provides an epilogue in which Joan reappears after her death.

In the history of theater, heroic drama occupies a large and important niche, cutting across Asian and western civilization, and across periods from the Greek golden age to the present.

Melodrama

The term *melodrama* means "song drama" or "music drama." Though it originally comes from the Greek, it usually refers to a theatrical form made popular by the French at the end of the eighteenth century and the beginning of the nineteenth. "Music" here refers to the background music that accompanied these plays, similar to the music played along with silent films and to background music in sound films.

In early melodrama, a premium was put on surface effects, especially those creating suspense, fear, nostalgia, and other strong emotions in the audience. The heroes and heroines of melodrama were clearly delineated and stood in sharp contrast to the villains; the audience sympathized with the good characters and despised the bad ones. Melodrama had easily recognized stock characters: the threatened woman, the sidekick (a comic foil to the hero), and the promiscuous fallen woman who repents but is still punished for her wicked past. The fate of the fallen woman is an example of the highly moral tone of traditional melodrama: the conflict between good and evil was clearly and firmly established, and virtue was always victorious. In order to keep the audience's interest, melodrama—both past and present—has a suspenseful plot, with a climax at the end of each act. Today, melodramas on television, such as adventure stories, detective stories, and cop shows, have a climax—a car crash, a sudden confrontation, a discovery of important evidence—just before each commercial break.

Most types of nineteenth-century melodrama have modern equivalents. Domestic melodrama has a counterpart in television soap opera. Frontier melodrama has become the western. Crime melodrama is now the popular mystery or detective show. Nautical melodrama, which dealt with sailors and pirates, was the forerunner of the swashbuckler or underwater film. Equestrian melodrama, which featured horses performing spectacular tricks, was the ancestor of various television and film melodramas starring animals.

Domestic or Bourgeois Drama

In the eighteenth and nineteenth centuries, there was a marked rise in the importance of ordinary men and women. With the industrial revolution and the expansion of trade, the merchant class came very much to the forefront and began to replace kings, queens, and the nobility—dukes and duchesses, earls and countesses—as both social and political leaders. With the emergence of this new class of ordinary citizens, there was a call for drama dealing not with royal families but with people from everyday life. As a result, drama began to change.

In England in 1731, George Lillo (1691–1739) wrote *The London Merchant,* about a merchant's apprentice who is led astray by a prostitute and betrays his good-hearted employer. This play, like others that came after it, overstated the case for simple working-class virtues; but it dealt with recognizable people from the daily life of Britain, and audiences welcomed it.

From these beginnings, *bourgeois* or *domestic drama* developed throughout the balance of the eighteenth century and the whole of the nineteenth, until it achieved a place of prominence in the works of Ibsen, Strindberg, and later writers such as Arthur Miller, Tennessee Williams, and Lorraine Hansberry. Problems of society, struggles within a family, dashed hopes, and renewed determination are characteristic of domestic drama. *Domestic* means "related to the household or the family," and most of the plays in this category deal with people from everyday life—usually the members of a family—in their own homes.

In the last 150 years, domestic drama has replaced both classical tragedy, as written by the Greeks and the Elizabethans, and heroic drama as the predominant type of serious drama. Domestic drama that is serious but has a happy ending has replaced heroic drama; and domestic drama with an unhappy ending that is sufficiently penetrating or profound has become a modern form of tragedy.

Tragicomedy

Drama has often combined serious and comic material in the same play, and at times in the past there have been dramas classified as tragicomedies. It was in the twentieth century, however, that the genre of tragicomedy came to the forefront. What exactly is *tragicomedy?*

Traditionally, comedy has been set in opposition to tragedy or serious drama: serious drama is sad, comedy is funny; serious drama makes people cry, comedy makes them laugh; serious drama arouses anger, comedy brings a smile. The two, however, are not always as clearly separated as this polarity suggests. For instance, a great deal of serious drama has comic elements. Shakespeare included comic characters in several of his serious plays: the drunken porter in *Macbeth,* the gravedigger in *Hamlet,* and Falstaff in *Henry IV, Part 1* are examples. One of the best-known of all medieval plays, *The Second Shepherds' Play,* concerns the visit of the shepherds to the manger of the newborn Christ child. While they are spending the night in a field, Mak, a comic character, steals a sheep and takes it to his house; he and his wife put it into a crib, pretending that it is their baby (a parody of Christ in the manger). When the shepherds discover what Mak has done, they toss him in a blanket, and after this horseplay the serious part of the story resumes.

Such alternation of serious and comic elements is a practice of long standing, but *tragicomedy* does not refer to plays which simply shift from serious to comic and back again. In tragicomedy, the point of view is itself mixed; the overall or prevailing attitude is a *synthesis,* or fusion, of the serious and the comic. One eye looks through a comic lens and the other through a serious lens; and the two points of view are so intermingled as to become one—like a food which tastes sweet and sour at the same time.

Shakespearean Tragicomedy

In addition to his basically serious plays and his basically comic plays, Shakespeare wrote others, such as *Measure for Measure* (1604) and *All's Well That Ends Well* (1602), which seem to be a combination of tragedy and comedy. Because they do not fit neatly into one category or the other, these plays have been dubbed *problem plays.* The "problem," however, arises largely because of a difficulty in accepting the tragicomic point of view, for these plays have many attributes of a fusion of tragic and comic. In *Measure for Measure,* for instance, Angelo—a puritanical, austere man—condemns young Claudio to death for having made his fiancée pregnant. When Claudio's sister, Isabella, comes to plead for her brother, Angelo is overcome by passion and tries to make Isabella his mistress. Angelo's sentencing of Claudio is serious, but the bitter irony which arises when Angelo himself is guilty of even worse "sins of the flesh" is comic. The result is a situation that is simultaneously tragic and comic.

TRAGICOMEDY: A MIXTURE OF THE SERIOUS AND THE COMIC
During the twentieth century, a form of drama that has come very much to the forefront is tragicomedy, in which serious and humorous elements are intermingled and fused. This genre reflects the confusing and complex nature of today's world. A good example of tragicomedy—and one of the first in modern drama is Uncle Vanya *by Anton Chekhov. The title character is tragic and comic at the same time. This scene shows Derek Jacobi (left, as Vanya) and Roger Rees in a production at the Roundabout Theatre in New York.* (© Joan Marcus)

Modern Tragicomedy

In the modern period—during the last hundred years or so—tragicomedy has become a predominant form. A statement made by the Danish philosopher Søren Kierkegaard (1813–1855) as early as 1842 can serve to set the tone for the tragicomic attitude: "Existence itself, the act of existence, is a striving and is both pathetic and comic in the same degree."

The plays of Anton Chekhov, written at the end of the nineteenth century, reflect this spirit. Chekhov called two of his major plays comedies; but Stanislavski, who directed them, called them tragedies—a confusion arising from Chekhov's mixture of the serious and the comic. One illustration of Chekhov's approach is found in a scene at the end of the third act of his play *Uncle Vanya,* first produced in 1899. Vanya and his niece, Sonya, have worked and sacrificed for years to keep an estate going in order to support her father, a professor. At the worst possible moment, just when Vanya and Sonya have both been rebuffed by people they love, the professor announces that he wants to sell the estate, leaving Vanya and Sonya with nothing. A few moments later Vanya comes in to shoot the professor. He waves his gun in the air like a madman and shoots twice, but he misses both times and then collapses on the floor. In this scene, Vanya and Sonya are condemned to a lifetime of drudgery and despair—a grim fate—but Vanya's behavior with the gun (it is doubtful that he honestly means to kill the professor) is wildly comic.

After World War II, a new type of drama emerged called *theater of the absurd,* and many absurdist plays can be considered tragicomedy. They probe deeply into human problems and cast a dark eye on the world; yet they are also imbued with a comic spirit—among other traditional manifestations of humor, they include juggling, acrobatics, clowning, and verbal nonsense. Three important absurdist playwrights are Eugène Ionesco, Samuel Beckett, and Harold Pinter. (Beckett's play *Waiting for Godot* will be discussed in detail in Chapter 15.) Pinter has called his plays *comedies of menace,* suggesting their juxtaposition of the serious and the comic. His characters are often pursued and persecuted by unknown people and forces, but the action also has a comic component.

In tragicomedy, a smile is frequently cynical, a chuckle may be tinged with a threat, and a laugh is sometimes bitter. In the past, the attitude which produced such combinations was the exception rather than the rule, but in our day it seems far more prevalent—and relevant. As a result, tragicomedy has taken its place as a major genre alongside more traditional approaches.

In this chapter we have examined the point of view—tragic, comic, tragicomic—that informs the theater experience. The person who initially gives a theater experience a point of view is the playwright, or others who create a text. The creators incorporate into the text specific language, attitudes of characters, and chains of events, and these elements determine the nature of the play. In preceding chapters, we considered other elements of theater: acting, directing, audiences, criticism, theater spaces, and visual and aural aspects. In Chapter 9, we will see how all these elements of theater are brought together in an actual production.

SUMMARY

An essential element of theater is a dramatic text or script created by a playwright, or by someone else functioning as a playwright.

An important aspect of a dramatic text is the point of view, which determines *genre*—a French term for "type" or "category." The two oldest and best-known theatrical genres are tragedy and comedy.

Particular societies as well as individual playwrights are often predisposed to a tragic point of view. For example, two historical periods conducive to tragedy were the fifth century B.C. in Greece and the period from the late sixteenth to the early seventeenth century in the European Renaissance.

Comedy may take a variety of forms, including farce, burlesque, satire, domestic comedy, comedy of manners, and comedy of ideas.

Although tragedy and comedy are the two fundamental genres, there are other important genres, including heroic drama, melodrama, domestic or bourgeois drama, and tragicomedy.

THEATER **ON** THE WEB

Internet sites pertaining to dramatic structure are by and large educational and are focused on training for students of playwriting.

Playwrighting Seminars Homepage   http://www.vcu.edu/artweb/playwriting/seminar.html

Richard Toscan of Virginia Commonwealth University posts online seminars about playwriting.

Screenwriter and Playwright's Homepage   http://www.teleport.com/~cdeemer/scrwriter.html

Charles Deemer is a playwright in the Pacific northwest who manages this page of resources for writers.

Aristotle Poetics Butcher Translation   http://libertyonline.hypermall.com/Aristotle/Poetics.html

This site posts a full translation of Aristotle's famous treatise on drama.

What specific information about character development can you find at each of these sites? Do modern seminars advocate principles written about in *The Poetics* to teach character development? What can you find about developing different kinds of dramatic structures? How is structure for screenwriting different from structure for theatrical plays? Are there similarities?

United Stage   http://unitedstage.com

International consortium of theater professionals who believe that playwrights must direct the first production of their plays to fully realize their vision.

Browse this site and discuss: Do you think a playwright must direct their plays in order to realize their vision? Would Aristotle agree with this consortium's view? Use specific examples from *The Poetics* to support your argument.

Photo 4 (© Peter Guither/Illinois Shakespeare Festival)

The scene designers create drawings and models to help the director visualize the setting. Drawings that show what the set will look like are renderings. Blueprints for how the scenery and all its elements are to be arranged are known as ground plans. The director reviews these drawings and signs off on the design concept. Once the director and designer are in agreement, construction drawings are made so that the setting can be built. For the Shakespeare Festival, the technical director works with the designer to create the construction drawings.

The sets then must be built to the specifications in the drawings. Seen in **photo 2** are the drawings being reviewed by a crew member. In **photo 3,** a member of the construction crew is seen building a set piece. **Photo 4** is of a rendering for the set for *Shrew,* designed by Peter Beudert.

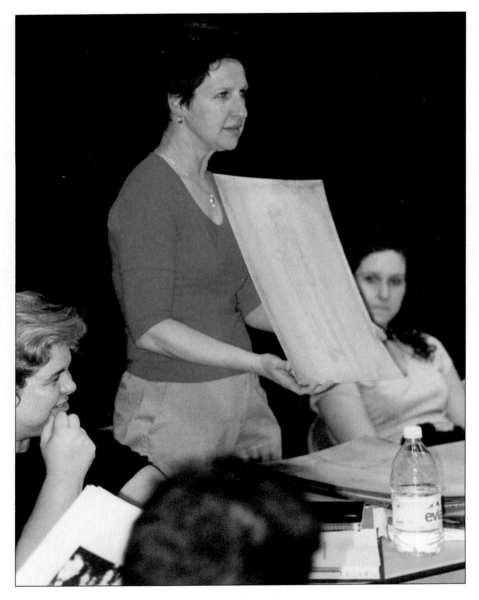

Photo 5 (© Peter Guither/Illinois Shakespeare Festival)

The costume designer also creates renderings for the director to review. Once the director has approved of the costume design concepts, the costume designer meets frequently with the construction team to discuss the designs and any unusual needs or problems. In **photo 5,** Kathryn Rohe, one of the Shakespeare Festival's designers, is shown in a meeting with the costume construction team.

Photo 6 (Abigail Wurster © Peter Guither/Illinois Shakespeare Festival)

Again, like sets, costumes are either pulled from stock or built. While the Shakespeare Festival has an extensive collection of historic clothing, many new costumes are still constructed. Because three shows are being staged each summer, the artistic director and the directors must consult carefully with the costume staff to make certain that there is enough time to create the clothing for all the productions. Actors must be measured for either the altering of pulled costumes or the construction of new ones.

In **photo 6,** a costume is being built from scratch in the Shakespeare Festival's costume shop.

The artistic director also hires stage managers and scene, costume, sound, and lighting designers for each production, as well as the summer technical director and production manager to oversee the construction and running of the season. The university provides personnel to supervise the scene and costume shops. These areas then hire staff/people to support the construction of scenery and costumes, the hanging of lights, and the running of the shows during the season.

Photo 7 (© Peter Beudert/Illinois Shakespeare Festival)

Photo 8 (Brad Hellwig © Peter Guither/Illinois Shakespeare Festival)

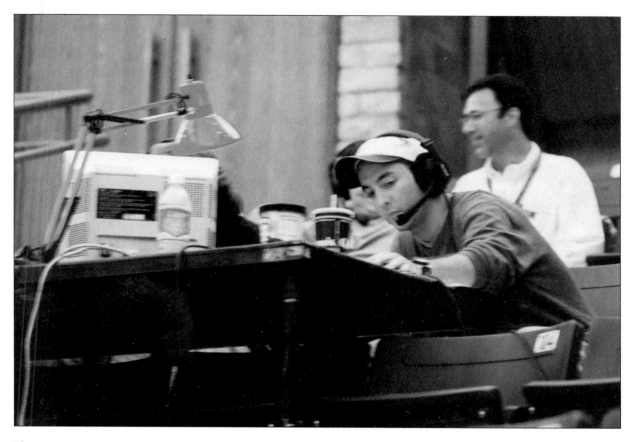

Photo 9 (Jim Juhl operating light and sound boards; © Peter Guither/Illinois Shakespeare Festival)

The lighting designer also needs to communicate to the director and to the technicians what the lighting for the production will be like. The designer does this by creating a plot. For the Shakespeare Festival, a general plot for all three outdoor shows is created, and then adaptations are made for each production.

Seen in **photo 7** is the partial lighting plot for the indoor production of *The Taming of the Shrew*. Should the weather force the cancellation of the outdoor performance, the indoor space on the campus of Illinois State University must be ready to accommodate the staging.

Hanging of the lights is an arduous task. Hundreds of lights must be hung in the outdoor and indoor theaters; they must also be focused according to the light plot. Seen in **photo 8** is a crew member hanging lights before the start of the technical and dress rehearsals. In **photo 9,** another crew member reviews cues for sounds and lights on a computer.

Photo 10 (Left to right: Kathleen Logelin, Courtney Clonch, Faith Hurley, Joan Marie Lauckner; © Peter Guither/Illinois Shakespeare Festival)

Photo 11 (Left to right: Courtney Clonch, Joseph Thompson, Faith Hurley, Drew Vidal; © Peter Guither/Illinois Shakespeare Festival)

While the designing of the production is going on, the actors are in intensive rehearsals. Each day, the company rehearses two shows or 4-hour time periods. After the first two shows of the season are opened, the third show, which has had minimal rehearsal, goes into intensive rehearsal and opens 2 weeks later. At that time, all three shows are presented in rotating repertory.

Seen in **photo 10** are actors rehearsing a scene. In addition, there are also rehearsal calls for special needs such as fight choreography. In **photo 11,** a dance rehearsal is under way.

Before the show opens, there are technical rehearsals that focus on all the design and technical elements and then dress rehearsals, when costumes are added and the show is run as if it were actually in performance. Seen in **photo 12** is a dress rehearsal for *The Taming of the Shrew.*

Photo 12 (Left to right: Courtney Clonch, Faith Hurley, Kathleen Logelin, Michael Burns; © Peter Guither/Illinois Shakespeare Festival)

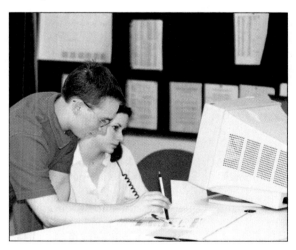

Photo 13 (Left to right: Tim Holbrook, Rebecca Goodrich; © Peter Guither/Illinois Shakespeare Festival)

There are many people who work behind the scenes at the Illinois Shakespeare Festival. These include people who provide literary advice, the dramaturgs, as well as those who deal with publicity and ticket sales. Seen in **photo 13** is a box office manager demonstrating procedures for processing the 12,000 tickets that will be sold. This photo captures the computerized system used so that tickets can be printed and sales can be tracked.

Photo 14 (© Peter Guither/Illinois Shakespeare Festival)

After 5 weeks of rehearsal, the first two shows of the summer open. Shown here is a production photo of *The Taming of the Shrew.* As can be seen in **photo 14,** all of the elements have come together: directing, acting, scene design, costuming, and lighting design.

These are just a few representative members of the entire festival staff.

There are also a large number of individuals who are hired to work in the business management area of the festival. The general manager hires the staff that is responsible for publicity and marketing. These staffers develop strategies to market the entire festival as well as the individual shows. In addition, they will also publicize the many auxiliary events staged as part of the festival. One of the most popular is the greenshow, which is presented an hour before each performance and includes picnicking on the lawn in front of the theater and a comic skit satirizing the evening's full-length play, as well as madrigal singers performing Renaissance music, to attract family audiences. The general manager also hires a house manager who will make certain that all the issues connected to audience accommodation are dealt with every evening. Many other personnel are also employed in the management area, including ticket salespeople (who are supervised by a box office manager), concessions staff, and ushers. In addition, staff members are hired to design, write, and produce the festival's souvenir program, including a company photographer. Overall, the Illinois Shakespeare Festival employs almost one hundred people each summer.

Below are just a few of the Shakespeare festivals around the country that can be found on the Web.

Illinois Shakespeare Festival   http://www.orat.ilstu.edu/isf.html

A source of entertainment and education for audiences who delight in seeing Shakespeare's work performed beneath a canopy of stars.

Oregon Shakespeare Festival   http://www.orshakes.org

Presents an eight-month season of eleven plays—five by Shakespeare and six by classic and contemporary playwrights—in repertory in three theaters.

Texas Shakespeare Festival   http://www.texasshakespeare.com

In residence on the campus of Kilgore College, this festival offers a summer season of Shakespearean works for the community.

Alabama Shakespeare Festival   http://www.asf.net

ASF produces fourteen world-class productions annually, including classical works, contemporary plays, lavish musicals, and new works commissioned by the festival's Southern Writers Project.

New Jersey Shakespeare Festival   http://www.njshakespeare.org

The state's only professional theater company dedicated to the presentation of Shakespeare's work.

How are these festivals similar? How are they different? Consider the following in your discussion: Are they all seasonal (summer-stock)? How many are associated with an academic institution? In what kind of community are they located? Are they all professional organizations? How many present plays other than Shakespeare's? Where do they get their performers? How long have they been in business? What is each festival's target audience?

Can you make any conclusions about the target audience of each festival from your discovery?

Theater Tradition and Theater Today

OUTLINE

10. Greek and Roman Theater

11. Asian and Medieval Theater

12. Renaissance Theater

13. Theater from 1660 to 1875

14. Modern Theater: 1875 to 1945

15. Modern Theater: 1945 to 1990

16. Contemporary Trends

In Part II, we explore the theater of the past and the theater today. The two are inextricably linked: the contemporary theater builds on theater from the past, both the Western tradition which began in Greece and Rome as well as the Eastern tradition which began in India, China and Japan many centuries ago. Seen in this photo is the reconstructed Roman Colosseum at night. This arena originally housed Roman popular entertainments, such as gladiator battles. Today it sometimes functions as a playhouse for spectac-ular theatrical presentations and continues to play a role in the contemporary theater.

(Pierpaolo Cito/AP/Wide World Photos)

Chapter 10

Greek and Roman Theater

Origins of Theater

Greece

   Background: The Golden Age of Greece

   Theater and Culture: Greek Theater Emerges

Timeline: *Greece*

Living History: *Antigone*

   Greek Tragedy

Play Synopsis: *King Oedipus*

   Greek Comedy

   Theater Production in Greece

   Dramatic Criticism in Greece: Aristotle

   Later Greek Theater

Rome

   Background: Rome and Its Civilization

   Theater and Culture in Rome

   Popular Entertainment in Rome

Timeline: *Rome*

   Roman Comedy: Plautus and Terence

Living History: *The Menaechmi*

   Roman Tragedy: Seneca

   Making Connections: Greek and Roman Popular Arts

   Dramatic Criticism in Rome: Horace

   Theater Production in Rome

   Decline of Roman Theater

Summary

◄ SOPHOCLES'S *OEDIPUS REX*

Sophocles's Oedipus Rex *is considered the greatest surviving classical Greek tragedy. The play is frequently revived and audiences continue to debate the questions it raises about self-determination and excessive pride. An intriguing production of* Oedipus Rex *was recently produced by the Greek National Theatre at the Roman Colosseum. Seen here is Greek actor Grigoris Valtinos as Oedipus during the final tragic scene. (Pierpaolo Cito/AP/Wide World Photos)*

The ancient civilizations of Greece and Rome have had a profound impact on western civilization. Their innovations in the arts, architecture, culture, science, philosophy, law, engineering, and government shaped much of later thought and practice. The theaters of Greece and Rome laid the foundations of many traditions of today's western theater. Although Greek and Roman theater, like Greek and Roman society, were quite distinct, the theatrical practices of both influenced later generations of theater artists. Before turning to these two remarkable eras, however, we should first briefly discuss some of the possible origins of theater.

Origins of Theater

No one knows how theater began, or where or when it originated. We do know, however, that the impulse to create theater is universal among humans. There is evidence that in every culture and every historical period, people have used elements of theater to communicate, to educate, and to entertain.

One element of theater is storytelling: this, along with other elements, is an important part of religious observances and rituals—formal, repeated ceremonies—in cultures around the world. An example is found in ancient Egypt, where there was an elaborate ritual concerning the god Osiris. Osiris became a ruler of Egypt, married his sister Isis, was murdered by his brother, and was eventually avenged and resurrected. This ceremony, retelling the story of Osiris, was performed over a period of nearly 2,000 years, from around 2500 B.C. to 550 B.C., at a sacred place called Abydos.

Another recurring theatrical element is costuming. Throughout central and western Africa, for example, striking and imaginative costumes and masks are used in a variety of ceremonies. Among the Kuba People in Zaire, there is a dance that marks the initiation into manhood. The central figure in this ceremony is the Woot, a mythical hero who wears an enormous headdress and a mask made of feathers, plumes, shells, and beads.

RITUAL THEATER OF AFRICA
Most ceremonies—whether in Africa, for instance, or among Native Americans, or in southeast Asia—have a strong theatrical component. This includes masks, costumes, repeated phrases, music, and dancing. Shown here is a Kuba initiation rite in Africa. (National Museum of African Art, Eliot Elisofon Archives, Smithsonian Institution)

In certain societies, rituals, religious ceremonies, and storytelling have been combined and transformed into theatrical events. In western culture, the first place where this occurred was ancient Greece.

Greece

Background: The Golden Age of Greece

There are times in history when many forces come together to create a remarkable age. Such a time was the fifth century B.C. in Athens, Greece, when there were outstanding achievements in politics, philosophy, science, and the arts, including theater. This era has come to be known as the *classical period* and also as the *golden age* of Greece. There are good reasons for calling it a golden age: important accomplishments were made in many fields.

For example, Greece was then a collection of independent city-states, and Athens—the most important—is credited with being the birthplace of democracy (although only male citizens had a voice in politics and government). There were advances in other areas as well. Greek philosophers, such as Socrates and Plato, tried to explain the world around them; Herodotus transformed history from a simple account of events into a social science. Also, a number of important mathematical and scientific discoveries were made: for instance, the Greek mathematician Pythagoras formulated a theorem that remains one of the cornerstones of geometry; and Hippocrates formulated an oath for physicians which is the one still taken today. Moreover, the classical Greeks were remarkable artists and architects: Greek sculpture from this period is treasured in museums around the world, and buildings such as the Parthenon—the temple that sits atop the Acropolis—remain models for architects.

Theater and Culture: Greek Theater Emerges

Of particular importance to Greek theater were the ceremonies honoring Dionysus—the god of wine, fertility, and revelry. Later, Greek drama was presented in honor of Dionysus, and most (though not all) historians believe that Greek drama originated out of the dithyrambic chorus, a group of fifty men who sang and danced a lengthy hymn praising Dionysus.

A performer named Thespis is customarily credited with transforming these songs into drama in the sixth century B.C., by stepping out of the *chorus* and becoming an actor. He moved from simply reciting a story to impersonating a character and engaging in dialogue with members of the chorus. The contribution of Thespis is reflected in the term *thespian,* which is often used as a synonym for "stage performer."

Theater and Religion.   Greek theater was intimately bound up with Greek religion. Over the centuries, the Greeks had developed a religion based on worship of a group of gods, of whom Zeus and his wife, Hera, were the leaders. Annual festivals were held in honor of the gods, and theater became a central feature of

Greece
Year, B.C.

Theater		Culture and Politics

800 — Age of Homer (800 B.C.)

600

Thales of Miletus begins natural philosophy (physics) (ca. 585 B.C.)

575

Peisistratus, tyrant of Athens (560 B.C.)

555

Play contests begin in Athens (534 B.C.)

525 — Pythagoras flourishes; Doric temples of southern Italy and Sicily (ca. 525 B.C.)

Athenian democracy (510 B.C.)

Comedy introduced to City Dionysia (487 B.C.) — Pindar begins to write odes (500 B.C.)
Aeschylus introduces second actor (ca. 471 B.C.) **500** — Persian Wars (499–478 B.C.)
Battle of Marathon (490 B.C.)

Sophocles introduces third actor (ca. 468 B.C.) — Socrates born (470 B.C.)

475 — Pericles begins rise to power: age of Pericles (462–429 B.C.)
Aeschylus's *Orestia*; introduction of skene (458 B.C.) — Hippocrates born (460 B.C.)

Prizes for tragic acting awarded (449 B.C.) **450** Beginning of Parthenon; Herodotus flourishes (447 B.C.)
Dramatic activities incorporated into Lenaia (ca. 442 B.C.) — Phidias dies (500–435 B.C.)

Sophocles' *King Oedipus* (ca. 430 B.C.) **425** Peloponnesian Wars (431–404 B.C.)
Athenian fleet destroyed (404 B.C.)
Euripides' *Trojan Women* (415 B.C.) — Spartan hegemony begins (404 B.C.)

Aristophanes' *Lysistrata* (411 B.C.) **400** Trial and execution of Socrates (399 B.C.)

Aristotle born (384–322 B.C.)

375 Plato's *Republic* (ca. 375 B.C.)
Spartan hegemony ends (371 B.C.)

350 Theban hegemony ends (371–362 B.C.)

Aristotles's *Poetics* (ca. 335–323 B.C.) — Philip II, king of Macedonia (352 B.C.)
Theater of Dionysus completed (ca. 325 B.C.) — Alexander succeeds Philip II; in 335 B.C.
From this period to ca. 100 B.C., Greek **325** occupies Greece
theaters built throughout Mediterranean (320 B.C.) — Hellenistic culture spreads throughout eastern Mediterranean (ca. 320 B.C.)

Menander's *Dyskolos* (316 B.C.) **300**

Artists of Dionysus recognized (277 B.C.)

275

THEATER AND RELIGION

Throughout its history theater has often had a close association with religion. This is true of both western and eastern theater. The Greek and Roman theaters were often allied with religious festivals, and an important segment of the medieval theater dealt directly with religious subjects. The chief Greek theater festival honored the god Dionysus, who was the subject of a play by Euripides called The Bacchae. *Shown here is a scene from a version of the play done by the Great Lakes Theater entitled* The Bakkhai, *directed by Gerald Freedman, with Dionysus (Jeremy Webb) in the background and Pentheus (Charles Tuthill). (© Roger Mastroianni)*

certain festivals. In Athens, a spring festival called the **City Dionysia,** honoring the god Dionysus, incorporated tragic drama in 534 B.C. and comedy ca. 487–486 B.C. This festival lasted several days, including three days devoted to tragedies, and had a time set aside for five comedies. *Satyr plays* were also performed. A few days after the festival, awards were given, the festival operation was reviewed by a representative body, and people who had behaved improperly or disrespectfully were judged and penalized.

Since theater was a religious and civic event, the organization of dramatic presentations was undertaken by the government. Eleven months before a festival, an appointed official of the city-state would choose the plays to be presented and would appoint a *choregus*—the equivalent of a modern-day producer—for each of the selected playwrights. In the early days of Greek dramatic festivals, the tragic playwrights themselves functioned as directors. A playwright would choose the actors and supervise the production, working with the chorus and conferring with the actors about their roles.

Theater and Myth. What kind of stories were told in the plays written for the festivals? Where did the writers find these stories? The answer in most cases is Greek myths.

A *myth* is a story or legend handed down from generation to generation. Frequently, myths are attempts to explain human and natural phenomena: the changing of the seasons, for example, and cataclysmic occurrences like earthquakes and civil wars. Myths also deal with extreme family situations: one branch of a family opposing another, or a difficult relationship between a husband and wife or between parents and children. In every culture, certain myths have a strong hold because they seem to sum up a view of human relationships and of the problems and opportunities life presents to individuals. Greece had a multitude of myths. One good example is found in the ninth century B.C., in the works of the poet Homer. Homer recounts the war between the Greeks and the Trojans in the *Iliad* and the return from the war of the Greek hero Odysseus in the *Odyssey*. These and other myths furnished the stories for Greek drama.

Greek Tragedy

The most admired form of drama at the Greek festivals was tragedy. Approximately 900 tragedies were produced in Athens during the fifth century B.C., of which thirty-one have survived—all by three dramatists: Aeschylus, Sophocles, and Euripides.

Tragic Dramatists: Aeschylus, Sophocles, and Euripides. Aeschylus (525–456 B.C.) is considered the first important Greek dramatist, and therefore the first important western dramatist. He began writing at a time when a theater presentation would be performed by a large chorus of fifty men and a single actor. In his own dramas, however, Aeschylus called for a second actor, who could play different parts when he put on different masks. This made possible a true dramatic exchange between characters and was the start of drama as we know it. In another innovation, Aeschylus reduced the size of the chorus to twelve, making it more manageable.

The dramas of Aeschylus dealt with noble families and lofty themes and were praised for their lyric poetry as well as their dramatic structure and intellectual content. He was the acknowledged master of the *trilogy*—three tragedies that make up a single unit. The best-known of his trilogies is the *Oresteia* (458 B.C.): the saga of Agamemnon, a hero of the Trojan war who, when he returns home, is murdered by his wife, Clytemnestra. She in turn is killed by their children, Electra and Orestes.

Sophocles (ca. 496–406 B.C.), who lived through most of the fifth century B.C., built on the dramatic form which Aeschylus had begun. He raised the number in the chorus to fifteen, where it was to remain. More important, he realized that an additional, third actor—who, again, might play several parts—would allow enormous flexibility. Because each actor, by wearing different masks in turn, could play two or three parts, the use of three actors meant that a play could have

Thematically, *Oedipus* raises questions that have provoked philosophical discussions for centuries: questions fate, pride and the ironic nature of human events.

Greek Comedy

As we've noted, part of the seven-day City Dionysia was devoted to comedy, and comedies by five playwrights were presented during the festival. Later in the fifth century, a separate festival in the winter was devoted solely to comedy.

Greek comedy of this period has come to be known as **Old Comedy** to distinguish it from a different kind of comedy which took hold at the end of the fourth century B.C. and is called **New Comedy**. The only surviving Old Comedies were written by Aristophanes (ca. 448–ca. 380 B.C.).

Old Comedy always makes fun of social, political, or cultural conditions, and its characters are often recognizable personalities; the philosopher Socrates is only one of a number of prominent figures satirized in the plays of Aristophanes. The modern counterpart of Old Comedy is political satire in films, in television programs such as *Saturday Night Live,* and in the routines of "insult" comedians in nightclubs and on television.

In Old Comedy, the satire is underlined by fantastical and improbable plots; this is an aspect of the comic premise, discussed in Chapter 8. In *Lysistrata,* for instance, Aristophanes condemns the Peloponnesian war, which Greece was then fighting; the women in the play go on a sex strike, refusing to sleep with their husbands until the men stop the war.

GROUND PLAN OF A TYPICAL GREEK THEATER
The theaters of ancient Greece were set into hillsides which made natural amphitheaters. At the base of the seating area was a circular space (orchestra) in which the chorus performed; at the center of the orchestra was an altar (thymele). Behind the orchestra was a temporary stage house (skene), at each side of which was a corridor (parodos) for entrances and exists.

Audience

Altar

Orchestra

Parodos, or entrance

Parodos, or entrance

Skene, or scene house

Unlike tragedies, most Old Comedies do not have a climactic structure. For example, they do not take place within a short span of time or in one locale, and they often have a large cast of characters. They also have two scenes not found in tragedy. One is a debate, called an *agon,* between two forces representing opposite sides of a political or social issue. The other is a choral section, known as a *parabasis,* addressed directly to the audience; it makes fun of the spectators in general and of specific audience members.

During the Greek Hellenistic era, which began in the fourth century B.C., Old Comedy gave way to New Comedy. Instead of the political, social, and cultural satire of Old Comedy, New Comedy dealt with romantic and domestic problems. We will study this kind of drama when we look at Roman comedy—a direct outgrowth of New Comedy.

Theater Production in Greece

Greek drama, as we have noted, was staged in *amphitheaters.* An amphitheater was cut out of the side of a hill and held between 10,000 and 17,000 spectators. At the base of the hillside was a circular playing area called the *orchestra,* and behind this was a scene house. The chorus made its entrances and exits on each side of the scene house through an aisle called a *parodos.* This is the first recorded example of the *thrust stage,* discussed in Chapter 4. The standard scenic setting for Greek tragedy was a palace, and simple devices were used to indicate locales and to move characters on- and offstage.

GREEK MECHANE AND EKKYKLEMA

A conjectural reconstruction of Greek stage machinery: on the left, a crane used for flying in characters located on a side wing (paraskenion) of the scene building. On the right, a mechane higher up on the roof of the skene. The ekkyklema below was a platform on wheels used to bring out characters from inside the building.

All the characters in Greek drama, male and female, were portrayed by men. The performers, particularly the chorus members, had to be accomplished at singing and dancing as well as vocal projection. The actors may have been paid, and after 449 B.C. an acting contest was introduced.

The major element in Greek costuming was the mask, worn by all performers. The mask covered the entire head and included hairstyle and distinctive facial features such as a beard. Masks indicated the emotional state of the characters and also made it possible for male actors to play female characters.

Dramatic Criticism in Greece: Aristotle

In the fourth century B.C., roughly 100 years after Sophocles was at the height of his powers as a playwright, the first significant work of dramatic criticism—*The Poetics*—appeared. Its author was Aristotle (384–322 B.C.). Aristotle, like Socrates and Plato, was an important Greek philosopher;

The Menaechmi

Rome, 184 B.C. It is 184 B.C., and many of the inhabitants of the city of Rome are on their way to attend performances at a spring festival in honor of Jupiter. Their mood today is happy and ebullient, because they are about to see a comedy by Plautus, whose plot twists and comic invention have made his works favorites with everyone.

The Romans are heading toward a large, temporary wooden theater building, seating several thousand, that has been erected next to a temple of Jupiter. All theater productions in Rome now take place during religious festivals, and all the theaters are near temples. A Roman theater—unlike the Greek theaters in the lands Rome has conquered—is a single unit, built on level ground, with the stage house attached directly to the ends of a semicircular audience area. In front of the stage house is a long platform stage; and in front of that is a half-circle surrounded by the audience.

The group converging on the theater consists of people from all walks of life. Plautus himself has remarked that a Roman audience is a genuine mixture: in addition to well-to-do middle- and upper-class citizens, it includes government officials and their wives; children with nurses; prostitutes; slaves—in short, virtually every social group. Because this is a state festival, admission is free.

Magistrates of the state have received a grant to produce today's plays and have engaged acting troupes to present individual plays. Each troupe is under the direction of a manager, and one of these managers has bought from Plautus a play called *The Menaechmi* and has arranged for the costumes, music, and other production elements.

As the Romans enter the theater, they see two doors onstage: one opens on the house of Menaechmus of Epidamnus (the Greek city in which Plautus has set his play); the other is the door to the house of Erotium, a woman with whom Menaechmus is having a love affair that he is trying to keep secret from his wife. The stage represents the street in front of the two houses; at one end is an exit to the port, and at the other end is an exit to the center of town.

An actor comes onstage to deliver a prologue. He asks the audience members to pay careful attention to what Plautus has to say, and then he outlines the background of the story: how the Menaechmi twins were separated when they were infants and how the twin who grew up in Syracuse is just now returning to try to find his long-lost brother. As in many of Plautus's plays, most of the dialogue is sung, somewhat like the musical numbers in twentieth-century musical comedies.

When the play opens, Menaechmus is shown to be the despair of his jealous wife. He confides to "Sponge," a parasite, that he has stolen his wife's dress, hiding it under his own clothes—and is going to give it to his mistress, Erotium. At Erotium's house he suggests that in return for the dress, she invite them to dinner. Menaechmus exits.

Meanwhile, the twin from Syracuse has arrived with his slave, Messenio. His master gives Messenio a purse full of money for safe-keeping. At that point, Erotium steps out of her house and, mistaking the Syracuse twin for Menaechmus, makes advances to him, by which he is totally confused. Not knowing he is a twin, she is equally confused by his odd behavior. Meanwhile, the two servants of the twins are constantly confused with one another as well.

Finally, the Syracuse twin does enter the house of Erotium to have dinner, and later leaves with the dress that his twin brother Menaechmus had previously given her. Menaechmus comes back just in time to have his wife demand that he return her dress. He goes to Erotium to retrieve the dress, only to be told by her that she has already given it to him. In short, he is rebuffed by both his wife and his mistress.

The play continues like this, with the two brothers constantly being confused for one another by everyone, including the wife, the mistress, the father, and the two servants. Confusion and slapstick comedy abound until the end of the play, when everything is resolved.

ROMAN COMEDY
Based on Greek New Comedy, the Roman version, which stressed domestic travails shown in comic fashion, has been the basis for comedy running through the entire western tradition, right up to the point of today's television situation comedies. One of the most popular adaptations of ancient Roman comedy is the musical A Funny Thing Happened on the Way to the Forum, *with book by Burt Shevelove and Larry Gelbert and music and lyrics by Stephen Sondheim. Shown here is a scene from a recent Broadway production which starred the actress Whoopi Goldberg (far left). (© Joan Marcus)*

the most popular being the parasite who lives off others and is motivated mainly by sensuality. Courtesans, lovers, and overbearing parents were also favorite characters. Most of the dialogue was meant to be sung. Plautus's comedies are farces, and they use such farcical techniques as mistaken identity. A good example of mistaken identity is found in *The Menaechmi.*

The Roman comic writer who followed Plautus was Terence (ca. 185–159 B.C.). Although Terence's plots are as complicated as those of Plautus, his style is more literary and less exaggerated. Terence's *Phormio* (161 B.C.) dramatizes the attempts of two cousins, named Antipho and Phaedria, to overcome their fathers' objections to their lovers. The plot complications and stock characters are similar to those found in *The Menaechmi,* but *Phormio* is less farcical and slapstick and gives more emphasis to verbal wit.

Roman Tragedy: Seneca

The most notable tragic dramatist of the Roman period was Seneca (ca. 4 B.C.–A.D. 65). Seneca's plays appear to be similar to Greek tragedies but in fact are quite distinct. His chorus is not integral to the dramatic action; and—unlike Greek dramatists, who banished violence from the stage—Seneca emphasizes onstage stabbings, murders, and suicides. In addition, supernatural beings often appear in the dramatic action.

Although his plays were rarely performed, Seneca's influence on later periods is noteworthy. Shakespeare, for example, was greatly influenced by Seneca's

Making Connections:

Greek and Roman Popular Arts

GLADIATOR BATTLES
Shown here is a Roman mosaic depicting a gladiator battling a leopard. Such battles between human combatants and animals were extremely popular, particularly during the Roman Empire. (© Archivo Iconografico, S.A./Corbis)

While we focus on the great dramas and comedies created during the Greek and Roman eras, we should not forget that there was a great tradition of popular entertainment during these time periods. The types of popular arts that flourished during these eras were to have a great influence on popular culture through our own times.

During the classical Hellenistic Greek eras, we know that there were traveling mimes who performed throughout the Greek world. Historians believe that mime may have developed in the fifth and fourth centuries B.C., but there is a great deal of debate over how to define the form. Greek mime is often described as dealing with domestic and sexual situations in a popular and highly bawdy manner, though it may have first been a form that parodied mythological figures and stories.

Mimes sometimes performed by themselves, but by the Hellenistic era they were usually organized into troupes. Mime was never introduced into the festivals and was seen as a lower form of theatrical art. Women eventually were performers in mime troupes, and frequently the actors in this type of popular entertainment, especially in the Hellenistic era, appeared without masks. In order to survive economically, mime troupes traveled extensively. For that reason, it is often argued that Greek mime performers influenced the development of Roman theater and popular entertainments.

Roman theater had great competition in the popular arts that were available to the Roman public. Mime troupes continued to perform in Roman times. The Romans also developed a form referred to as *pantomime,* in which a single male dancer interpreted classical literature, sometimes accompanied by a chorus that chanted and musicians.

But the Romans also organized even greater spectacles. As we have noted, they created huge circuses, stadiums, and amphitheaters for popular arts. Some of the circuses, for example, had tracks for chariot races. Stadiums held animal battles, battles between gladiators, and fights between humans and animals. As we noted earlier in the chapter, the Circus Maximus and the Colosseum were erected for just such events.

In modern times, we can see many similarities to the popular arts of Greece and Rome. Stand-up comedians and small troupes of comics entertain us regularly in events that are very reminiscent of the early mimes. Sports arenas, indoors and outdoors, house gladiator-like battles, such as football and boxing. And many of these events are highly theatrical, mixing pregame, half-time and postgame performances, into already highly theatricalized sports.

dramatic style; in fact, *Hamlet*—which has much onstage violence and includes a supernatural character (the ghost of Hamlet's father)—is often described as influenced by a Senecan revenge tragedy.

Dramatic Criticism in Rome: Horace

Like Roman drama, Roman dramatic criticism was based on the work of others, especially Aristotle. Horace (65–8 B.C.), sometimes called the "Roman Aristotle," outlined his theory of correct dramatic technique in *Ars poetica* (*The Art of Poetry*). Horace argued that tragedy and comedy must be distinct genres, or types, of drama, and that tragedy should deal with royalty, while comedy should depict common people. He also stressed that drama should not just entertain but should also teach a lesson.

Theater Production in Rome

Roman production practices differed slightly from those of Greece. Roman festivals were under the jurisdiction of a local government official who hired an acting troupe. The *dominus*, or head, of a troupe—who was usually the leading actor—made financial arrangements, bought dramas from playwrights, hired musicians, and obtained costumes. Acting companies had at least six members, all male; and the Romans ignored the three-actor rule of Greek theater. Roman acting technique emphasized detailed pantomime and broad physical gestures, necessitated by the size of Roman theaters; it also stressed beautiful vocal delivery. The Romans did not greatly value versatility in actors; rather, they admired performers who specialized in one type of role and refined their characterizations of stock figures. Facial expression was unimportant, since full linen head masks were worn—only mime performers appeared without masks.

As we've seen, Roman theaters were based on Greek models. The Romans did not construct a permanent theater until 55 B.C. Thus there were no permanent spaces for presenting the works of Plautus and Terence, the best-known Roman playwrights. Instead, temporary wooden structures, probably similar to the later permanent ones, were erected.

A Roman theater had the same three units as a Greek theater: (1) a semicircular, sloped seating area; (2) an orchestra; and (3) a stage house, called the *scaena*. The Roman structures, however, were different from classical Greek theaters in that they were freestanding buildings with the tiered audience section connected to the stage house to form a single unit. The sloped, semicircular audience seating area was often larger than its Greek counterpart; the average capacity of a Roman theater was around 25,000.

The Roman orchestra, which was also semicircular (rather than circular as in Greek theaters), was rarely used for staging; rather, it was used for seating government officials or, in some theaters, was flooded for sea battles.

In front of the stage house was a large raised stage about 5 feet high whose area varied from approximately 100 feet by 20 feet to 300 feet by 40 feet. The stage house itself was a unique feature of the Roman theater structure. Two or three stories high, it was used for storage and dressing space, and a roof extended from the scene building over the stage to protect the actors from the weather. Two side wings connected the stage house to the audience area. The facade of the stage house—the *scaena frons*—was elaborate and ornate, with statuary, columns, recesses, and three to five doorways. Because of its emphasis on the raised stage and the facade behind it, the Roman theater moved to a point somewhere between the thrust stage of the Greek theater and later proscenium stages.

Decline of Roman Theater

In the fourth century after Christ, it was clear that the Roman empire was beginning to fall apart. In 330, Emperor Constantine established two capitals for the empire: Rome in the west and Constantinople in the east. From that point on, the center of gravity shifted to Constantinople, and the city of Rome became less and less important.

THE ROMAN THEATER AT ORANGE

The Romans built theaters throughout their empire, which circled the Mediterranean Sea. One of the best-preserved, built in the first or second century after Christ, is at Orange in France, near the center of town. Note the semicircular orchestra, the large stage area, and the stage house at the back, with its ornate facade with niches for statues and other adornments. (Giraudon/Art Resource)

GROUND PLAN OF TYPICAL ROMAN THEATER

Roman theaters, in contrast to Greek theaters, were free-standing structures—all one building—with the stone stage house connected to the seating area, known as the cavea. The orchestra was a semicircle instead of a full circle as in Greek theaters. The stage was long and wide, and the stage house was several stories high with an elaborate facade.

The downfall of Rome was marked in A.D. 476 by the unseating of the western Roman emperor by a barbarian ruler. It had probably been caused by the disintegration of the Roman administrative structure and the sacking of Roman cities by northern barbarians; but in any case the fall of the empire also meant the end of Roman theater.

Another important factor in the decline of Roman theater was the rise of Christianity. From the outset, the Christian church was opposed to theater because of the connection between theater and pagan religions and because the church fathers felt that evil characters portrayed onstage taught immorality to audiences. In addition, the sexual content of Roman entertainments offended church leaders. As a result, the church issued various edicts condemning theater and in A.D. 398 decreed that anyone who went to the theater rather than to church on holy days would be excommunicated.

After the invaders from the north had plundered the cities of the Roman empire, no large centers of culture remained. People scattered, and in many places the buildings that had housed government offices, schools, and performing spaces were abandoned. The plays of the Greek and Roman dramatists and the writings of Aristotle and Horace were lost or forgotten. The tradition of theater that had stretched virtually unbroken for nearly 1,000 years—from the Greeks in the fifth century B.C. through the early centuries of the Christian era—was at an end. In the western world, theater as an organized activity would not appear again until the medieval period, many centuries later.

SUMMARY

The impulse to create theater is universal. Elements of theater exist in rituals and ceremonies in Africa, in Asia, in Europe, and wherever else human society develops.

On the European continent, Greek theater set the stage for all western theater to follow, with the tragedies of Aeschylus, Sophocles, and Euripides and the dramatic form known as climactic structure. Aristotle's *Poetics* marked the development of serious criticism of drama and theater. With Aristophanes' Old Comedies, the Greeks were leaders in comedy as well. Classical Greek theater buildings were large outdoor spaces built into hillsides, which accommodated audiences attending religious festivals. All the performers were male, and the chorus was an integral element of all classical Greek drama and theater. During the later Hellenistic period in Greece, New Comedy, which was concerned with domestic and romantic situations, prepared the way for almost all later popular comedy.

The Romans borrowed many Greek conventions, including the introduction of drama and theater into religious and civic festivals, but they emphasized domestic and romantic comedies, as in the plays of Plautus and Terence. The tragedies of Seneca are noteworthy because of their influence on later playwrights.

Roman theaters were usually huge outdoor buildings. In Roman playhouses (unlike Greek theaters), all the structural elements were connected, and the most significant element was a large raised stage with an ornate facade.

THEATER ON THE WEB

In studying theater history, it is helpful to have online resources to enhance your understanding of the relationship between theater and culture during each historical period. The following links provide more information about the Greek and Roman period discussed in this chapter.

Project Perseus: Texts and Translations   http://www.perseus.tufts.edu/Texts.html
Scholarly Greek texts with English translations, including nearly all the surviving
   Greek dramas.

Internet Classics Archive   http://classics.mit.edu
Over 400 searchable works of classical literature.

Didaskalia Ancient Theater Today   http://didaskalia.berkeley.edu
An electronic source for the latest developments in performance of Greek and
   Roman drama, dance, and music.

Classical Drama Sites   http://www.webcom.com/shownet/medea/cldrama.html
A host of links to classical drama and ancient theater sites.

Maecenas: Images of Ancient Greece and Rome   http://wings.buffalo.edu/AandL/
   Maecenas/index.html
Images of ancient Greece and Rome, free for noncommercial downloading and use.

After browsing these resources, develop a bibliography of sites that you could use if you were a scenic designer doing research for a historical replication of a production of *The Menaechmi*. Consider the historical context, art, architecture, analysis of the play, acting conventions, and performance spaces.

Chapter 11

Asian and Medieval Theater

Asia

    Background: Asian Theater

    Theater in India

Timeline: *Asia*

    Theater in China

    Theater in Japan

Living History: *Sotoba Komachi*

Play Synopsis: *Sotoba Komachi*

The Middle Ages

    Background: Medieval Europe

    Theater and Culture in the Middle Ages

Timeline: *Middle Ages*

    Medieval Drama: Mystery, Miracle, and Morality Plays

Living History: *Noah's Ark*

    Medieval Theater Production

Summary

◀ NŌ THEATER

The traditional Nō theater, with its stylized performance, use of masks, and exquisite costumes, continues to be popular in Japan today. Seen here is a photo from a production of Taihei Shojo, *staged in Kyoto, Japan.* (Courtesy of Inoue Corp. U.S.A.)

After the fall of Rome, the highly developed theater of Greece and Rome disappeared. However, as we shall see, wandering players kept the theatrical tradition alive in western society for the 500 years after the fall of the Roman Empire. Then, between A.D. 1000 and 1500, new types of theater, many connected to the church, developed.

At the same time, in the Asian world various classical forms of theater arose, many of which had strong connections to Asian religions.

Asia

Background: Asian Theater

When we turn to the theater of Asia, we have moved half a world away from the theater of Greece and Rome as well as the Middle Ages. These two cultures—east and west—knew nothing of each other at the time. Nevertheless, theater had begun in parts of Asia during a period of nearly 1,000 years—from roughly A.D. 350 to 1350—when there was little organized theater in Europe.

Each of the three great Asian traditions—Indian, Chinese, and Japanese—reached a high point at a time when religion and philosophy were central in the culture. As a result, the focus of these traditional theaters has remained to some extent religious and philosophical, even though the societies themselves changed and were modernized. In addition, the three great cultures created and sustained forms of theater in which there was a unique synthesis of many facets of theatrical art—acting, mime, dancing, music, and text. We will understand the development of Asian theater more clearly as we examine these three theaters in turn, beginning with the theater of India.

Theater in India

Indian history has been described as a succession of immigrations into the Indian subcontinent from the north. Though early traces of civilization in Indian history go back to 3000 B.C., it was 1,000 years later, when the Aryans came into southern India and left behind works in Sanskrit, that the basis of the great Indian literary traditions was established.

Around 400 B.C., Buddhism, the religion of eastern and central Asia that follows the teachings of Buddha, reached a peak of development. By roughly 240 B.C., India was united under Buddhist rule, but a period of disorder and confusion followed for several centuries, until around A.D. 320, when the Guppy dynasty began to reunite the nation. Hindu culture entered its golden age at this time, and it was during the next centuries that the great Sanskrit dramas were written and performed.

Sanskrit Drama. What remains from the tradition of this golden age, beginning in the fourth century after Christ, is a group of plays written in Sanskrit—the language of the noble classes—for performance in various court circles. These plays draw on themes from Indian epic literature. The most celebrated playwright of the classic period is Kalidasa (ca. fifth century after Christ), whose play *Shakuntala* is a lengthy love idyll on various classic themes.

Although their texts have been preserved, no information remains on how the Sanskrit plays were acted. We do, however, have descriptions of a typical theater in which they were performed. It was 96 feet long and 48 feet wide, divided equally into stage and auditorium, and the seating capacity was probably about 400. There were four pillars in the auditorium—one white, one yellow, one red, and one blue—indicating where members of different castes were to sit. A curtain divided the stage into two parts: one part for the action and the other for dressing rooms and a backstage area. Scenery was evidently not used, although elaborate costumes probably were. Dance, symbolic gestures, and music played an important part in the productions. The plays often use fixed characters, such as a narrator and a clown.

Not only playwriting but also dramatic criticism reached a peak during the great period of Sanskrit theater. The best-known work of criticism is the *Natyasastra*, probably written sometime between 200 B.C. and A.D. 200. In addition to discussing the content and philosophy of Sanskrit drama, it also serves as a dictionary of theatrical practices.

Later Indian Drama.   By the end of the ninth century, the golden age of Hindu culture had faded. By the twelfth century, the Arabs had begun to invade India; and with that series of invasions, the Hindu Sanskrit tradition disappeared. However, folk dramas and dance dramas, based on epic materials from Sanskrit drama and Indian myths, remained popular.

In more recent times—during the past three centuries—an interesting form of dance drama, called *kathakali,* has been prominent in southwestern India. It is

KATHAKALI: INDIAN DANCE DRAMA
Much Asian drama includes a large element of dance. A prime example is kathakali, a dramatic form found in southwestern India. In kathakali, stories of strong passions, the furies of gods, and the loves and hates of extraordinary human beings are told in dance and mime. Notice the makeup and stylized costume and headdress. (© Djamdjian Manuel/Liaison Agency)

Asia
Year, A.D.

Theater

Natyasastra, major critical work of Indian Sanskrit drama (ca. 200 B.C.–200 A.D.)

Sanskrit drama highly developed in India (320–600)

Shakuntala, famous Sanskrit drama by Indian author Kalidasa (400)

The Little Clay Cart, Indian Sanskrit drama attributed to King Shudraka (5th century)

Academy of the Pear Garden, school for dancers and singers, founded in China (714)

Development of professional theater companies in China (960)

Decline of Sanskrit drama (1150)

Indian dance drama, puppet plays, and folk plays (late 12th century)

Scholars and artists work in popular theater in China (13th century)

Zeami Motokiyo (1363–1444): development of nō drama

Literary and romantic drama develops during Ming period in China (1368–1664)

In Japan, kabuki first performed in Kyoto (1600–1610)

Nō becomes an aristocratic entertainment and rigidly codified (1650)

Kabuki becomes popular form of theater (1675–1750)

Bunraku (puppet theater) established in Japan (1685)

Chikamatsu Monzaemon begins writing for bunraku theater (1686)

Peking opera, a less literary and more theatrical form, becomes dominant in China (1875)

Culture and Politics

Spread of Buddism in India. In India, trade with China, Egypt, Rome, southeast Asia. Gandhara school of art flourishes. (180 B.C.–150 B.C.)

Goldern age of classical Sanskrit in India (300–500)

Earliest known use of zero and decimals occurs in India (600)

T'ang dynasty in China (618–907)

Travels in India of Xuan Zang, Chinese pilgrim and chronicler (630–644)

Song dynasty in China (960–1279); flowering of arts, literature, and scholarship

Civil strife in Japan leads to military government (1100)

Beginning of Muslim rule in India (1192)

Marco Polo visits court of Kublai Kahn, Beijing, China (1271); Polo visits Kayal, southern India (1288)

Yuan dynasty in China (1271–1368)

Rule of Yoshimitsu (r. 1395–1408) in Japan; years of stability followed by civil wars

Ming dynasty in China (1368–1644)

First Europeans visit Japan (1542)

Period of national unification in Japan (1568–1600)

Rule of Shah Jahan in India; construction of great buildings, including Taj Mahal (1628–1657)

Ch'ing dynasty in China (1644–1911)

Meiji restoration in Japan (1869); new ruler sponsors exchanges with west

Time markers

300
500
700
900
1100
1300
1500
1700
1900

produced at night by torchlight, on a stage approximately 16 feet square covered with a canopy of flowers. Kathakali heightens certain elements of Sanskrit drama, presenting violence and death onstage in dance and pantomime. The stories revolve around clashes between good and evil, with good always winning. A language of 500 or more gestural signs has been developed to tell these stories.

Theater in China

Chinese civilization can be traced back to at least 2000 B.C., when a unified culture spread over large parts of what is now the People's Republic of China. By 200 B.C., a centralized imperial system had been developed; and China was provided with a central government that continued to remain effective, through many long periods of stability, until modern times.

The early development of theater, like that of many other forms of art in China, was linked to the patronage of the imperial court. Records of court entertainments go back as far as the fifth century B.C., and ancient chronicles mention other theatrical activities such as skits, pantomimes, juggling, singing, and dancing—early Chinese versions of popular entertainments.

The court of the emperors during the Tang period (A.D. 618–906) was one of the high points of world culture. At this time there was in the capital a kind of actors' training institute known as the Pear Garden, which firmly established a tradition of training theatrical performers. During the Song dynasty (960–1279)—the last dynasty before the coming of the Mongols—various court entertainments contributed to the development of a form called *variety plays*. Documents record the existence of traveling theatrical troupes, some permanent playhouses, and theatrical activity that involved not only performers, dancers, and singers but also shadow puppets and marionettes.

Chinese Theater in the Yuan Dynasty. A synthesis of art and popular tradition came in the dramas of the Yuan period (1271–1368). The Yuan dynasty, which followed the Song, became well known in the west through the writings of the Italian explorer Marco Polo. During this period China was ruled not by a Chinese emperor but rather by a Mongol, Kublai Khan, whose grandfather Genghis Khan had conquered the country.

The fusion of popular culture with the high culture of literary intellectuals resulted in an outpouring of drama in the Yuan dynasty—the late thirteenth and early fourteenth centuries. Yuan drama was usually written in four acts—or four song sequences, since these plays used a great deal of music. Rather than writing an original drama, a playwright would compose a dramatic text to suit the rhythms and meter of familiar popular music. Usually, the leading character—the protagonist—sang all the music in any given act. Unfortunately, none of the music has survived.

The poetic content of these plays was considered the central factor in their success. Because of its lyrical nature, Yuan drama had only a small number of characters, and subplots and other complexities were avoided. The topics chosen by Yuan playwrights ranged from love and romance to religion, history, and even crimes and lawsuits.

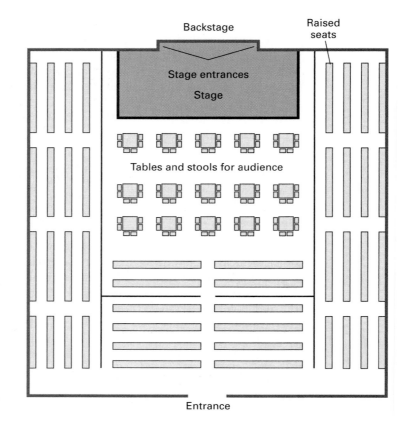

GROUND PLAN OF A TRADITIONAL CHINESE THEATER

Diagrammed here is the arrangement for seating in Chinese theater for the period from the seventeenth through the nineteenth centuries. Before that, performances were held in teahouses; when permanent theaters were built, tables with chairs around them were retained in the section nearest the stage. Women and commoners sat at the sides and back.

Perhaps the most famous of the plays that have survived from this period is *The Romance of the Western Chamber,* actually a cycle of plays, by Wang Shifu (fl. late thirteenth century). These dramas chronicle the trials of two lovers—a handsome young student and a lovely, well-born girl—who became the models for thousands of imitations down to the present century.

Relatively little is known about how Yuan plays were produced, but it is thought that the actors and actresses were professionals, and that performers of each sex occasionally played both male and female roles. The performers were organized into troupes, some of which were run by women. Most of the theater buildings seem to have been built for outdoor use and were not roofed over. Curtains and such properties as swords and fans were used, but there is no evidence of scenery. Much of the color of the performances came from elaborate costumes and stylized makeup.

Chinese Theater in the Ming Dynasty. By the end of the Yuan period, theater in China had reached a very high level. However, with the overthrow of the Mongols and the establishment of the Ming dynasty (1368–1644), a Chinese emperor was restored to the throne, and he reinstated traditional patterns of social behavior. This meant that dramatists reverted to writing only for the elite, and theater lost contact with the broad public.

Still, a new dramatic form, which expanded the structure of Yuan drama, emerged in the Ming period. One of the best-known plays of this type was *Lute Song* by Gao Ming (ca. 1301–1370), which dealt with questions of family loyalties; its main character is a woman whose husband has abandoned her.

By the middle of the sixteenth century, Manchu peoples would begin to advance southward into northern China; and in the middle of the seventeenth century, they—like the Mongols before them—would conquer the country. This period of foreign rule was to last until the dissolution of the empire in 1912. The Manchu rulers enjoyed Chinese culture, including theater, and continued to support the sort of lavish literary productions that had become a tradition among the elite. On the other hand, popular theater was often suppressed, and its scripts were destroyed, for political or moral reasons.

Peking (Beijing) Opera. In the nineteenth century, elements of folk theater and other genres popular among ordinary people formed the basis for a new form of popular theater which in the west was called *Peking opera* or—more recently— *Beijing opera.* (The city whose name is now transliterated as Beijing was for many years known to westerners as Peking. Peking opera is also called by other Chinese

PEKING (BEIJING) OPERA
A highly formalized type of theater, Beijing (or Peking) opera was developed in China in the nineteenth century. It is not like western grand opera; rather, it is popular entertainment. Beijing opera is filled with song, dance, and acrobatics. It makes wide use of symbols—with, for instance, a table standing for a mountain—and is performed in highly colorful and stylized costumes like the one shown here. Also, note the theatrical headdress and makeup. (© Dean Conger/ Corbis)

names, including *jingju* and *xiqu*. Although mindful of the rationale for each of these, we will use the traditional term: Peking opera.) Peking opera is not like the grand opera we know in the west; though it combines music and theater, it is also based on dance and even acrobatics.

The theater space traditionally used for Peking opera is something like a modern dinner theater: audience members are seated at tables and eat and drink during performances. In its staging, Peking opera stresses symbolism. The only furniture onstage is usually a table and several chairs, but these few items are used with imagination. The table and chairs, for instance, may represent a dining hall, a court of justice, a cloud, or a mountain. A tripod holding incense indicates a palace. When a script calls for a long journey, the performers walk around the stage in a circle. Costumes and makeup are highly lavish, ornate, and colorful, and they too serve symbolic functions. The colors and patterns of makeup, for example, signal to the audience what type of character a performer is playing. Performance style emphasizes symbolic movement and piercing vocal patterns.

NŌ PERFORMANCE TODAY
Traditional Nō theater is still performed in Japan and other parts of the world, and its stylized acting, minimalist settings, ornate costumes, and distinctive masks are still used. Shown here is a recent performance staged in San Francisco. (Robert A. Isaacs/Photo Researchers)

Theater in Japan

Although the civilization of Japan is younger than that of China, its heritage is long and complex. By the fifth century after Christ, the southern portions of the country were consolidated and a series of capitals were established in the vicinity of present-day Kyoto. By that time, the Japanese had developed a religion called Shinto ("Way of the Gods"), which was closely bound to nature and spirit worship. With the growing influence on the Japanese aristocracy of the Tang dynasty in China (A.D. 618–906), Buddhism became a prevailing influence in Japan, first in court circles and then in the country as a whole. Both Shinto and Buddhism had a strong influence on the development of theater in Japan. The first great period in the history of Japanese theater occurred in the fourteenth century, not long after similar developments in China. The sudden and remarkable development of *nō*—one of three great traditional forms of Japanese theater—came about when popular stage traditions and high learning joined forces.

Nō. In the fourteenth century in Japan, there were a number of roving troupes of actors who performed in a variety of styles, some popular and even vulgar but others having genuine artistic merit. One of the artistic troupes was directed by the actor Kan'ami (1333–1384), whose son Zeami Motokiyo (1363–1443) was one of the finest child actors in Japan. A performance by the troupe

Sotoba Komachi

1413, Kitano temple, Japan The year is 1413. In Japan, at the Kitano temple, a platform stage, with a floor of polished wood, has been set up. There is also a wooden walkway, or bridge, on which actors can move to the stage from a dressing room set up in one of the temple buildings. The spectators are on three sides of this platform stage.

The actor performing today is Zeami. He is 50 years old and has been under the patronage of the shogun of Japan since he was 12. Zeami's father, Kan'ami, was a renowned actor before him, and Zeami has carried his father's art to even greater heights. He has studied different acting styles, perfected his own technique, trained other actors, and written plays for them to perform.

The theater he has fashioned from all this is called *nō*; it has elements of opera, pantomime, and formal, stylized dance. In nō theater, the main character, who wears a beautifully carved, hand-painted wooden mask, recites his or her adventures to the constant accompaniment of several onstage musicians. Toward the end of the play, the chief actor will perform a ritualistic dance which includes symbolic gestures of the head and hands and stomps of the feet on the wooden floor.

The crowd is gathered today for a special reason. Usually, Zeami performs only in a restricted theater space for the shogun and members of his court, or at a temple for a select audience. But here at the Kitano temple, performances will go on for 7 days and will be open to everyone; as one later commentator will explain: "All were admitted, rich and poor, old and young alike."

As with all nō performances, several plays will be presented each day. The play the audience awaits now, *Sotoba Komachi*, was written by Zeami's father. In it, Zeami portrays a woman. (As in ancient Greek theater, all the performers in nō are men.) The legend of Komachi is as well-known to the audience as the story of Antigone was to the Greeks. Komachi, a beautiful but cruel woman, is pursued by a man named Shii no Shosho. She tells him that he must call on her for 100 nights in a row, and for 99 nights he comes, in all kinds of weather. But on the hundredth night he dies. On that night a snowstorm is raging and he falls exhausted, to die on her doorstep.

When the play begins, we see two priests enter. As they discuss the virtues of following Buddha, they come upon an old woman. This is Zeami in the mask and wig of Komachi in old age. She is a wretched woman approaching her hundredth birthday. Komachi tells how she was once beautiful but has lost her beauty and grown old. She argues with the priests about religion and then reveals who she is. She recounts the story of what she did to Shosho.

As the play progresses, the audience watches Zeami's performance with rapt attention. At one point, his character becomes possessed: the spirit of Shosho takes over Komachi, and Zeami acts this out in pantomime, to a musical accompaniment. At times, he acts out Komachi's part while her lines are chanted by a chorus of ten or twelve men sitting at the side of the stage. At another point, Komachi is dressed as Shosho and becomes him, feeling his death agony. Zeami performs this sequence as a mesmerizing, frightening dance. At the end of the play, the spirit of Shosho leaves Komachi, and she prays to Buddha for guidance and for a peaceful life in the hereafter.

The audience members, who have heard a great deal about Zeami but have never before seen him perform, watch in awe. Throughout, he plays the various parts with astounding grace, subtlety, and understatement, developed through years of training and performance. The segments when he lets go—as in Shosho's death agony—are all the more effective because of their contrast with the measured quality of the rest. For the audience, the play is a revelation of how moving a theatrical performance can be— an experience unlike any they have had before.

was seen by Ashikaga Yoshimitsu (1358–1408), the shogun of Japan, a man of wealth, prestige, and enormous enthusiasm for the arts. Fascinated by what he saw, he arranged for Zeami to have a court education to develop his art.

When Zeami succeeded his father as head of the troupe, it remained attached to the shogun's court in Kyoto. With a patron of this caliber, Zeami was able to devote himself to all aspects of theater: composing plays, training actors (there were no actresses in Zeami's theater), and constantly refining his own acting style. Under Zeami's direction, nō became the dominant form of serious theater in his own time, and it would remain dominant for 200 years—well past 1600. In fact, the elegance, mystery, and beauty of nō have continued to fascinate the Japanese, and the tradition, passed on from teacher to disciple, is still carried on today.

The stories on which nō plays were based often came from literary or historical sources. One particularly notable source was a famous novel, Lady Murasaki's *The Tale of Genji*, written around 1220; it depicted court life during the Heian period (794–1185). Many nō dramas show a strong influence of Buddhism. *Sotoba Komachi*, written by Kan'ami and revised by his son Zeami, is one in which this influence is most pronounced (this was the play performed by Zeami at the Kitano temple in 1413). In fact, its title indicates a Buddhist connection: *Sotoba Komachi* can be translated as "Sotoba on the Stupa," and a stupa is a monument to Buddha.

The nō stage has remained roughly the same since the time of Zeami and his successors. The stage has a bridge, called a *hashigakari,* which leads from the actors' dressing room offstage to the stage proper. The bridge is normally around

GROUND PLAN OF A TRADITIONAL NŌ THEATER

The nō theater of Japan— a stylized theater originally for the upper classes— began nearly 600 years ago. It was performed outdoors; a ramp at the left led from a dressing room to the wooden platform stage. Spectators sat on two sides of the stage, to the left and in front.

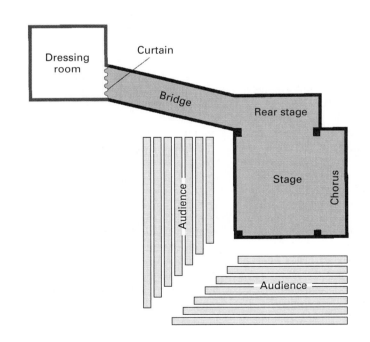

SOTOBA KOMACHI (14TH CENTURY)

By Kan'ami, (1333–1384)

Characters

First priest
Second priest
Ono-no-Komachi
Chorus

Background

Sotoba Komachi is based on a fable. Ono-no-Komachi is a woman who was once a famous courtesan. At the time when she is young and at the apex of her beauty—and also extremely haughty and proud—a man named Shii-no-Shosho falls deeply in love with her; he ardently pursues and courts her, hoping to win her favor and her love. Komachi, however, mocks and rejects Shosho. She will not even let him enter her house, though she tells him that if he will come to her doorstep for a hundred consecutive nights, she will admit him on the hundredth. For ninety-nine nights, Shosho comes faithfully to the entrance to her house. Each night, he cuts a new notch on the "shaft-bench" of his chariot. On the hundredth night, a terrible snowstorm is raging; he fights his way through it, but by the time he reaches her doorstep, he is so exhausted that he dies there.

The text of a nō drama is usually about the length of a western one-act play. It is important to note that in a nō drama like *Sotoba Komachi,* there is very little action or conflict of the kind found in the west. Most of the text is recited or sung to musical accompaniment; most of the stage movements are formal and ritualistic, as in stylized dance such as ballet.

The Play

The play seems to take place in autumn—a gloomy season when the days are growing shorter. Komachi is now distraught, unhappy, and very old: in fact, she is approaching her hundredth year—a symbolic echo of her suitor's last, fatal visit to her doorstep on the hundredth night. In her final years, she has become destitute, her friends have deserted her, and her mind has begun to fail.

An early section of the play presents a theological debate between Komachi and a priest. Moving unsteadily across the stage, Komachi appears to sit on a fallen stone that the priest says is a Buddhist stupa (monument). The priest accuses Komachi of profanation—of desecrating the stupa. She argues that there can be no sacrilege in her act because all things in life and nature are holy, including even a wrecked life such as hers. She insists that the ruined monument and the ruined old woman have a great deal in common. This notion will be a recurrent theme.

Although Komachi appears to win this religious argument, she is then quickly struck by madness. She imagines that she is once more in the storm that raged on the hundredth night of her lover's visits, and that he is once again lying dead at her feet.

At this point the character of Komachi mimes the release of her emotions in a wild, mad dance which is one of the high points of the drama, theatrically fusing words, music, and movement. The priest narrates the past occurrence while the performer playing Komachi physicalizes it, using highly symbolic gestures and movements. For a brief time during this dance, she relives the glorious days of her youth, becoming young again.

Komachi's agony as she gives release to her emotions is an expiation of her sins. At the conclusion of the play, there is an indication that she will receive a form of salvation. This idea is embraced in an overall theme: that ultimately—in the cosmic vision of life—evil and good, self-gratification and purity become one.

20 feet long, depending on the size of the theater; the main playing space is about 18 feet square, is roofed, and has a ceremonial pine tree painted on the rear wall. At the back of the playing space is a narrow section for four or five musicians, who accompany the play. Nō theaters were originally outdoors, but a modern nō theater is placed inside a larger shell as though it were a giant stage set.

Nō actors move in a highly stylized way that has important elements of both dance and pantomime. During the performance of a nō text, the actors alternate sections of chanting with a heightened speech that might best be compared to recitative in western opera.

Costumes made for nō are usually of great elegance, and the masks worn by the chief character are among the most beautiful, subtle, and effective ever created for any theater.

Bunraku: Puppet Theater.   Nō remained the most popular theatrical form during Japan's long medieval period. Civil wars and other disturbances, however, caused increasing political disarray until in 1600 a general, Tokugawa Ieyasu, unified the country. All through the long Tokugawa period (1600–1868), Japan was unified and at peace, but this period of calm was purchased at a price. Alarmed at the political maneuvering of Japan's growing number of Christians—who had been converted by European missionaries—the Tokugawa family outlawed Christianity and cut Japan off from any extensive contact with either China or Europe until the middle of the nineteenth century. Peace did bring, however, a

JAPANESE BUNRAKU: PUPPET THEATER

Bunraku—puppet theater—became a popular form in Japan in the 1600s. In bunraku, unlike traditional western puppet theater, the puppeteers are in full view of the audience; they are always dressed in black. Often, the story is delivered by a chanter, with the puppets dramatizing the action. Since the puppets today are very complex, there may be more than one puppeteer controlling each of them, as is the case in the photo shown here, with the men in black to the right and left of the two characters. (Japan National Tourist Organization)

rapid development of commerce and trade and a growing merchant class, which demanded its own entertainment.

The first of the new popular forms of theater to flourish was a puppet theater known as *bunraku*. Bunraku is a highly unusual type of theater featuring musicians and a chanter who tells the story and creates the voices of all the characters. The puppets which enact the drama are today approximately two-thirds of human size and are operated by men dressed in black who move the puppet's head, arms, and body. The puppeteer's black outfit is a convention: it signifies that the audience should consider him invisible. Bunraku first became popular in the early seventeenth century and is still performed in Japan today.

The first and undoubtedly the best of the writers for bunraku, Chikamatsu Monzaemon (1653–1725), contributed enormously to the transformation of this popular theater into a true art form. Chikamatsu wrote both historical plays and domestic dramas dealing with life in his own day; his domestic dramas have remained popular to the present time. His emphasis on ordinary people was new to the Japanese stage and foreshadowed later developments in European theater.

Kabuki.   Shortly after bunraku had become established, a new form of popular theater—*kabuki*—developed, in the early and middle seventeenth century. Legend has it that kabuki was originated by an actress, Okuni, who lived around the end of the sixteenth century. Kabuki drew its material from plays written for nō and bunraku; the exaggerated gestures of kabuki are often attributed to the fact that in its early phases a conscious attempt was made to imitate puppets. Despite these exaggerated and stylized gestures, though, kabuki was less formal and distant than nō, which remained largely the theater of the court and nobility. Kabuki quickly became a tremendously popular form of theater, and it remains a favorite of Japanese audiences today.

Kabuki was performed first by all-female troupes, then by boys, and finally—beginning in 1652—by all-male companies. Kabuki actors are trained from childhood in singing, dancing, acting, and physical dexterity. The actors who play women's parts are particularly skillful at suggesting the essence of a feminine personality through stylized gestures and attitudes. The costumes and makeup are elegant as well as colorful. Musicians—sometimes onstage, sometimes offstage—generally accompany the stage action.

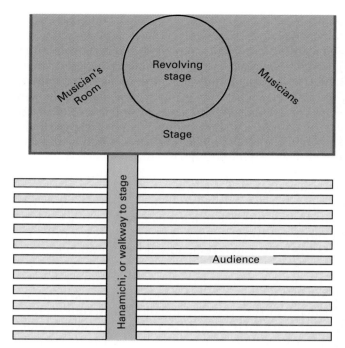

A KABUKI THEATER

Kabuki, a 400-year-old Japanese theater, is performed today in elaborate spaces with staging devices that include onstage turntables for shifting scenery. As shown in this ground plan, the stage covers the entire front of the theater and is approached by a ramp—the hanamichi—on which performers make dramatic entrances and exits.

The stage used for kabuki performances underwent various changes during the history of the art, but the same principles were observed after the middle of the nineteenth century. The stage is long and has a relatively low proscenium. Kabuki features elaborate and beautiful scenic effects, including the revolving stage, which was developed in Japan before it was used in the west. Another device used in kabuki is the *hanamichi,* or "flower way," a raised narrow platform connecting the rear of the auditorium with the stage. Actors often make their entrances on the hanamichi and occasionally perform short scenes there as well.

The Middle Ages

Background: Medieval Europe

The period from A.D. 500 to 1500 in western history is known as the *Middle Ages* or the *medieval* era. Within that thousand years, the period from the years 500 to 1000 in Europe is sometimes called the *dark ages* because so much of the civilization of the preceding thousand years was in eclipse. Today, many historians feel that *dark ages* is a misnomer, and that we should speak instead of the early Middle Ages and the later Middle Ages.

At the start of the early Middle Ages, following invasions from the north and the dissolution of Roman civilization, cities were abandoned and life throughout southern and western Europe became largely agricultural. The nobility controlled local areas, where most people worked as vassals. Gradually, several hundred years after the fall of the Roman empire, towns began to emerge, and with them trade and crafts. Learning also slowly revived. The strongest force during this period was the Roman Catholic church, which dominated not only religion but education and frequently politics as well.

Theater and Culture in the Middle Ages

During the early part of the Middle Ages there were some scattered traces of theatrical activity, most of these based on the popular entertainments of Greece and Rome—traveling jugglers, minstrels, and mimes. In the late tenth century a nun in a convent in Germany, Hrosvitha of Gandersheim (ca. 935–1001), wrote religious plays based on the dramas of the Roman writer Terence. Though her plays were probably not produced, it is still remarkable that she created drama almost in a vacuum. (Hrosvitha has recently been rediscovered by feminist critics and others.)

Middle Ages
Year, A.D.

Theater		Culture and Politics

475

"Dark ages" (476–1000)

Traveling performers (ca. 500–925)

525

Justinian becomes Byzantine emperor (527)

575

Mohammed born (ca. 570)

625

675

Trulian Synod attempts to end performances in Byzantium (692)

725

Charles Martel defeats Muslims near Poitiers (732)

775

Charlemagne crowned emperor of Holy Roman Empire (800)

825

Beginning of Romanesque architecture (ca. 830)

875

Earliest European reference to a collar in the harness of a horse which would allow the drawing of heavy loads and plow (920)

Quem quaeritis trope (ca. 925)

925

Hrosvitha, a nun, writes Christian comedies based on Terence (ca. 970)

975

Beowulf (1000)

1025

First Crusade (1095)

1075

Beginning of Gothic architecture (1140)

Vernacular religious drama flourishes: Peak of medieval theater (ca. 1350–1550)

Black death apparently originates in India (1332)

Second Shepherd's Play (ca. 1375)

1125

Boccaccio's *Decameron* (1353)

Pride of Life (ca. 1400)

The Castle of Perseverance (ca. 1425)

1325

Urban VI in Rome; Clement VII at Avignon (1378)

Actor playing Judas at Metz almost dies while being hanged (1437)

Peasant revolt in England (1381)

1375

Pierre Patelin (ca. 1470)

Chaucer dies (1400)

Hans Sachs born (1494)

1425

Gutenberg invents printing by movable type (ca. 1450)

Everyman (ca. 1500)

Constantinople falls to the Turks (1453)

Cycle staged at Mons (1510)

1475

Copernicus born (1473)

Jean Bouchet, pageant master, directs cycle at Poitiers (1508)

Martin Luther born (1483)

John Heywood's *Johan Johan* (1533)

1525

Columbus crosses the Atlantic (1492)

Essentially, though, theater had to be reborn in the west during the latter part of the Middle Ages. Interestingly, key elements of the new theater first appeared in the church, which had suppressed theater several hundred years earlier. In certain portions of the church service, priests or members of the choir played the roles of characters from the Bible. Gradually these small segments, which were spoken in Latin, were enlarged, and became short dramas—known as *liturgical dramas*—enacted in the church. One reason the church supported these dramas so strongly was that most people in the Middle Ages could not read or write, and such plays were an excellent way to teach them stories from the Bible as well as moral lessons.

Later in the Middle Ages, *vernacular drama* developed. The language of these later plays was not Latin but the everyday speech of the people. Like the brief church plays, vernacular dramas dealt with biblical stories and other religious stories. The vernacular dramas, however, were more elaborate and were usually presented as a series of one-act dramas. Also, they were presented not inside churches but in town squares or other parts of cities. Historians continue to debate whether vernacular drama evolved from liturgical drama or developed independently.

Medieval Drama: Mystery, Miracle, and Morality Plays

Three types of religious vernacular plays were popular in the medieval period. *Mystery* or *cycle plays* dramatized a series of biblical events that could stretch from Adam and Eve in the garden of Eden, Noah and the flood, and Abraham and Isaac to the stories of Christ in the New Testament. *Miracle plays* dramatized the lives of the saints. *Morality plays* such as *Everyman* (ca. 1500) used religious characters and religious themes to teach a moral lesson. Virtually all the plays were short—the equivalent of a one-act play today—and mystery and miracle plays were often strung together to form a series, known as a *cycle*.

INTEREST IN MEDIEVAL MYSTERY PLAYS IS STILL STRONG
In 1999, the Royal National Theatre in London presented this very successful staging of The Passion, *with Joe Duttine as Jesus. As can be seen here, contemporary directors often build on anachronisms already present in medieval drama to make references to modern society. Note the costumes of the guards accompanying Jesus.* (© Donald Cooper/PhotoStage, England)

Chapter 12

Renaissance Theater

Italy

Background: The Renaissance Era

Italian Theater: Commedia dell'Arte

Timeline: *Italian Renaissance*

Living History: *Commedia dell'Arte*

Italian Dramatic Rules: The Neoclassical Ideals

Theater Production in Italy

England

Background: Elizabethan England

Elizabethan Drama

Timeline: *English Renaissance*

Elizabethan Theater Production

Living History: *Hamlet*

Making Connections: The Popular Arts of Shakespeare's Time

Theater after Elizabeth's Reign

Spain

Background: The Spanish Golden Age

Spanish Drama

Timeline: *Spanish Golden Age*

Living History: *The King, The Greatest Alcalde*

Theater Production in Spain

France

Background: France in the Seventeenth Century

French Drama: The Neoclassical Era

Timeline: *Neoclassical France*

Living History: *Tartuffe*

Theater Production in France

Summary

◀ MEASURE FOR MEASURE

The plays of William Shakespeare, the leading English Renaissance dramatist, continue to be immensely popular. There are frequent productions of his plays and many have been adapted into films. Stage and film directors often set his work in a contemporary context in order to engage their audiences. Seen here is a production of Shakespeare's dark comedy Measure for Measure, *staged in contemporary dress by the Hudson Valley Shakespeare Festival. (Sara Krulwich/NYT Pictures)*

Renaissance is a term that means "rebirth" and refers to an awakening of the arts and learning in the western world, which occurred during the period stretching roughly from the late fourteenth through the early seventeenth century. The center of activity was Italy, which at this time was made up of a group of independent city-states. The Renaissance was also prevalent a short time later in England, Spain, and France. During the Renaissance, theater blossomed in these countries. Before we discuss the theatrical innovations of this time period, however, let us first examine social and cultural changes.

Italy

Background: The Renaissance Era

European politics changed markedly during the Renaissance. There was a rise of kings and princes, and merchants became key economic figures. As these people's wealth increased, they had leisure time to fill and also became eager to display their fortunes; consequently, they often hired artists to create lavish works for them.

Renaissance art is noticeably different from medieval art. During the Middle Ages, painting and sculpture had religious subjects. Renaissance artists, on the other hand, treated their subjects as human beings with whom we can identify. A good example is the statue of David by the Italian sculptor Michelangelo: the figure of David looks like a real person, not an otherworldly religious image. Painting also became more realistic through the use of oils and perspective, a technique which gives the illusion of three-dimensional depth on a flat canvas. In Renaissance literature, the major movement was *humanism,* which imitated the Greeks and Romans and focused on human beings rather than the gods. The printing press, which appeared in Europe in the 1450s, made this literature available to great numbers of people.

The Renaissance was also a period of exploration and invention. Discoveries in North and South America brought new wealth to Europe; at the same time, scientific advances revolutionized western ideas about of the position of humanity in the universe. For example, the Italian astronomer Galileo proved that the sun, not the earth, is the center of the solar system.

The Renaissance also saw remarkable developments in theater, especially in Italy, England, Spain, and France.

Italian Theater: Commedia dell'Arte

Italy, which led the way in Renaissance painting and sculpture, also saw radical transformations in its theater between 1550 and 1650. These were chiefly in improvisational theater, acting, dramatic criticism, theater architecture, and scene design. The written drama of the Italian Renaissance is less significant: much of it was modeled after Greek and Roman plays and presented at academies or at the homes of wealthy patrons, and almost none of it left a lasting mark. *Opera,* of course, is of great significance: it was invented during the Italian Renaissance by people who believed they were recreating the Greek tragic style, which had fused music with drama; and in fact it is the only Italian Renaissance theatrical form that

Italian Renaissance
Year, A.D.

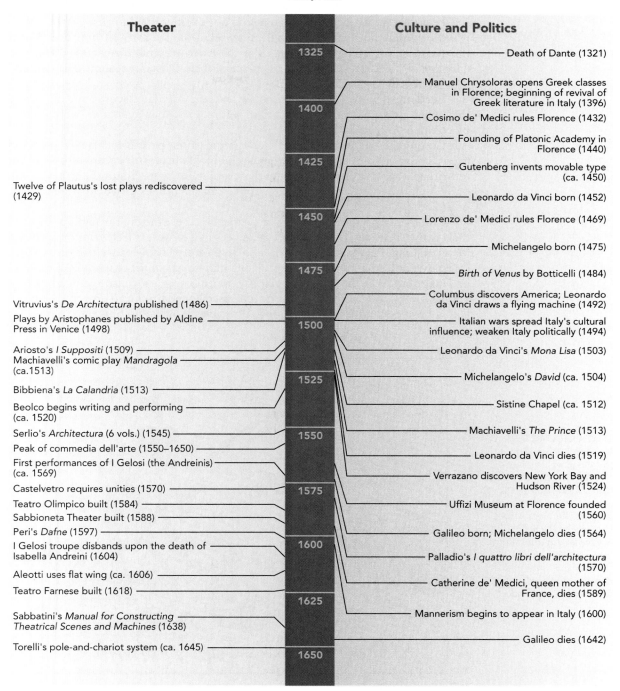

Theater

Culture and Politics

Year	
1325	Death of Dante (1321)
1400	Manuel Chrysoloras opens Greek classes in Florence; beginning of revival of Greek literature in Italy (1396)
	Cosimo de' Medici rules Florence (1432)
	Founding of Platonic Academy in Florence (1440)
1425	Gutenberg invents movable type (ca. 1450)

Twelve of Plautus's lost plays rediscovered (1429)

Leonardo da Vinci born (1452)

1450 — Lorenzo de' Medici rules Florence (1469)

Michelangelo born (1475)

1475 — *Birth of Venus* by Botticelli (1484)

Columbus discovers America; Leonardo da Vinci draws a flying machine (1492)

Vitruvius's *De Architectura* published (1486)

Plays by Aristophanes published by Aldine Press in Venice (1498)

1500 — Italian wars spread Italy's cultural influence; weaken Italy politically (1494)

Leonardo da Vinci's *Mona Lisa* (1503)

Ariosto's *I Suppositi* (1509)
Machiavelli's comic play *Mandragola* (ca.1513)

Michelangelo's *David* (ca. 1504)

1525 — Sistine Chapel (ca. 1512)

Bibbiena's *La Calandria* (1513)

Machiavelli's *The Prince* (1513)

Beolco begins writing and performing (ca. 1520)

Leonardo da Vinci dies (1519)

Serlio's *Architectura* (6 vols.) (1545)

1550 — Verrazano discovers New York Bay and Hudson River (1524)

Peak of commedia dell'arte (1550–1650)

First performances of I Gelosi (the Andreinis) (ca. 1569)

Uffizi Museum at Florence founded (1560)

Castelvetro requires unities (1570)

1575 — Galileo born; Michelangelo dies (1564)

Teatro Olimpico built (1584)

Sabbioneta Theater built (1588)

Palladio's *I quattro libri dell'architectura* (1570)

Peri's *Dafne* (1597)

1600 — Catherine de' Medici, queen mother of France, dies (1589)

I Gelosi troupe disbands upon the death of Isabella Andreini (1604)

Aleotti uses flat wing (ca. 1606)

Mannerism begins to appear in Italy (1600)

Teatro Farnese built (1618)

1625 — Galileo dies (1642)

Sabbatini's *Manual for Constructing Theatrical Scenes and Machines* (1638)

Torelli's pole-and-chariot system (ca. 1645)

1650

has survived. However, opera is usually considered a part of music because the *libretto*—its text—is often secondary to the music.

If, however, the Italian Renaissance is not distinguished for its written drama it did originate an important, and immensely popular form of improvisational theater, closely related to many of our popular performance forms today. This was *commedia dell'arte*—"comedy of professional artists." Commedia dell'arte thrived in Italy from 1550 to 1750.

In commedia, performers had no set text; they invented words and actions as they went along. *Scenarios*—short plot outlines without dialogue—were written by company members.

Commedia companies, usually consisting of ten performers (seven men and three women), were traveling troupes; the most successful companies were often organized by families. Commedia companies were adaptable: they could perform in town squares, in theater spaces, in the homes of wealthy merchants, or at court.

Commedia performers played the same stock characters throughout most of their careers. Among the popular comic personages were a lecherous, miserly old Venetian man, Pantalone; a foolish scholar, Dottore; a cowardly, braggart soldier, Capitano; and sometimes foolish servants known as *zanni,* of whom Arlecchino, or Harlequin, was the most popular. Commedia scenarios also included serious young lovers. All commedia characters used standard *lazzi*—repeated bits of comic business, usually physical, and sometimes bawdy and obscene.

STOCK CHARACTERS
Comedy in particular features stock or stereotypical characters who have clearly identifiable traits, gestures, styles of dress and qualities. This was particularly true in Italian commedia dell'arte. Shown here are two such characters: Scapino and Zerbino. (Victoria and Albert Museum, London)

Scapino.   Cap: Zerbino

Commedia dell'Arte

1500s, Rome The time is the late 1500s; the place is a town square in Rome. Set up in the square is a wooden platform stage with a backdrop at the rear. This backdrop, or curtain, not only forms the scenic background of the action on the platform but also provides a hidden space in which the performers can adjust their costumes and from which they can make their entrances and exits.

A crowd is beginning to gather, and people are trying to get the best position to see the performance that is about to begin. In front of the stage, people are already standing several rows deep; at the sides the audience members push closer, but they won't be facing the stage directly. As the spectators look around, they can see that the audience represents a cross section of Roman citizens.

There is great anticipation in the air, because the performers are members of one of the best-known theater companies in Italy—a troupe called I Gelosi, led by Francesco and Isabella Andreini. The ten members of the company have perfected commedia dell'arte, a form of improvisational comedy which has become the most popular type of theater in Italy.

Commedia is different from many other kinds of theater. There is no script in the usual sense. There is an outline of the action— the characters portrayed in a scene, what happens, how the scene develops—but the dialogue is not written out. The lines the characters speak are not provided.

The performers, therefore, improvise their speeches—that is, they make them up as they go along. This, plus the fact that the movements also are improvised, adds a great air of immediacy to the production. It is most challenging to the performers, and this makes the presentation all the more exciting for those now assembled to watch.

Soon the performance is under way, and the fun begins. The story is partly about an actress who is pursued by every man—unmarried or married—in town, and partly about the adulterous intrigues of her pursuers' wives. There are insults, cases of mistaken identity, and plans gone wrong, and people's misbehavior is exposed.

The characters are stock figures: an old Venetian merchant, a foolish pedant, a cowardly braggart soldier, comic servants, and young lovers. All the characters except the lovers wear masks, most of which are half masks covering the upper part of the face. Each character wears a costume which makes him or her easily recognizable: the pedant, for instance, wears academic robes; the captain wears a uniform; the young lovers are fashionably dressed. One source of great pleasure in watching the performance is seeing these pompous, self-important characters get their comeuppance during the course of the action.

The servants are a special delight. They are known as *zanni* and are usually of two types. The first, called Buffetto and various other names, is a clever, domineering intriguer who motivates the plot through various schemes. The other, even better known, is Arlecchino, or Harlequin. He wears a patchwork outfit of many colors, is given to pratfalls, and is often the victim of knockdown physical humor. Frequently, the servants outwit their masters and help the young lovers get together.

One plot twist operates around the notion that older characters attempt to thwart the desires of the young lovers, and it is only at the conclusion that the lovers achieve their objective.

The spectators crowded around the platform, knowing that the performers are improvising, are amazed at how quick on their feet the performers are and how readily they respond to the dialogue thrown at them.

The interaction of the performers is very physical. In one scene, a master beats a servant with a stick, which is hinged with a flap to make an exaggerated sound when it hits the servant's backside. In another scene, a soldier challenges a lover to a duel and becomes hopelessly entangled with his own sword; at times his sword sticks out from between his legs, taking on a sexual connotation. The more entangled he becomes, the louder the audience laughs.

At the end of the play, as they make their way home, audience members talk among themselves, sometimes laughing out loud as they recall highlights of the performance.

Commedia characters wore traditional costumes, such as Harlequin's patchwork jacket and Dottore's academic robes. A significant addition to Harlequin's costume was the *slapstick,* a wooden sword used in comic fight scenes; today, we still use the term *slapstick* for comedies emphasizing physical horseplay. Masks, usually covering part of the face, were a significant element of commedia costumes. The young lovers, however, did not wear masks.

Italian Dramatic Rules: The Neoclassical Ideals

In terms of drama, critics rather than playwrights proved influential in the Italian Renaissance. Italian critics formulated dramatic rules—known as the **neoclassical ideals**—which were to dominate dramatic theory through much of Europe for nearly 200 years.

One overriding concern of the neoclassicists was *verisimilitude,* by which they meant that drama should be "true to life." Their verisimilitude, however, was not the kind of realism we find in modern drama. The neoclassicists wanted stock dramatic situations and stock characters but insisted that these be recognizable and verifiable from real life.

Another concern of the neoclassicists—in fact, their most famous mandate—was their insistence on three **unities:** unity of *time,* of *place,* and of *action.* The unities grew out of the desire for verisimilitude. Unity of time required that the dramatic action in a play should not exceed 24 hours. Unity of place restricted the action of a play to one locale. Unity of action required that there be only one central story, involving a relatively small group of characters; this meant that there could be no subplots. The three unities are often mistakenly attributed to Aristotle, though in fact he had suggested only unity of action.

The neoclassicists interpreted genre very narrowly. For many of them, tragedy dealt with royalty, comedy with common people; tragedy must end sadly and comedy happily; and the two genres must never be mixed.

The function of all drama, the neoclassic critics insisted, was to teach moral lessons. Also, they held, characters must be morally acceptable to the audience.

There were numerous other rules. Onstage violence was forbidden, for instance; and the neoclassicists banished the chorus and supernatural characters. They were also opposed to the **soliloquy**—a monologue through which a character reveals thoughts by speaking them aloud.

While there were significant differences among the various Italian critics, they were all highly *prescriptive,* telling authors how to write in order to create great drama. The rules of the neoclassical critics were to have particular influence on playwrights in France during the seventeenth century.

Theater Production in Italy

Another significant contribution of the Italian Renaissance was made by architects who revolutionized theater construction. Two buildings in particular illustrate the gradual development of Italian theater architecture, and fortunately both are still standing.

The oldest surviving theater built during the Italian Renaissance—the Teatro Olimpico in Vicenza, which opened in 1584—was designed as a miniature indoor Roman theater. Its auditorium, accommodating approximately 3,000 spectators, had curved benches connected to the *scaena*, or stage house; this arrangement created a semicircular *orchestra*. There was a raised stage, about 70 feet wide by 18 feet deep, in front of the scaena. The ornate facade of the scene house, patterned after the Roman scaena frons, was designed to look like a street. There were five openings in the facade—three in the back wall and one on each side. Behind each opening was an alleyway or street scene that seemed to disappear in the distance. To achieve an effect of depth, in each alleyway there were three-dimensional buildings—houses and shops—which decreased in size as they were positioned farther and farther away from the opening onstage.

The most renowned theater building of the Italian Renaissance was the Teatro Farnese in Parma, completed in 1618. The Farnese had a typical court, or academic, theater auditorium, with raised horseshoe seating that accommodated about 3,500 spectators. What was revolutionary in the Teatro Farnese was its *proscenium-arch* stage. Despite the term *arch*, a proscenium opening is usually a rectangular frame. Realistic scenery can be placed much more effectively behind such a frame than in any other type of theater; thus the proscenium arch, along with Renaissance innovations in scene design, became an impetus for greater theatrical realism. (See Chapter 4 for a fuller discussion of the proscenium-arch theater.)

TEATRO FARNESE
Completed in 1618, the Teatro Farnese was the first theater with a proscenium arch—the opening behind which scenery and stage machinery are concealed. The horseshoe shaped auditorium held 3,500 spectators, and a semi-circular orchestra was placed between audience and stage. The view here is from the stage to the audience area. (© Ruggero Vanni/Corbis)

SETTING BY GIACOMO TORELLI
Torelli's elaborate stage machinery and designs were influential in Italy and France, and his method of scene shifting—the pole-and-chariot system—became standard in continental Europe. Note the ornateness of this perspective design. (Bibliothèque Nationale, Paris)

When we move from the stage to the auditorium, we find that the major changes occurred in the public opera houses of Venice. These were proscenium-arch houses, but—unlike court or academy theaters—they were commercial ventures which needed as many paying customers as possible; thus they required a larger audience area. Opera houses were therefore designed with "pit, boxes, and galleries," which had already been used in France, England, and Spain. It was their combination of a "pit, box, and gallery" auditorium with a proscenium-arch stage that made the Venetian opera houses innovative. This kind of proscenium-arch theater with pit, box, and gallery seating would later become the standard theater space throughout the western world and would remain so for over 200 years.

The *pit,* in which audience members stood, was an open area on the house floor extending to the side and back walls. Built into the walls were tiers of seating. The lower tiers were usually the most expensive; they were divided into separate private *boxes* and were frequented by the upper classes. The upper tiers, which were called *galleries,* had open bench seating. The pit—a raucous area where the spectators ate, talked, and moved around—and the galleries were the least expensive accommodations.

Advances in scene design during the Italian Renaissance were no less impressive than architectural innovations. *Perspective* drawing, which creates an illusion of depth and which had become an important feature of Renaissance art, was introduced into theater.

The earliest painted-perspective scenery was clumsy and not easy to shift; as a result, by the early 1600s flat wings were used to create painted-perspective settings. In this arrangement, a series of individual wings on each side of the stage, parallel to the audience, were placed in a progression from the front to the back of the stage and enclosed at the very back by two shutters that met in the middle. The final element in these perspective settings was provided by overhead borders—strips across the top of the stage that completed the picture.

The method of scene shifting used with settings of this kind is often referred to as the *groove system* because the wings and shutters were placed in parallel grooves on and above the stage floor. The major problem with this system was coordinating the removal of the flat wings by scene shifters at each groove position. This problem was solved with an innovative scene-changing system

GROOVE SYSTEM OF SCENE CHANGES

During the Italian Renaissance, the groove method of shifting scenery was perfected. Along the sides of the stage, in parallel lines, scenery was set in sections. At the back, two shutters met in the middle. Together, these peices formed a complete stage picture. When one set of side wings and back shutters was pulled aside, a different stage picture was revealed.

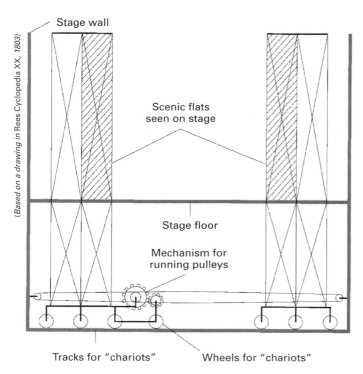

Stage wall

Scenic flats
seen on stage

Stage floor

Mechanism for
running pulleys

Tracks for "chariots"   Wheels for "chariots"

POLE-AND-CHARIOT SYSTEM
This method of changing wings and back shutters was developed by Torelli. When a series of wheels and pulleys below the level of the stage—attached on frameworks to the scenery above—were shifted, the scene changed automatically. Because the mechanisms were interconnected, scene shifts could be smooth and simultaneous.

developed by Giacomo Torelli (1608–1678) and known as the ***pole-and-chariot*** system. Poles attached to the flats continued below the stage floor, where they were connected to wheels ("chariots") in tracks. In this way, the flats could be moved offstage smoothly; by connecting a series of ropes and pulleys, the entire set could be removed by turning a single winch. The pole-and-chariot system was adopted and used throughout much of the world for over two centuries.

England

Background: Elizabethan England

The English Renaissance is often called the *Elizabethan* period, because its major political figure was Elizabeth I, who reigned during the 45 years from 1558 to 1603. Throughout the English Renaissance, explorations abroad were undertaken, and language and literature flourished. The English were intrigued by language—Queen Elizabeth herself was an amateur linguist—and at the heart of the English Renaissance in literature and the arts was theater.

Elizabethan Drama

Christopher Marlowe and the "Mighty Line". One of the most important of the Elizabethan playwrights was Christopher Marlowe (1564–1593), who advanced the art of dramatic structure and contributed a gallery of interesting characters to English drama; he also perfected another element that was to prove central to later Elizabethan plays: dramatic poetry. Critics speak of Marlowe's "mighty line," by which they mean the power of his dramatic verse. The meter of this verse is iambic pentameter, which has five beats to a line, with two syllables to each beat and the accent on the second beat. In Marlowe's hands, dramatic verse in iambic pentameter developed strength, subtlety, and suppleness, as well as great lyric beauty.

Marlowe wrote several important plays, including *Doctor Faustus* (ca. 1588), *Tamburlaine* (Parts 1 and 2; ca. 1587), and *Edward II* (ca. 1592), but his promising career as a dramatist was unfortunately cut short when he was stabbed to death in a tavern brawl in 1593 at the age of 29.

English Renaissance
Year, A.D.

Theater

Culture and Politics

Year	
1050	
1225	
1250	
1275	
1300	
1325	
1450	
1475	
1500	
1525	
1550	
1575	
1600	
1625	
1650	

Culture and Politics

Norman conquest (1066)

Magna Carta (1215)

Oxford University flourishes (ca. 1260)

Roger Bacon's *De Computo Naturali* (1264)

100 Years' War (1338–1453)

War of Roses (1455–1485)

Henry VIII reigns (1509)

Thomas More's *Utopia* (1516)

Elizabeth I, queen of England, rules (1558–1603)

Sir Walter Raleigh's expedition to Virginia (1584)

Execution of Mary, Queen of Scots (1587)

Defeat of Spanish armada (1588)

James I begins reign (1603)

Jamestown, Virginia, founded (1607)

Hudson claims part of North America for United Provinces (1609)

King James Bible (1611)

Thirty Years' War begins (1618)

Francis Bacon's *Novum Organum* (1620)

Charles I begins reign (1625)

Charles I dissolves Parliament (1629)

English civil war (1642)

Charles I beheaded (1649)

Theater

Sackville and Norton's *Gorboduc*: first English tragedy (1561)

Master of Revels made licenser of plays and companies; James Burbage's Earl of Leicester's Men founded (1574)

The Theater built by James Burbage; first Blackfriars opened (1576)

Kyd's *Spanish Tragedy* (ca. 1587)

Marlowe's *Doctor Faustus* (ca. 1588)

Alleyn's Lord Admiral's Men and Burbage's Lord Chamberlain's Men, the major companies in London (1594)

Second Blackfriars built by James Burbage (1596)

Globe Theater built (1599)

Shakespeare's *Hamlet* (ca. 1600)

Lord Chamberlain's Men become the King's Men (1603)

Johnson's *Volpone* (1606)

Webster's *Duchess of Malfi* (ca. 1613)

Inigo Jones designs masques (ca. 1620)

Jacobean playwrights flourish (ca. 1620)

John Ford's *'Tis a Pity She's a Whore* (ca. 1633)

Parliament closes British theaters (1642)

William Shakespeare: A Playwright for the Ages. William Shakespeare (1564–1616) appeared on the theater scene around 1590, just after Marlowe had made his debut. Shakespeare was a native of Stratford-upon-Avon (a town about 85 miles northwest of London); his father was a prosperous glove maker and town alderman, and his mother—Mary Arden—was the daughter of a prominent landowner and farmer. Shakespeare was educated in Stratford; he then married Anne Hathaway, who was several years older than he and who bore him three children.

At some point after the third child was born, Shakespeare left his family and went to London, where he worked first as an actor and shortly after that as a playwright. As a dramatist, he worked with elements that had been established in early Elizabethan drama—Senecan dramatic devices; the platform stage; powerful dramatic verse; source material from English history, Roman history and drama, and Italian literature; and the episodic plot structure that had its roots in medieval theater. He fused these elements into one of the most impressive bodies of plays ever created.

Shakespeare was an expert in many aspects of theater. As an actor and a member of a dramatic company, the Lord Chamberlain's Men (which was London's leading troupe), he understood the technical and business elements of theater. As a writer, he excelled in several genres, including tragedy, comedy, and history. His tragedies include *Romeo and Juliet* (1595), *Julius Caesar* (1599), *Hamlet* (1601), *Othello* (1604), *Macbeth* (1605–1606), and *King Lear* (1605–1606). His comedies include *The Comedy of Errors* (1592), *A Midsummer Night's Dream* (1595), *As You Like It* (1599), and *Twelfth Night* (1601). Among his well-known histories are *Richard III* (1592–1593); *Henry IV, Parts 1 and 2* (1597–1598); and *Henry V* (1599).

His verse, especially the power of his metaphors and the music of his language, is extraordinary; and his characters are so well-rounded and carefully detailed that they often seem like living people. He was also a master of plot construction, notably episodic plot structure—which, as we have seen, stands alongside climactic structure as one of the two main forms that have been predominant throughout the history of western theater.

The Globe Theater, where his plays were produced, burned in 1613; after that, Shakespeare retired to Stratford and became one of its leading citizens. He died 3 years later.

Elizabethan Theater Production

Public Theaters.   The plays of Shakespeare, Marlowe, and their contemporaries were performed primarily in *public theaters.* Between the 1560s and 1642, at least nine open-air public theaters were built just outside the city of London. The reason for their being located just outside the city limits was to avoid government restrictions. All levels of society attended productions at the public theaters. The most famous public theater was the Globe, because it was the home of Shakespeare's plays.

In recent years, sections of the foundations of the Globe and another theater, the Rose, have been rediscovered and excavated. Also, a replica of the original Globe was erected near the site of the original theater. It opened for performances in 1997.

Hamlet

1600, London It is early afternoon on a day around the year 1600. In London, England, people from many parts of the city are gathering along the north bank of the Thames River to be carried by boat across to its south bank. There is a special excitement in the air because most of those crossing the Thames are headed for the Globe Theater, to see the first public performance of a new play by William Shakespeare called *Hamlet*.

The Globe is one of the newest and finest playhouses serving London. The reason it is on the other side of the Thames, outside city limits, is that officials in London have forbidden theatrical performances inside the city. The first permanent theaters in England have been built to the north of London or across the Thames to the south, outside the jurisdiction of city officials.

When the spectators arrive at the theater—well over 2,000 people all together—they can pay a penny at the main door to get in, or they can use another entrance for the more expensive accommodations. Those who use the main door move into a central courtyard, open to the sky, where they will stand during the performance around three sides of a platform stage at one end of the courtyard. Those who can afford to pay more enter one of three levels of covered gallery seats surrounding the stage and courtyard on three sides. By

paying even more, the nobility can sit on cushioned seats in boxes next to the stage. Food and drink—apples, nuts, water, ale— are being sold throughout the playhouse.

As the audience gathers, there is a great deal of conversation about the play. Some audience members already know something about *Hamlet;* they are familiar with earlier versions of the story, and they know that *Hamlet* will be a revenge play—one of their favorite types of drama. There is keen interest, too, because *Hamlet* is by William Shakespeare, a favorite playwright; and its star is Richard Burbage, who is considered by many people the finest actor in England.

At two o'clock, the play begins. Two sentinels standing watch on the parapet of a castle appear onstage, soon to be joined by Horatio, a friend of Hamlet's; the three men discuss a ghost that has been appearing every night. All of a sudden, the ghost is there: it is the ghost of Hamlet's father, and it is played by Shakespeare himself, who is also an actor with the company. Horatio and the sentinels are frightened; the ghost stays briefly and then disappears.

The scene shifts to the interior of the castle: King Claudius enters. He is the brother of Hamlet's father, the dead king, and he has married Hamlet's mother, Queen Gertrude. Onstage, too, are the other principals of the play,

including Hamlet, who is dressed in black and stands apart from the others.

The action of the play is full of twists and turns. In the next scene, Hamlet himself sees the ghost of his father, who says that Hamlet must avenge his murder at the hands of his brother, Claudius. Hamlet later has a group of strolling players present a drama which proves that Claudius did murder Hamlet's father. In a later scene, Hamlet thrusts his sword through a curtain in his mother's bedroom, thinking that Claudius is hiding behind it, but the person concealed there turns out to be someone else.

As the plot continues to unfold, the audience is enthralled—all the way to the end, when almost everyone is killed: Hamlet and Laertes in a duel, Gertrude by poisoning, Claudius by stabbing. Throughout the play, the audience enjoys not only the action and suspense but also the memorable lines and speeches. Several times Hamlet stands alone onstage delivering a soliloquy.

On the way back across the Thames, after the play is over, and all evening, the audience members will continue to discuss *Hamlet*. They would like to see it again because there is more to it than they were able to take in at one viewing; they want to live through it once more to feel the thrill of the action and to sort out their thoughts about what it means.

The stage of a public theater—a raised platform surrounded on three sides by the audience—was closer to a contemporary thrust stage than to a proscenium stage. This platform stage was a neutral playing area which could become many different places in quick succession: a room in a palace, a bedroom, a street, a battlefield. When one group of characters left the stage and another group entered, this generally signaled a change of scene. Sometimes the characters announced where they were; at other times, the location was apparent from the action.

AN ELIZABETHAN PLAYHOUSE

This drawing shows the kind of stage on which the plays of Shakespeare and his contemporaries were first presented. A platform stage juts into an open courtyard, with spectators standing on three sides. Three levels of enclosed seats rise above the courtyard. There are doors at the rear of the stage for entrances and exits and an upper level for balcony scenes.

GROUND PLAN OF THE FORTUNE THEATER

The only English Renaissance theater for which we have a number of specific dimensions is the Fortune. From the builder's contract we know the size of the stage, the standing pit, the audience seating area, and the theater building itself. The building was square; the backstage area ran along one side; the stage was rectangular; and the audience—both standing and sitting—three sides.

In the stage floor were trapdoors. Behind the raised platform was the stage house, known as the *tiring house.* This three-story building served as a place for changing costumes as well as for storing properties and set pieces. The stage house was also the basic scenic piece in an Elizabethan public theater.

There is a great deal of debate over the configuration of the tiring house, but it is usually argued that the first level had two doorways, one on each side; and that entrances and exits through these doors indicated scene changes. For plays with scenes in which characters were concealed, there was probably an inner stage on the first level, either as part of the tiring house or within a freestanding structure. If such a special area did not exist, possibly one of the doors provided a place for concealment.

Another feature of the Elizabethan playhouse was an upper playing area for balcony scenes. No one knows for certain what the upper playing area looked like, but it might have been an inner area on the second level of the tiring house or part of a freestanding structure at the rear of the stage. The third level of the stage house, referred to as the *musicians' gallery,* probably housed the musicians who provided accompaniment for the plays. A roof, which protected the stage, extended out from the stage house. In some theaters it was supported by pillars; in others, it was suspended from the back. A flag was flown from the top of the stage house on days when a performance was taking place.

The exact shape of public theaters varied. It is estimated that their audience capacity was between 1,500 and 3,000—the larger number is now more widely accepted. Spectators were accommodated in the *yard, boxes,* and *galleries.* On the ground floor, in front of and on the sides of the stage, was the standing area, known as the *yard;* the lower-class audience members who stood there were known as *groundlings.* The galleries were usually three tiers of seating ranged on three sides around the stage. One tier was divided into boxes, known as *lords' rooms* because they were frequented by the wealthy; the undivided tiers were equipped with bench seating. Spectators—even those at the back wall of the galleries—were never very far from the actors.

Private Theaters.   Elizabethan *private theaters* were indoor spaces, lit by candles and high windows. The term *private* in this context often causes confusion, because today it would imply that certain classes were excluded. In Elizabethan England, however, private theaters were open to the general public, though they were usually smaller (seating about 600 to 750 spectators) and therefore more expensive than public theaters.

The pit of a private theater, which faced the stage in only one direction, had backless benches. The platform stage extended to the side walls, with galleries and boxes facing the stage on three sides.

Scenery and Costumes in Elizabethan Theaters. The Elizabethans did not use painted scenery in their public or private theaters, and the stage space did not represent a specific locale. Instead, the extensive, episodic nature of Elizabethan drama required scenes to be changed rapidly. Sometimes actors coming onstage would bring out minimal properties, such as a throne, to suggest a locale.

Costuming followed the conventions and traditions of medieval English theater. While their dramas exhibit a great deal of historical and geographical variety, the Elizabethans were not overly concerned with accuracy; most costumes were simply contemporary clothing.

English Actors and Acting Companies. Throughout the English Renaissance, the monarchy exerted considerable legal control over theater, and the number of acting companies was restricted by law.

Elizabethan acting companies—each of which had approximately twenty-five members—were organized on a *sharing plan.* There were three categories of personnel in a company: *shareholders, hirelings,* and *apprentices.* Shareholders, the elite members of the company, received a percentage of the troupe's profits as payment. Hirelings were actors contracted for a specific period of time and for a specific salary, and they usually played minor roles. Apprentices—young performers training for the profession—were assigned to shareholders. There were no female performers; women's roles were played by boys. Since the plays had many characters, doubling of roles was common.

What style of acting was used by the Elizabethans continues to be debated, particularly how "realistic" it was—that is, how close to the speech and gestures of everyday life. Many of the conventions of the period, such as dramatic verse, seem to suggest a departure from realistic style.

An English company would rarely perform the same play on two consecutive days, and each company had to be able to revive plays in its repertoire on very short notice. Thus the primary concern was not so much a carefully realized production as expert delivery of lines. Actors were provided with *sides,* which contained only their own lines and cues rather than the full script, and improvisation must have been used frequently. *Plots*—outlines of the dramatic action of the various plays—were posted backstage so that performers could refresh their memories during performances. Rehearsals were run by playwrights or leading actors;

THE SWAN THEATER
This drawing of an Elizabethan playhouse is a copy of a sketch made by a Dutch visitor to London in 1596. While the sketch shows the platform stage, tiring house, and galleries, controversial questions remain. Is the sketch complete? If so, where is the space for concealed characters? Who are the people in the "gallery"? Is this a rehearsal or a performance? (University Library, Utrecht)

Making Connections:

The Popular Arts of Shakespeare's Time

Bear baiting was a popular entertainment during Shakespeare's lifetime. Arenas were constructed for this form of entertainment, in which bears were attacked by trained dogs. What is even more remarkable is that this entertainment continued to attract audiences into the early nineteenth-century. Shown here is an illustration of bear baiting in Westminster, London in the 1820s. (© Hulton-Deutsch Collection/Corbis)

When we review the history of the English Renaissance theater, we often forget that Shakespeare and his contemporaries had to battle with the popular arts for London's audience members. Two of the most popular were bearbaiting and cockfighting.

Bearbaiting consisted of a bear being chained in the middle of an arena and then attacked by trained mastiff dogs. Points were scored depending on where the dogs struck the bear. The entertainment was probably developed out of the Roman animal entertainments and the tradition of baiting bulls during the Middle Ages.

In the 1500s, bearbaiting became a commercial entertainment in London. Up until 1574, there were two baiting rings in that city. During Shakespeare's time, there was one extremely popular arena: the Bear Garden. The Bear Garden was allowed to present bearbaiting on Sundays, when the

theaters were closed. Sunday attendance was so great that in 1583, parts of the building collapsed because of the large number of spectators.

Shakespeare comments on the popularity and theatricality of bearbaiting in his comedy *The Merry Wives of Windsor* (1600). The comedic character Slender comments about how much he loves the sport of bearbaiting and the audience's admiration for the great bear Sackerson:

> I love the sport well, but I shall as soon quarrel at it as any man in England. You are afraid if you see the bear loose, are you not? . . . I have seen Sackerson loose twenty times, and have taken him by the chain; but I warrant you, the women have so cried and shrieked at it, that it passed.

This form of entertainment remained popular through the English Restoration and was not made illegal until 1835.

The Cockpit, also known as the Phoenix, was opened in 1609 as an indoor space to house cockfights, another animal entertainment. Spectators would watch and bet on cocks, which were trained to fight with each other. The Cockpit became one of the best-known private, or indoor, theaters in the late English Renaissance after it was remodeled in 1616.

The popularity of cockfighting continued into the eighteenth-century English world. For that matter, the sport was popular in the early American colonies. George Washington, in his diaries, comments on attending cockfights in the new world.

Given the great competition for audiences, it is clear that the stage fights, violence, and slapstick comedy that abound in English Renaissance drama were techniques employed to combat the popularity of these other forms of entertainment.

and since rehearsal time was minimal, the prompter (who stood just offstage) became an indispensable part of the productions.

Theater after Elizabeth's Reign

After Elizabeth I died in 1603, the great Elizabethan dramatists, including Shakespeare and Ben Jonson (1572–1637), continued to write plays. Ben Jonson's comic masterpiece *Volpone,* for example, was staged in 1606. In contrast to Shakespeare, Jonson championed a more literary approach to drama.

James I succeeded Elizabeth; his reign is known as the *Jacobean* period. *The Duchess of Malfi* (ca. 1613–1614), by John Webster (ca. 1580–ca. 1630), is probably the most renowned Jacobean tragedy. These later tragedies were usually very melodramatic and emphasized violence and spectacle.

Another development in English drama in the early 1600s was a mixing of serious and comic elements. Such plays generally had many of the qualities of tragedy but ended happily. Francis Beaumont (ca. 1584–1616) and John Fletcher (1579–1625), two playwrights who often collaborated with each other, excelled at this form.

An elaborate type of entertainment featured at court during the reign of James I and his successor Charles I, and not found in either public or private theaters, was the *masque.* Masques were ornate, professionally staged, mythological allegories intended to praise the monarch; they were embellished by music and dance,

JACOBEAN DRAMA *Following Shakespeare and other Elizabethan dramatists, the dramatists in the period of James I (1603-1625) wrote more melodramatic tragedies. A good example is* The Changeling *by Thomas Middleton (1580-1627) and William Rowley (1558-1625). Shown here is a scene from a production directed by Robert Woodruff and produced by the Theater for a New Audience in New York City, with Melissa Bowen and Reg E. Cathey in foreground. (© Gerry Goodstein)*

and they frequently used amateur performers from the court. In the first decade of the seventeenth century, Inigo Jones (1573–1652), a designer who had studied in Italy, began to introduce the Italian style of theater architecture and scene design into English court masques.

James I was succeeded by Charles I in 1625. Though Charles I was not deposed—and beheaded—until 1649, the English Renaissance ended in 1642. By then, a civil war had begun between supporters of Charles I and the Puritan-backed Parliament. The Puritans were vehemently opposed to theater; they believed that playgoing was an inappropriate way to spend one's leisure time and that theater was a den of iniquity, teaching immorality. In 1642, the Puritans outlawed all theatrical activity.

Spain

Background: The Spanish Golden Age

THE SPANISH GOLDEN AGE
Two men were the major playwrights of the Spanish Golden Age: Calderón de la Barca and Lope de Vega. It was a period—partly coinciding with the Elizabethan era in England—in which theater flourished in Spain. The actor here, John Ortiz, is appearing as Segismundo in the Hartford Stage Company's production of Sueño, an adaptation of Calderon's Life is a Dream *by Josè Rivera.* (© T. Charles Erickson/Hartford Stage)

The period from about 1550 to 1650 is known as the Spanish golden age. During this rich period, Spain, which had a formidable navy, became a leading world power, primarily because of its exploration and conquest of the new world. Spain also remained a devoutly Catholic nation in the face of the Protestant Reformation which had swept much of the rest of Europe. In order to keep Spain Catholic, the church instituted the Inquisition, a type of court that punished any seeming religious heresy. During this period a popular theater, which incorporated both religious and popular secular forms, flourished.

Spanish Drama

Spain was one of England's chief rivals in the late sixteenth and early seventeenth centuries. At the same time that the two nations competed with one another, there were many similarities in their theaters. One important difference, however, is that the Spaniards—unlike the English—adopted the techniques of medieval religious drama and continued to produce medieval dramas throughout their golden age and beyond: until 1765, in fact.

Secular drama, which flourished between 1550 and 1700, developed in Spain side by side with religious drama and was created by the same artists. Full-length secular plays, known as *comedias,* usually dealt with themes of love and honor; the leading characters were often minor members of the nobility. Comedias were

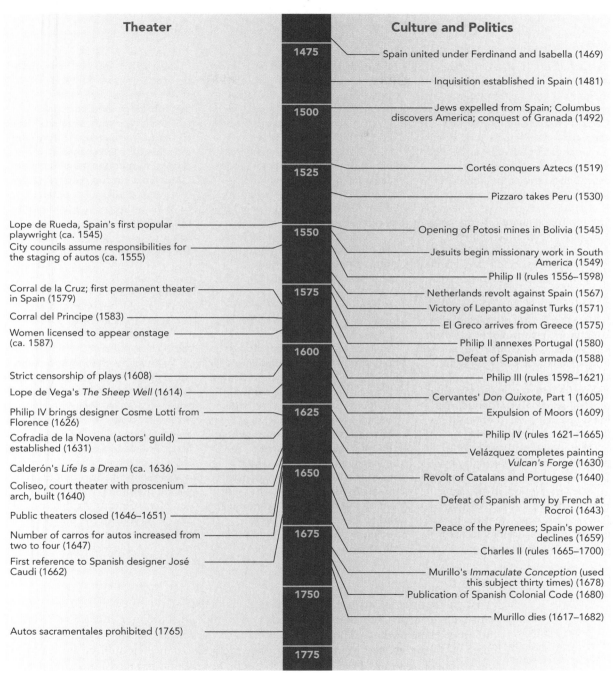

Spanish Golden Age
Year, A.D.

Theater

Culture and Politics

| 1475 | Spain united under Ferdinand and Isabella (1469) |

Inquisition established in Spain (1481)

| 1500 | Jews expelled from Spain; Columbus discovers America; conquest of Granada (1492) |

| 1525 | Cortés conquers Aztecs (1519) |

Pizzaro takes Peru (1530)

Lope de Rueda, Spain's first popular playwright (ca. 1545)

City councils assume responsibilities for the staging of autos (ca. 1555)

| 1550 | Opening of Potosi mines in Bolivia (1545) |

Jesuits begin missionary work in South America (1549)

Philip II (rules 1556–1598)

Corral de la Cruz; first permanent theater in Spain (1579)

Corral del Principe (1583)

Women licensed to appear onstage (ca. 1587)

| 1575 | Netherlands revolt against Spain (1567) |

Victory of Lepanto against Turks (1571)

El Greco arrives from Greece (1575)

Philip II annexes Portugal (1580)

| 1600 | Defeat of Spanish armada (1588) |

Strict censorship of plays (1608)

Lope de Vega's *The Sheep Well* (1614)

Philip III (rules 1598–1621)

Cervantes' *Don Quixote*, Part 1 (1605)

Philip IV brings designer Cosme Lotti from Florence (1626)

Cofradia de la Novena (actors' guild) established (1631)

Calderón's *Life Is a Dream* (ca. 1636)

Coliseo, court theater with proscenium arch, built (1640)

Public theaters closed (1646–1651)

Number of carros for autos increased from two to four (1647)

First reference to Spanish designer José Caudi (1662)

| 1625 | Expulsion of Moors (1609) |

Philip IV (rules 1621–1665)

Velázquez completes painting *Vulcan's Forge* (1630)

| 1650 | Revolt of Catalans and Portugese (1640) |

Defeat of Spanish army by French at Rocroi (1643)

| 1675 | Peace of the Pyrenees; Spain's power declines (1659) |

Charles II (rules 1665–1700)

Murillo's *Immaculate Conception* (used this subject thirty times) (1678)

| 1750 | Publication of Spanish Colonial Code (1680) |

Murillo dies (1617–1682)

Autos sacramentales prohibited (1765)

| 1775 | |

The King, The Greatest Alcalde

1620, Madrid It is four o'clock on a lovely spring afternoon in 1620. In Spain, a new full-length play by the Spanish playwright Lope de Vega is about to be performed at the Corral del Principe, one of two public theaters in Madrid. The audience has paid two entrance fees, one to the company presenting the play and the second to a charity supporting the city's hospital. The fee to the charity is one reason why government and church officials allow theater in Madrid.

As the audience gathers inside the *correl,* there is great excitement about the performance that will soon begin. Those standing in the patio are a bit noisy. Many of the spectators have bought nuts, fruit, and spiced honey from the *alojero.* People in the pit are jostling for the best vantage point; people in the galleries are exchanging pleasantries, speaking to friends, and looking around the theater to see who is here this afternoon.

The audience is particularly excited to attend a new play by Lope de Vega. Some years ago, in 1609, Lope argued, in an essay titled "The New Art of Writing Plays in This Age," that the most important measure of success in theater is the audience's enjoyment.

He has certainly passed his own test, for he is the most popular playwright of the day. The play about to be seen, *The King, The Greatest Alcalde,* promises to be filled with thrilling episodes.

Now the performance begins. First, before the actual play, there is a comic prologue. Then comes the play itself. It is a *comedia:* in Spain, this is the term for any full-length nonreligious play, serious or comic. *The King, The Greatest Alcalde* is serious, but it also has comic elements. It is about a farmer who promises his daughter Elvira to a peasant, Sancho. Sancho seeks approval for the marriage from his lord, Don Tello. Don Tello agrees, but when he sees Elvira, he wants her for himself. He postpones the wedding and kidnaps Elvira. As the play unfolds, it seems to have all the ingredients of a sparkling drama: a clash between peasants and the nobility, a wronged peasant, a kidnapping, a beautiful maiden in distress. The boisterous spectators in the pit are especially vocal in responding to each twist and turn of the plot and to the mixture of comedy and suspense, but the entire audience finds itself caught up in the story.

The actors and actresses in the theater company play fifteen speaking roles and some nonspeaking parts, and the audience responds enthusiastically to the performances. Though the play has thirteen scenes in different locations, all of its action takes place on the platform stage. It is easy to follow the action, because—through a combination of dialogue and properties, such as a throne—the playwright and the performers let the spectators know exactly where they are in every scene. The scenes are divided into three acts; during intermissions between the acts, the spectators are also entertained by short comic pieces and musical interludes.

As the play continues, Sancho appeals to the king to help him regain Elvira from Don Tello; after several complications, the king arrives, in disguise. When the king discovers that Don Tello has forcibly seduced Elvira, he orders Don Tello to marry her and then has him executed so that Elvira will be honorably widowed and can marry Sancho. At this conclusion, everyone in the audience—in the galleries as well as the pit—is pleased that justice has been done.

written in three acts, and like English Renaissance plays, they were extensive or episodic in form. Comedias mix serious and comic subject matter and are very similar to modern melodrama. Thus if Spanish plays of the golden age are very close to Elizabethan drama in their dramatic form, they seem closer in their subject matter to the swashbuckling films of the 1940s, to romantic novels, and to television soap operas.

Besides full-length plays, the Spaniards developed many popular, short, farcical forms. A short farce of this kind would be presented on the same program with a comedia.

The major playwrights of this period were Lope de Vega (1562–1635) and Calderón de la Barca (1600–1681). Lope de Vega was born within a year of Shakespeare and was a remarkable playwright—one of the most prolific dramatists of all time. He is said to have written 1,500 plays (although 800 is a more realistic figure); 470 of them survive, one of the best-known being *The Sheep Well* (ca. 1614). One of Calderón's most famous plays is *Life Is a Dream* (ca. 1636).

Theater Production in Spain

The Corrales. Nonreligious plays by writers like Lope de Vega and Calderón were staged in public theaters known as *corrales* (the plural of *corral*). Corrales were constructed in existing courtyards; like Elizabethan public theaters, they were open-air spaces with galleries and boxes protected by a roof. These courtyard theaters were temporary at first but later became permanent spaces. The two most famous were both in Madrid: the Corral de la Cruz (1579) and the Corral del Principe (1583).

A SPANISH CORRAL
This drawing is based on John J. Allen's research on the corral del Principe in Madrid. Note the various elements of the corral: the year (patio), the seating areas (boxes and galleries), and the platform stage with the tiring house behind it. Note also that in front of the yard there were benches or stools and that seats are set up at the side of stage. In addition, notice how similar the face of the building behind the stage was to the facade of the Elizabethan tiring house.

THE CLASSIC SPANISH STAGE
The corrales were outdoor, courtyard theaters used for the presentation of secular drama during the Spanish Golden Age. These playhouses were similar to the public theaters of the English Renaissance. A corral, that was uncovered accidentally in 1955, is shown here in Almagro, Spain. A theater festival is staged in this space every year. (Javier Rodriguez/COVER)

The stage in a corral was a platform erected opposite the entrance to the yard. Access to the yard was usually through a street building; there were also several entranceways for other seating areas. The yard floor or *patio* was primarily an area for standing and, like the pit of an Elizabethan public theater, was a raucous area. At the front of the yard, near the stage, a row of stools—later, a few benches—were set up, separated from the rest of the yard by a railing.

In the back wall opposite the stage, above the main entranceway in the yard, was a gallery for unaccompanied women known as the *cazuela;* it had its own separate entrance and was carefully guarded to prevent men from entering. Above the cazuela, there was a row of boxes for local government officials; above these boxes was a larger gallery for the clergy. Along the side walls of the yard were elevated benches and above them windows protected by grills from which a play could be viewed. On the next level were boxes which extended out from the buildings around the courtyard. A fourth floor had cramped boxes with low ceilings. At the back of the yard, on one side of the main entrance, was a refreshments box, the *alojero,* from which food and drinks were sold.

A corral held about 2,000 spectators: 1,000 places for men, 350 for women, and the rest reserved boxes and other accommodations for government officials and the clergy.

Scenic conventions in Spain were similar to those in England. A two-story facade behind the platform stage was the basic scenic construction; a curtain, props, and flats might be used in conjunction with this facade. There were three openings for entrances, exits, and scenes of concealment, as well as an upper playing area. The facade, therefore, served the same function as the Elizabethan tiring house. Spoken dialogue was also used to indicate locale.

Spanish Acting Companies. In Spain during the golden age, acting troupes consisted of sixteen to twenty performers. Unlike Elizabethan companies, these Spanish companies included women. In many places on the European continent—in contrast to England—women had been allowed to act in medieval religious drama, and the inclusion of women in Spanish companies during the Renaissance was an outgrowth of this custom. The church, though, did not support the use of female performers; as a result, the Spanish government was forced to impose stringent restrictions on women working in the theater—for instance, only a woman who was married or otherwise related to an actor in a troupe could be employed. Most Spanish acting troupes were *compañias de parte*—sharing companies, like those of Elizabethan England. Some companies, however, were organized by a manager who contracted performers for a specific period of time.

France

Background: France in the Seventeenth Century

Renaissance theater did not reach its zenith in France until the seventeenth century, later than in Italy, England, or Spain. This was partly due to a religious civil war taking place in France between Catholics and Protestants, a war that was finally brought to an end in 1594 when Henry IV formulated the Edict of Nantes, which offered religious tolerance to Catholics and Protestants. With religious and political stability established in the seventeenth century, French society was able to flourish under Louis XIV, who ruled from 1643 to 1715. Among France's significant accomplishments during this period was exploration of the new world, particularly in Canada and the Louisiana Territory of the United States.

During this period, French society was greatly influenced by the innovations of the Italian Renaissance. As we shall see, French theater in the seventeenth century adopted and adapted many of the Italian theatrical innovations.

TARTUFFE BY MOLIÈRE
The most famous comic playwright of the French Renaissance—and one of the best comic playwrights of all time—was Molière. He was particularly masterful at creating characters who carried an idea or obsession to excess. Here Elmire (left, played by Michele Farr) kicks Orgon (played by Richard Kinter), her foolish husband, who has been duped by the religious hypocrite Tartuffe. The scene is from a production at the Utah Shakespearean Festival. (John Running/© Utah Shakespearean Festival)

French Drama: The Neoclassical Era

The most important seventeenth-century French dramatists were Molière, noted for his comedies, and two authors known for tragedy: Pierre Corneille and Jean Racine.

Among all the French neoclassical playwrights, the one who exerts the most influence on modern theater is Molière (Jean-Baptiste Poquelin; 1622–1673). Molière was not only a dramatist but also an actor and the leader of a theatrical troupe. His first theater venture in Paris was a failure, and so he toured the provinces for 12 years, learning first-hand the techniques of theater and perfecting his craft as a dramatist. He then returned to establish himself as France's leading actor-manager and playwright, specializing in comedies of character.

Molière's work was strongly influenced by Italian commedia dell'arte. In plays like *Tartuffe* (1664), *The Misanthrope* (1666), *The Miser* (1668), and *The Imaginary Invalid* (1673), he creates exaggerated character types and makes fun of their eccentricities. The title character in *The Miser,* for example, is a man so greedy and so possessive of his money that he becomes paranoid when he thinks anyone knows where he has hidden it; in protecting his treasure, he even turns against his children. Molière was a master of slapstick as well as more subtle kinds of comedy, and he frequently used a *deus ex machina* to resolve his contrived plots.

Pierre Corneille (1606–1684) began his career writing comedies but soon turned to tragedy. His play *The Cid,* which opened in 1636, became a huge success. It aroused opposition from intellectuals because it did not follow the neoclassic rules established by Italian critics; despite this, it remained enormously popular and was presented frequently not only in France but in other European countries. Corneille, however, stopped writing plays for 4 years. Because of the controversy, when he resumed playwriting, he adhered more closely to the neoclassical rules.

Jean Racine (1639–1699) was the other great writer of tragedy in seventeenth-century France. Unlike Corneille, he was comfortable with the neoclassic rules from the start; all of Racine's tragedies adhere to these rules.

One of Racine's best-known tragedies, *Phaedra* (1677), is based on a play by Euripides. In Racine's version, Phaedra, queen to King Theseus, falls in love with her stepson, Hippolytus. Upon hearing that Theseus has died, she admits her love to Hippolytus, who reacts with disgust. When Phaedra discovers that Theseus is not dead, she allows her maid to spread the rumor that it was Hippolytus who

FRENCH NEOCLASSICAL DRAMA

The two major playwrights of French neoclassic drama were Pierre Corneille and Jean Racine. Both, in their separate ways, perfected a French version of classic tragedy. Racine's Phaedra, is probably the best known neoclassic tragedy. Shown here is a scene from a Comédie Française production with Martine Chevallier as the title character and Eric Genovèse as the stepson. (Roger-Viollet/Liaison Agency)

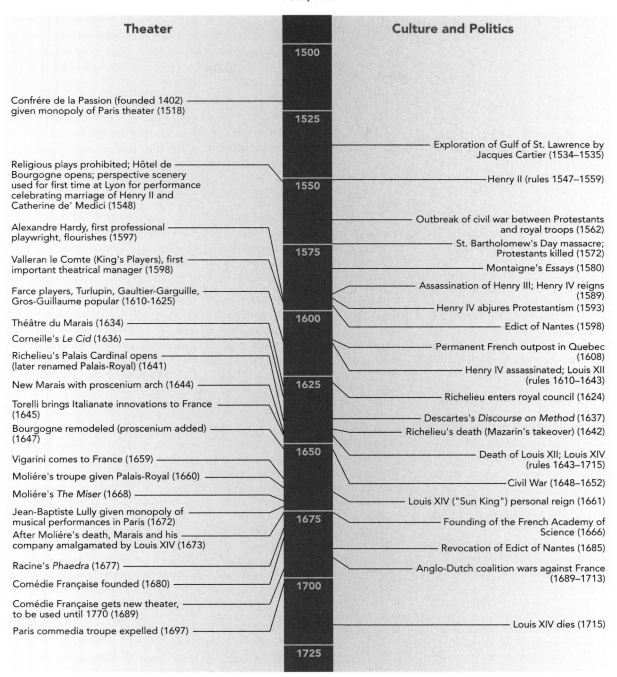

Neoclassical France
Year, A.D.

Theater		Culture and Politics

1500

Confrére de la Passion (founded 1402) given monopoly of Paris theater (1518)

1525

Exploration of Gulf of St. Lawrence by Jacques Cartier (1534–1535)

Religious plays prohibited; Hôtel de Bourgogne opens; perspective scenery used for first time at Lyon for performance celebrating marriage of Henry II and Catherine de' Medici (1548)

1550

Henry II (rules 1547–1559)

Outbreak of civil war between Protestants and royal troops (1562)

Alexandre Hardy, first professional playwright, flourishes (1597)

St. Bartholomew's Day massacre; Protestants killed (1572)

1575

Valleran le Comte (King's Players), first important theatrical manager (1598)

Montaigne's *Essays* (1580)

Assassination of Henry III; Henry IV reigns (1589)

Farce players, Turlupin, Gaultier-Garguille, Gros-Guillaume popular (1610-1625)

Henry IV abjures Protestantism (1593)

Théâtre du Marais (1634)

Edict of Nantes (1598)

1600

Corneille's *Le Cid* (1636)

Permanent French outpost in Quebec (1608)

Richelieu's Palais Cardinal opens (later renamed Palais-Royal) (1641)

Henry IV assassinated; Louis XII (rules 1610–1643)

New Marais with proscenium arch (1644)

1625

Richelieu enters royal council (1624)

Torelli brings Italianate innovations to France (1645)

Descartes's *Discourse on Method* (1637)

Bourgogne remodeled (proscenium added) (1647)

Richelieu's death (Mazarin's takeover) (1642)

1650

Death of Louis XII; Louis XIV (rules 1643–1715)

Vigarini comes to France (1659)

Civil War (1648–1652)

Moliére's troupe given Palais-Royal (1660)

Louis XIV ("Sun King") personal reign (1661)

Moliére's *The Miser* (1668)

Jean-Baptiste Lully given monopoly of musical performances in Paris (1672)

1675

Founding of the French Academy of Science (1666)

After Moliére's death, Marais and his company amalgamated by Louis XIV (1673)

Revocation of Edict of Nantes (1685)

Racine's *Phaedra* (1677)

Anglo-Dutch coalition wars against France (1689–1713)

Comédie Française founded (1680)

1700

Comédie Française gets new theater, to be used until 1770 (1689)

Paris commedia troupe expelled (1697)

Louis XIV dies (1715)

1725

Tartuffe

1669, Paris The date is February 9, 1669. At the Palais-Royal theater in Paris, France, spectators are eagerly awaiting a performance of *Tartuffe*, written by France's best-known comic playwright and actor, Molière.

Tartuffe has already been the cause of an enormous controversy. Molière first read it 4 years ago to King Louis XIV at his palace at Versailles; the king liked it, but before it could be presented publicly, it provoked an uproar. The reason is its subject matter. The title character of the play, Tartuffe, is a religious hypocrite. He pretends to be very pious and wears clothing that looks like a religious habit, but he is actually interested in acquiring money and seducing women. He has come to live in the house of Orgon, a wealthy man who has been completely taken in by Tartuffe's false piety.

The people who oppose the presentation of *Tartuffe* include a number of religious figures (one of them is the archbishop of Paris) who say that it is an attack on religion. Molière, however, insists that his play is not an attack on religion, but rather an attack on people who hide behind religion and exploit it.

The audience is aware that until now the opposition has been successful in keeping *Tartuffe* out of theaters; the king did not dare authorize its presentation as long as the forces against it were so strong. So far, the play has been presented only once, in the summer of 1667, and then for only one night. The king was out of the country at that time, and in his absence the religious authorities had it closed down. Now, however, *Tartuffe* has finally been given royal approval, and today's performance is to be its official public unveiling.

The Palais Royal theater, where Molière's troupe performs, is a rectangular space with a stage at one end and galleries on three sides around it. It accommodates almost 1,500 people: 300 stand in a "pit" in front of the stage, about 700 sit in a raised amphitheater behind the pit, about 330 sit in the galleries, 70 stand at the very back, and 50 wealthy nobles sit on the sides of the stage itself. Having spectators onstage is customary in French theaters but makes things very difficult for the performers.

The stage is fitted with wings and shutters, like Italian Renaissance theaters, and scenery can be changed with a pole-and-chariot system. For *Tartuffe*, however, there will be no scene changes: the entire action takes place in the drawing room of Orgon's house.

Well aware of all the scandal and debate, the audience feels a rush of anticipation as this performance of *Tartuffe* begins. Once it is under way, though, the spectators realize that the controversial figure of Tartuffe does not even make an appearance for two full acts. Rather, it is the figure of Orgon, played by Molière himself, on whom they first concentrate. The spectators see that Orgon is thoroughly duped and pays no attention to the members of his family when they tell him how dishonest and disreputable Tartuffe is.

Finally, in the third act, Tartuffe makes his entrance. He is challenged by Orgon's family, but Orgon remains loyal to him. Only when Orgon learns for himself the awful truth about Tartuffe does he realize his error. This occurs in a scene in which Orgon, hiding under a table, hears Tartuffe try to seduce his wife. The wife has led Tartuffe on, and he exposes himself as a genuine scoundrel. As the audience members watch the scene, they think it is one of the funniest they have ever seen.

Orgon's discovery of Tartuffe's true nature seems to come too late: at this point, Orgon has already handed his house and his fortune over to Tartuffe, disinheriting his own children. At the end of the play, though, the king intervenes. This is the same Louis XIV who in real life has intervened on Molière's behalf so that the play can be presented.

A few weeks from now, both king and playwright will be vindicated: *Tartuffe* will be performed twenty-eight times in a row—an unprecedented number—and will show every sign of becoming a classic comedy.

made amorous advances to Phaedra, rather than the other way around. Hearing the rumor and believing it, Theseus invokes a god to kill his son Hippolytus, after which a heartbroken Phaedra takes poison—before she dies, however, she reveals the truth.

Racine's *Phaedra* is a perfect example of climactic plot structure: it has only a few characters, and the action takes place in one room at one time. Furthermore, Racine's masterful handling of poetry and emotion established a model to be followed in France for the next three centuries.

Theater Production in France

The French were the first Europeans after the Romans to construct a permanent theater building. This was the Hôtel de Bourgogne, completed in 1548. The Bourgogne was built by the Confraternity of the Passion, a religious order that had been granted a monopoly for the presentation of religious drama in Paris. When religious drama was outlawed—in the same year that the Bourgogne was completed—the Confraternity rented its space to touring companies.

The Hôtel de Bourgogne, a long, narrow building with a platform stage at one end, was the sole permanent indoor theater building in Paris for nearly a century, until the Théâtre du Marais opened in 1634. The Marais was a converted indoor tennis court. Such indoor courts were long and narrow—like the Bourgogne—and had galleries for spectators (court tennis was a popular sport); thus they could be transformed into theaters very easily.

The Italian influence on French theater architecture became evident in 1641, when Cardinal Richelieu, a leading political figure, erected the Palais Cardinal, renamed the Palais-Royal after his death. This is the theater that Molière's troupe eventually used. The Palais Cardinal was the first proscenium-arch theater in France and also had Italian-style machinery to shift scenery. Following the

GROUND PLAN OF THE COMÉDIE FRANÇAISE
The French national theater company performed in this playhouse for 81 years, beginning in 1689. The theater had a proscenium-arch stage with machinery for scene shifts, and a horseshoe-shaped auditorium for improved sight lines. The parterre was where audience members stood; the amphitheater contained bleacherlike seating.

Wings and shutters

Benches for audience

Amphitheater (raised gallery)

Stage

Orchestra

Parterre (standing pit)

Benches for audience

Galleries and boxes in side walls

construction of Richelieu's theater, the Théâtre du Marais and the Hôtel de Bourgogne were remodeled in the 1640s into proscenium-arch theaters. Painted-perspective wing-and-shutter scenery—shifted by the pole-and-chariot system—was used in the two remodeled theaters.

Early French proscenium-arch theater buildings differed slightly from those of the Italian Renaissance: in the back wall opposite the stage was an *amphithéâtre*, an undivided gallery with inexpensive bleacherlike seating. In both the Marais and the Bourgogne, there was probably a small upper stage, raised 13 feet above the main stage, which was used for special effects such as flying. At the close of the seventeenth century, upper-class audience members were frequently seated on-stage.

In the 1650s, Louis XIV's interest in ballet brought this form of entertainment back into prominence at court. To satisfy the royal taste for elaborate ballets and to prepare for Louis's marriage, a new court theater was built, known as the Salle des Machines ("Hall of Machines"). It was completed in 1660 and was the largest playhouse in Europe: 52 feet wide and 232 feet long. The auditorium took up only 92 feet of the 232-foot length, leaving 140 feet for the stage and its machinery. The backstage equipment included one piece of machinery on which the entire royal family and all their attendants—well over 100 people—could be "flown" into the space above the stage. Because of its unsatisfactory acoustics, its size (especially backstage), and the expense of producing spectacles, the Salle des Machines was rarely used after 1670.

Another major theater building of the French neoclassical period was the Comédie Française, which housed the national theater. The French national theater had been founded by Louis XIV in 1680, but the company did not move into its own building until 1689. The interior of the Comédie Française featured a horseshoe-shape construction, which meant that the sight lines were significantly better than those in other French spaces of the time.

Acting companies in French neoclassical theaters were organized under a sharing plan and had women members who could become shareholders. Rehearsals were supervised by the playwright or a leading performer or both, but troupes spent little time on rehearsals. Once a play was introduced, the troupe was expected to be able to revive it at a moment's notice, and the bill at theaters was changed daily.

The Renaissance in Italy, England, Spain, and France saw significant—even revolutionary—changes in theatrical practices. Many of these practices will be built on as we look at developments in theater between 1660 and 1875, in Chapter 13.

SUMMARY

During the Italian Renaissance, the neoclassical rules for drama were formulated. Commedia dell'arte developed as a popular theater, based on stock characters, repeated pieces of comic business, and recognizable costumes. Painted-perspective scenery, which could be changed easily, and the proscenium-arch theater were both introduced, leading to greater verisimilitude—truth to life—in theater.

During the English Renaissance—the Elizabethan age—the great plays of Shakespeare and his contemporaries were being staged. Outdoor public theaters and indoor private theaters accommodated these extensive-form dramas through the use of an unlocalized platform stage and a flexible tiring house, or stage house. Brilliant poetic language also helped set the action.

In Spain during its golden age, the secular dramas of Lope de Vega and Calderón de la Barca were performed in corrales, theaters built in courtyards. Corrales used many of the same staging conventions as Elizabethan theaters.

In French neoclassical theater, the tragic dramas of Corneille and Racine and the comedies of character by Molière were clearly patterned after traditions established in the Italian Renaissance. French theater architecture and design were also based on Italian models.

THEATER ON THE WEB

Links to cultural information about western Europe are readily available on the Internet.

Records of Early English Drama (REED)   http://www.chass.utoronto.ca/~reed/reed.html

A leading scholarly resource for early medieval and Renaissance drama.

Lope de Vega (1562–1635)   http://www.imagi-nation.com/moonstruck/clsc33.html

Offers a biography of the Spanish playwright, plus links to all his works currently in print.

Molière in English   http://moliere-in-english.com

Find plays by Molière in new English language adaptations.

Internet Shakespeare Editions: Home Page   http://castle.uvic.ca/shakespeare

Provides texts of the plays, with research materials and extensive background information on both specific plays and the playwright.

I Sebastiani   http://www.iSebastiani.org

Hosted by the I Sebastiani commedia troupe, with links to other historical and contemporary commedia dell'arte troupes.

Using historical information found at these sites, create a list of historical events that could have influenced Shakespeare, de Vega, and Molière. Discuss whether or not you think commedia influenced any or all of these playwrights. Discuss whether or not you think their plays are relevant today.

Chapter 13

Theater from 1660 to 1875

The English Restoration

    Background: England in the Seventeenth Century

    Restoration Drama: Comedies of Manners

Timeline: *English Restoration*

Living History: *The Country Wife*

    Theater Production in the Restoration

Play Synopsis: *The Way of the World*

The Eighteenth Century

    Background: A More Complex World

Timeline: *Eighteenth Century*

    Eighteenth-Century Drama: New Dramatic Forms

Theater Production in the Eighteenth Century

Living History: *The Marriage of Figaro*

The Nineteenth Century

    Background: A Time of Social Change

    Theater in the Nineteenth-Century Life

Timeline: *Nineteenth Century, 1800–1875*

    Nineteenth-Century Dramatic Forms

Making Connections: *Nineteenth-Century Popular Theatrical Arts*

    Theater Production in the Nineteenth Century

Summary

◄ CARLO GOZZI'S *THE KING STAG*

Two popular Italian playwrights of the eighteenth century were Carlo Goldoni and Carlo Gozzi. Seen here is a theatrical production of Gozzi's The King Stag, *staged by avant-garde director Andrei Serban for the American Repertory Theatre at Harvard. The production has been remounted many times since its premiere in 1984. The costumes, puppets, masks, choreography were by Julie Taymor, who directed* The Lion King. *The actors in this scene are Richard Grusin and Lynn Chausow.*
(© Richard Feldman)

The period from 1660 to 1875 saw radical transformations in western society. Revolutions and nationalism led to changes in governments and the establishment of new nations. Mechanization and new technology transformed work, the workplace, and economic classes. Innovations in modes of transportation made travel easier, both within nations and internationally. Theater mirrored the social, political, and economic issues of the times, and it too was transformed. In this chapter, we will examine the theater of England in the late seventeenth century as well as developments in worldwide theater in the eighteenth and nineteenth centuries.

The English Restoration

Background: England in the Seventeenth Century

After a bitter civil war lasting from 1642 to 1649, Charles I of England was removed from the throne by the Puritans and beheaded. For the next 11 years, England was a Commonwealth, governed by Oliver Cromwell with a Parliament that had been purged of all his opponents.

When Cromwell died in 1658, his son was unable to keep control of the government; and in 1660 Charles II, who had been living in exile in France, was invited by a newly elected Parliament to return and rule England. The monarchy was thus restored, and this period in English history—usually dated from 1660 through 1700—is therefore called the *Restoration*.

During the period of the Commonwealth, many members of the English nobility had been exiles in France; when the English monarchy returned, these people took back with them the theatrical practices they had seen there.

Restoration Drama: Comedies of Manners

The theaters that reopened in England represented a fusion of Elizabethan, Italian, and French stage conventions. This gave a unique flavor to every aspect of Restoration theater: texts, theater buildings, and set designs.

The best-known Restoration comedies, many of which were influenced by the French dramatist Molière, are referred to as **comedies of manners**. They poked fun at the social conventions of the upper class of the time and satirized the preoccupation of English aristocrats with reputation: most of the upper-class characters in these plays are disreputable. Emphasizing witty dialogue and filled with sexual intrigue and innuendo, the plays took an amoral attitude toward human behavior, including sex. Audiences consisted primarily of members of the nobility and the upper class, the same people whom the playwrights were satirizing.

In their dramatic structure, Restoration comedies combine features of Elizabethan theater and the neoclassical theater of Italy and France. For example, in *The Country Wife* by William Wycherley (1640–1715), the action is far more unified than in a Shakespearean play, with fewer scene shifts. But it does move

FEMALE PLAYWRIGHTS IN THE RESTORATION
There were a number of significant female playwrights during the Restoration. Among them was Aphra Behn, whose works are now frequently revived in the contemporary theater. Seen here is a production of her most famous comedy of intrigue, The Rover, *as staged at Illinois State University.* (© Peter Guither)

from place to place, involves many characters, and even has a subplot. The characters are stock types, with names which usually describe their distinctive personality traits. Fidget and Squeamish are nervous about their reputations; Pinchwife is a man who doesn't want his wife pinched by other men; and Sparkish is a fop who mistakenly believes himself to be a real "spark," witty and fashionable.

Other types of Restoration comedies included comedies of humours, and comedies of intrigue. Comedies of humours followed the tradition of Ben Jonson, in which characters have one trait overshadowing all others. Comedies of intrigue featured daring exploits of romance and adventure and had complicated plots. One of the most successful writers of this type of comedy was a woman, Aphra Behn (1640–1689), whose most famous play is *The Rover* (1677).

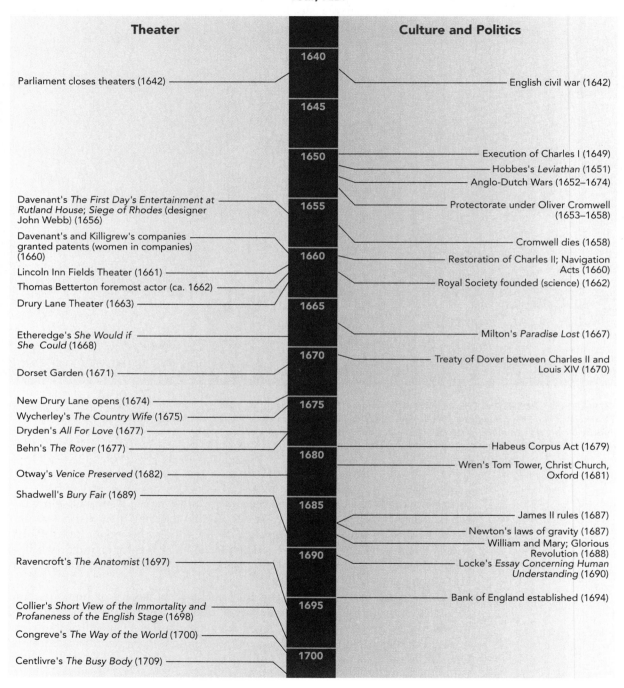

English Restoration
Year, A.D.

Theater		Culture and Politics

1640

Parliament closes theaters (1642) — English civil war (1642)

1645

1650

Execution of Charles I (1649)

Hobbes's *Leviathan* (1651)

Anglo-Dutch Wars (1652–1674)

Davenant's *The First Day's Entertainment at Rutland House; Siege of Rhodes* (designer John Webb) (1656) — **1655** — Protectorate under Oliver Cromwell (1653–1658)

Davenant's and Killigrew's companies granted patents (women in companies) (1660)

Cromwell dies (1658)

1660

Restoration of Charles II; Navigation Acts (1660)

Lincoln Inn Fields Theater (1661)

Royal Society founded (science) (1662)

Thomas Betterton foremost actor (ca. 1662)

Drury Lane Theater (1663)

1665

Etheredge's *She Would if She Could* (1668)

Milton's *Paradise Lost* (1667)

1670

Treaty of Dover between Charles II and Louis XIV (1670)

Dorset Garden (1671)

New Drury Lane opens (1674)

1675

Wycherley's *The Country Wife* (1675)

Dryden's *All For Love* (1677)

Behn's *The Rover* (1677)

1680

Habeus Corpus Act (1679)

Wren's Tom Tower, Christ Church, Oxford (1681)

Otway's *Venice Preserved* (1682)

Shadwell's *Bury Fair* (1689)

1685

James II rules (1687)

Newton's laws of gravity (1687)

William and Mary; Glorious Revolution (1688)

1690

Ravencroft's *The Anatomist* (1697)

Locke's *Essay Concerning Human Understanding* (1690)

Bank of England established (1694)

Collier's *Short View of the Immortality and Profaneness of the English Stage* (1698) — **1695**

Congreve's *The Way of the World* (1700)

1700

Centlivre's *The Busy Body* (1709)

The Country Wife

1675, London, England It is a raw, overcast day in January 1675, and two young men—members of the nobility—set forth to the theater in London. They are making their way to the new Drury Lane Theater. Another theater once stood at the site of the Drury Lane, but it burned in 1672; the new theater, designed by the architect Christopher Wren and erected on the same spot, opened only a year ago, in 1674.

The play they will see is a new one, by William Wycherley, called *The Country Wife*. They anticipate that they will hear witty, rapier-like exchanges between the characters, and doubtless many double-entendres: clever lines which operate on two levels, one ordinary and the other decidedly sexual.

It is just after two o'clock in the afternoon. The play will not begin until 3:30, but the young men want to arrive at the theater early—to talk to their acquaintances, to flirt with the attractive young women who sell oranges and other things to eat, and even to go backstage to try to see the actresses. As they arrive at the playhouse, the young men join a carefree, pleasure-loving crowd.

The new Drury Lane—a building 58 feet wide by 140 feet long—seats 650 people, some in a pit facing the stage, others in boxes and galleries along the sides and back. Its stage is a platform about 34 feet deep; the front half of the stage is open, and the back half—framed by a proscenium—contains the scenic elements.

When the performance begins, the first person onstage is an actor named Charles Hart, who delivers a prologue; then the play itself starts. Hart plays a character called Horner, who spreads the rumor that he has been rendered impotent by a venereal disease he contracted while abroad. Horner's doctor, Quack, substantiates the rumor, and Horner uses this "cover story" to gain access to his acquaintances' wives; because of his supposed condition, the husbands will regard him as no threat. The wife he most desires is Margery Pinchwife, a naive woman whose husband usually keeps her locked away in the country and tries to disguise her as a boy when they are in town. Coming upon Pinchwife and the disguised Margery in the street, Horner realizes that the "boy" is a woman in a man's clothing and takes advantage of the situation to make amorous advances, hugging and kissing her in front of her husband, who can do nothing. During the course of the dramatic action, a subplot develops: Horner's friend Harcourt steals Pinchwife's sister Alithea away from her intended husband, Sparkish.

The young male spectators are particularly taken with Elizabeth Bowtell, who plays Margery. In France and Spain, women have appeared onstage for some time; but England forbade actresses until 1660—only a few years ago—and seeing them now is a novelty that strongly appeals to the men in the audience. Moreover, ever since women have been allowed to perform onstage in England, a favorite dramatic device is to have a woman dress as a man; parts that require this kind of cross-dressing are called *breeches roles*. Seeing a woman's legs—which are usually hidden under wide skirts—has a strong sexual fascination.

The audience is also titillated by the sexual references, especially by a scene which is to become famous—the "china closet" scene. In this scene, Horner and Lady Fidget are in a room offstage while Lady Fidget's husband is onstage listening to their conversation. Horner and Lady Fidget are supposed to be examining Horner's collection of china, but the audience soon realizes that though Horner is speaking about china, he is actually making love to Lady Fidget while her husband stands by in ignorance. Then another woman, Mrs. Squeamish, arrives, and she too asks to see Horner's china. When Horner tells Mrs. Squeamish he has no more, the audience knows that china has become a code word for sex and that Horner is unable at that moment to make love.

At the conclusion of the play, Horner's scheme has been successful: he has made love not only to Margery but to the other wives as well.

RESTORATION DRAMA: COMEDIES OF MANNERS
During the period of the English Restoration, beginning in 1660, the most popular plays were comedies which satirized the upper classes with their gossip, emphasis on dress and decorum, infidelity, conspiracies and the like. One of the most famous plays to emerge from the period was The Country Wife by William Wycherly in which a man disguises his wife as a boy in hopes of discouraging other men from pursuing her, but the main character takes advantage of this ploy to initiate an affair with the woman. Shown here is a scene from a production of the play at the New Jersey Shakespeare Festival with performers Peter Bradbury and Sue Brady. (© Gerry Goodstein)

Another well-known Restoration comic playwright is William Congreve (1670–1729). Congreve's *The Way of the World* (1700) is often considered a bridge between Restoration comedy and the later, more traditional morality of eighteenth-century English sentimental comedy. In eighteenth-century English comedy, as we will see, the sinful are punished and the virtuous are rewarded. Like Restoration comedy, *The Way of the World* has a number of characters involved in adulterous affairs, as well as the traditional stock characters, but its two young lovers, Mirabell and Millamant, are united, while the wicked characters, Fainall and Marwood, are punished.

Many Restoration comedies, including *The Country Wife,* indicate that audiences of that era, unlike today's audiences, were quite spirited during theatrical presentations. The fop Sparkish in *The Country Wife* describes how audience members bought fruit from the "orange wenches" (some of whom were prostitutes), spoke back to the performers, arranged assignations, and attended theater to be seen rather than to see the play. These extratheatrical activities increased attacks on theater by religious leaders, who were generally opposed to theater anyway.

Theater Production in the Restoration

Performers and Acting Companies. In theater production, the most obvious difference between the English Renaissance and the Restoration was the appearance of women on the English stage for the first time.

Another change was that in London the sharing plan followed by companies like Shakespeare's almost disappeared during the Restoration. Instead, London performers were hired for a specific period of time at a set salary. In order to increase the set wage, an actor or actress was provided with a yearly *benefit,* a performance of a play from which he or she kept all the profits. The benefit system was used in English theater from the Restoration through the nineteenth century.

The Restoration also saw the emergence of theatrical entrepreneurs who were often part owners of theater buildings and companies. The rise of the entrepreneur as a powerful theatrical force was, of course, a step in the development of modern theater business, with its independent theater owners and producers.

THE WAY OF THE WORLD (1700)

By William Congreve, (1670–1729)

(Victoria and Albert Museum, London)

Chief Characters

Mirabell, *in love with Millamant*
Millamant, *niece of Lady Wishfort*
Lady Wishfort, *enemy of Mirabell*
Fainall, *in love with Mrs. Marwood*
Mrs. Fainall, *Fainall's wife and daughter of Lady Wishfort*
Mrs. Marwood, *friend to Fainall*
Sir Wilfull Witwoud, *Lady Wishfort's nephew*
Another Witwoud, *follower of Millamant*
Waitwell, *Mirabell's servant*
Foible, *Lady Wishfort's maid*

Background

The play takes place among members of the upper class in London in the late seventeenth century. The society it depicts is highly artificial and values gossip, intrigue, deception, seduction, and sparkling conversation above everything else.

Act 1: A chocolate shop. Mirabell complains to Fainall that his attempt to win the love of Millamant is not succeeding because Millamant's aunt and guardian, Lady Wishfort, has turned against him. Lady Wishfort is infatuated with Mirabell but she feels he has not been attentive enough. Witwoud and Petulant, followers of Millamant, join the conversation.

Act II: In St. James Park, Mrs. Fainall and Mrs. Marwood are talking when Fainall and Mirabell join them. (Mrs. Fainall is Mirabell's mistress, though he really loves Millamant.) When Mirabell and Mrs. Fainall are alone, Mrs. Fainall complains that she detests Fainall, whom Mirabell compelled her to marry. Though disappointed in Mirabell, Mrs. Fainall's passion for him leads her to help him in his next scheme, even though it involves her mother, Lady Wishfort. Mirabell wants to marry the beautiful and wealthy Millamant, but her aunt is jealously withholding her consent. With Mrs. Fainall's collaboration, Mirabell arranges to have his servant, Waitwell, in the guise of an imaginary uncle called Sir Rowland, pay court to Lady Wishfort. Then, since Mirabell already has accomplished a secret marriage between Waitwell and Lady Wishfort's maid, Foible, he declares his intention to expose the scandal. He will remain silent only if he can have Millamant and her fortune.

Act III: With the scheme perfected, the scene shifts to Lady Wishfort's house: Foible tells Lady Wishfort that a man known as Sir Rowland has seen her picture and is infatuated with her. A meeting is arranged but their plot is overheard by Mrs. Marwood, another of Mirabell's conquests and herself a crafty schemer. Mrs. Marwood promptly persuades Lady Wishfort that Millamant should be married to Sir Wilfull Witwoud, a rich and amiable dunce. Fainall agrees to Mrs. Marwood's plan: she will write a letter exposing "Sir Rowland" as a fraud.

Act IV: Lady Wishfort is unnerved as she awaits the bogus Sir Rowland. Meanwhile, Mirabell and Millamant discuss a commonsense "contract" they believe a husband and wife should agree to, for their marriage to succeed. The action then returns to Lady Wishfort and the arrival of "Sir Rowland." He begs for an early marriage, declaring that his nephew, Mirabell, will poison him for his money if he learns of the romance. The jealous Lady Wishfort promptly agrees. Then Mrs. Marwood's letter arrives, but Sir Rowland declares it to be the work of Mirabell.

Act V: Lady Wishfort learns that she is being deceived and turns on her maid Foible. The frightened Foible confesses that Mirabell conceived the whole plot, and Lady Wishfort is planning a dire revenge when more trouble comes: Fainall, her son-in-law, demands that his wife turn over her fortune to him, or else he and Mrs. Marwood will reveal to the world that Mrs. Fainall was Mirabell's mistress before her marriage and that she continues to be. Lady Wishfort is reflecting upon this new humiliation when Mirabell comes asking for forgiveness.

Mirabell offers a compromise: if Lady Wishfort will permit her niece to marry him, he will contrive to save Mrs. Fainall's reputation and fortune. Lady Wishfort agrees. Mirabell then tells her, "As regards your daughter's reputation, she has nothing to fear from Fainall . . . He and Mrs. Marwood . . . have been and still are lovers . . . And as regards your daughter's fortune, she need have no fear on that score, either: acting upon my advice, . . . she has made me the trustee of her entire estate." Cries Fainall: "'Tis outrageous!" Says Mirabell: "'Tis *The Way of the World*."

DRURY LANE THEATER
This reconstruction of the Drury Lane Theater in the Restoration period shows Christopher Wren's design for the Theatre Royal, Drury Lane, 1674. Note the pit for the audience and the two doors on each side of the stage. (from Richard Leacroft, in the Theatre, Roy Publishers, p. 34)

Government and Theater. When English theater was restored in 1660, Charles II issued patents to two entrepreneurs, William Davenant and Thomas Killigrew (1612–1683), which in effect gave them a monopoly on presenting theater in London.

By the early eighteenth century, this monopoly would become unenforceable, however; and in 1737 Parliament was to pass the Licensing Act, a new attempt to regulate London theater. Under this act, only two theaters—Drury Lane and Covent Garden—were authorized to present drama for "gain, hire, or reward," and the lord chamberlain became responsible for licensing plays.

Theater Architecture. During the Restoration, there were three theaters of note in London: Drury Lane (1663); Lincoln Inn Fields (1661), a converted tennis court; and Dorset Garden (1671). Though the interiors of these theaters were distinct, all three showed a unique fusion of Italian and Elizabethan features.

All Restoration theaters were indoor proscenium-arch buildings. The area for the audience was divided into pit, boxes, and galleries and had a total seating capacity of about 650. The pit, which had backless benches to accommodate spectators, was raked—or slanted—for better sight lines.

The Restoration stage was highly unusual in that it was divided into two equal halves by the proscenium arch. In the seventeenth century, only English theaters had this extended apron, and most historians believe that it was a vestige of the

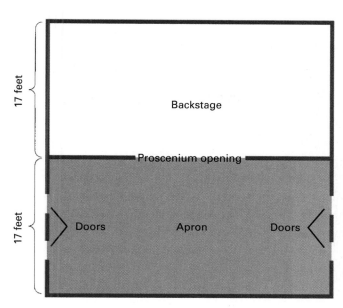

GROUND PLAN OF A RESTORATION STAGE

This stage was an unusual combination of English and Italian Renaissance stages. The Restoration saw the introduction of the Italianate proscenium arch into public playhouses in England. However, the extended apron, equal in depth to the rear stage area, and the two proscenium doors on each side of the stage were vestiges of the Elizabethan platform stage and tiring house.

Elizabethan platform stage. The deep apron was a major performance area in Restoration theaters; the upstage area housed the scenery. The entire stage was raked to improve the spectators' sight lines.

Another unique element of the Restoration stage was the proscenium doors, with balconies above them. On each side of the stage there were two proscenium doors leading onto the forestage. These doors were used for exits and entrances, and for concealment scenes—scenes in which one character listens from out of sight, a popular device in Restoration comedy. The balconies above these doorways could be used for balcony and window scenes.

Scenery, Lighting, and Costumes. Restoration scenery and lighting also illustrate a fusion of Italian and English stage practices. The basic scenic components were wings, shutters—sometimes replaced by rolled backdrops—and borders for masking. The English rarely used the pole-and-chariot system for scene changes; instead, they used the groove system. Throughout the Restoration, companies kept collections of stock sets, painted in perspective; these were reused frequently, partly because it was expensive to have new scenery painted.

Because Restoration theaters were indoors, lighting was a major concern. During the late seventeenth century, theater performances were normally given in the afternoon so that the windows could provide some natural lighting. Candles were the source of artificial light; these were placed in chandeliers above the stage and the audience, and also in brackets attached to the fronts of the boxes. The stage and audience area were always lit, and footlights—candles on the floor along the front of the stage—were also used.

Restoration costuming followed the traditions of the English Renaissance and the French neoclassical era: contemporary clothing was used rather than historically accurate costuming.

The Eighteenth Century

Background: A More Complex World

Throughout Europe, the eighteenth century was a time of transition; as a result, the study of its history, including its theater history, becomes quite complex. As the world was slowly transformed into a global community, homogeneous, self-contained societies began to disappear. Increased manufacturing and international

Eighteenth Century
Year, A.D.

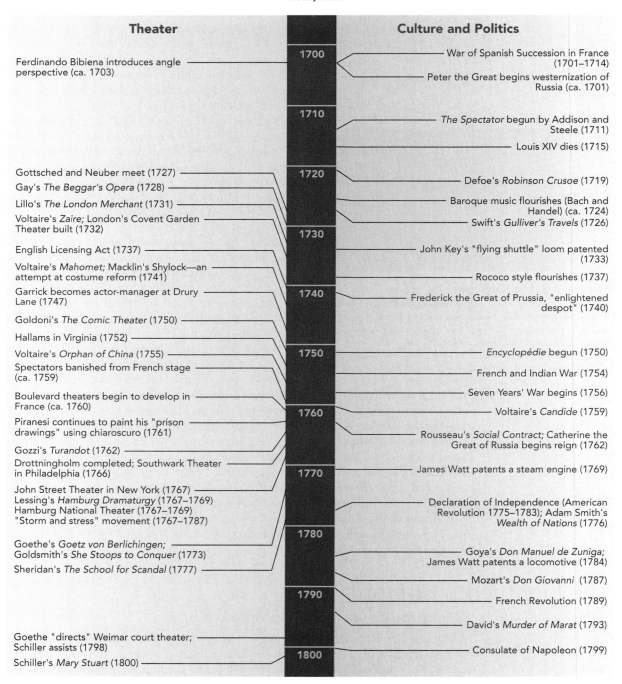

Theater		Culture and Politics

1700

Ferdinando Bibiena introduces angle perspective (ca. 1703)

War of Spanish Succession in France (1701–1714)

Peter the Great begins westernization of Russia (ca. 1701)

1710

The Spectator begun by Addison and Steele (1711)

Louis XIV dies (1715)

1720

Gottsched and Neuber meet (1727)

Gay's The Beggar's Opera (1728)

Defoe's Robinson Crusoe (1719)

Lillo's The London Merchant (1731)

Baroque music flourishes (Bach and Handel) (ca. 1724)

Voltaire's Zaire; London's Covent Garden Theater built (1732)

Swift's Gulliver's Travels (1726)

1730

English Licensing Act (1737)

John Key's "flying shuttle" loom patented (1733)

Voltaire's Mahomet; Macklin's Shylock—an attempt at costume reform (1741)

Rococo style flourishes (1737)

Garrick becomes actor-manager at Drury Lane (1747)

1740

Frederick the Great of Prussia, "enlightened despot" (1740)

Goldoni's The Comic Theater (1750)

Hallams in Virginia (1752)

Voltaire's Orphan of China (1755)

1750

Encyclopédie begun (1750)

Spectators banished from French stage (ca. 1759)

French and Indian War (1754)

Seven Years' War begins (1756)

Boulevard theaters begin to develop in France (ca. 1760)

Piranesi continues to paint his "prison drawings" using chiaroscuro (1761)

Voltaire's Candide (1759)

1760

Gozzi's Turandot (1762)

Rousseau's Social Contract; Catherine the Great of Russia begins reign (1762)

Drottningholm completed; Southwark Theater in Philadelphia (1766)

James Watt patents a steam engine (1769)

1770

John Street Theater in New York (1767)
Lessing's Hamburg Dramaturgy (1767–1769)
Hamburg National Theater (1767–1769)
"Storm and stress" movement (1767–1787)

Declaration of Independence (American Revolution 1775–1783); Adam Smith's Wealth of Nations (1776)

1780

Goethe's Goetz von Berlichingen; Goldsmith's She Stoops to Conquer (1773)

Goya's Don Manuel de Zuniga; James Watt patents a locomotive (1784)

Sheridan's The School for Scandal (1777)

Mozart's Don Giovanni (1787)

1790

French Revolution (1789)

David's Murder of Marat (1793)

Goethe "directs" Weimar court theater; Schiller assists (1798)

Consulate of Napoleon (1799)

1800

Schiller's Mary Stuart (1800)

trade affected populations worldwide. The major eighteenth-century mercantile powers were England and France, and decisions made in these two nations directly affected people in such places as North America, India, and Africa. One effect on Africa, for example, was a marked increase in the slave trade.

Because of the growth in trade, western Europe prospered more than ever before, and ingenious and daring investors of capital became extremely wealthy. Profits from colonial trade filtered down to the emerging middle class, which included merchants and others in commercial enterprises and which now became a social as well as a political force.

There were so many new developments in learning and philosophy that the eighteenth century is called the *age of enlightenment*. The search for knowledge was supported by the educated middle class, and though France was its center, the enlightenment had international reverberations.

Two major political and social upheavals, the American Revolution (1775–1783) and the French Revolution (1789–1799), were based on ideals of the enlightenment. Unfortunately, the ideals of the French Revolution were compromised by the Reign of Terror; instead of liberty, equality, and fraternity, the French in 1799 wound up with Napoleon.

Much of the new knowledge that characterized this era had practical applications. Inventions of the late eighteenth century facilitated the industrial revolution in the nineteenth century; the flying shuttle, the spinning jenny, and the cotton gin revolutionized the textile industry. James Watt's improved steam engine revolutionized manufacturing and transportation.

In the arts of the late seventeenth and early eighteenth centuries, the predominant style was *baroque*. Baroque painters emphasized detail, color, and ornamentation to create a more total visual illusion. Renowned baroque composers achieved unity of mood and continuity of line, but their music—like baroque painting—was filled with movement and action.

The complexity of eighteenth-century society was mirrored in an extremely complex theater that crossed many national boundaries and saw the rise of many new theatrical forms.

Eighteenth-Century Drama: New Dramatic Forms

The eighteenth century did not produce outstanding drama; rather, this was a time when new dramatic forms began to appear.

In terms of genre, for instance, many eighteenth-century plays deviated from traditional definitions of tragedy and comedy. The *drame,* a new French form, was a serious play that did not fit the neoclassical definition of tragedy. *Bourgeois* ("middle-class") *tragedy* and *domestic tragedy* are eighteenth-century examples of drame. Bourgeois and domestic tragedies ignored the neoclassical requirement that the chief characters be kings, queens, or nobles; their new tragic heroes and heroines were members of the emerging middle class. These plays were frequently sentimental and melodramatic, and they usually reflected eighteenth-century middle-class morality, with the virtuous being rewarded and the wicked

SENTIMENTAL COMEDY
In the 18th century in England a few types of comedy emerged which were much less amoral than Restoration comedy. One was "laughing comedy," which satirized middle-class social pretensions and values. A good example of the form is She Stoops to Conquer *by Oliver Goldsmith. The scene here is from the Illinois Shakespeare Festival.* (© Max Gerwick/Illinois Shakespeare Festival)

punished. By the close of the century, such melodrama was being written in France, Germany, and England.

The English and the French originated additional dramatic forms during this period. In England these included the satirical **ballad opera,** popularized by the success of *The Beggar's Opera* (1728) by John Gay (1685–1732), and *sentimental comedy.* Sentimental comedy of eighteenth-century England, like Restoration comedy, was comedy of manners, except that it reaffirmed middle-class morality. In later sentimental comedy, a closer balance was struck between upholding middle-class virtues and making fun of social pretensions. The major examples of this later form are *The Rivals* (1775) and *The School for Scandal* (1777) by Richard Brinsley Sheridan (1751–1816). In the emerging American theater, *The Contrast* (1787) by Royall Tyler (1757–1826) was patterned after Sheridan's sentimental comedies.

There were opponents of sentimental comedy, the best-known being the English dramatist Oliver Goldsmith (ca. 1730–1774), who wrote two plays: *The Good Natur'd Man* (1768) and *She Stoops to Conquer* (1773). Goldsmith advocated "laughing comedy," which would force audiences to laugh at their own eccentricities and absurdities.

In France, the *boulevard theaters* of Paris—so named because they were located on the Boulevard du Temple—invented many types of musical entertainments catering to popular tastes.

In the late eighteenth century, many German playwrights revolted against the neoclassical ideals. The playwright and critic Gotthold Ephraim Lessing

(1729–1781), for example, questioned the neoclassicists' interpretation of Aristotle and admired Shakespeare's dramaturgy. German admiration for Shakespeare and the Elizabethans culminated in the *Sturm und Drang* (**storm and stress**) movement, in which dramatists patterned their works on Shakespeare's extensive episodic structure, his mixture of genres, and his onstage violence. "Storm and stress"—which included such plays as *Goetz von Berlichingen* (1773) by Johann Wolfgang von Goethe (1749–1832) and *The Robbers* (1782) by Friedrich Schiller (1759–1805)—was the forerunner of nineteenth-century romanticism.

In Italy during the mid-eighteenth century, there was a struggle between the playwrights Carlo Goldoni (1707–1793) and Carlo Gozzi (1720–1806) over what direction commedia dell'arte should take: Goldoni wanted to make it less artificial, while Gozzi wanted to make it even more fantastic. Their stylistic battle foreshadows the split between realists and antirealists in the nineteenth century.

Theater Production in the Eighteenth Century

Government and Theater. In certain countries—such as England, France, and the independent German states—the eighteenth century was marked by governmental attempts to regulate theater. Frequently, however, ingenious theatrical entrepreneurs found ways to outwit the government and get around its restrictions.

We noted earlier that in 1737 the English parliament issued the Licensing Act, which restricted the presentation of drama in London to the Drury Lane and Covent Garden theaters and made the lord chamberlain responsible for licensing plays. Numerous theater practitioners tried to circumvent this act. Some managers, for example, simply opened unlicensed houses, hoping that the act would not be vigorously enforced. The manager of one unlicensed theater claimed that his audiences were paying admission to hear concerts and that his plays were being presented as a free extra.

In eighteenth-century France, the government restricted what types of plays could be produced and granted monopolies to certain theaters. In fact, the new popular entertainments presented in the boulevard theaters were invented to get around monopolies awarded to other theaters. There was also some government subsidization of theater: the Opera, the Comédie Française (the home of nonmusical drama), and the Comédie Italienne (the home of commedia dell'arte and, later, of comic opera) were the three major Parisian theaters subsidized in this way. In 1791, the leaders of the French Revolution abolished the earlier theatrical restrictions.

In Germany, government intervention in theater was of a somewhat more positive nature. Eighteenth-century Germany was not unified but consisted of several independent states, and German theater—which was struggling to become established at that time—became an important artistic force in the last part of the century. Subsidized theaters were organized in several German states, and this provided stability for theater artists, though it also meant that the government could wield control over the content of plays.

THE THEATER AT DROTTNINGHOLM, SWEDEN

This theater still has the same sets and stage machinery that were used when it was built as a court playhouse in the eighteenth century. It is an excellent example of an Italianate proscenium theater with the pole-and-chariot system for changing scenery. Each summer, period productions are staged, such as the one shown here: Iphegenia in Aulis. *(© Bengt Wanselius/ Drottningholms Slottsteater)*

STAGE MACHINERY AT DROTTNINGHOLM

Since this building still has the machinery found in an Italianate proscenium theater of the eighteenth century, productions there today continue to use the same technology. Here, contemporary stagehands use its pole-and-chariot system to execute a scene change. (Drottningholms Slottsteater)

Eighteenth-Century Theater Architecture. The basic configuration of eighteenth-century continental theaters followed the Italian Renaissance tradition; but to accommodate the new middle-class audiences, both continental and English theaters became larger. The interiors were usually egg-shaped, to improve sight lines. In England, playhouses moved more toward the continental model: the apron shrank to about 12 feet, and the area behind the proscenium became much deeper.

Throughout Europe—in such countries as Germany, Russia, and Sweden—theater buildings proliferated during the eighteenth century. From our own point of view, one of the most significant theater buildings of this period is Drottningholm in Sweden, erected in 1766 as part of the royal summer palace outside of Stockholm. Drottningholm was boarded up in the 1790s and remained closed until the twentieth century, when it was reopened. Today tourists there can explore a perfect working example of an eighteenth-century theater.

In the United States, during the colonial era and after the American Revolution, permanent theaters were constructed following the English model.

The Marriage of Figaro

1784, Paris, France It is a brisk spring day in May of 1784. In Paris, the Comédie Française is giving a performance in its new theater building, which opened 2 years ago. With great expectations, Parisians depart early so that they can arrive at the theater before the starting time, 5:30. Tonight they are to see Beaumarchais's new play *The Marriage of Figaro*.

The Comédie Française is noted not only for traditional neoclassical drama but also for new drama by French authors. At this performance, there will be dance presentations between the acts of the play and also a short, comic afterpiece following *The Marriage of Figaro*. Not since *Tartuffe* has there been such controversy over a play.

The Marriage of Figaro—set in Spain—is about an older man's attempt to seduce a servant girl, and its key character is a comic servant; Beaumarchais introduced his characters several years ago, in *The Barber of Seville*. The real point of *The Marriage of Figaro* is social and political satire, and it is this that is controversial. Because of the controversy, the king, Louis XVI, has refused to give his permission for its production. Despite this, however, it has been performed continuously since its opening in April and is clearly a success. People who were present on the opening night have reported that the theater was filled hours beforehand and that some of the audience members had brought food with them so that they would not have to risk losing their seats by leaving the theater to eat.

As the spectators enter the theater, they are struck by its size and beauty. Remarkably, everyone in the audience now has a place to sit. In earlier French theaters, the pit in front of the stage had no seats, and people in that area stood during performances; in fact, people in the old seatless pits would move about and socialize. The new seats are controversial—Parisians enjoyed the social ambience of the old pit, and one of the leading playwrights of the day, Louis Sébastian Mercier, has publicly criticized the addition of benches. The audience area is egg-shaped; this configuration, at least, will be welcome, making it easier for everyone in the audience to see the action onstage. Like older theaters, the new Comédie Française has three rows of boxes with a row of galleries above those. Spectators who cannot afford the more expensive sections take their place in the pit, sitting on the new benches.

When the curtain rises, the spectators are impressed at once by the stage, which is large and very deep. However, it has a smaller apron than the company's previous theaters had: the actors and actresses must all perform behind the proscenium arch. The scenery is painted and will be changed by wings and shutters. As the play begins, the spectators are very excited, because they are seeing performers they have heard much about.

The plot of *The Marriage of Figaro* is full of intrigue, unexpected twists, and great comic moments. Figaro, the servant, is engaged to marry Suzanne, who is also a servant; but his master, Count Almaviva, wants to sleep with her himself. The count has been unfaithful to his wife, and we watch with great enjoyment the various complications that develop as he tries to conquer another woman but is thwarted. At the end of the play, the count is exposed in his plotting and is humiliated; he pledges fidelity to his wife, and Figaro and Suzanne are brought together.

As the Parisians walk home, they relive many of the comic moments in the play. Yet they also understand why this seemingly simple, farcical work has caused such a political furor. It is the master who is ridiculed and frustrated: despite his social rank, his machinations are futile and his clever servants outwit him. Clearly, Beaumarchais is questioning the social structure of France. Some people are saying that this play threatens society with the same kind of revolution that has taken place in the new world. Are these people right? Was the king right to be concerned about the political implications of this comedy? These questions remain long after the evening at the Comédie Française.

Scenery, Lighting, and Costumes.

In the eighteenth century, as in the Renaissance, Italy was the birthplace of many scenic innovations. The most influential Italian designers and theater architects of the period were the Bibienas—an extended family that included several generations of designers. One innovation by the Bibienas was *angular* or *multipoint perspective*. Previously, the painted sets used during the Italian Renaissance pulled the eye to a central vanishing point and appeared to be totally framed and enclosed by the proscenium arch. In the Bibienas' designs, the eye was attracted to various vanishing points, and the set seemed to extend beyond the proscenium. Typically, the Bibienas' designs were grandiose, lavish, and ornate.

Elsewhere, Italian influence was pervasive in eighteenth-century scene design. Most continental theaters used wing-and-shutter settings, painted in perspective and shifted by Torelli's pole-and-chariot mechanism. Additional elements occa-

A BIBIENA SET DESIGN

During the eighteenth century, one family dominated scene design in Europe: the Bibiena family, whose second, third, and fourth generations carried on the tradition begun by Giovanni Bibiena. This engraved stage design by Giuseppi Bibiena (1696–1757) is typical of the family's work, with its vast scale, ornateness, and elegance, and its perspective vista disappearing in several directions. (Victoria and Albert Museum, London) sionally incorporated into the painted designs included (1) borders at the top to mask the fly space; (2) *ground rows* (silhouette cutouts along the stage floor); (3) large scenic cutouts, such as painted trees, which could be shifted by the pole-and-chariot system; (4) rolled backdrops, which replaced the shutters; and (5) *act drops*—curtains at the front of the stage.

A few historians have argued that sometime between the Renaissance and the eighteenth century, Italian designers also introduced the **box set:** the use of flats to create three sides of a room onstage. We will look at the development of the box set more closely when we discuss nineteenth-century theater.

There were also experiments with stage lighting in the late 1700s, including attempts to mask lighting sources, to use silk screens for coloring, and to replace candles with oil lamps and other sources. These lighting sources were not easily controlled, however, and the auditorium as well as the stage had to remain lit.

Unlike scenery and lighting, theatrical costuming remained undeveloped throughout most of the eighteenth century. Actors and actresses—who often provided their own wardrobes—believed that the chief criterion for a costume was to show the performer off to the best advantage. Daring theater artists throughout Europe experimented with historically accurate costuming, but their attempts rarely resulted in the kind of historical reconstructions we see today.

Acting in the Eighteenth Century. If the plays of the eighteenth century were not noteworthy, the performers often were. This was an age that glorified star performers. All across Europe, successful actors and actresses developed dedicated followings.

The predominant approach to acting in the eighteenth century was *bombastic,* emphasizing the performer's oratorical skills. More often than not, performers addressed their lines to the audience rather than the character to whom they were supposed to be speaking. Standardized patterns of stage movement were necessary because rehearsal time was limited and bills were changed frequently.

In the midst of these conventional practices, however, there were some innovators. Among those who rebelled against the bombastic, conventionalized style were the English actors Charles Macklin (ca. 1700–1797) and David Garrick (1717–1779). Macklin and Garrick rejected formal declamation, stereotyped patterns of blocking (prescribed movements onstage), and singsong delivery of verse. They both favored individualized characterizations and wanted more careful rehearsal procedures.

The Emergence of the Director. In terms of the future, possibly the key development during the eighteenth century was the first emergence of the modern director. Before then, playwrights or leading performers normally doubled as directors of stage business, and actual directing was minimal; furthermore, little time was spent on preparing a production in rehearsal. What was missing in theater was someone to oversee and unify stage productions, assist performers, and ensure the appropriateness of visual elements. Two eighteenth-century figures are often considered the forerunners of the modern stage director because they assumed these responsibilities: the English actor David Garrick and the German playwright, poet, and novelist Johann Wolfgang von Goethe.

Between 1747 and 1776, David Garrick was a partner in the management of the Drury Lane Theater and was therefore responsible for all major artistic decisions. As the company's leading performer, he championed a more natural style of acting and argued for careful development of characters' individual traits as well as for thorough preparation and research; and his work as a director was in keeping with these theories of acting. In contrast to the usual eighteenth-century custom, Garrick's rehearsals were quite extended, sometimes lasting for weeks. Garrick was also a strict disciplinarian: he required his performers to be on time, to know their lines, and to act during rehearsals—not simply recite—moreover, he established penalties for infractions of these rules. As part of his reform of stage practices, Garrick also banished spectators from the stage.

Goethe, unlike Garrick, was not restricted by commercialism, nor was he an actor in the company he directed. In 1775, Goethe—by then a famous author—was invited to oversee the court theater at Weimar in Germany. Initially, Goethe did not take his theater duties seriously, but by the 1790s he had become enthusiastic about the theater and had become a *régisseur,* or dictatorial director. (*Régisseur* is the French term for "director.")

Goethe rehearsed for lengthy periods and expected his performers to work as an ensemble; like Garrick, he penalized those who broke his rehearsal rules. He

DAVID GARRICK IN VENICE PRESERVED

The eighteenth century was an era of great stars, some of whom paid close attention to details of performance and costuming to achieve a greater sense of reality. David Garrick, seen here in a production at Drury Lane in 1762 of a tragedy by Thomas Otway (1652–1685), was considered the finest English actor of his day. (Victoria and Albert Museum, London)

Part 2   Theater Tradition and Theater Today

established rules for stage movement and vocal technique—he worked on instituting a uniform stage speech rather than a variety of dialects—and he also set rules for his performers' behavior in their personal lives. He even laid down rules for the conduct of his audiences; the only appropriate audience reactions, he insisted, were applause and withholding applause. Our modern tradition of audience decorum can be traced back to Goethe.

Goethe did not advocate a completely natural style of acting; he believed, for instance, that performers should speak facing the audience rather than each other. He used routine blocking patterns, although he did emphasize careful stage composition, that is, the pictorial arrangement of performers onstage. Goethe oversaw settings and costumes and believed in historical accuracy.

The Nineteenth Century

Background: A Time of Social Change

Major social changes took place in the period from 1800 to 1875, including the industrial revolution—which entailed the replacement of hand tools and human power by machinery, the development of the factory, and an expansion of the urban working class. The industrial revolution also involved technological advances such as steam power, expanded means of transportation, and new modes of communication. Another major development was the rise of nationalism.

There was also intellectual ferment. Two especially significant theoretical works were Charles Darwin's *Origin of Species* (1859) and Karl Marx's *Das Kapital* (*Capital;* 1867). Darwin's work, which dealt with evolution, questioned traditional religious concepts; Marx's work questioned the capitalist system, which was the driving economic force of the industrial revolution.

These societal transformations had a major impact on the nature of theater. Nineteenth-century theater built on the innovations of the eighteenth century and paved the way for modern theater.

Theater in Nineteenth-Century Life

Before examining specific transformations in drama and production techniques during the nineteenth century, we should look at the unique place theater held at that time. Between 1800 and 1875, the dramatic arts exploded. The masses who filled the fast-growing cities demanded theater; it was a passion, a fad, and also a seeming necessity for these new audiences. Nineteenth-century theater, therefore, was a true popular entertainment that attracted huge numbers of spectators and helped audiences to forget—momentarily, at least—the cares and drudgery of daily life. The escapist dramas of the period were written quickly and often not too well, but they were immensely popular and reflected social concerns.

Nonliterary forms of entertainment also attracted the masses. The American public, for example, supported such popular arts as the *minstrel show, burlesque, variety,* and *circus.* Throughout the nineteenth century, concert halls, saloons, and playhouses presented collections of entertainments—including songs, dances,

Nineteenth Century, 1800 to 1875
Year, A.D.

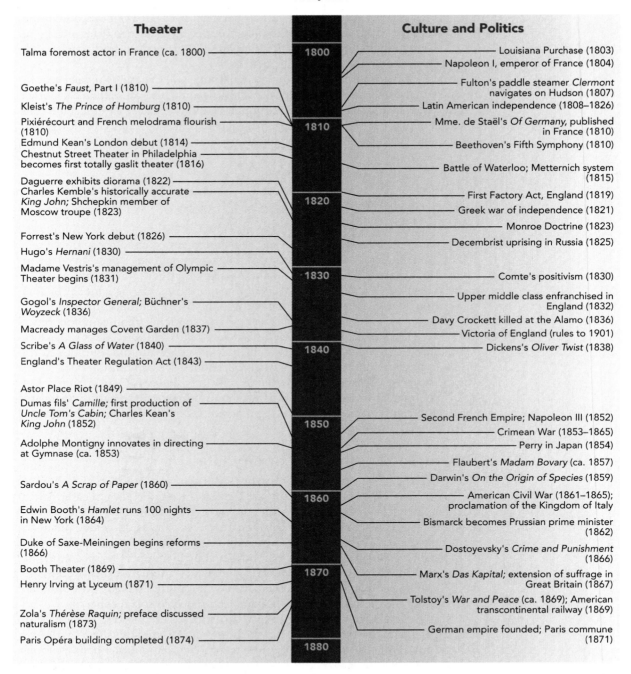

Theater

Talma foremost actor in France (ca. 1800)

Goethe's *Faust*, Part I (1810)

Kleist's *The Prince of Homburg* (1810)

Pixiérécourt and French melodrama flourish (1810)

Edmund Kean's London debut (1814)

Chestnut Street Theater in Philadelphia becomes first totally gaslit theater (1816)

Daguerre exhibits diorama (1822)

Charles Kemble's historically accurate *King John*; Shchepkin member of Moscow troupe (1823)

Forrest's New York debut (1826)

Hugo's *Hernani* (1830)

Madame Vestris's management of Olympic Theater begins (1831)

Gogol's *Inspector General*; Büchner's *Woyzeck* (1836)

Macready manages Covent Garden (1837)

Scribe's *A Glass of Water* (1840)

England's Theater Regulation Act (1843)

Astor Place Riot (1849)

Dumas fils' *Camille*; first production of *Uncle Tom's Cabin*; Charles Kean's *King John* (1852)

Adolphe Montigny innovates in directing at Gymnase (ca. 1853)

Sardou's *A Scrap of Paper* (1860)

Edwin Booth's *Hamlet* runs 100 nights in New York (1864)

Duke of Saxe-Meiningen begins reforms (1866)

Booth Theater (1869)

Henry Irving at Lyceum (1871)

Zola's *Thérèse Raquin*; preface discussed naturalism (1873)

Paris Opéra building completed (1874)

Culture and Politics

Louisiana Purchase (1803)

Napoleon I, emperor of France (1804)

Fulton's paddle steamer *Clermont* navigates on Hudson (1807)

Latin American independence (1808–1826)

Mme. de Staël's *Of Germany*, published in France (1810)

Beethoven's Fifth Symphony (1810)

Battle of Waterloo; Metternich system (1815)

First Factory Act, England (1819)

Greek war of independence (1821)

Monroe Doctrine (1823)

Decembrist uprising in Russia (1825)

Comte's positivism (1830)

Upper middle class enfranchised in England (1832)

Davy Crockett killed at the Alamo (1836)

Victoria of England (rules to 1901)

Dickens's *Oliver Twist* (1838)

Second French Empire; Napoleon III (1852)

Crimean War (1853–1865)

Perry in Japan (1854)

Flaubert's *Madam Bovary* (ca. 1857)

Darwin's *On the Origin of Species* (1859)

American Civil War (1861–1865); proclamation of the Kingdom of Italy

Bismarck becomes Prussian prime minister (1862)

Dostoyevsky's *Crime and Punishment* (1866)

Marx's *Das Kapital*; extension of suffrage in Great Britain (1867)

Tolstoy's *War and Peace* (ca. 1869); American transcontinental railway (1869)

German empire founded; Paris commune (1871)

1800
1810
1820
1830
1840
1850
1860
1870
1880

Part 2 Theater Tradition and Theater Today

acrobatics, and animal acts—on one bill; these developed into the popular variety and vaudeville presentations at the turn of the century and the early twentieth century. The renowned popularizer of the circus, P. T. Barnum (1810–1891), merits special mention. Barnum developed the art of spectacular advertising to attract audiences to his entertainments; when he became involved with the circus in the 1850s, he advertised it as the "greatest show on earth." The wide variety of attractions to which audiences responded in the nineteenth century is a prime example of the tradition of popular entertainments of which we have spoken in earlier chapters.

The increase in numbers of spectators and types of entertainments resulted in the construction of more and larger playhouses throughout the western world. With improvements in rail transportation, the dramatic arts were also brought to new places and new audiences.

The passion that audiences felt for theater helps to explain several infamous theater riots, which reflected not only the intense emotional involvement of audiences but also pervasive social upheavals. The most violent of the nineteenth-century riots occurred outside New York's Astor Place Theater in lower Manhattan and grew out of rivalry between the English star William Charles Macready (1793–1873) and the American star Edwin Forrest (1806–1872). Forrest, who was noted for his portrayals of melodramatic heroes, had made an unsuccessful English tour; he blamed its failure on Macready, whose performance style was more subtle and realistic. When Macready appeared at the Astor Place Theater on May 8, 1849, Forrest's working-class fans prevented the performance.

ASTOR PLACE RIOT
This riot, in New York in 1849, was the result of nationalistic fervor and the passionate involvement of theater audiences. The riot broke out when working-class fans of the American star Edwin Forrest attacked the theater in which the English actor William Charles Macready, who had supposedly insulted Forrest, was performing. (The Metropolitan Museum of Art, bequest of Edward W. C. Arnold, 1954)

GOETHE'S FAUST
The greatest nineteenth-century romantic drama was Goethe's Faust, *which is written in two parts. It follows the pattern of episodic Shakespearean drama and deals with the temptation of Faust by Mephistopheles. Shown here is a scene from Peter Stein's full-length production staged in Germany in 2000. (© Ruth Walz)*

Macready was persuaded by his aristocratic admirers to appear again two nights later, on May 10, but this performance brought out a mob of 15,000 who assembled outside the playhouse and began to attack it. The infantry was called out to disperse the mob, and by the time the riot ended, twenty-two people had been killed.

The popularity of theater between 1800 and 1875 has not been equaled in modern times. Partial parallels could be drawn to movies and television, which present similar kinds of entertainment, attract mass audiences, and feature popular stars. Still, the passion of nineteenth-century audiences has rarely been aroused by other forms of entertainment. In our own time, the only equivalent might be the emotional intensity of audiences at rock concerts.

Nineteenth-Century Dramatic Forms

Two major forms of drama that came to the fore between 1800 and 1875 were romanticism and melodrama.

Romanticism. *Romanticism,* influenced by the German "storm and stress" movement, was a revolutionary literary trend of the first half of the nineteenth century. The most noted romantic dramas of the period were Goethe's *Faust* (Part 1, 1808; and Part 2, 1831) and Victor Hugo's *Hernani* (1830).

The romantics were revolutionary partly because they rejected the neoclassical rules; in fact, they rejected all artistic rules, believing that genius creates its own rules. Since many of the romantics adopted Shakespeare's structural techniques, their plays were episodic and epic in scope; but unlike Shakespeare, they were often more interested in creating dramatic mood and atmosphere than in developing believable plots or depth of character. The romantic hero was frequently a social outcast—a bandit, for example—who sought justice, knowledge, and truth. One of the most common romantic themes was the gulf between human beings' spiritual aspirations and their physical limitations.

Melodrama. Another dramatic form that came to the forefront in the nineteenth century was melodrama. As was discussed in Chapter 8, *melodrama* literally means "song drama" or "music drama"—a reference to the background music that accompanied these plays.

In nineteenth-century melodrama, the emphasis was on surface effects, especially effects evoking suspense, fear, nostalgia, and other strong emotions in the audience. The conflict between good and evil was clearly established: melodramatic heroes and heroines stood in sharp contrast to villains, and the audience sympathized with the good characters and despised the bad ones. Virtue was always victorious.

To hold the audience's interest, melodramas had suspenseful plots, with a climactic moment at the end of each act (the modern equivalent would be a television drama which has a car crash or a sudden confrontation just before a commercial break). Since melodrama is primarily an escapist form, visual spectacle and special effects were important.

THE WELL-MADE PLAY

A type of drama that came to prominence in the nineteenth century was the well-made play, meaning a play that was carefully constructed and featured unity of action and often unity of time and place as well. It incorporated a tightly managed plot with a strong cause-and-effect sequence of events. An example is The Heiress, *adapted by Ruth and Augustus Goetz from a book by Henry James. Shown here in a Lincoln Center Theater production is Cherry Jones in the title role and Jon Tenney as a duplicitous suitor who takes advantage of her.* (© T. Charles Erickson)

The Well-Made Play. Many popular melodramas of the nineteenth century had a structure described by the term *well-made play.* In the twentieth century, this term came to mean a play which builds mechanically to its climactic moments and is intended mainly to arouse the audience's interest in these contrived climaxes, rather than create truthful characterizations or emotions. When critics today describe a play as *well-made,* they are often being condescending. However, in the nineteenth century the term was complimentary: a well-made play was one that represented excellent craft, and the term itself implied admiration for all well-crafted goods of the industrial revolution. It is also true that this kind of structure was sometimes used creatively by later dramatists.

A well-made play has a tightly constructed cause-and-effect development, and its action often revolves around a secret known to the audience but not to the characters. The opening scenes carefully spell out the necessary background information, or *exposition.* Throughout the play, the dramatic action is clearly foreshadowed, and each act builds to a climax. In the major scene, known as the *obligatory scene,* the opposed characters confront each other in a showdown. The plot is carefully resolved so that there are no loose ends.

The two most famous writers of well-made plays were both French: Eugène Scribe (1791–1861) and Victorien Sardou (1831–1908).

Making Connections:

Nineteenth-Century Popular Theatrical Arts

POPULAR ARTS
During the nineteenth century, a significant number of highly theatrical popular entertainments developed. Among these was the circus. The American entrepeneur, P. T. Barnum, was a key innovator in developing the circus as we know it today. Seen here are female trapeze artists, performing in 1890. (Library of Congress)

As we have noted, it is hard to distinguish between the popular entertainments of the nineteenth century and the theater of that era. Many of the popular forms were presented in theaters, and many traditional dramas were adopted for spaces that usually held mass audience entertainments.

The nineteenth century saw an explosion of museums, musical halls, and circuses. The American who was world-renowned for his ability to draw mass audiences was P. (Phineas) T. (Taylor) Barnum (1810–1891), who in 1841 opened the American Museum, in which he exhibited human curiosities and also staged concerts and plays, including many temperance melodramas. Later, in the early 1870s, Barnum was also instrumental in developing the three-ring circus as we know it today. But even before Barnum, there were circus rings that housed clowns, equestrian performances, trained animal acts, and pantomimes. In the early nineteenth century, dramas staged on horseback were presented in many of these spaces.

The music halls of England served food and drink and had a small platform stage for popular song and dance presentations. A master of ceremonies moved the show along, providing comic interludes. By the end of the 1800s, these early music halls evolved into theatrical spaces dedicated exclusively to the presentation of these musical performances.

The nineteenth century also saw the development of many other forms of popular entertainments, including wild west shows, vaudeville, and minstrelsy. *Wild west* shows (or exhibitions), popular in the last quarter of the nineteenth century, presented heroic figures of the west as well as Native Americans, most often to audiences in the eastern United States who had little real contact with that world.

Minstrel shows were variety shows that featured white performers wearing blackface, and caricaturing African Americans. Later in the nineteenth century, there were African American minstrel troupes. Vaudeville was a series of variety acts—music, sketches, juggling, animal acts—that made up an evening's entertainment.

The intertwining of the popular arts and theater made the two almost indistinguishable. Furthermore, many of the popular forms developed in the nineteenth century continue to have an impact on our performance arts. For example, the well-known Canadian circus troupe Cirque du Soleil stages productions that break the boundaries between a popular art and theater. Television has incorporated the tradition of vaudeville and variety.

Theater Production in the Nineteenth Century

EDWIN BOOTH

An outstanding actor of the nineteenth century was Edwin Booth, famous for his portrayal of Hamlet (shown here), and other Shakespearean characters, as well as for building his own theater. As a performer, he was renowned for the depth of character, as well as grace and freedom from mannerisms with which he imbued the parts he played. In an age of stage posturing, he adopted a more natural approach in his roles. (Corbis-Bettmann)

Performers and Acting. Even more than in the eighteenth century, the nineteenth century was an era of great stars; performers throughout the world were idolized by the audiences who flocked to see them. Some of these performers amassed—and frequently lost—fortunes, and a number of them were not only national but international figures. Major changes in the business and art of acting were caused partly by the rise of the star performer.

During the nineteenth century, the traditional *repertory company,* a troupe of actors and actresses performing together for a set period of time in a number of plays, gradually disappeared. Early in the century, touring stars had performed with local repertory companies, but as transportation improved, not only stars but full productions—known as *combination companies*—began to tour, replacing the local repertory troupes. At about the same time, the long run became more common: popular plays might run for more than 100 consecutive performances.

Most performers of the period acted in the classical, romantic, and melodramatic styles. Many, however, moved toward modern realism: they were dedicated to true-to-life acting, in which stage movements, vocal patterns, and characterizations reflected the everyday world. Among such more realistic performers were the American Edwin Booth (1833–1893) and the Italian Eleonora Duse (1858–1924).

Nineteenth-Century Developments in Directing. The art of directing, pioneered by David Garrick and Johann Wolfgang von Goethe in the eighteenth century, was refined and developed in the nineteenth century. The goal of innovative nineteenth-century directors was to create a unified stage picture, particularly by allotting more time for rehearsal and paying more attention to production details. Many of them also experimented with historical accuracy in scenery and costuming, and some asked for a more realistic style of performance.

ELEONORA DUSE
Duse was the great Italian actress of the late nineteenth and early twentieth century. She was known for her more realistic acting style. The English playwright George Bernard Shaw considered her a greater performer than Sarah Bernhardt. (Culver Pictures)

In England and the United States, numerous performer-managers took great interest and care in creating stage productions. On the European continent, a number of people significantly developed the art of directing, including two Germans—the opera composer Richard Wagner (1813–1883) and George II (1826–1914), duke of Saxe-Meiningen—who were not actors within their companies and thus were closer to our modern idea of the director.

Wagner's concept of a totally unified artwork—the *Gesamtkunstwerk*—controlled by one person influenced twentieth-century theories of "total theater" and directing. He believed that an opera, which is made up of many musical and theatrical elements, needs a controlling figure to unify it. He insisted that this figure must have dictatorial control; at his Bayreuth Festspielhaus, he put this theory into practice, becoming its *régisseur,* or "director." Wagner's innovations for increasing stage illusion are particularly important. Musicians were forbidden to tune their instruments in the orchestra pit, and audiences were not supposed to applaud during the course of a presentation. Wagner is also often credited with being the first director to extinguish the house lights in order to focus the audience's attention on the stage.

In 1866, the duke of Saxe-Meiningen—a small state in northwestern Germany—took control of his court theater; and between 1874 and 1890 he made the Meiningen Players the most renowned company in the world. A major reason for his ability to organize such a successful theatrical venture was his enormous wealth, but this was not the only reason. Assisted by his wife and an actor in the company, he revolutionized stage production. He rehearsed for extensive periods of time, refusing to open a show until he believed it was ready. He was opposed to the star system and employed mostly young performers. His productions were especially famous for intricately planned crowd scenes and were also admired for their historically accurate settings and costumes. Because his company toured frequently to other countries, the duke's theatrical innovations became well known throughout Europe and his work had a marked influence on later directors of realistic drama.

Nineteenth-Century Theater Architecture. Between 1800 and midcentury, many playhouses were enlarged to meet the demands of the expanding lower-class urban audiences. By the 1860s, however, there was a shift away from the construction of huge theaters—a shift caused by the development of playhouses in European and American urban centers that catered to specific segments of society.

The traditional proscenium arch and "pit, box, and gallery" arrangement dominated theater buildings in the nineteenth century; but in a few cases the pit had comfortable individual seats and thus was equivalent to the modern *orchestra.*

In the United States, the Booth Theater was completed in 1869 for the renowned American Shakespearean actor Edwin Booth. This is often cited as the first modern theater in New York City. Instead of a pit and galleries, it had a modern orchestra area and balconies, although there were boxes on both sides of the proscenium arch. The seats were individual armchairs. The stage in Booth's theater was revolutionary: it was not raked, and it had no grooves. Scenery could be raised from the basement by elevators or dropped in ("flown in") from above, and scenic pieces were often supported by braces. The fly space was high enough to accommodate scenic drops without their being rolled up.

Another innovative nineteenth-century theater building, the Bayreuth Festspielhaus, built for Richard Wagner, opened in 1876. This theater also broke with the earlier "pit, box, and gallery" tradition. Wagner wanted seating that would not emphasize class distinctions, and so his theater had 1,300 individual seats in thirty raked rows, forming a fan-shaped auditorium. Audiences exited at the ends of the rows, an arrangement known as *continental seating*. There was also a 300-seat balcony and a sunken orchestra pit. All seats in this house cost the same.

Scenery, Costumes, and Lighting. Eighteenth-century experiments with realistic devices and conventions in scenery and costuming were carried even further in the nineteenth century. Historical accuracy in sets and costumes became more common with the increasing availability of works of historical research. This new knowledge about the past—combined with the fascination with antiquity that characterized the nineteenth century—led various theater artists, including the duke of Saxe-Meiningen, to mount historically accurate productions. In Saxe-Meiningen's presentations, costumes were carefully researched and authentic materials were used, regardless of their cost. The same careful attention was given to the settings the duke designed.

Wing-and-shutter settings shifted by pole-and-chariot or groove systems gradually disappeared during the nineteenth century, as alternatives to painted sets were introduced. The most significant alternative was the ***box set,*** an arrangement in which flats are cleated together at angles—rather than set up parallel to the audience—to form the walls of a three-dimensional room. As noted previously, the box set may have been introduced as early as the Renaissance, but it was in the nineteenth century that box sets revolutionized scene design. Between 1800 and 1875, a number of theatrical artists used this three-dimensional setting, often furnishing it with practical elements, such as doors and windows.

During this same period, the technology of the industrial revolution was introduced into theater. New means of scene shifting were developed: by the close of the century, the *elevator stage* (which allows sections of a stage floor, or even the entire floor, to be raised or lowered) and the *revolving stage* were perfected. The latter is a large turntable on which scenery is placed; as it moves, one set turns out of sight and another is brought into view.

Nineteenth-century technology also revolutionized stage lighting. In 1816, Philadelphia's Chestnut Street Theater became the world's first playhouse to be completely gaslit. Gaslight allowed control of the intensity of lighting in all parts of the theater; and by the middle of the century, the *gas table*—the equivalent of a modern dimmer board—enabled one stagehand to control all the stage lighting.

**NINETEENTH-CENTURY
THEATER
ARCHITECTURE**
*Significant changes took
place in theater architecture
in the 1800s. The
illustration of Covent
Garden in London (top)
shows a typical "pit, box,
and gallery" theater of the
era. The illustration of
Wagner's Bayreuth
Festspielhaus (bottom),
however, shows that by
1876 significant
transformations were
occurring.* (Victoria and
Albert Museum, London)

Thomas Edison's incandescent lamp, invented in 1879, further revolutionized stage lighting. By 1881, London's Savoy Theater was using incandescent lighting, though some other playhouse may actually have used it earlier. Electricity, of course, is the most flexible, most controllable, and safest form of theater lighting.

By 1875, theater was about to enter the modern era: the seeds of theatrical realism—as well as of reactions against realism—had been gradually planted since the Renaissance. In Chapter 14, we turn to the beginnings of the modern era: the development of realism and early reactions against the new realistic theater. In Chapter 15 we explore these and other developments in modern theater.

SUMMARY

The theater of the English Restoration combined aspects of English and continental Renaissance theater. Restoration drama had elements of both Elizabethan theater and the French theater of Molière. The Restoration stage also had native and continental elements: its modified proscenium came from French and Italian practice, but its elongated apron came from Elizabethan theaters.

In the eighteenth century, there were many attempts throughout Europe to break away from the Italianate tradition. Theaters were still constructed as proscenium-arch spaces, but their shapes and sizes changed. Revolutionary authors—especially the "storm and stress" dramatists of the late 1700s—abandoned the neoclassical ideals. Many new genres which ignored the Italian Renaissance rules were developed, including bawdy Restoration comedy, sentimental comedy, middle-class tragedy, drame, and ballad opera.

There were also attempts in the 1700s to develop unity in production; these included some primitive experiments with historical accuracy, and—especially notably—the directorial controls instituted by David Garrick and Johann Wolfgang von Goethe.

The nineteenth century was the bridge to our modern era. Comfortable modern proscenium-arch theaters, such as Booth's Theater and the Bayreuth Festspielhaus, were built. Principles of modern directing were developed and were clearly manifested in the work of the duke of Saxe-Meiningen. Historical accuracy in costuming and settings as well as expanded use of the box set added to theatrical illusionism. Theater was also affected by technological advances, such as gas lighting.

THEATER ON THE WEB

Links to eighteenth- and nineteenth-century theater are found at various sites.

Baroque   http://history.evansville.net/baroque.html/Literature and Drama
A collection of dramatic, historical, and social sites focusing on the baroque (and Restoration) period.

Theatre Resources, 18th Century   http://artsci.washington.edu/drama/jw18th.html
This site contains articles on costume, theaters, and a range of arts popular in the eighteenth century.

World of London Theatre, 1660 to 1800   http://web.nwe.ufl.edu/~craddock/lonthe1.html
A project at the University of Florida describing the theaters and the social environment of London during the Restoration.

Theatre Ephemera   http://www.neiu.edu/~rghiggin/ephem/Ephemera.html
A collection of photographs primarily from nineteenth-century theater in the United States, including playwrights, actors, productions, and theater buildings.

Imagine that you are a costume designer working on a production of Dickens's *A Christmas Carol* that will be performed in the historical Ford theater in Washington, D.C., during the winter holiday season. Use these resources to create a bibliography of links to historical articles, links to images, and links to specific information about the play. Annotate the bibliography to indicate the relevance of each link to your production.

Modern Theater: 1875 to 1945

The Birth of Realism
  Background: The Modern Era
Timeline: 1875 to 1915
  Theatrical Realism
  Realistic Playwrights
Play Synopsis: A Doll's House
  Realism and Naturalism
  Producers of Realism:
  Independent Theaters
Living History: The Sea Gull
  Realistic Theater between
  1915 and 1945

Timeline: 1915 to 1945
Departures from Realism
  Antirealist Playwrights: Ibsen,
  Strindberg, and Wedekind
  Symbolism
  Antirealist Designers: Appia
  and Craig
  Russian Theatricalism:
  Meyerhold
  Early Eclectics
  Departures from Realism:
  1915–1945
Totalitarianism, the Second
World War, and Theater
Summary

◀ HEDDA GABLER

Realistic drama was the first controversial movement of the late nineteenth century. A leading realist was the Norwegian playwright, Henrik Ibsen. One of Ibsen's important and controversial plays was Hedda Gabler *in which the heroine rebelled against the domestic life she was forced to lead. Shown here in the title role is Martha Plimpton. The production was by the Long Wharf Theatre. (© T. Charles Erickson)*

317

In the modern era, usually defined as 1875 to the present, the arts have, as always, mirrored changes occurring in society; in theater, these developments have been reflected in a great diversity of types of theater. Theater in the modern period has become increasingly eclectic and experimental. Avant-garde theater appears alongside more conventional theater, and new plays are produced while classics from the past also enjoy great popularity.

In the theater of the modern era, four major strands stand out. The first strand is realism; the second is departures from realism; the third is a continuation of traditional theater from the past—comedies, tragedies, melodramas, and spectacular extravaganzas that nineteenth-century audiences applauded; and the fourth is postmodern experimentation and forms, which seem to defy traditional categorization. In Chapters 14, 15, and 16 we will discuss all four of these strands as they developed chronologically.

In this chapter, we will begin our examination of how these four approaches developed in modern theater between 1875 and 1945.

The Birth of Realism

Background: The Modern Era

Modern theater began with the plays of three dramatists: the Norwegian Henrik Ibsen; the Swede August Strindberg; and the Russian Anton Chekhov. Their works also reflect the period when they were written—the *modern era,* which began in the late nineteenth century and continues to this day. Their plays also ushered in the techniques and the outlook that characterized western theater throughout most of the twentieth century.

In the mid-nineteenth century, profound changes began to occur in religion, philosophy, psychology, and economics. Ideas were put forth that were to challenge long-held beliefs about who we are and how we relate to the world around us. In 1859, Charles Darwin published *The Origin of Species,* which challenged the concept that human beings are special and created by God in his own image. In 1867, Karl Marx's *Das Kapital* questioned the fundamentals of capitalism. In 1900, Sigmund Freud's *Interpretation of Dreams* suggested that we are not in complete control of our actions or even our thoughts: frequently, Freud claimed, the subconscious as much as the conscious mind influences our behavior. In 1905, Albert Einstein presented the first part of his theory of relativity, which stated that many aspects of the universe which we consider fixed and immutable are subject to variation and change; by extension, people questioned whether other aspects of life are also relative rather than absolute or permanent. One result of this series of intellectual, religious, and moral challenges was that societies which had been unified now became fragmented.

Along with fragmentation, the first half of the twentieth century was marked by tremendous unrest, in both Europe and Asia. This era of unrest was ushered in by World War I, which lasted from 1914 to 1918 and resulted in 8.5 million deaths. Unrest also contributed to the Russian Revolution of 1917, which led to the establishment of the Soviet government and a costly civil war.

AUGUST STRINDBERG
*Along with Ibsen, the Swedish dramatist
August Strindberg was a pioneer in developing
modern realistic drama. These playwrights
revolutionized the theater of the late
nineteenth century by dealing with taboo
subject matter in a manner that mirrored
everyday life. Much of their work was
controversial and could not be produced
in state or commercial theaters.* (Theatre
Collection, Museum of the City of New York)

MISS JULIE
*An early, important realistic play by Strindberg
was* Miss Julie. *Driven, neurotic, and torn
between the conventional life in which she was
brought up and her desire for total freedom, the
title character is a woman of extremes. In this
scene, Laura Knight (on the right) is Julie, William
Church is the servant with whom she has a fateful
encounter, and Kristin Proctor is the cook.*
(© Richard Feldman/A.R.T. Institute for Advance
Theatre Training)

sexes: men and women vie with each other and attempt to dominate one another.
In the end, one of them is destroyed—the man in *The Father* and the woman in
Miss Julie. Also, Strindberg's characters are subject to the neuroses and anxieties
that have characterized so much of twentieth-century life.

Strindberg took realistic drama closer to naturalism, a type of realism we will
discuss shortly. In a famous preface to *Miss Julie,* he outlined how he hoped to
make the play even more lifelike than Ibsen's plays. He wanted no intermission,
so that the audience would remain absorbed in the action; he made his characters
multidimensional, giving them complex, contradictory features; he wanted the
scenery to be real, with genuine pots and pans sitting on the kitchen shelves instead of being painted on backdrops as they had been before; and he wanted the
dialogue to be interrupted and fragmentary—again, as it is in real life.

THE CHERRY ORCHARD BY CHEKHOV

The Russian dramatist Anton Chekhov created a type of modern realistic drama which has had a profound influence in the past century. Subtle, low-key, it avoided melodramatic elements but probed deeply and movingly into the hearts and souls of the characters he depicted. His final masterpiece was The Cherry Orchard *in which the main character, Madame Ranevskaya, unable to adjust to modern times, loses the family home and her precious cherry orchard. Shown here is Marina Neyolova as Ranevskaya in a production by Moscow's Sovremennik Theater. (Courtesy of the Russian-American Arts Foundation)*

Anton Chekhov. The third significant playwright in the birth of modern realism is the Russian Anton Chekhov (1860–1904), whose play *The Sea Gull* (1896) was at first a failure but was later successfully revived by the Moscow Art Theater. He wrote three other major plays: *Uncle Vanya* (1899), *The Three Sisters* (1900), and *The Cherry Orchard* (1904).

Chekhov introduced important variations to the realism of Ibsen and Strindberg. He moved away from melodramatic elements such as the suicides in Ibsen's *Hedda Gabler* and Strindberg's *Miss Julie*. He also dealt with a full gallery of characters—often twelve or fourteen rather than five or six—and he orchestrated his characters in such a way that their stories overlapped and echoed one another. Chekhov also developed a blend of tragedy and comedy, creating a genre—often referred to as *tragicomedy*—that has characterized much of modern drama; tragicomedy is discussed in Chapter 8.

Realism and Naturalism

Naturalism is a form of theater that developed alongside the realism of Ibsen, Strindberg, and Chekhov; it can be seen as a subdivision of realism or an extreme form of realism. The naturalistic movement began in France in the nineteenth century and spread to other European countries. In naturalism, everything on stage—characters, language, properties, settings, costumes—should seem to have been lifted directly from everyday life. Dramatic action should never seem contrived, but rather should look like a "slice of life."

Many of the naturalists believed that the most appropriate subject matter for drama was the lower class, and they frequently focused on the sordid and seamy aspects of society, in order to confront audiences with social problems and instigate reforms. The most famous naturalistic theorist and playwright was the French author Émile Zola (1840–1902).

Naturalism is a more stringent form than realism. One reason is its insistence on showing the stark side of life; the other is that its action cannot be shaped by the same kind of artistic techniques used in realism. Realism can use symbols and can structure events in a way that is often more aesthetically satisfying. In fact, the naturalists' extreme position ultimately prevented their movement from being more influential; realism was seen as a more viable theatrical form. In its original form, then, naturalism did not last long, though some of its ideas have shown up often in later drama as well as in films and on television, including recent reality-based TV series.

Producers of Realism: Independent Theaters

At the time when they were first written, realistic and naturalistic works were seen by the mainstream as too controversial for production; in England, for example, the lord chamberlain refused licenses to many of these works. Also, such plays were not considered commercially viable. In order to overcome this problem, a number of independent theaters were established throughout Europe. They were exempted from government censorship because they were organized as subscription companies, with theatergoers being treated like members of a private club. These independent theaters were not striving for commercial success; they presented their plays to small audiences interested in new dramatic forms.

The best-known of these independent theaters were the Théâtre Libre (Free Theater), founded in Paris in 1887 by André Antoine (1858–1943); the Freie Bühne (Free Stage), founded in Germany in 1889 by Otto Brahm (1856–1912); and the Independent Theater, founded in London in 1891 by J. T. Grein (1862–1935). In 1892, the year after its founding, the Independent Theater introduced the Irish-born George Bernard Shaw (1856–1950) to the London public by producing his first play, *Widower's Houses*. (As a theater critic, Shaw defended the realists and naturalists; he believed that drama should inspire social reform. Unlike the works of other realists, however, many of his own socially conscious dramas are comedies.)

NATURALISM

An extreme form of realism is naturalism which attempts to put on stage an unflinching, almost documentary version of people and events as they are encountered in real life. An early example is Thérèse Raquin, an 1873 drama by Émile Zola, in whose preface Zola stated the tenets of naturalism. Here we see Elizabeth Marvel and Sean Haberle in a version of the play produced by the Classic Stage Company. (© T. Charles Erickson)

The Sea Gull

1898, Moscow It is the evening of December 17, 1898, and the Moscow Art Theater is about to give its first performance of *The Sea Gull* by the Russian playwright Anton Chekhov. Backstage, the actors and actresses are nervous—so nervous that just before the curtain is to rise, most of them have taken valerian drops, a tranquilizer. Constantin Stanislavski, the director of the play, who is also playing the role of Trigorin— a bored commercial writer—finds it difficult to control a twitch in his leg.

The reason for their anxiety is easy to understand. The author, Anton Chekhov, who trained to be a doctor, is one of the best-known short-story writers in Russia. So far, however, his dramatic work has not met with the same approval as his stories. In fact, when *The Sea Gull* was first produced 2 years ago in Saint Petersburg, the performance was a fiasco, not because of the play but because the company presenting it had not rehearsed and had produced it very badly. So devastated was Chekhov by the experience that after the performance he left the theater in despair and swore never again to write plays or even to let *The Sea Gull* be performed.

One reason why the company in Saint Petersburg failed to give a decent performance of *The Sea Gull* is that the play was quite different from anything they were accustomed to. It takes place on a Russian country estate and is about two generations of actresses and writers. The leading female character, Madame Akardina, is a vain, self-absorbed actress. Her son Treplev, an ideal-istic young writer, is in love with Nina, a young woman who aspires to be an actress. Akardina's lover, Trigorin, with whom Nina falls in love, is a successful writer but dissatisfied with his life. (This is the character Stanislavski is now playing in Moscow.) A number of other people are also involved with these four main characters, and one of the unusual aspects of the play is that the characters' lives are all closely intertwined. This orchestration of a group of characters is unlike previous nine-teenth-century dramas. Another unusual aspect is an absence of melodramatic confrontations and developments, such as the murders, suicides, and sudden plot twists that had been staples of most nineteenth-century theater. Rather, the action is subtle, modulated, and true to life.

Interestingly, the same lifelike qualities that have confused so many people have attracted a playwright and producer named Vladimir Nemirovich-Danchenko— a cofounder, with Stanislavski, of the Moscow Art Theater. Nemirovich-Danchenko and Stanislavski want their theater to be different from any other, and Nemirovich-Danchenko feels that *The Sea Gull* is just the kind of play that will set it apart. However, when he first asked Chekhov to let the Moscow Art Theater present this play, Chekhov adamantly refused, because of the debacle in Saint Petersburg. It has taken all of Nemirovich-Danchenko's powers of persuasion to win Chekhov's consent.

All this explains why there is so much at stake tonight in Moscow, as Act I of *The Sea Gull* begins. Chekhov himself is so worried about the outcome that he is not even here; he is far away, in Yalta—partly because of ill health, it is true, but also because of his nervousness.

Now the performers are halfway through Act I, but they cannot tell how the audience is responding. When the act ends, they are greeted by a monumental silence. Fearing failure, the actress Olga Knipper (who will later become Chekhov's wife) fights desperately to keep from breaking into hysterical sobs. Then, all of a sudden, the silence is broken; the audience breaks into thunderous, tumultuous applause. In the words of an eyewitness: "Like the bursting of a dam, like an exploding bomb, a sudden deafening eruption of applause broke out." The applause goes on and on, and Stanislavski dances a jig. The same reaction will greet the next three acts.

Both Chekhov and the Moscow Art Theater have triumphed, and a new chapter in modern theater has begun. So significant is this event that a century later the symbol on the curtain of the Moscow Art Theater will still be a sea gull.

Possibly the most influential of the late-nineteenth-century theaters dedicated to realism was the Moscow Art Theater, which mounted a landmark production of *The Sea Gull* as well as Chekhov's other major plays. Founded in 1898 by Constantin Stanislavski (1863–1938) and Vladimir Nemirovich-Danchenko (1858–1943), it continues to produce drama today and celebrated its centennial in 1998.

In addition to giving the world an important theater, the Moscow Art Theater provided the first systematic approach to realistic acting: that of Constantin Stanislavski. The ***Stanislavski method,*** discussed in detail in Chapter 2, has formed the basis for most realistic acting in the twentieth century. Naturally, there have been variations, additions, and challenges to Stanislavski's approach, but his emphasis on the performer's immersing himself or herself in a role, preparing mentally and physically for a role, and maintaining both relaxation and concentration onstage has remained a cornerstone of realistic acting.

Realistic Theater between 1915 and 1945

Producing Organizations in the United States.   During the early decades of the twentieth century—after the initial objections and censorship had eased—realistic plays began to be presented commercially in both Europe and the United States. In the United States, however, for a long time small, independent groups like those that developed in France, Germany, and England produced these plays.

These small American theaters were part of what was called the *little theater* movement, which flourished between the two world wars. The Provincetown

THE GROUP THEATER'S
AWAKE AND SING
Clifford Odets's play, produced in 1935, is an example of a realistic social drama dealing with American concerns of the 1930s. It is an intense family drama set in a Bronx apartment during the depression, and it required the realistic acting for which the Group Theater was noted. (Billy Rose Theatre Collection, New York Public Library for the Performing Arts, Astor, Lenox, and Tilden Foundations)

1915 to 1945
Year

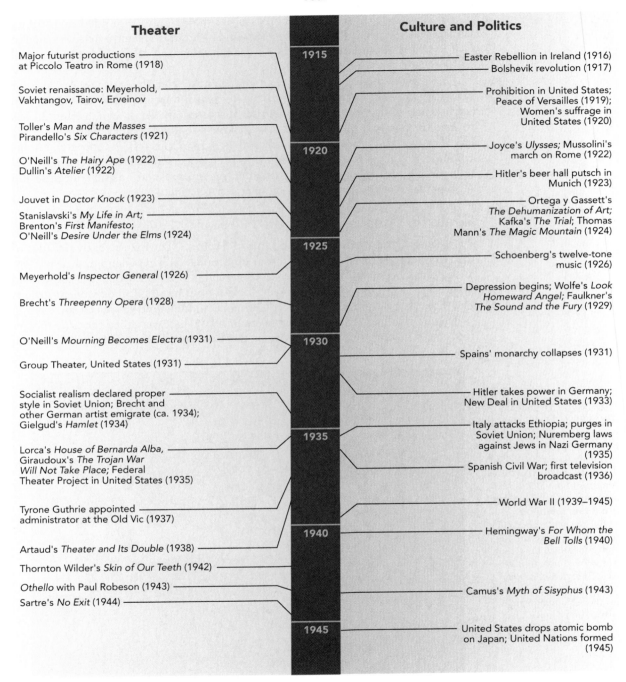

Theater

Major futurist productions at Piccolo Teatro in Rome (1918)

Soviet renaissance: Meyerhold, Vakhtangov, Tairov, Erveinov

Toller's *Man and the Masses* Pirandello's *Six Characters* (1921)

O'Neill's *The Hairy Ape* (1922) Dullin's *Atelier* (1922)

Jouvet in *Doctor Knock* (1923)

Stanislavski's *My Life in Art*; Brenton's *First Manifesto*; O'Neill's *Desire Under the Elms* (1924)

Meyerhold's *Inspector General* (1926)

Brecht's *Threepenny Opera* (1928)

O'Neill's *Mourning Becomes Electra* (1931)

Group Theater, United States (1931)

Socialist realism declared proper style in Soviet Union; Brecht and other German artist emigrate (ca. 1934); Gielgud's *Hamlet* (1934)

Lorca's *House of Bernarda Alba*, Giraudoux's *The Trojan War Will Not Take Place*; Federal Theater Project in United States (1935)

Tyrone Guthrie appointed administrator at the Old Vic (1937)

Artaud's *Theater and Its Double* (1938)

Thornton Wilder's *Skin of Our Teeth* (1942)

Othello with Paul Robeson (1943)

Sartre's *No Exit* (1944)

Culture and Politics

Easter Rebellion in Ireland (1916)
Bolshevik revolution (1917)

Prohibition in United States; Peace of Versailles (1919); Women's suffrage in United States (1920)

Joyce's *Ulysses*; Mussolini's march on Rome (1922)

Hitler's beer hall putsch in Munich (1923)

Ortega y Gassett's *The Dehumanization of Art*; Kafka's *The Trial*; Thomas Mann's *The Magic Mountain* (1924)

Schoenberg's twelve-tone music (1926)

Depression begins; Wolfe's *Look Homeward Angel*; Faulkner's *The Sound and the Fury* (1929)

Spains' monarchy collapses (1931)

Hitler takes power in Germany; New Deal in United States (1933)

Italy attacks Ethiopia; purges in Soviet Union; Nuremberg laws against Jews in Nazi Germany (1935)

Spanish Civil War; first television broadcast (1936)

World War II (1939–1945)

Hemingway's *For Whom the Bell Tolls* (1940)

Camus's *Myth of Sisyphus* (1943)

United States drops atomic bomb on Japan; United Nations formed (1945)

Years: 1915, 1920, 1925, 1930, 1935, 1940, 1945

Playhouse, the Neighborhood Playhouse, and the Washington Square Players, all founded in 1915 as alternatives to commercial theater, often presented experimental, nonrealistic work; they also offered a haven for controversial or unknown realistic drama. The Provincetown Playhouse, in particular, supported the early work of the playwright Eugene O'Neill (1888–1953).

In terms of realism, the most important producing group between World War I and World War II was the Group Theater, a noncommercial company in New York's Broadway district. The Group Theater was dedicated to presenting socially relevant drama and to introducing Stanislavski's system in the United States. Its founding members were Lee Strasberg (1901–1982), Cheryl Crawford (1902–1986), and Harold Clurman (1901–1980); and its acting company included a number of performers who became well-known in movies as well as on the stage. Its resident playwright was Clifford Odets (1906–1963), a leading realist in the 1930s; Odets's plays include *Awake and Sing* (1935) and *Golden Boy* (1937). The Group Theater disbanded in 1941, but its influence on realistic acting, directing, and playwriting continued for many years.

One additional experiment in American theater between the wars should be noted. During the depression, President Franklin Delano Roosevelt established the Works Progress Administration (WPA), which organized governmentally subsidized agencies to put the unemployed back to work. The Federal Theater Project, headed by Hallie Flanagan Davis (1890–1969), a college professor, was one of these agencies. For 4 years the Federal Theater Project supported theatrical ventures throughout the United States and helped revitalize interest in theater outside New York City. The Federal Theater also assisted aspiring African American theaters and artists, supporting, for example, an all-black production of *Macbeth* directed by Orson Welles (1915–1985). The government, for political reasons, discontinued funding the project in 1939 (many members of Congress had claimed that the project was sympathetic to communism).

After World War II, small theaters in New York (off-Broadway and off-off-Broadway) and elsewhere continued to produce difficult, controversial realistic plays, as well as experimental avant-garde works.

Realistic Playwrights between the Wars. Playwrights in many countries throughout the twentieth century continued the realistic drama initiated by Ibsen, Strindberg, and Chekhov. In Europe, for example, two Irish playwrights who had a strong impact on realism were John Millington Synge (1871–1909), in plays like *Riders to the Sea* (1904); and Sean O'Casey (1884–1964), in such works as *Juno and the Paycock* (1924) and *The Plough and the Stars* (1926).

In the United States, Eugene O'Neill wrote a number of realistic plays early in his career, including *Anna Christie* (1921) and *Desire Under the Elms* (1924). After writing experimental plays through much of the 1920s and 1930s, O'Neill later returned to realism and wrote what many consider his finest plays: *The Iceman Cometh* (1939), *A Moon for the Misbegotten* (1947), and *Long Day's Journey into Night* (produced in 1957). Another well-known realistic playwright of the 1930s and 1940s was Lillian Hellman (1905–1984).

Chapter 14 Modern Theater: 1875 to 1945

Departures from Realism

In spite of its substantial impact on our contemporary theater, as well as on film and television, theatrical realism is often seen as having serious limitations. Since the time when realism became pervasive, there have been playwrights and theorists who considered it too confining, including some of the early realists themselves. One impetus for experimenting with departures from realism is that realistic drama excludes a number of effective, long-standing theatrical devices, such as music, dance, symbolism, poetry, fantasy, and the supernatural. Some authors argue that theater can never truly be realistic, that the conventions of the art are always apparent.

From the outset of realism, then, there has been a strong countermovement of *departures from realism* or *antirealism*. Let us, therefore, turn our attention to the many artists who between 1875 and 1945 departed from the realistic traditions.

Antirealist Playwrights: Ibsen, Strindberg, and Wedekind

As we noted earlier in this chapter, Ibsen and Strindberg are remembered most for their realistic plays, but late in their careers they moved away from realism. In plays like *The Master Builder* (1892) and *When We Dead Awaken* (1899), Ibsen adopted many of the tenets of symbolism, discussed below; and August Strindberg's later antirealistic dramas, such as *A Dream Play* (1902) and *The Ghost Sonata* (1907), have been especially influential. As its title indicates, *A Dream Play* evokes the world of dreams. It deals with many of the same concerns as Strindberg's realistic drama—the destructiveness of marriage, materialism, and the class struggle. But as Strindberg says in his explanatory note to *A Dream Play*, these are dramatized in "the disconnected but apparently logical form of a dream. Everything can happen; everything is possible and likely."[1]

The German dramatist Frank Benjamin Wedekind (1864–1918), in such plays as *Spring's Awakening* (1891), combined symbolist and grotesque elements with realistic—sometimes controversial—subject matter.

Symbolism

The leading antirealistic movement between 1880 and 1910 was *symbolism.* Its major proponents were French, but it influenced playwrights and practitioners in many other countries. The symbolists believed that drama should present not mundane, day-to-day activities but the mystery of being and the infinite qualities of the human spirit. They called for poetic theater in which symbolic images rather than concrete actions would be the basic means of communicating with the audience. Probably the most renowned symbolist authors were Maurice Maeterlinck (1862–1949) in Belgium and Paul Claudel (1868–1955) in France.

Symbolist plays often seem to take place in a dreamworld, and their most important dramatic goal is not to tell a story but rather to evoke atmosphere and mood. The symbolists, unlike the realists, did not try to create individual characters; instead, symbolist characters are figures representative of the human condition. The symbolists also argued against realistic scenic detail, believing that a stage picture should have only the bare essentials necessary to evoke a dramatic universe.

DEPARTURES FROM REALISM
August Strindberg, toward the end of his career, wrote plays that departed from the realistic style. These dramas were forerunners of many of the avant-garde texts of the later twentieth century. His A Dream Play *uses the structure of a dream to break many of the conventions of realistic drama. Seen here is Penny Downie as Agnes and George Raistrick as the Lawyer, in the Royal Shakespeare Company's staging of the play. (© Donald Cooper/PhotoStage, England)*

In one way, at least, the symbolists were like the realists: both needed independently organized theater companies to produce their plays. In France, two independent theater companies were dedicated to antirealistic drama and production style. The Théâtre d'Art was organized by Paul Fort (1872–1960) in 1890; when it closed 3 years later, the Théâtre de l'Oeuvre was established by Aurélien-Marie Lugné-Poë (1869–1940), who had acted for Fort and for André Antoine at the Théâtre Libre. Possibly the most notorious of Lugné-Poë's presentations was

---

[1]August Strindberg, *A Dream Play*, trans. Walter Johnson. In *Anthology of Living Theater*, edited by Edwin Wilson and Alvin Goldfarb, McGraw-Hill, New York, 1998, p. 225.

ALFRED JARRY'S *UBU THE KING*
Jarry's play, written in 1896, is often cited as a forerunner of many antirealist movements of the twentieth century. It is an insane takeoff of King Oedipus *and a number of Shakespeare's histories and tragedies. Shown here is a production at Lincoln Center in New York.* (Billy Rose Theatre Collection, New York Public Library for the Performing Arts, Astor, Lenox, and Tilden Foundations)

not a symbolist work but a play by Alfred Jarry (1873–1907) called *Ubu the King* (1896), a takeoff in comic-book style on Shakespeare—in particular, on *Julius Caesar, Macbeth,* and the history plays. The farcical plot details how the bungling and gluttonous Ubu conspires to take over as ruler of Poland and is later dethroned by the assassinated king's only surviving son. The play's opening word, "Merdre," a takeoff on the French slang term for feces, created an immediate furor, as did many of its other scatological references.

In Ireland, the Abbey Theater and the poet William Butler Yeats (1865–1939), who was also a playwright, were associated with early symbolist drama.

Antirealist Designers: Appia and Craig

Scene designers also contributed to the departure from realistically based representations of life. Adolphe Appia (1862–1928) and Edward Gordon Craig (1872–1966), in particular, were able to present many of the symbolists' theories visually. Most of Appia's and Craig's ideas remained only in the form of sketches or drawings, but these ideas had great significance for twentieth-century scene design.

Appia (who was born in Switzerland) and Craig (who was English) both argued against photographic reproduction as a basic goal of scene design; they believed that a setting should suggest a locale but should not reproduce it. Both used levels and platforms to design spaces that would be functional for the performer. Moreover, both took full advantage of the introduction of electricity and used light as an integral visual element. Most of their designs are extremely atmospheric, stressing contrasts between light and dark.

Appia and Craig influenced many of the leading twentieth-century American designers; for example, devices such as Craig's *unit set*—a single setting which can represent various locales—have been especially important.

Russian Theatricalism: Meyerhold

The reaction against realism also influenced a number of Russian artists who rejected the principles of Constantin Stanislavski and the Moscow Art Theater. Possibly the most influential was Vsevolod Meyerhold (1874–1940), who was the leading Russian antirealist between 1905 and 1939 and frequently experimented with *theatricalism.* Theatricalists liked to expose the devices of theater, such as the way stage machinery works, to make the audience conscious of watching a performance; they also borrowed techniques from the circus, the music hall, and similar entertainments.

ADOLPHE APPIA'S DESIGN FOR *IPHIGENIA IN AULIS*
Appia's ideas of lighting and scenery were revolutionary. He moved from realistic settings to the use of shapes and levels which would serve as acting areas. He was also among the first to realize the vast possibilities of modern lighting techniques. (Billy Rose Theatre Collection, New York Public Library for the Performing Arts, Astor, Lenox, and Tilden Foundations)

The list of Meyerhold's innovations and experiments is astounding, and much of what was called avant-garde in the second half of the twentieth century can be traced back to his experiments early in the century. Meyerhold's theater was a director's theater: he was literally the author of his productions, and he frequently restructured or rewrote classics. He searched for suitable environments for his presentations, arguing for the use of *found spaces*—that is, spaces (such as streets, factories, and schools) not originally meant for theater. He experimented with, and theorized about, multimedia in stage productions.

Meyerhold also attempted to train his performers physically by using techniques of commedia dell'arte, the circus, and vaudeville. He devised an acting system known as *biomechanics,* which emphasized external, physical training; the implication of biomechanics was that the performer's body could be trained to operate like a machine. Meyerhold argued that through physical actions performers can evoke the necessary internal responses in themselves and audiences. Meyerhold's sets, known as *constructivist* settings, provided machines for his performers to work on; these settings consisted of skeletal frames, ramps, stairways, and platforms and often looked like huge Tinkertoys.

Early Eclectics

Some theater artists in the early twentieth century tried to bridge the gap between realism and antirealism. These practitioners—known as *eclectics*—were not doctrinaire; instead, they argued that each play should define its own form. Eclectic directors included the Austrian Max Reinhardt (1873–1943) and the Russian Yevgeny Vakhtangov (1883–1922).

Departures from Realism: 1915–1945

The period from 1915 to 1945—from World War I to the end of World War II—was, as we noted earlier, turbulent, and these were also turbulent years for theater, which reflected the chaotic world scene. Many theatrical innovators broke sharply with realism, which by then had become the most popular form of theater. A number of new antirealistic movements developed in continental Europe, including expressionism, futurism, dada, and surrealism, and these movements, though they were most influential in the visual arts, also had an important impact on avant-garde theater. Some artistic movements were associated with political ideologies. Expressionism and epic theater, for example, supported socialism; others, such as futurism, supported fascism.

Before we turn to such movements, we should mention briefly an influential playwright whose work does not fit into any of the usual categories: the Italian dramatist Luigi Pirandello (1867–1936). In his play *Six Characters in Search of an Author* (1921), Pirandello has six characters from an unfinished play existing in a playwright's mind enter a theater and interrupt a rehearsal, in the hope that the troupe will act out their unfinished story. In the course of the action—as in several of his other plays—Pirandello deals very theatrically with questions of appearance versus reality and art versus life.

Expressionism. *Expressionism,* which flourished in Germany at the time of World War I, was a movement in art and literature in which the representation of reality was distorted in order to communicate inner feelings. In a painting of a man, for example, the lines in his face would be twisted to indicate the turmoil he feels inside.

Expressionism in drama has well-defined characteristics. Expressionist plays are often highly subjective; the dramatic action is seen through the eyes of the protagonist and therefore frequently seems distorted or dreamlike. Many of these plays have common themes, such as the dehumanization of the individual by society and the deterioration of the family. The protagonist in a typical expressionist play is a Christlike figure who journeys through a series of incidents that may be causally unrelated. Characters are representative types, often given titles—such as Man, Woman, or Clerk—rather than names. The language of the plays is telegraphic, with most speeches consisting of one or two lines; but these speeches alternate with long lyrical passages. Many expressionist playwrights were politically motivated, supporting socialist and pacifist causes, though some were apolitical.

The major German expressionist playwrights were Georg Kaiser (1878–1945) and Ernst Toller (1893–1939). Shortly after expressionism flourished in Europe, its influence was felt in the United States—for example, in some of Eugene O'Neill's plays, including *The Emperor Jones* (1922).

In its pure form, the expressionist movement was short-lived, lasting only about 15 years, but many expressionistic techniques found their way into the mainstream of modern theater.

Futurism, Dada, and Surrealism.   Although futurism and dada—two other nonrealistic movements that emerged around the time of World War I—had less impact than expressionism on theater, the aesthetic principles of both movements have influenced avant-garde theater artists from the 1960s to the present.

Futurism originated in Italy in 1909. Unlike the expressionists, the futurists idealized war and the machine age. They attacked artistic ideals of the past, ridiculing them as "museum art" and arguing that new forms had to be created for new eras. They sought a "synthetic" theater of short, seemingly illogical dramatic pieces and argued against the separation of performers and audience. They also believed that audiences should be confronted and antagonized.

Dada, which originated in Switzerland in 1916, was a short-lived movement that never really caught on. Reacting against World War I, the dadaists argued that art should mirror the madness of the world. Like the futurists, they railed against museum art and wanted to confuse and antagonize their audiences. Unlike the futurists, however, they were not concerned with glorifying war or machines.

Surrealism, an outgrowth of dada, began in 1924. One of its major exponents was André Breton (1896–1966), and its center was France. Surrealists argued that the subconscious is the highest plane of reality and attempted to re-create its workings dramatically. Many of their plays seem to be set in a dreamworld, mixing recognizable and fantastic events.

Antirealistic Theorists: Artaud and Brecht.   The two most influential theatrical theorists in Europe between the world wars were Bertolt Brecht and Antonin Artaud. Both reacted vehemently against the principles of Stanislavski and the aesthetics of realistic theater.

Antonin Artaud (1896–1948), who was French and who had originally been associated with the surrealists, proposed a *theater of cruelty* in the 1930s. He argued that western theater needed to be totally transformed because its literary tradition, which emphasized language, was antithetical to its ritualistic origins. Artaud believed that western theater artists should study the stylized Asian theaters. He also asserted that there were "no more masterpieces," by which he meant that

PAUL ROBESON IN EUGENE O'NEILL'S *THE EMPEROR JONES*
This play, like many of O'Neill's dramas of the early 1920s, uses expressionistic techniques. The audience sees the drama through the eyes of the protagonist, a black dictatorial ruler of a Caribbean island who is fleeing his people in the jungle. (Billy Rose Theatre Collection, New York Public Library for the Performing Arts, Astor, Lenox, and Tilden Foundations)

Chapter 14   Modern Theater: 1875 to 1945

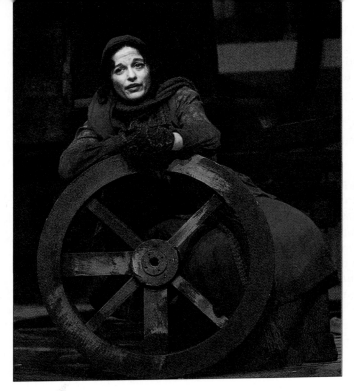

BERTOLT BRECHT

Brecht's epic theories and plays continue to be part of contemporary theater; his concepts, including alienation and historification, continue to be debated and are still influential. Brecht's personal life has been no less controversial than his work: recent scholarship suggests that some of his work was plagiarized and that his political stance was perhaps hypocritical. Shown here is the title character from one of his best-known plays, Mother Courage and Her Children, *with Elise Stone as Mother Courage in a production by the Jean Cocteau Repertory of New York City.* (© Gerry Goodstein)

the classics should be produced not for their historical significance but only if they were still relevant to contemporary audiences. For Artaud, a text was not sacred but could be reworked in order to point up its relevance.

Artaud's theater of cruelty is characterized by its emphasis on the sensory. He did not literally mean that theater artists should be cruel to their audiences or physically brutalize them—although some avant-garde theater artists in the 1960s interpreted cruelty as actual physical confrontation with spectators. He felt, instead, that the viewers' senses should be bombarded. (A contemporary example of such sensory involvement would be a multimedia presentation or a sound and light show at a rock concert.) Artaud, like many of the antirealists who preceded him, wanted to reorganize the theater space to make the audience the center of attention.

Bertolt Brecht (1898–1956), who was German, developed what he called **epic theater,** though he was not the first to use that term or the first to use epic techniques. Brecht's major plays—including *Mother Courage* (1937–1941), *The Good Person of Setzuan* (1938–1940), and *The Caucasian Chalk Circle* (1944–1945)—were written between 1933 and 1945, while he was in exile from Hitler's Germany. As a director, Brecht worked with the Berliner Ensemble in East Berlin from 1949 until his death in 1956, making an international impact. His theories, most of which were formulated in the 1930s but frequently revised, have influenced many contemporary playwrights and directors.

As the term *epic theater* implies, Brecht's plays are epic in scope. They are, accordingly, episodic in structure: they cover a great deal of time, shift locale frequently, and have intricate plots and many characters. Brecht, an ardent socialist, believed that theater could create an intellectual climate for social change, and the goal of his epic theater is to instruct. He felt that for theater to teach successfully, the audience should not be emotionally hypnotized but should be involved intellectually. He believed that a production should force the audience to remain emotionally detached—or *alienated*—from the dramatic action. To prevent emotional involvement, Brecht's works are highly theatrical; the audience is always made aware of being in a theater. A narrator is frequently used to comment on the dramatic action, for example. To alienate the audience, Brecht also used a technique he referred to as *historification.* Many of his plays, such as *Mother Courage,* are set in the past, but it is apparent that he is really concerned with contemporary events paralleling the historic occurrences.

Totalitarianism, the Second World War, and Theater

As might be expected, the rise of totalitarianism and the outbreak of World War II in 1939 curtailed the development of European theater and drama. Theatrical activity did not cease altogether, but in totalitarian societies—particularly the Soviet Union under Stalin and Germany under Hitler—government-supported theaters became instruments of propaganda. Courageous artists attempted to attack these regimes; for the most part, though, experimentation and freedom of expression were suppressed. The totalitarian rulers saw realistic art as easier to manipulate and to use for propaganda. Furthermore, they saw individual experimentation as dangerous because it implied freedom. Therefore, the fascists and communists vigorously attacked many of the artists who experimented with forms that departed from realism.

In Spain, for example, the playwright Federico García Lorca (1898–1936)—author of *Blood Wedding* (1933), *Yerma* (1934), and *The House of Bernarda Alba* (1936)—was killed by Franco's forces during the civil war. Productions of García Lorca's works, which poetically dramatized the oppression of Spanish women, were not allowed in Spain until after Franco's death in 1975.

Numerous German theater artists, because of their religion or politics, had to flee Germany after Adolf Hitler's takeover in 1933. They included the directors Max Reinhardt and Erwin Piscator (1893–1966) as well as the playwrights Bertolt Brecht and Ernst Toller. Many artists who opposed the Third Reich but did not leave were interned in the Nazi concentration camps.

Still, theatrical artists did resist totalitarianism; the most vivid example of such resistance was the theater organized by inmates of the Nazi concentration camps. In camps in conquered territories during World War II, such as Auschwitz, there were surreptitious entertainments in the barracks: these improvised presentations consisted of literature and drama recited from memory, satirical skits, and traditional songs. In the camp at Theresienstadt, in Czechoslovakia, satirical plays, operas, and cabaret entertainments were written and openly staged; this was allowed because the Nazis were using Theresienstadt as a "model" camp—they brought the Red Cross and foreign officials there in order to discredit rumors of atrocities. Most of the artists who passed through Theresienstadt were later sent to extermination centers.

In Chapter 15, we will continue to see how the strands of our modern theater developed during the period immediately following World War II until about 1990.

SUMMARY

Modern theater began in the late nineteenth century with the realistic plays of Henrik Ibsen, August Strindberg, and Anton Chekhov. In realism, events onstage mirror observable reality in the outside world. The characters speak, move, dress, and behave as people do in real life; they are seen in familiar places such as living rooms, bedrooms, and kitchens.

One appeal of realism is that audiences can identify with and verify people and events onstage. One disadvantage of realism is that it excludes a number of traditional theatrical devices, such as poetry, music, ghosts, and special effects. Despite this drawback, however, realism is so effective that it has been a dominant theatrical form of the past hundred years.

Because of its uncompromising presentation of life, realism was initially produced not commercially but by small independent theaters. As it became more widely accepted, it entered the mainstream of theater.

In the twentieth century, Synge and O'Casey in Ireland, O'Neill and Hellman in the United States, and many other playwrights worldwide wrote powerful realistic drama.

From 1875 until the 1945, there were also significant movements which departed from realism: these included symbolism, expressionism, futurism, dada, surrealism, and epic theater. Among practitioners who attempted to transform theater were the designers Appia and Craig as well as the director Meyerhold. Key theories arguing against realism are Artaud's theater of cruelty and Brecht's epic theater.

These movements have made audiences reevaluate realism, particularly since many "antirealistic" techniques were eventually fused into more traditional dramas and commercial productions.

THEATER ON THE WEB

Here is a sampling of modern playwrights and performers who can be found on the Web.

Anton Chekhov (1860–1904)   http://www.imagi-nation.com/moonstruck/clsc6.htm

Brief biography of the Russian dramatist Anton Chekhov, plus links to all his works currently in print.

Ibsen.net   http://www.ibsen.net

A large collection of links devoted to the playwright, maintained by the municipality of Skien in Norway, Ibsen's home.

Strindberg   http://www.extrapris.com/astrindberg.html

Offers a biography of the Swedish playwright, interviews, and images of his paintings and drawings.

International Brecht Society   polyglot.lss.wisc.edu/german/brecht

This site is maintained as a service to scholars, critics, students, and theater people interested in the works and thought of Brecht.

Footlight Notes   http://members.tripod.com/FootlightNotes/index.html

An electronic zine about the history of popular entertainment in theater from the 1850s to the 1920s.

After reviewing these links, compare and contrast the theater scene in northern and eastern Europe with that of western Europe and the United States. Cite specific links to productions and personalities. Discuss how the social and political climate in each region contributed to the body of theatrical work from the early modern era.

Chapter 15

Modern Theater: 1945 to 1990

Postwar Realistic Theater

Background: The Postwar Era

Timeline: *1945 to 2000*

American Selective Realism

Play Synopsis: *Death of a Salesman*

The "Angry Young Men" in England and Documentary Drama in Germany

Experimentation and Departures from Realism: 1945 to 1980

Living History: *Waiting for Godot*

Existentialism and Theater of the Absurd

Experimental Theater

Play Synopsis: *Waiting for Godot*

Postwar Eclectics

Developments in Postwar American Theater

African American Theater

Musical Theater

Alternatives to Commercial Theater

Making Connections: *Film and the Other Mass Media*

Summary

◀ TENNESSEE WILLIAM'S *ORPHEUS DESCENDING*

After World War II, there were many new movements in dramatic literature. During this time period, playwrights also mixed various styles to create their own unique dramas. The American playwright Tennessee Williams mixed realistic technique with a haunting poetic style. Orpheus Descending is an example of such a play. While not successful in its original productions, the play has been revived frequently. A very successful production, starring Helen Mirren, was staged by the Donmar Warehouse in London in 2000. (© Donald Cooper/PhotoStage, England)

Theater experienced a turbulent period from 1945 through the 1990s. There was an explosion of experimentation, with new, nonrealistic avant-garde trends developing one after another. Because these movements are so close to our own lifetime, we are unable to evaluate their historical significance conclusively. It is clear, however, that established theatrical and dramatic forms have been questioned and reworked, and that movements such as absurdism and environmental theater have forced us to redefine our concept of drama and theater. While we review many international developments during this time period, we will also highlight the turbulent American theater scene.

Postwar Realistic Theater

Background: The Postwar Era

After World War II, which ended in 1945 with the defeat of Germany and Italy in Europe and Japan in Asia, there was again hope for peace. The period after World War II was different from the period after World War I. For one thing, the atom bomb—which had been dropped on two cities in Japan at the close of World War II—and later the hydrogen bomb—had been developed. These weapons were potentially so deadly that a stalemate developed between the superpowers controlling them, the United States and the Soviet Union.

At the end of World War II, the Soviet Union had annexed many nations in eastern and central Europe into an association known as the Warsaw Pact. There was also an association among western nations known as the North Atlantic Treaty Organization (NATO). Between these two blocs there developed what came to be called a *cold war*. The cold war was to last for decades, not ending until the countries of eastern Europe moved away from communist and Soviet domination in 1989 and 1990 and the Soviet Union was dissolved at the end of 1991.

The end of World War II did not mean the end of military conflicts. Between 1945 and 1990 there were numerous other wars, including the Korean war, the Israeli-Arab conflicts in the middle east, the Vietnamese war, a Soviet-led war in Afghanistan, the Persian Gulf war, the Bosnian-Serb war in the former Yugoslavia, and the Rwandan civil war in Africa.

There was also a great deal of social unrest, including civil rights movements by underrepresented groups such as African Americans, women, and homosexuals. This has been a violent era, marked by assassinations, revolutions, and attempts by dictatorial regimes to put down revolutions—as in the Soviet bloc and in China.

Another development of the postwar period was a striking increase in the industrial power of two of the defeated nations: Germany and Japan. Economically and politically, the world became more interdependent, with developments in one part of the world—such as environmental pollution or the price of oil—directly affecting other areas around the globe: Central and South America, for instance, as well as Europe, Asia, and the United States.

Meanwhile, inventions continued at a rapid pace: nuclear power, for example, and computer technology, which revolutionized many aspects of life. Earlier,

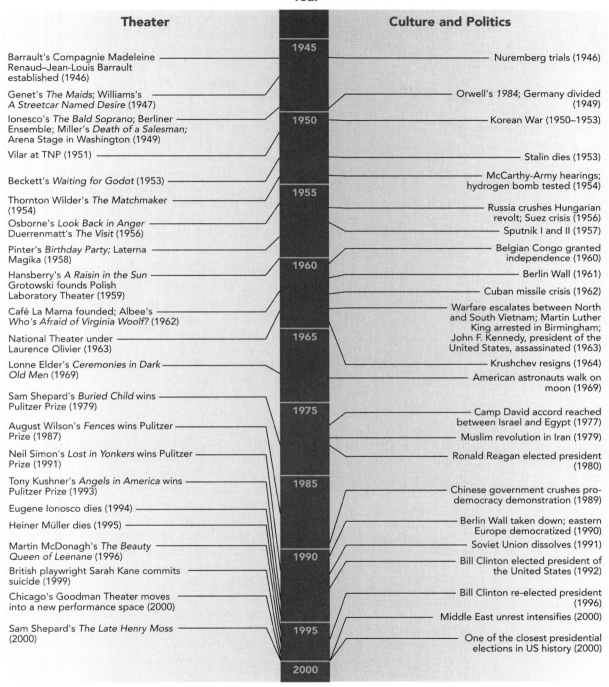

Theater

Barrault's Compagnie Madeleine
Renaud–Jean-Louis Barrault
established (1946)

Genet's *The Maids*; Williams's
A Streetcar Named Desire (1947)

Ionesco's *The Bald Soprano*; Berliner
Ensemble; Miller's *Death of a Salesman*;
Arena Stage in Washington (1949)

Vilar at TNP (1951)

Beckett's *Waiting for Godot* (1953)

Thornton Wilder's *The Matchmaker*
(1954)

Osborne's *Look Back in Anger*
Duerrenmatt's *The Visit* (1956)

Pinter's *Birthday Party*; Laterna
Magika (1958)

Hansberry's *A Raisin in the Sun*
Grotowski founds Polish
Laboratory Theater (1959)

Café La Mama founded; Albee's
Who's Afraid of Virginia Woolf? (1962)

National Theater under
Laurence Olivier (1963)

Lonne Elder's *Ceremonies in Dark
Old Men* (1969)

Sam Shepard's *Buried Child* wins
Pulitzer Prize (1979)

August Wilson's *Fences* wins Pulitzer
Prize (1987)

Neil Simon's *Lost in Yonkers* wins Pulitzer
Prize (1991)

Tony Kushner's *Angels in America* wins
Pulitzer Prize (1993)

Eugene Ionosco dies (1994)

Heiner Müller dies (1995)

Martin McDonagh's *The Beauty
Queen of Leenane* (1996)

British playwright Sarah Kane commits
suicide (1999)

Chicago's Goodman Theater moves
into a new performance space (2000)

Sam Shepard's *The Late Henry Moss*
(2000)

Culture and Politics

Nuremberg trials (1946)

Orwell's *1984*; Germany divided
(1949)

Korean War (1950–1953)

Stalin dies (1953)

McCarthy-Army hearings;
hydrogen bomb tested (1954)

Russia crushes Hungarian
revolt; Suez crisis (1956)

Sputnik I and II (1957)

Belgian Congo granted
independence (1960)

Berlin Wall (1961)

Cuban missile crisis (1962)

Warfare escalates between North
and South Vietnam; Martin Luther
King arrested in Birmingham;
John F. Kennedy, president of the
United States, assassinated (1963)

Krushchev resigns (1964)

American astronauts walk on
moon (1969)

Camp David accord reached
between Israel and Egypt (1977)

Muslim revolution in Iran (1979)

Ronald Reagan elected president
(1980)

Chinese government crushes pro-
democracy demonstration (1989)

Berlin Wall taken down; eastern
Europe democratized (1990)

Soviet Union dissolves (1991)

Bill Clinton elected president of
the United States (1992)

Bill Clinton re-elected president
(1996)

Middle East unrest intensifies (2000)

One of the closest presidential
elections in US history (2000)

1945
1950
1955
1960
1965
1975
1985
1990
1995
2000

this period saw the development of jet airplanes, television, and many advances in medical science.

At the same time, tremendous problems remained: economic inequality and conflicts between rich and poor in many nations, assaults on the environment, persistent racial prejudice, and starvation and homelessness in many parts of the world.

Clearly, then, western society after World War II was left with many haunting questions. How could the civilized world have engaged in a war that resulted in over 35 million deaths? How could rational societies undertake genocide? Would the atom bomb lead to annihilation of the human race? How could wealthy societies continue to have large numbers of poverty-stricken people? How could racism continue to survive? Questions like these have forced western society to reevaluate its most cherished beliefs.

American Selective Realism

Between 1945 and 1990, there were many playwrights who continued to refine the realistic form and who created new types of dramas based on the earlier innovations of Ibsen, Chekhov, and Strindberg. One such trend was selective realism.

After World War II, two important American writers were Tennessee Williams (1911–1983) and Arthur Miller (1915–   ). Williams's important realistic plays include *A Streetcar Named Desire* (1947) and *Cat on a Hot Tin Roof* (1954)—both of which won the Pulitzer Prize—and *The Night of the Iguana* (1961). Miller's realistic works include *All My Sons* (1947) and *A View from the Bridge* (1955).

Some critics suggest that Miller and Williams write in a form known as *selective realism*—a type of realism that heightens certain details of action, scenery, and dialogue while omitting others. For example, in Miller's *Death of a Salesman* (1949), the playwright highlights selected elements of the world of the main character, Willy Loman—elements which symbolize his downfall. Moreover, scenes in Willy's mind and scenes from the past are interspersed with

THE RIDE DOWN MT. MORGAN BY ARTHUR MILLER
An American dramatist who carried forward the realistic tradition of Ibsen, Arthur Miller also employed selective realism (in Death of a Salesman*) and historical drama. Miller's* The Ride Down Mt. Morgan, *which was produced off-Broadway in New York in 1998, is an example of selective realism. Seen here are Katy Selverstone and Patrick Stewart in a photograph from the later Broadway production of that play.* (© Joan Marcus)

scenes in the present. *Death of Salesman* is set in a recognizable, realistic world, but the elements have been carefully chosen to underline thematic concerns. Tennessee Williams combines the theatrical device of a narrator with realistic scenes in his play *The Glass Menagerie* (1945).

DEATH OF A SALESMAN (1949)

Arthur Miller, (1915–   )

(AP/Wide World Photos)

Chief Characters

Willy Loman
Linda, *his wife*
Biff, *his older son*
Happy, *his younger son*
Bernard, *Biff's friend*
the Woman, *Willy's mistress*
Charley, *a neighbor, Bernard's father*
Uncle Ben, *Willy's brother*

Setting and Time

Willy Loman's house in New York, and various other locations in New York and Boston. The present and flashbacks to the past.

Background

Willy is an aging traveling salesman who doesn't produce much business anymore. Many of his friends and business contacts are dead; his sons are not the successes he expected them to be—Biff, for example, was a football star but did not graduate from high school. Willy has a tendency to daydream. Linda is a devoted wife and mother, trying desperately to keep her husband and family from falling apart.

Act I: Willy arrives home unexpectedly, having cut short a sales trip. He tells Linda that he kept driving off the road. Linda tells Willy that he should persuade the company to let him work in New York rather than travel. Willy expresses disappointment about his son Biff, who has just returned home after living as a drifter in the west. Meanwhile, in their bedroom upstairs, Biff and Happy discuss their concern about their father and an old dream of starting their own business.

Downstairs, Willy moves into a scene from the past in which he brags to young Biff about what a great

salesman he is. Bernard, a neighbor who is the same age as Biff, is a good student. Because he idolizes the athletic Biff, Bernard wants to help Biff study so that he can pass his exams. Willy puts Bernard down as the "studious type" and tells Biff that personality will get him further than studying. Willy, in a different flashback, is shown in Boston with the Woman, with whom he is having an affair. Back in the present, Willy and his neighbor Charley have a minor confrontation during which Willy speaks out loud to his brother Ben's ghost. In Willy's fantasy, Ben is a successful self-made man who once, years ago, offered Willy a chance to go with him, a chance which Willy refused.

Linda defends Willy and asks Biff to try to get along better with him. She confesses that she thinks Willy is trying to kill himself. Willy confronts Biff about his career and is rude to Linda while Biff stands up for her. Later, Biff finds rubber tubing attached to a gas line in the basement—a suicide device that Willy is evidently planning to use.

Act II: The next morning. Willy seems optimistic about the future: Biff represents Willy's final chance to prove that he himself has not been a total failure. He believes that Biff's former boss will give Biff a job. Also, Linda thinks that Willy has taken the rubber hose away and is no longer contemplating suicide, but later she finds out that Biff removed it.

The scene shifts to Willy's office, where he meets with his boss, Howard Wagner, and asks to be assigned to the New York office. Willy is aggressive but becomes desperate when Howard refuses his request and then

fires him. Willy leaves in despair and vents his frustration on Ben's ghost.

The scene shifts to Charley's office, where Willy and Charley's son, Bernard, now a successful lawyer, discuss the time when Biff failed mathematics. Willy blames Biff's failures on that one incident. Bernard says that he always wondered why Biff didn't go to summer school after he failed. Willy is evasive and asks Charley for a loan; but when Charley offers him a job, Willy turns it down, out of pride. Meanwhile, Biff and Happy are in a restaurant waiting for Willy. Biff tells Happy that he had an unsuccessful meeting with his ex-boss; but Willy, when he arrives, won't let Biff tell the real story—Willy wants to hear an upbeat version, though he admits to the boys that he himself has been fired. The scene shifts to the past and Willy's hotel room in Boston; because he has failed in school, the young Biff shows up unannounced and finds Willy with the Woman. He decides that everything Willy stands for is false, and returns home beaten. Back in the present, Happy and Biff leave Willy alone in the restaurant, distraught and fantasizing.

At home, Linda accuses her sons of deserting Willy. Willy, still caught up in his fantasies, has returned home to plant a garden at night. He tells Ben about his insurance policy—the $20,000 would help Biff get on his feet.

Back in the present, Biff tells Willy that he has finally come to realize the truth about himself and tries to make Willy see the truth also. Alone, Willy gets into his car, drives off, and kills himself in an automobile accident. At his funeral, Linda expresses her sorrow and confusion.

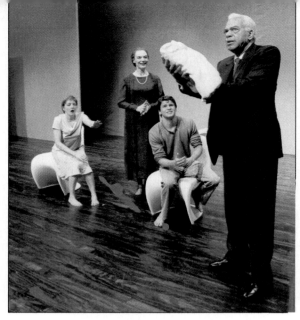

THE SELECTIVE REALISM OF ALBEE

Among the American playwrights who have effectively combined realism with other forms such as symbolism and expressionism is Edward Albee. His most recent drama, The Play About the Baby, *shows how difficult it is to categorize contemporary drama. Seen here are Rebecca Harris, Marian Seldes, David Burtka, and Earle Hyman in the minimalist environment for this play.* (© T. Charles Erickson/Alley Theatre, Houston)

Throughout the twentieth century, the end of realism has been pronounced periodically, but the form has continued with great vigor to the present day. In 1962, another American writer, Edward Albee (1928–   ), joined the list of important realists with his play *Who's Afraid of Virginia Woolf?* (1962). Albee's style is highly enigmatic, however, and some of his plays—such as *Three Tall Women,* which won the Pulitzer Prize in 1994—mix realistic and nonrealistic techniques. Albee's most recent work, *The Play About the Baby,* opened at the Royal Court Theatre in London in 1998. Several outstanding American playwrights of the 1970s and 1980s wrote powerful plays using realistic techniques.

The "Angry Young Men" in England and Documentary Drama in Germany

In England in the 1950s, a group of antiestablishment playwrights known collectively as the ***angry young men*** dealt with the dissolving British empire, class conflict, and political disillusionment. Most of the dramas by the "angry young men" are in the traditional realistic form, slightly modified. The most famous of these plays was *Look Back in Anger* (1956) by John Osborne (1929–1994).

A German movement of the 1960s called *documentary drama* has also been influential. Documentary dramas are based on historical documents, which give an air of authenticity and historical reality. The goal of documentary drama was to convince audiences that they were watching history unfold, even when these dramatists had modified the documents for dramatic or political effect. One of the most famous documentary dramas was *The Investigation* (1965) by Peter Weiss (1916–1982), which dramatizes the war crimes trials of people who had been guards at a Nazi extermination camp. Today, docudramas—as they are sometimes referred to—are popular as made-for-television movies.

Experimentation and Departures from Realism: 1945 to 1980

The period from 1945 to 1980 saw a great deal of experimentation with theatrical forms and techniques. Much of this experimentation was inspired by political unrest and by a desire to question political authority through the questioning of traditional theatrical practices, styles, and techniques. One of the first of the nontraditional forms to develop immediately after World War II, theater of the absurd, was born out of the unanswerable questions this horrific conflict had left in the minds of the survivors.

Waiting for Godot

1957 California The setting is San Quentin prison in California on November 19, 1957. In the prison's North Dining Hall, a stage is set up where a group from the Actors' Workshop will perform Samuel Beckett's *Waiting for Godot*. It will be the first performance at the prison in over forty years.

The Actors' Workshop is a theater group dedicated to performing provocative, experimental, avant-garde works by both national and international playwrights. Its members have made a name for themselves not only in the San Francisco area but throughout the United States. When performing, they work closely together as an ensemble.

The performers today are nervous, not only because they are performing in a penitentiary, but also because of the play itself. *Waiting for Godot* is a drama without much action, and is filled with literary and religious references. It has already baffled intellectuals in Europe and the United States: how, the actors wonder, will a group of restless prisoners react to it?

The setting is described simply as "A country road. A tree." In actuality, it is a barren plain. The two central characters, Vladimir and Estragon, who are also known as Didi and Gogo, are tramplike clowns who are waiting for the Godot figure. They have the vague expectation that somehow, if and when he comes, Godot will be able to help them. It is never stated who Godot is: he may be God, he may be someone else, or he may not even exist. While they wait, they try to break the painful monotony of their boring lives with bickering and occasional vaudeville routines.

The difficulty of the play is compounded by the fact that the second act seems to be almost the same as the first act. In both acts, Vladimir and Estragon try to entertain themselves; they move between hope and despair; they engage in vaudeville routines and philosophical speculation.

Meanwhile, two other characters, Pozzo and Lucky, appear. Pozzo is an overbearing creature who treats Lucky as his slave. Lucky, who has been mute, toward the end of the first act suddenly makes a long speech filled with legal terms. In the second act, the roles of Pozzo and Lucky are somewhat reversed, as Pozzo has become blind.

There is not the usual progress or story line expected in a traditional play. There is no building of suspense, no careful development of characters, no sudden plot twist, no big payoff at the end. In short, the play defies most of the conventional notions of both the content and the structure of drama.

At the end of the play, Godot's identity still has not been revealed, nor has he ever appeared. Instead, a young messenger arrives at the close of both the first and second acts and announces that while Godot will not come that day, he will no doubt come the next.

The members of the Actors' Workshop have been acting together for a long time and when they approach a play, they take their time, exploring the text, becoming familiar with the characters, and engaging in improvisation as they develop a performance. Even with this background they are apprehensive as they approach the performance at San Quentin. These, after all, are prisoners, not a sophisticated, intellectual audience, and this material is difficult for even the most scholarly spectators.

With these difficulties in mind, the performers from the Actor's Workshop begin their presentation. Shortly after the performance is under way, they have an indication that the production will go over better and be more readily understood than they had anticipated. Within the first few minutes, the audience grows quiet. A group of men sitting on some steps who had planned to leave early become engrossed and stay.

To the surprise of the performers, the audience sits in rapt attention. The prisoners follow the play closely from beginning to end and seem to understand what is happening. After the performance is over, it is clear that the prisoners have understood much of what they have seen—perhaps more than other audiences might understand. These prisoners, waiting out their sentences in boredom and frustration, have intuitively connected with the men onstage who wait for the unknown Godot, who never comes.

Existentialism and Theater of the Absurd

Existentialism is a philosophy most clearly articulated by two Frenchmen, Jean-Paul Sartre (1905–1980) and Albert Camus (1913–1960), who were reacting, among other things, to World War II. Existentialists believe that existence has little meaning; that God does not exist; that humanity is alone in an irrational universe; and that the only significant thing an individual can do is accept responsibility for his or her own actions. Both Camus and Sartre wrote plays illustrating these beliefs. The best-known are Sartre's *The Flies* (1943), an adaptation of the Greek *Oresteia*; and *No Exit* (1944), in which hell is equated with other people.

In the early 1950s, a theatrical approach emerged which combined existentialist philosophy with revolutionary, avant-garde dramatic form. Although not an organized movement, it was called ***theater of the absurd*** by the critic Martin Esslin (1918–   ). Esslin pointed out that the playwrights in this group have certain qualities in common: one is the notion that much of what happens in life is ridiculous or absurd and cannot be explained logically; another is the belief that this ridiculousness or absurdity should be reflected in dramatic action. Among the writers taking this approach are Samuel Beckett (1906–1989), Jean Genet (1910–1986), Eugène Ionesco (1912–1994), Edward Albee, and Harold Pinter (1930–   ).

Absurdist playwrights present our existence, including human relationships and human language, as futile or nonsensical. To reinforce this theme, they use seemingly illogical dramatic techniques. Their plots do not have either traditional climactic structure or episodic structure. Frequently, nothing seems to happen: the plot moves in a circle, concluding in the same way it began. The characters are not realistic, and the settings are sometimes strange and unrecognizable. The language is often telegraphic and sparse; the characters fail to communicate.

THEATER OF THE ABSURD: BECKETT'S *WAITING FOR GODOT*
One of the plays typifying the spirit of alienation and loneliness of drama after World War II *is* Waiting for Godot, *about two men waiting to be saved by someone who never comes. Shown here are the tragicomic protagonists—Vladimir, played by Jeremy Geidt (left); and Estragon, played by Alvin Epstein (right)—in a production at Boston's American Repertory Theatre.* (© Richard Feldman)

Waiting for Godot (1953) by Samuel Beckett is probably the most famous of these enigmatic, nontraditional dramas. As in many absurdist dramas, the plot is cyclical: the action in Act II appears to start over, with nothing having changed since Act I. The two main characters, Vladimir and Estragon, spend their time waiting; they accomplish nothing and are unable to take control of their lives. The other two men, Lucky and Pozzo, also have no control over their destiny; fate reverses their roles, transforming one from master into servant and the other from servant into master.

Beckett referred to *Waiting for Godot* as a "tragicomedy in two acts," a description that reveals his tragicomic view of the human condition. Human inaction is comical but has tragic consequences.

Experimental Theater

After absurdism, there were further attempts to supersede traditional theater practices. These experiments, carried out in Europe and the United States in the 1960s and 1970s, went in many directions—a reflection, no doubt, of the fragmentation of modern life. The experiments included happenings, multimedia, and environmental theater.

Happenings, Multimedia, and New Technology.   Two significant developments of the 1960s and 1970s were happenings and experiments with multimedia.

Happenings were what the name suggests: unstructured events that occurred with a minimum of planning and organization. The idea—especially popular in the 1960s—was that art should not be restricted to museums, galleries, or concert halls but can and should happen anywhere: on a street corner, in a grocery store, at a bus stop.

Multimedia is a joining of theater with other arts—particularly dance, film, and television. In work of this sort, which is still being produced, live performers interact with sequences on film or television. The idea here is to fuse the art forms or to incorporate new technology into a theatrical event. A current form that combines theater, dance, and media is called *performance art.*

Any discussion of departures from realism after World War II must also take into account new technology in scene and lighting design (see Chapters 5 and 6). The Czechoslovakian designer Josef Svoboda (1920–), for example, experimented with such elements as projections, multimedia, movable platforms, and new materials, including plastics. Computer technology as well has been incorporated into many modern theater buildings and lighting systems.

Environmental Theater.   The term *environmental theater* was coined in the 1960s by the American director and teacher Richard Schechner (1934–); many characteristics of environmental theater, however, had developed out of the work and theories of earlier avant-garde artists, including Vsevolod Meyerhold and Antonin Artaud. Proponents of environmental theater treat the entire theater space as a performance area, suggesting that any division between performers and

WAITING FOR GODOT (1953)

Samuel Beckett, (1915–   )

(AP/Wide World Photos)

Chief Characters

Estragon, Vladimir, Lucky, Pozzo
Boy

Setting and Time

A country road with a tree. The
present.

Background

Estragon and Vladimir have been
coming to the same bleak spot every
day for some time to wait for an
unknown person called Godot. It is
a crossroads, bare except for a small
leafless tree in the background. While
the men wait, they pass the time
discussing the nature of humankind,
religion, what they did yesterday, or
anything else on their minds.

Act I: Estragon is trying to pull off
his boot when Vladimir enters. The
two men discuss where Estragon
spent the night and that he was
beaten again. Vladimir relates the
tale of the two thieves crucified with
Christ and explains that current
religious scholars cannot agree on
what happened to the thieves. As
Estragon paces, the scene is punctu-
ated by pauses , which enhance the
feeling of waiting. Occasionally the
men talk of leaving and then decide
that they cannot leave because they
are waiting for Godot. They consider
leaving each other; they argue; they
make up. They discuss hanging
themselves from the tree but decide
that they can't do it because the
limbs are slender and might break.

At the point when they have
decided not to do anything, two
other men, Pozzo and Lucky, enter.
Lucky is carrying heavy baggage and
wears around his neck a rope held
by Pozzo. Pozzo jerks occasionally
on the rope and barks commands to
Lucky, who responds mechanically.
Pozzo sits, eats, and smokes his pipe.
Estragon asks why Lucky doesn't
put down the bags, and Pozzo
explains that Lucky wants to impress
Pozzo so that Pozzo will keep him.
Pozzo says that it would be best to
kill Lucky; this makes Lucky cry.

Estragon tries to comfort Lucky,
and Lucky kicks him. As the sky
changes from day to night, Pozzo
tells Lucky to dance, which he does.
Pozzo tells Lucky to think, and Lucky,
who has been silent until this moment,
goes into a long, incoherent tirade
which agitates the others. When they
take Lucky's "talking hat" off, he
stops talking and collapses in a heap.
The men say good-bye, but no one is
able to leave. Pozzo finally gets up
and exits—with Lucky in the lead,
wearing the rope around his neck. A
boy enters, telling Vladimir and
Estragon that Godot will not come
today but will surely come tomorrow.
After he exits, the moon suddenly
rises. Estragon says he will bring
some rope the next day so that they
can hang themselves. They talk
about parting but don't part. The
curtain falls.

Act II: The next day at the same
time, in the same place. The scene
opens with Estragon's boots and
Lucky's hat onstage. The small tree,
which was bare, now has four or
five leaves. Vladimir enters in an
agitated state, paces back and forth,
and begins to sing. Estragon enters,
apparently in a foul mood. He and
Vladimir embrace, and Estragon
says that he was beaten again the
night before—but he can't remember
what happened the day before.

They discover Estragon's boots,
which seem to be the wrong color.
They discuss leaving but can't leave
because they are waiting for Godot.
Estragon takes a nap, and Vladimir
sings a lullaby. They discover the hat
and do a comic hat-switching
routine. They hear a noise and think
that finally Godot is coming. They
are frightened and rush around
excitedly. Nothing happens; no one
comes. Pozzo, now blind, enters
with Lucky. Lucky stops short, falls,
and brings Pozzo down with him.
Pozzo calls for help, but Vladimir
and Estragon think Godot has
arrived. They discover that it is
Pozzo and Lucky. Vladimir and
Estragon try to help Pozzo up, but
they fall also. Finally, everyone gets
up. Estragon goes to Lucky and,
kicking him, hurts his own foot.
Lucky gets up and gathers his things
together; he and Pozzo exit.

Estragon tries to take off his
boots and then falls asleep as
Vladimir philosophizes. The boy
enters, tells Vladimir that Godot will
not come that night but will come
the next night, and exits. The sun
sets, and the moon rises quickly.
Vladimir and Estragon talk again of
hanging themselves on the tree, but
they have no rope. They test the
strength of Estragon's belt, but it
breaks and his pants fall to the
ground. Vladimir says, "Well? Shall
we go?" Estragon says, "Yes, let's
go"—but they do not move.

viewers is artificial. For every production, spatial arrangements are transformed. (See the discussion of created and found spaces in Chapter 4.)

To Schechner, we should note, not only the theater space but also the dramatic text is subject to such transformation: a text is not sacred or even essential, and both improvisation and reworking of an existing drama are permissible.

The major influence on Schechner's theories is the Polish director Jerzy Grotowski (1933–1999). Works staged by Grotowski with the Polish Laboratory Theater from its founding in 1959 until 1970 had many characteristics of environmental theater. For each production, the theater space and the performer-audience relationship were arranged to conform to the play being presented. According to Grotowski, the essence of theater is interaction between live performers and audiences—hence his emphasis on reorganizing spatial arrangements. In his production of *Kordian* (1962), for instance, the space resembled a mental institution, with spectators scattered among the beds and patients (the performers). In his version of *Doctor Faustus,* the theater space was filled with two large dining tables at which audience members sat as if attending a banquet given by Faustus. As is true of Schechner, for most of Grotowski's productions existing scripts were radically modified by the performers and director. The acting style was externally based, emphasizing body and voice rather than emotions.

Grotowski called his theater *poor theater,* meaning poor in scenery and special effects. It relied on the performers for its impact. (Grotowski's stress on the importance of the environment and nonverbal aspects of performance, has a strong affinity with the ideas of Antonin Artaud.)

Postwar Eclectics

It would be impossible to list every postwar European theatrical innovator. We can, however, note that there are numerous directors who borrow from various kinds of theatrical experiments—*eclectics* whose work incorporates a range of avant-garde techniques.

The English director Peter Brook (1925–) is a well-known contemporary eclectic. In staging Peter Weiss's *Marat/Sade* (1964), Brook applied concepts borrowed from Artaud's theater of cruelty. His production of Shakespeare's *Midsummer Night's Dream* (1970) was clearly influenced by Meyerhold's experiments with biomechanics and circus arts; for example, the fairy gods appeared on trapezes. Since 1971, when he became director of the International Center for Theater Research in Paris, Brook has tried to avoid what he calls "deadly" commercial theater, which does not allow for experimentation. Among his productions are a stripped-down version of the opera *Carmen;* a production of *The Cherry Orchard,* without intermission; and *The Man Who,* based on a popular book of case studies by a neurologist. Brook has explained his theories about theater in his book *The Empty Space* (1968).

The work of Peter Brook and other postwar eclectics is indicative of the incorporation of nonrealistic techniques into more traditional, commercial theater.

Developments in Postwar American Theater

We will now look at two important forms of theater that came to prominence in the United States in the years following World War II: African American theater and musical theater. After that, we will consider "alternative" forms of theater in the United States.

African American Theater

As we noted in Chapter 1, there are many theaters that appeal to diverse audiences with specific political viewpoints, concerns about gender, and sexual orientations. The diversity of American theater is also reflected in dramatic art created for and by the many ethnic and racial groups in our complex society; in this century, for example, there have been significant Italian, Jewish, German, Asian, and Hispanic theaters. Many historians note that the development of the realistic tradition in American theater at the beginning of the twentieth century was clearly aided by immigrants from eastern Europe, many of whom were Jewish. In addition, German immigrants who fled the Nazis during the 1930s and 1940s undertook experiments with departures from realism in American theater.

African American theater—also referred to as *black theater*—is a prime example of a theater which reflects the diversity of American culture and the contributions of a particular group to that culture. African American theater is theater written by and for black Americans or performed by black Americans. It partakes of two important traditions. One is the western theater tradition, in which actors like Paul Robeson (1898–1976) and writers like Lorraine Hansberry (1930–1965) have been significant. The other is a tradition that traces its origin to theater in Africa and the Caribbean.

Since African American theater has a long history, it will be helpful to trace its development from its beginnings so that we can better understand its significance and impact on our contemporary theater.

African American Theater in the Nineteenth Century.

In American drama of the eighteenth and nineteenth centuries, comic black servants—who spoke a thick dialect, shuffled slowly, and wore ill-fitting costumes—were popular characters. These roles, however, were usually enacted by white performers; it was rare to see black performers on the American stage in the nineteenth century.

An exception was the African Grove Theater—a black company founded in New York during the 1820–1821 season by William Brown (an African American) and the West Indian actor James Hewlett. The company was particularly noted for Shakespearean plays. Hewlett was the first black to play Othello, and the renowned actor Ira Aldridge (ca. 1806–1867) made his stage debut with the company. Here, too, the drama *King Shotaway* (1823)—believed to be the first play written and performed by African Americans—was presented. The African Grove closed in 1827, however, after attacks by white audience members.

IRA ALDRIDGE AS OTHELLO

Ira Aldridge was an African American artist of the early nineteenth century who, because of racial segregation in the United States, was compelled to work abroad. Aldridge became a renowned Shakespearean actor in Europe, in such countries as England, Poland, and Russia. This illustration shows him in his most famous role, the Moor in Shakespeare's Othello. *(Billy Rose Theatre Collection, New York Public Library for the Performing Arts, Astor, Lenox, and Tilden Foundations)*

Short of abandoning their profession, African American performers in the nineteenth century were faced with two choices: accepting roles as stupid servants or going to Europe, where racism against blacks was not so virulent. Ira Aldridge, for one, performed in England, Russia, and Poland in the plays of Shakespeare, receiving great acclaim.

The *minstrel show* was a popular nineteenth-century form which caricatured blacks. The performers were usually white entertainers dressed in colorful costumes, with their faces blackened and eyes and mouth enlarged by white and red lines. The minstrel show comprised comic and sentimental songs, skits, jigs, and shuffle dances. While the vast majority of nineteenth-century minstrel performers were white, there were a few black minstrel companies, some of which, ironically, also performed in blackface.

African American Theater from 1900 to 1950. At the turn of the century, the popular syncopated rhythms of ragtime had a strong influence on the emerging musical theater and served as a bridge for a number of talented African Americans. Bob Cole (1864–1912) and William Johnson (1873–1954) conceived, wrote, produced, and directed the first black musical comedy, *A Trip to Coontown* (1898). The comedians Bert Williams (ca. 1876–1922) and George Walker (1873–1911) and their wives joined composers and writers to produce musicals and operettas such as *In Dahomey* (1902) and *Abyssinia* (1906), in which Americans for the first time saw blacks on the Broadway stage without burnt-cork makeup, speaking without dialect, and costumed in high fashion.

The early twentieth century also saw the formation of African American stock companies. The most significant was the Lafayette Players, founded in 1914 by Anita Bush (1894–1938). By the time it closed in 1932, this company had presented over 250 productions and employed a number of black stars.

Black performers and writers were also making inroads into commercial theater in the 1920s. Twenty plays with black themes were presented on Broadway in this decade, five of them written by African Americans, including *Shuffle Along* (1921), with lyrics and music by Noble Sissle (1889–1975) and Eubie Blake (1883–1983). The decade also saw some black performers achieve recognition in serious drama, among them Charles Gilpin (1878–1930), Paul Robeson, and Ethel Waters (1896–1977).

The depression forced black performers to find other ways of earning a living or to invent ingenious ways to create their own theater. There were a few Broadway productions of plays by blacks, such as the folk musical *Run Little Chillun* (1933) and *Mulatto* (1935) by Langston Hughes (1902–1967).

Possibly the most significant development for black theater during the 1930s was the Federal Theater Project, discussed in Chapter 14. This project, which was meant to help theater artists through the depression, formed separate black units in twenty-two cities which mounted plays by black and white authors and employed thousands of African American writers, performers, and technicians. The Federal Theater Project created a new generation of African American theater artists who would develop the theater of the 1940s and 1950s.

The 1940s saw a stage adaptation, in 1941, of the controversial novel *Native Son* by Richard Wright (1908–1960), directed by Orson Welles for his Mercury Theater. Other important Broadway ventures included Paul Robeson's record run of 296 performances in *Othello* in 1943, and *Anna Lucasta* (1944), adapted by Abram Hill (1911–1986).

African American Theater since 1950. The 1950s saw an explosion of black theater that would continue over the next five decades. *Take a Giant Step* by Louis Patterson (1922–   ), a play about growing up in an integrated neighborhood, premiered in 1953. In 1954, the playwright-director Owen Dodson (1914–1983)—a significant figure in black theater since the 1930s—staged *Amen Corner* by James Baldwin (1924–1987) at Howard University.

Off-Broadway, the Greenwich Mews Theater began casting plays without regard to race and also produced *Trouble in Mind* (1956) by Alice Childress (1920–1994)—the first play by an African American woman to receive a commercial production. Possibly the most important production of the postwar era was *Raisin in the Sun* (1959) by Lorraine Hansberry. It is about a black family in Chicago, held together by a God-fearing mother, who is planning to move into a predominantly white neighborhood where the family will be unwelcome. The son loses money in a get-rich-quick scheme but later assumes responsibility for the family. Hansberry's play was directed by Lloyd Richards (1922–   ), the first black director on Broadway. Richards later became head of the Yale School of Drama, where in the 1980s he nurtured the talents of the black playwright August Wilson (1945–   ), author of *Ma Rainey's Black Bottom* (1984), *Fences* (1985), *Joe Turner's Come and Gone* (1986), *The Piano Lesson* (1990), *Seven Guitars* (1995), and *Jitney* (2000).

From 1960 to the 1990s, there was an outpouring of African American theater, much of it reflecting the struggle for civil rights. Amiri Baraka (1934–   ) came to theatergoers' attention in 1964 with *Dutchman,* a verbal and sexual showdown between an assimilated black male and a white temptress, set in a New York subway. His plays *The Slave* (1965), *The Toilet* (1965), and *Slave Ship* (1970) also deal with the political, sociological, and psychological dilemmas confronting blacks. Among other significant plays of these two decades were Lonne Elder's *Ceremonies in Dark Old Men* (1969); Charles Gordone's *No*

Place to Be Somebody (1969); Douglas Turner Ward's *Day of Absence* (1970); and Charles Fuller's *A Soldier's Play* (1981), which won a Pulitzer Prize for drama.

In 1970 the Black Theater Alliance listed over 125 producing groups in the United States. While only a few of these survived the decade, many had a significant impact. The Negro Ensemble Company, founded in 1967, holds the contemporary record for continuous production by a professional black theater company. The New Lafayette Theater, which operated from 1966 until 1972, introduced the playwright Ed Bullins (1935–), experimented with black ritual, and published the journal *Black Theater*.

In addition to the emergence of these producing organizations, another major change in the 1970s was the presence of a larger black audience at Broadway theaters, which accounted for a significant number of commercial African American productions, such as *Don't Bother Me, I Can't Cope* (1972), *The Wiz* (1975), and *Bubbling Brown Sugar* (1976). This trend continued in the 1980s and 1990s with such hits as *Black and Blue* (1989), *Jelly's Last Jam* (1992), and *Bring in da' Noise, Bring in da' Funk* (1996).

In the past decade, African American artists have continued to make an impact on commercial and noncommercial theater. For example, George C. Wolfe (1955–), author-director of *The Colored Museum* (1986), *Spunk* (1990), *Jelly's Last Jam*, and *Bring in da' Noise, Bring in da' Funk* also directed both parts of the award-winning *Angels in America*. Since 1993, Wolfe has been artistic director of the Public Theater, a renowned off-Broadway theater founded by the New York producer Joseph Papp (1921–1991).

BRING IN DA' NOISE

A late twentieth-century African American success is the musical Bring in da'Noise, Bring in da' Funk, *a piece depicting the black experience in terms of tap dancing. Created by performer-choreographer Savion Glover and director George C. Wolfe, it was first presented at the Joseph Papp Public Theater and then moved to Broadway.* (© Michal Daniel)

Musical Theater

American theater has long been dominated by a popular commercial theater that appeals to the masses. The rich history of this popular theater is often ignored because of a bias toward what some critics refer to as "high art" theater. Many contemporary historians and critics have pointed out that popular theater, which appeals to the masses, is worthy of study and has influenced many authors and theater artists who work outside the commercial mainstream. Possibly the most popular and distinctive theatrical form developed in America is the *musical.*

Antecedents. In the nineteenth century, melodrama used music to accompany the action of plays. Singing and dancing also played a key role in other forms of nineteenth-century theatrical entertainment, such as *vaudeville* and *burlesque.* In its later phases, burlesque became synonymous with vulgar sketches and "girlie shows," including striptease; but for most of the nineteenth century, burlesque featured dramatic sketches and songs that satirized or made fun of other theatrical forms. Vaudeville was a series of variety acts—music, sketches, juggling, animal acts—that made up an evening's entertainment. Another type of musical production that flourished in the nineteenth century was the minstrel show, a variety show which featured white performers wearing blackface.

The Black Crook, produced in 1866, is considered a significant forerunner of the modern musical. This was a melodrama whose plot was so far-fetched that the producer had little faith in it. However, just at this time a nearby theater in which a French ballet troupe was to perform burned down, and the producer of *The Black Crook* quickly hired the French dancers as part of his own production. The combination of drama and dance, much to everyone's surprise, proved to be immensely successful.

Another form that developed in the late nineteenth century was *operetta*. An operetta is a romantic musical piece featuring melodic solos, duets, and choruses interspersed with spoken dialogue. Examples of operetta include the works of W. S. Gilbert (1836–1911) and Arthur Sullivan (1842–1900), such as *The Pirates of Penzance* (1879) and *The Mikado* (1885). The American composer Victor Herbert (1859–1924) also composed operettas, such as *Naughty Marietta* (1910).

American Musicals from 1900 to 1940. In the early twentieth century, the musical shows of George M. Cohan (1878–1942), such as *Little Johnny Jones* (1904) and *Forty-Five Minutes from Broadway* (1906), had songs with an American flavor and more realistic dialogue and better plot development than earlier musicals. Cohan's shows moved a step closer to today's "book" musicals—musicals that tell a story. (The dialogue and action of a musical are sometimes called the *book*, though the term *libretto* is also used.)

Around the time of World War I and in the period following, a truly native American musical began to emerge. It featured a story that was typically frivolous and silly, and very popular songs with hypnotic lyrics and melodies; these successful songs were played over and over and became known as *standards*. Among the famous composers of this period were Irving Berlin (1888–1989), Jerome Kern (1885–1945), George Gershwin (1898–1937), Cole Porter (1891–1964), and Richard Rodgers (1902–1979). Matching the inventiveness of the composers were the lyricists, including Ira Gershwin (1896–1983), who wrote lyrics for many of his brother's tunes; and Lorenz Hart (1895–1943), who teamed up with Richard Rodgers. Berlin and Porter wrote their own lyrics.

GEORGE M. COHAN'S *FORTY-FIVE MINUTES FROM BROADWAY*
Cohan was a leading figure in the development of the American musical at the beginning of the twentieth century. He wrote book, music, and lyrics for his musicals and also performed in them. In Cohan's work, music and plot lines were better integrated than they had been in earlier musicals. Cohan was one of the first writers to focus on American subjects, and his characters and stories were also more down-to-earth. (Billy Rose Theatre Collection, New York Public Library for the Performing Arts, Astor, Lenox, and Tilden Foundations)

SHOW BOAT

When Show Boat *opened in 1927, it began a new chapter in the history of the American musical. The chorus line was eliminated, miscegenation (a romance between a white man and a black woman) was treated for the first time, and other problems facing African Americans were touched on. Also, it had a glorious score by Jerome Kern and Oscar Hammerstein. Shown here is the revival staged by Harold Prince in 1993—a Canadian production that then moved to Broadway.* (Michael Cooper/Live Entertainment of Canada Inc.)

In 1927, Oscar Hammerstein II (1895–1960), who wrote the lyrics and libretto, and Jerome Kern, who composed the music, combined some of the best aspects of operetta and musical comedy to create *Show Boat*. The story was thoroughly American, rather than an exotic romantic fable, and it dealt with serious material—including the love story of a black woman and a white man. It was also innovative in that the songs were carefully integrated into the plot, and the chorus line was eliminated. There have been several versions of *Show Boat* and numerous revivals, underscoring its historical significance; a spectacular revival in 1993 was staged by the director Harold Prince (1928–   ).

Another milestone of musical theater was Gershwin's *Porgy and Bess* (1935), with a book by DuBose Heyward (1885–1940). Set in the African American community of Charleston, South Carolina, it is even more realistic than *Show Boat;* and its score is so powerful that some people consider it an opera rather than a musical. (In fact, *Porgy and Bess* has been performed in a number of opera houses.)

The High Point of American Musicals.   *Oklahoma!*—which was produced in 1943 and brought the team of Rodgers and Hammerstein together for the first time—heralded a significant era of the American book musical. *Oklahoma!* has been praised for seamlessly fitting together story, music, lyrics, and dances so that tone, mood, and intention became a unified whole. Its choreography, by Agnes deMille (1905–1993), included a famous ballet sequence and influenced many later choreographers in musical theater, including Jerome Robbins (1918–1998) and Bob Fosse (1927–1987). Rodgers and Hammerstein went on to create other significant musicals such as *Carousel* (1945), *South Pacific* (1949), *The King and I* (1951), and *The Sound of Music* (1959).

Among other notable musicals during the 1940s and 1950s were Irving Berlin's *Annie Get Your Gun* (1946), based on the life of Annie Oakley; Cole Porter's musical version of *The Taming of the Shrew*, called *Kiss Me Kate* (1948);

THE GOLDEN AGE OF AMERICAN MUSICALS
The two decades beginning in 1943—with the production of Oklahoma!—*was an illustrious period for new American musicals. Works by Irving Berlin, Cole Porter, Lerner and Loewe, and Rodgers and Hammerstein created then are still produced frequently today. A good example is* Kiss Me, Kate, *revived on Broadway in the 1999, a scene from which is shown here, with Marin Mazzie and Brian Stokes-Mitchell.* (© Joan Marcus)

Guys and Dolls (1950) by Frank Loesser (1910–1969); *My Fair Lady* (1956), by the librettist and lyricist Alan Jay Lerner (1918–1986) and the composer Frederick Loewe (1904–1988), based on George Bernard Shaw's *Pygmalion* (1913); and *West Side Story,* a modernization of *Romeo and Juliet* which was created by the composer Leonard Bernstein (1918–1990), the lyricist Stephen Sondheim (1930–), and the librettist Arthur Laurents (1918–). Many of these have recently had successful Broadway revivals, including *Annie Get Your Gun,* starring Bernadette Peters (1948–) in 1999, and *Kiss Me Kate* later in that same year.

Some commentators believe that *Fiddler on the Roof* (1964)—with music by Jerry Bock (1928–), lyrics by Sheldon Harnick (1924–), and book by Joseph Stein (1912–)—marks the end of this era of book musicals. *Fiddler on the Roof,* about a Jewish family whose father attempts to uphold tradition in a Russian village where the Jewish community faces persecution, was directed and choreographed by Jerome Robbins.

American Musicals since 1965.

One example of changes in the musical following *Fiddler on the Roof* was the rock musical *Hair* (1967), by Galt McDermot (1928–) and Gerome Ragni (1942–), which had no actual story line and was a celebration of the antiestablishment lifestyle of the 1960s.

After *Hair,* the musical scene became increasingly fragmented, with fewer and fewer book musicals being written. In place of book musicals, there were other approaches, one being the *concept musical,* in which a production is built around an idea rather than a story. Two examples, both composed by Stephen Sondheim and directed by Harold Prince, are *Company* (1970) and *Follies* (1971). Two of Sondheim's more recent works, *Sunday in the Park with George* (1985) and *Into the Woods* (1988), can also be considered concept musicals, though in *Passion* (1994), Sondheim returned to the traditional book musical.

Another significant trend in musicals of the 1970s and 1980s is the ascendancy of the choreographer as director, providing the vision for a musical. *A Chorus Line* was developed by the director-choreographer Michael Bennett (1943–1987). Jerome Robbins, director of *West Side Story* and *Fiddler on the Roof,* is generally recognized as the leading director-choreographer in the United States. Other significant director-choreographers were Gower Champion (1920–1980), who was responsible for *Hello Dolly!* (1964) and *42nd Street* (1980); Bob Fosse, who directed *Sweet Charity* (1966) and *Pippin* (1972); and Tommy Tune (1939–), who directed *Nine* (1982), *Grand Hotel* (1989), and *The Will Rogers Follies* (1991). A recent example of the director-choreographer is Susan Stroman, responsible for *The Producers* (2001).

Still another trend of the past three decades has been the emergence of British composers and lyricists. The leading figure in this movement is the composer Andrew Lloyd Webber (1948–), who, with the lyricist Tim Rice (1944–), wrote *Jesus Christ Superstar* (1971) and *Evita* (1979). Webber has also written *Cats* (1982), *The Phantom of the Opera* (1987), and *Sunset Blvd.* (1993). Two other lavish musicals that originated in Britain are *Les Misérables* (1987) and *Miss Saigon* (1989).

After a period when elaborate, large-scale British musicals seemed to dominate the scene in the United States as well as abroad, new musicals began appearing in the mid-1990s that were created by international teams of artists. A good example is Aida, *with music by British pop composer, Elton John, lyrics by Andrew Lloyd Webber's former partner Tim Rice, and staged by a leading American director, Robert Falls. Seen here is Heather Headley, in the title role, for which she won a Tony award.* (© Joan Marcus)

Along with British imports, there has also been a trend toward revivals of earlier musicals. However, in the late 1990s there was a sense that the American musical was rebounding. The popularity of George C. Wolfe's *Bring in da' Noise, Bring in da' Funk* and the huge success of *Rent* by Jonathan Larson (1960–1996), first off-Broadway in 1995 and then on Broadway in 1996, seemed to reawaken interest in the American form. *Rent,* an adaptation of the opera *La Bohème,* uses many musical forms (rock, jazz, Latin, opera) to tell a story about starving artists in the East Village of New York. Disney's musicals have also been highly successful, including *The Lion King* (1997) and *Aida* (1999). In 2001, the musical *The Producers,* based on the film, was an award-winning Broadway hit.

In addition, there seemed to be indications of a weakening of the British musical imports, such as the failure of Andrew Lloyd Weber's *Sunset Blvd.* (1993), which lost $30 million worldwide, and *Whistle Down the Wind,* which never reached New York after its tryout in Washington, D.C.

Alternatives to Commercial Theater

In an attempt to produce works that were more experimental, more controversial, or less appealing to mass audiences, American theater artists developed alternatives to commercial New York Broadway theater. These major alternatives are referred to as regional theater, off-Broadway, and off-off-Broadway.

Making Connections:

Film and the Other Mass Media

FILM AND THEATER
Theater and film have had a close relationship with many artists working in both media. A recent popular film, Shakespeare in Love, *created a comical, fanciful portrayal of Shakespeare and his theater. One of the authors of the screenplay was the renowned playwright, Tom Stoppard. Shown here are Colin Firth and Dame Judi Dench, in a scene from that film. Both actors are also successful stage performers.* (Photofest)

In the twentieth century, theater saw the development of competitors for audiences. The popularity of film, radio, and television affected theater. The relationship between film and theater is clearly apparent. Throughout the twentieth century, theater artists have been captured by the allure of film, which can provide greater financial success and international popularity.

The first motion picture camera was invented in Thomas Edison's laboratory in 1888. In 1895, two French brothers, Auguste and Louis Lumiére, developed the art of projecting film onto a larger screen. In the first decade of the twentieth century, films began to tell complete stories and were mass-presented. In the second decade of the century, full-length films were popularized and silent film stars, such as Charlie Chaplin, Buster Keaton, and Lillan Gish, were world-renowned. In addition, great film directors, such as D. W. Griffith, Sergei

Eisenstein, and Carl Dreyer, revolutionized the art of filmmaking.

With the advent of sound in 1927 and the development of color technology in the 1930s, film became even more competitive with theatrical art, stealing artists and audience members. In the last half of the twentieth century, film technology became even more sophisticated, with the development of wide screens, special effects, digital sound, and a host of other innovations.

Radio and television also became the home of dramatic entertainments. Radio developed at the turn of the twentieth century; by the 1920s, commercial broadcasts and networks were established. In the United States in the 1930s, radio soap operas, dramas, and comedies became popular escapes from the depression. One of the most famous radio dramatizations was Orson Welles's *War of the Worlds,* which, when it was broadcast in 1938, fooled many listeners

into believing that Earth had been attacked by aliens from outer space. (Welles and his actors were all theater personalities.) Radio presented these forms of dramatic entertainments throughout the 1940s.

Television usurped radio in the 1950s and became the popular competitor of both film and theater. Although the roots of television can be traced back to developments in the 1920s, and early television broadcasting began in the 1930s, television became a mass entertainment in the early 1950s. Like film, television became more popular with innovations such as color and the recently introduced high-definition digital television (HDTV). In all countries, television has attracted theater and film artists, again because of the promise of financial reward and international recognition.

The relationship between theater and all these media is quite clear. Theater artists frequently are lured away to perform in these media. Film, radio, and television often adapt dramatic materials into films. Think about all of the adaptations of Shakespeare's works into movies. There have been many filmed versions of *Hamlet* and *Romeo and Juliet,* for example. Some of these versions employ the original texts; some, such as *Romeo Must Die* (2000), use the plotline as the basis of a new contemporary entertainment.

Yet in recent years, there has also been a new phenomenon: the return of theater artists from these electronic media to the live art. Recent productions in London and New York starred well-known film actors who had begun their careers as stage performers. Kevin Spacey, Matthew Broderick (most recently in the musical version of *The Producers*), Liam Neeson, and Judi Dench are just a few of the actors who cross from film and television back to theater. Some critics suggest that actors return to the stage because of theater's unique quality: the intersection of live performers with the live audience.

Regional Theater. An important trend in the United States in the past half century has been the growth of major established regional theaters. (The phenomenon of important theaters established outside of major cities is, again, a worldwide trend.) A number of significant regional theaters were founded in the 1940s and 1950s, including the Alley Theatre in Houston, Texas, and the Arena Stage in Washington, D.C.; and resident professional theaters began to flourish in the 1960s and 1970s in large cities around the country—cities such as Boston, New Haven, Louisville, Milwaukee, Minneapolis, Seattle, San Francisco, Los Angeles, and San Diego. These are nonprofit rather than commercial theaters, but they employ professional performers, directors, and designers. They present the best dramas from the past as well as interesting new plays. In fact, in recent years nonprofit theaters have been the chief source of new works in the United States.

These established nonprofit theaters have produced the work of many significant playwrights and directors. Among the better-known playwrights are John Guare (1938–), Lanford Wilson (1937–), Marsha Norman (1947–), and Wendy Wasserstein (1950–). Directors emerging from these theaters include Mark Lamos (1946–), at the Hartford Stage Company in Connecticut; Arvin Brown (1940–) of the Long Wharf Theater in New Haven; Jon Jory (1938–)of the Actors Theater of Louisville; and Des McAnuff (1952–), who has directed at many regional theaters, including La Jolla Playhouse in California, which he headed for several years.

It is noteworthy that in New York City, a comparable group of permanent theaters have become an important force; among the best-known are the Manhattan Theater Club and Playwrights Horizons.

Off-Broadway, Off-Off-Broadway, and Alternative Regional Theaters. In New York City, *off-Broadway* theater began in the 1950s as an alternative to commercial Broadway, which was becoming increasingly costly. Off-Broadway theaters were smaller than Broadway theaters—most of them had fewer than 200 seats—and were located outside the Times Square neighborhood where the Broadway houses are situated. Because off-Broadway was less expensive than Broadway, it offered more opportunity for producing serious classics and experimental works.

In the 1960s and 1970s, however, off-Broadway itself became expensive and institutionalized. As a result, small independent producing groups had to develop another forum. The result was *off-off Broadway*. Off-off-Broadway shows are produced wherever inexpensive space is available—in churches, lofts, warehouses, garages—and are characterized by low prices and a wide variety of offerings. It is in these theaters, too, that much experimental work takes place: for example, productions in which performers create their own work and in which theater is combined with painting, dance, or television.

One important off-off-Broadway theater is Café LaMama; among the significant groups who have worked off-off-Broadway are the Living Theater, the Open Theater, the Performance Group, Mabou Mines, and the Wooster Group. All have experimented with physical performance techniques, improvisation, texts created by performers and directors, and environmental presentations.

Two experimental directors whose works were first seen off-off-Broadway are Robert Wilson (1944–   ) and Richard Foreman (1937–   ). Their work is typically unified by a theme or point of view determined by the director, and their material is often organized into units analogous to frames in television or film. Stunning theatrical images containing the essence of the ideas that interest these directors are often the key to their work.

Counterparts of the off- and off-off-Broadway movements have also sprung up in other major cities across the United States—Washington, Atlanta, Chicago, Minneapolis, Los Angeles, San Francisco, Seattle, and others—where small groups perform as alternatives to the larger, established regional theaters. In Chicago, for example, there was an explosion of "off-Loop" theaters in the 1970s. (Off-Loop refers to theaters located outside the Loop—commercial downtown Chicago.) One, Steppenwolf Theater, founded in 1976, whose original company included many actors who became well-known stars, including John Malkovich (1953–   ), Gary Sinise (1955–   ), and Laurie Metcalf (1955–   ), evolved into a leading established regional theater.

Presentations by these alternative theaters include classics, new plays, and experimental works. One particular virtue of such theaters and artists is that they can present productions of interest to specific groups—for example, feminist theater, labor theater, Hispanic theater, gay and lesbian theater, and African American theater.

Again, this trend of creating out-of-the-way alternative theaters outside the commercial centers of major cities is taking place worldwide. In London, for example, there is a long history of "fringe" theaters: theaters outside London's commercial West End, which were originally established to circumvent the English censorship laws and which present more experimental works.

Two Contemporary American Playwrights with Roots in Alternative Theater. Two American playwrights whose work was first presented in small alternative, non-profit theaters and who then became prominent in regional and off-Broadway theaters are Sam Shepard (1943–) and David Mamet (1947–). Like many of our contemporary playwrights, Shepard and Mamet mix concerns of high art—such as the plight of the American family and the demise of the American dream—with techniques borrowed from mass entertainments such as film, popular music, and melodrama. Also, they often blur the distinction between realism and abstraction.

Sam Shepard.   Shepard first developed his playwriting skills off-off-Broadway with works that fused surreal and absurdist styles and abandoned traditional plot structure and development. His later dramas include *Buried Child* (for which he won a Pulitzer Prize in 1979), *True West* (1980), *Fool for Love* (1982), *A Lie of*

SAM SHEPARD'S *FOOL FOR LOVE*
Sam Shepard is a playwright who came out of the off-off Broadway movement of the late 1960s and the alternative regional theatre scene of the 1970s. Shepard is best known for the plays he wrote in the late 1970s and early 1980s, that combine traditional family drama with explosive theatricality. One such play is Fool for Love, *shown here in a recent revival starring (left to right) Glenn Fleshler, Laila Robins, James Morrison, and Mark Hammer. (© T. Charles Erickson/The McCarter Theatre Center for the Performing Arts)*

the Mind (1985), *Simpatico* (1994), and *The Late Henry Moss* (2000). These plays cannot be categorized as strictly antirealistic or realistic, since they fuse abstraction and theatricality with recognizable characters and circumstances. Shepard's new plays deal with American mythology, the violence of American society, and the degeneration of the American family.

David Mamet. David Mamet came out of the Chicago theater scene. (Since the mid-1970s, Chicago has been the home of a number of significant alternative theater companies, including Victory Gardens, Wisdom Bridge, Body Politic, and Steppenwolf.) Mamet's plays have naturalistic language and settings and down-and-out characters whose struggles are clearly recognizable, but they do not provide the clear-cut exposition or dramatic resolutions of traditional realism. His plays, like Shepard's, attack many accepted ideals of American life. Among his best-known works are *American Buffalo* (1977), *Glengarry Glen Ross* (1983), *Oleanna* (1992), *The Cryptogram* (1994), *The Old Neighborhood* (1997), and *Boston Marriage* (1999).

In Chapter 16, our final chapter, we will examine some of the contemporary trends that developed in recent years of theater history. Many of these trends have set the stage for the theater of the twenty-first century.

SUMMARY

A number of theatrical movements were in evidence between 1945 and 1980. The absurdist dramas of Beckett, Ionesco, and Pinter have had a profound influence on contemporary playwriting. Other movements included the "angry young men" in England and documentary drama in Germany. The two leading American dramatists—Arthur Miller and Tennessee Williams—worked in a style that can be described as selective realism.

Happenings, multimedia, environmental theater, and poor theater forced theatergoers to reevaluate their traditional expectations about the performer-audience relationship and other aspects of drama.

African American theater artists wrote plays and organized production companies which focused on racial issues confronting American society. In the United States, the musical reached a golden age in the 1940s. At the same time, artists began to break away from commercialism, working off-Broadway, off-off-Broadway, and in regional and alternative theaters.

This is a small sample of websites dedicated to modern American theater.

American Drama   http://blues.fd1.uc.edu/www/amdrama
Online journal of American drama.

Tennessee Williams   http://www.imagi-nation.com/moonstruck/clsc9.htm
A biography of the American playwright Tennessee Williams, plus links to all his works in print.

Samuel Beckett Resources and Links   http://home.sprintmail.com/~lifeform/Beck_Links.html
A comprehensive grouping of links to online essays, reviews, analyses, and various other material related to the works of Samuel Beckett.

An Electronic Eugene O'Neill Archive   http://www.eoneill.com
An electronic forum for discussion of O'Neill's works and collected essays.

Rodgers and Hammerstein Organization   www.rnh.com
Founded by Richard Rodgers and Oscar Hammerstein II, this organization represents over 100 songwriters and authors.

Choose one of the links above and discuss in detail how that site could be used by the following theater professionals as a resource:

Actor

Dramaturg

Director

Designer

Audience member

Chapter 16

Contemporary Trends

The Beginning of a New Century

Today's Theater: Diversity and Eclecticism

    Asian American Theater

    Hispanic Theater

    Native American Theater

    Feminist Theater

Play Synopsis: *Fefu and Her Friends*

    Gay and Lesbian Theater

    Performance Art

    Postmodernism

    International Trends

    Two African Playwrights

Today and Tomorrow: A Look Ahead

Making Connections: *The Digital Arts*

Summary

◀ DIVERSITY OF FORMS

The contemporary theater is marked by a diversity of theatrical forms. Many of these forms are difficult to define. Performance art may be the hardest to categorize. A performance artist, whose work combines vaudeville, silent film clowning, commedia, and street performance, is Bill Irwin. Irwin is also a film and stage actor. He is seen here bringing his performance art skills to an adaptation of Beckett's Texts for Nothing, *presented at the Classic Stage Company. (© Dixie Sheridan)*

In this chapter we will examine important trends of contemporary theater. Our focus will be mainly on American theater, but much of what we discover will be representative of theatrical conditions in other parts of the world. We will focus most closely on theatrical movements and forms that reflect the great diversity of contemporary society, such as feminist theater, and those that embody continuing experimentation, such as postmodernism and performance art. Our ultimate goal in this chapter, however, will be to consider whether theater as we know it will survive in the twenty-first century.

The Beginning of a New Century

As we noted in Chapter 15, social unrest and violence marked the second half of the twentieth century. Worldwide political, economic, and cultural turmoil continued as the century ended—and, as always, the arts have continued to reflect the world in which they are being created.

To take just two examples, theater has been affected by the rise of political, religious, and social conservatism and, deeply, by AIDS. AIDS, a disease that destroys the body's immune system, began to reach alarming proportions in the 1980s, and it has been one reason for the growing activism of homosexual groups. A significant number of theater figures have died of AIDS, including the Broadway musical director Michael Bennett and the founder of the Ridiculous Theatrical Company, Charles Ludlam (1943–1987). Also, AIDS has been the subject of many plays, perhaps most notably the epic *Angels in America* by Tony Kushner (1965–   ).

Meanwhile, various conservative movements have attempted to question the advances made by gays, feminists, and other minorities, and conservative politicians worldwide have questioned government support of the arts.

Contemporary society has again been confronted by horrific genocide in Bosnia and Rwanda, forcing us to question whether there have been any real changes in moral outlook since World War II. While the fall of totalitarian communism was celebrated in eastern Europe, the world has also been troubled by continued poverty, crime, and intolerance toward racial minorities, even with a vibrant economy. There has also been increased tension and violence in the Middle East. At the same time, the American presidency, under Bill Clinton, was rocked by a number of scandals and impeachment hearings. In 2000, George W. Bush, while losing the popular vote, was elected President in a highly contested election.

Today's Theater: Diversity and Eclecticism

Two words that can characterize today's theater are *diversity* and *eclecticism*: diversity because the types of theater available to audiences are so wide-ranging and, as we noted in Chapter 1, because the audiences themselves are so diverse; and eclecticism because contemporary theater embraces such a wide variety of events.

Audiences today can see revivals of the best theater from the past: Greek, Elizabethan, French, and Spanish. They can see theater from Asia, Africa, and Latin America; new plays; and avant-garde and experimental works. There are productions in translation of the best new plays from other countries. What's more, these productions can be seen in a wide variety of theater environments: in outdoor as well as indoor theaters; in proscenium theaters and on thrust stages; in huge theaters seating 3,000 or 4,000 people; and in small theaters seating only 50 or 75.

One hallmark of contemporary theater is that all these strands exist simultaneously. This is an expression of its eclecticism. Forms of both realistic theater and departures from realism continue to flourish today. Alongside them are such diverse forms as musical theater, ethnic theater, political theater, feminist theater, and gay and lesbian theater.

As all this suggests, our contemporary theater is complex. If theater mirrors the society in which it is produced, then it is not surprising that ours is fragmented, reflecting the complexity of today's life. We have already surveyed African American theater in Chapter 15; we now turn our attention to other examples of diversity in contemporary theater.

Asian American Theater

For most of the nineteenth century and the first half of the twentieth century, Asians appeared in dramatic offerings strictly as stereotypes. With the coming of cultural and ethnic awareness in the 1960s and 1970s, things began to change. In 1965 several Asian American performers and directors founded the East West Players in Los Angeles. In 1973, two more groups were formed—the Asian Exclusion Act in Seattle and the Asian-American Theatre Workshop in San Francisco—and in 1977 the director-actor Tisa Chang (1945–   ) founded the Pan Asian Repertory Theatre in New York. These groups employed Asian American performers, produced dramas from the Asian cultural heritage, and emphasized new plays written by and for Asian Americans.

A number of plays by Asian American writers were produced in the 1970s and 1980s, including a memory play by Philip Kan Gotanda (1950–   ) called *Song for a Nisea Fisherman* (1980). A playwright who came to prominence in the 1980s was David Henry Hwang (1957–   ), son of first-generation Americans who immigrated from China to California. Hwang wrote several plays that won wide recognition, beginning with *FOB*, produced in 1980, and *The Dance and the Railroad*, produced in 1981. Later in the decade, in 1988, Hwang's *M. Butterfly* opened successfully on Broadway. Based on a true story, the play deals with a French diplomat who meets and falls in love with a Chinese opera singer who he thinks is a woman but turns out to be a man and a spy. A new play by Hwang, *Golden Child*, opened in the 1996–1997 theater season.

There has also been a movement to have more Asian Americans employed as performers in appropriate roles. Hwang and the actor B. D. Wong, who played the

PING CHONG'S *POJAGI*

Ping Chong is an Asian American theater artist who works in a variety of performance styles. Often referred to as a performance artist, his work mixes Eastern and Western theatrical elements to call into question the representation of Asians and Asian Americans in theater. Pojagi is part of Ping Chong's East-West series and focuses on Korean history. Shin Young Lee is shown here in the production staged off-off Broadway at La Mama. (© Tom Brazil)

Chinese opera singer in the original production of *M. Butterfly,* led a vigorous protest against the hiring of an English actor to play the leading role in the musical *Miss Saigon.* That battle was lost; but by 1996, when a revival of *The King and I* opened on Broadway, it had a large proportion of Asian American performers.

Hispanic Theater

Contemporary Hispanic theater in the U.S. can be divided into at least three groups: Chicano theater, Cuban American theater, and Puerto Rican or Nuyorican theater. All three address the experiences of Hispanics living in the United States, and the plays are sometimes written in Spanish but are usually in English.

Chicano theater, which originated primarily in the west and southwest, came to prominence during the time of the civil rights movements of the 1960s. The theater troupe known as El Teatro Campesino ("farmworkers' theater") grew out of the work of Luis Valdéz (1940–   ), who joined César Chavez in organizing farmworkers in California. Valdéz wrote *actos,* short agitprop pieces dramatizing the lives of workers. (The term *agitprop* means "agitation propaganda"; it was applied in the 1930s to plays with a strong political or social agenda.)

El Teatro Campesino became the prototype for other groups such as Teatro de la Gente ("people's theater"), founded in 1967; and Teatro de la Esperanza ("theater of hope"), begun in 1971 in Santa Barbara, California. Also in 1971, a network of these theaters across the country was established. In the 1990s a well-known theater, Teatro Vista, performed for Mexican and Hispanic communities in Chicago.

In 1978 Valdéz's play *Zoot Suit,* about racial violence in Los Angeles in 1943, opened in Los Angeles to considerable acclaim; it later moved to Broadway. Other plays about the Chicano experience followed, one of the most notable being *Roosters* (1987) by Milcha Sanchez-Scott (1955–), in which cockfighting is a metaphor used to explore Chicano concerns and family conflicts. Among other writers who have dealt with Chicano as well as wider themes is Arthur Giron (1937–), an American writer from Guatemala.

Cuban American theater developed chiefly in Florida. The Federal Theater Proj-

HISPANIC THEATER

Among the important theaters that represents the wide diversity of theater in the United States is Hispanic theater. Shown here is a production of a play entitled Zoot Suit *by Luis Valdez.* Zoot Suit *was the first play to be written and directed by a Chicano on Broadway. This production was staged by Chicago's Goodman Theatre, with Marco Rodriguez as Pachuco. (© Liz Lauren)*

ject of the 1930s resulted in fourteen Cuban American productions in 1936 and 1937. A highly regarded Cuban American dramatist who began to be produced in the 1970s was Maria Irene Fornes (1930–). Among the current generation of Cuban American writers who have emerged in the past quarter-century are Manuel Martin, Mario Peña, Dolores Prida, Iván Acosta, and Omar Torres. (Torres's work is centered in Miami and New York.)

Nuyorican is a term that refers to Puerto Rican culture, mostly in New York, but elsewhere as well. Works by playwrights with a Puerto Rican orientation began to be produced in the 1960s and 1970s by groups such as the Teatro Repertorio Español, the Puerto Rican Traveling Theatre, and the New York Public Theatre founded by Joseph Papp (1922–1991). The Nuyorican Poets' Café presented plays by a number of Hispanic writers, including an ex-convict, Miguel Piñero (1947–1988) whose *Short Eyes,* a harshly realistic portrait of prison life, proved to be very successful and won a number of awards in the 1973–1974 season. Today a new group of Puerto Rican playwrights has come to prominence, including Yvette Ramírez, Cándido Tirado, Edward Gallardo, and Juan Shamsul Alam.

Native American Theater

Native American (sometimes referred to as American Indian) theater tradition, which stressed ancient rituals and communal celebrations, differed from western theater in several respects. For one thing, it was infused with cosmic significance; for another, there was no audience as such: those observing were considered participants just as much as the principal performers. Much of this theater legacy was wiped out during the nineteenth century, along with much of Native American life itself. In recent years, though, there have been attempts to recapture lost rituals and traditions from among the 3 million native peoples and their 500 tribal cultures.

As for Native American life onstage, a movement began at somewhat the same time as other minority-oriented theaters to establish a true Native American theater. Two examples of groups that emerged in the late 1960s and early 1970s are the Red Earth Theatre in Seattle, Washington, and the Native American Theatre Ensemble in New York, headed by Hanay Geiogamah.

Later, a significant work was *Black Elk Speaks,* produced by the Denver Center Theatre Company in 1993. This was a collaboration between Native Americans and others, including Donovan Marley, the director of the Denver company; it was based on a healing vision experienced by Nicholas Black Elk, a Sioux born in 1863. At age 9, Black Elk fell into a coma lasting 12 days, during which he had a transforming dream: he saw that a sacred hoop, uniting all nations, was broken and had to be repaired. Sixty years later Black Elk related the vision in great detail to others who recorded it in a book; and it was this book which Marley, guided by advice from Native American elders, turned into the play.

NATIVE AMERICAN THEATER

The play Black Elk Speaks *is an example of the growing Native American theater. Based on a healing vision of Nicholas Black Elk, a Sioux, it was presented first by the Denver Center Theatre Company in a production shown here featuring Lorne Cardinal as Red Cloud.* (© Terry Shapiro)

Feminist Theater

In the United States, many female playwrights have questioned traditional gender roles and the place of women in American society. In the 1970s and 1980s, there were a number of successful female American playwrights. Representative works include *Fefu and Her Friends* (1977) by Maria Irene Fornes; *'Night, Mother* (1983) by Marsha Norman (1947–   ); *Crimes of the Heart* (1977) by Beth Henley (1952–   ); *The Heidi Chronicles* (1988), *The Sisters Rosensweig* (1992), and *An American Daughter* (1997) by Wendy Wasserstein; and *How I Learned to Drive* (1988) by Paula Vogel (1951–   ).

*In the last 30 years, a
number of playwrights and
theater companies have
treated contemporary issues
and concerns confronting
women. One of the most
notable dramatists is Maria
Irene Fornes. This is a
scene from her play* Fefu
and Her Friends, *which
focuses on eight women.
During its course, the
audience is divided into
four groups and taken to
four separate locations to
see different scenes. This
production was staged at
the Yale Repertory Theatre
and shown in this scene are
Julianna Margulies as Emma
and Joyce Lynn O'Connor
as Fefu. (© Gerry Goodstein)*

Suzan-Lori Parks (1964–   ) and Pearl Cleage (1948–   ) are two contemporary African American female playwrights whose works deal with issues of racism and feminism and whose work has been produced in regional and alternative theaters. Parks's *Venus* (1996), for example, depicts the life of a nineteenth-century black woman who was exhibited in England as a sideshow freak, the "Hottentot Venus." Parks's other critically acclaimed works include *The Death of the Last Black Man in the Whole Entire World* (1990) and *The America Play* (1993).

Pearl Cleage's best-known plays are the one-act *Chain* (1992) and *Flyin' West* (1992), which was produced by Atlanta's Alliance Theater Company; she has also created a number of performance pieces, a form that will be discussed later in this chapter.

Another female African American dramatist whose work is politically charged is Kia Corthron (1961–   ). Corthron's works, which include *Seeking the Genesis* (1996) and *Force Continuum* (2001), have been commissioned by leading regional and off-Broadway companies.

Feminist theater companies have forced audiences to reexamine their own gender biases and those of their society. Some scholars estimate that more than 100 feminist companies have been founded in the United States; these companies include At the Foot of the Mountain, Women's Experimental Theatre, and Omaha Magic Theater. One company, Split Britches, became well-known for its production of *Belle Reprieve* (1991), which made satiric references to Tennessee Williams's *A Streetcar Named Desire* and was created collaboratively with an English gay company, Bloolips.

FEFU AND HER FRIENDS (1977)

Maria Irene Fornes, (1930–   )

Characters
Fefu, Cindy, Christina, Julia, Emma Paula, Sue, Cecilia

Setting
A house belonging to Fefu and her husband in the New England countryside. Spring 1935.

Background
Eight women who went to college together gather for a day to visit and plan a collaborative presentation urging educational reform.

Part I
The living room: midday. Fefu tells Cindy and Christina, "My husband married me to have a constant reminder of how loathsome women are." As they discuss this provocative idea, Fefu picks up a shotgun, aims out the door, and fires at her husband. Fefu explains to her shocked friends that she plays a game with her husband—she shoots blanks at him and he falls down. He has told her that he may load the gun with real bullets someday.

Julia arrives in a wheelchair, then goes off to wash up. Cindy explains to Christina the bizarre accident that led to Julia's paralysis. Julia fell down at the moment a hunter had shot and killed a deer. Julia became delirious, talking about torturers who would kill her if she did not recant. The bullet had grazed her forehead, but the doctors found no spinal cord injury that would adequately explain her inability to walk. Fefu remembers that Julia used to be afraid of nothing.

Emma arrives wearing a theatrical Turkish dress. Paula and Sue are with her. The women decide that they will eat lunch and then rehearse their presentation. Emma concentrates on the theatrical elements, suggesting which colors the other women should wear. Emma, Fefu, Paula, and Sue exit.

Part II
For this section of the play, the audience is divided into four groups. Each group is taken to one of four different locations in Fefu's house and lawn, to observe one of four separate scenes, which are enacted simultaneously: "on the lawn," "in the study," "in the bedroom," and "in the kitchen." When these four scenes have been played once, each audience group rotates to the next location and the scenes are repeated. All the audience members see every scene, but not in the same order.

On the lawn: Fefu and Emma play croquet and agree that admission to heaven is probably determined by sexual performance on earth. Fefu leaves to fetch lemonade, while Emma recites a sonnet. Returning, Fefu is followed by Paula and Cecilia.

In the study: Christina and Cindy engage in idle conversation while reading. Christina says she is frightened by Fefu's unconventional behavior. Sue comes in, looking for Julia, and then goes off to look in the bedroom. Cindy describes a strange dream in which a doctor attacks her. Fefu comes through the room and invites them to play croquet.

In the bedroom: Wearing a white hospital gown, Julia rests on the floor. She hallucinates talking about the judges who have crippled her and have the power to kill her. She says Fefu is in danger. Sue comes with a bowl of soup for Julia.

In the kitchen: Sue heats soup. Paula explains her theory of how long an affair lasts. Sue puts a bowl of soup on a tray and exits. Cecilia enters, and she and Paula awkwardly discuss their past relationship. Fefu comes in for lemonade, and all three go out to play croquet.

Part III
For Part III, the entire audience reassembles and watches together.

The living room: Evening. All eight women are present. The women decide on the order of their presentation. Emma delivers her speech, on the importance of environment in education. Then all the women except Julia and Cindy go into the kitchen, but they run into and out of the living room having a water fight. When they return to the kitchen, Fefu is alone in the living room. Julia enters, walking, picks up the sugar bowl, and exits. Then, in her wheelchair, she reenters with the other women, who reminisce about their school days. After the other women go outside, Fefu confronts Julia about having seen her walk, but Julia denies this. Christina and Cecilia enter, and Fefu gets her gun. She exits and fires the gun. Julia puts her hand to her forehead, which is bloody. Fefu reenters with a rabbit she has killed, as Julia slumps in her chair—apparently dead.

Feminist theater has roots in the past. One significant forerunner, for example, was the American playwright Rachel Crothers (1878–1958). Crothers wrote and directed many successful plays from 1906 to 1937; all of them dealt with women's moral and social concerns, and most of them were set in urban high society. In the summer of 1995, the Looking Glass Theater in New York revived Crothers's *A Man's World* (1909), which attacks the double standard. Its heroine, a writer named Frank Ware, is raising the illegitimate son of a woman who died in childbirth. Frank has developed strong feelings against the code that allows fathers of such children to avoid responsibility; she then discovers that in this case the father is actually one of her own suitors—and she must choose between her love for him and her detestation of what he represents. Rachel Crothers's plays are skillful, entertaining comedies, but she always focused on the issue of sexual equality.

Feminist theater is, of course, also a worldwide phenomenon. There are many feminist playwrights and theater companies throughout the world. In England, for example, there are a number of significant female playwrights, including: Caryl Churchill (discussed later), Timberlake Wertenbaker (1946–   ), and Pam Gems (1925–   ).

Gay and Lesbian Theater

Lesbian theater groups can be part of feminist theater, but gay and lesbian theater is also a distinct movement.

A number of plays and performers, introduced homosexual and lesbian themes into theater before the 1960s. For example, in the nineteenth century and the early twentieth century there was a considerable amount of cross-dressing in performances: men often appeared in "drag" and women in men's clothing, raising questions about sexual and gender roles. Also, plays included material on this subject; one example is Lillian Hellman's *The Children's Hour* (1934), in which a presumed lesbian relationship between two schoolteachers was presented.

However, the play that first brought gay life to the forefront was *The Boys in the Band* (1968), by Mart Crowley (1935–   ). Crowley depicted a group of men living an openly gay life. Ironically, in 1969, the year after it opened, gay patrons of the Stonewall Inn in New York's Greenwich Village fought against police officers attempting to close the bar. This uprising, considered the beginning of the modern gay rights movement, changed attitudes of gay activists, who now rejected what they considered a stereotype of homosexuals depicted in *The Boys in the Band*. However, a significant New York revival for its thirteenth anniversary led to a reevaluation of the play's significance in the history of gay and lesbian theater in the United States.

GAY AND LESBIAN THEATER

Among the many alternative theaters that emerged in the last part of the twentieth century was theater centering on the gay and lesbian experience. Among the groups that became well known is the one shown here called The Five Lesbian Brothers. The actors are, from left to right, standing Babs Davy, Dominique Dibbell, Maureen Angelos, and Lisa Kron; and, in front, Peg Healey. The production shown is Brides of the Moon. *(© Joan Marcus)*

In the years that followed, complex gay characters were presented unapologetically. Plays in the 1970s and 1980s included *The Ritz* (1975) by Terrence McNally (1939–   ) and *Torch Song Trilogy* (1983) by Harvey Fierstein (1954–   ). Since then, more and more plays have dealt expressly with gay issues. In these dramas, not only is the lifestyle of gays and lesbians presented forthrightly, but frequently a gay or lesbian agenda is also put forward. In addition to a general concern for gay and lesbian issues, there is a sense of urgency engendered by the AIDS crisis. This has led to a number of significant dramas, including *The Normal Heart* (1985) by Larry Kramer (1935–   ), *As Is* (1985) by William M. Hoffman (1939–   ), Tony Kushner's two-part play *Angels in America* (1993–1994), and Terrence McNally's *Love! Valor! Compassion!* (1995).

"Gender-bender" groups such as the Cockettes and the Angels of Light in San Francisco and Centola and Hot Peaches in New York are an offshoot of gay and lesbian theater. An important company in New York was the Theater of the Ridiculous, founded by John Vaccaro, which developed an extraordinary writer and performer—Charles Ludlam (1943–1987). Ludlam rewrote the classics to include a good deal of wild parody and frequent cross-dressing; he also created the long-lived Ridiculous Theatrical Company.

Though a number of groups have not survived, individual performers and playwrights in gay and lesbian theater remain very much in the spotlight.

Performance Art

In the past three decades, a number of artists have experimented with forms that force audiences to confront certain issues: What is performance? What is theater? What is the subject of theatrical representation? Some of these artists are also political-minded; some are not. *Performance art* is one recent form that poses these questions and then some.

Performance art has two important antecedents: first, earlier avant-garde experiments of the twentieth century—such as dada, surrealism, and happenings, which stressed the irrational and attacked traditional artistic values and forms—and second, the theories of Antonin Artaud and Jerzy Grotowski.

During the past three decades, the term *performance art* has stood for various things. In its earliest manifestations, performance art was related on one hand to painting and on the other hand to dance. In the 1970s, one branch of performance art emphasized the body as an art object: some artists suffered self-inflicted pain, and some went through daily routines (such as preparing a meal) in a museum or in a theater setting. Another branch focused on *site-specific* or environmental pieces in which the setting or context was crucial: performances were created for specific locations such as a subway station, a city park, or a waterfront pier.

In some of the earliest forms of performance art, story, character, and text were minimized or even eliminated. The emphasis was not on narrating a story or exploring recognizable characters but rather on the visual and ritualistic aspects of performing. This type of theater was often the work of an individual artist who incorporated highly personal messages, and sometimes political and social messages, in the event. The overall effect was often like a constantly transforming collage. As might be expected, there was, as mentioned earlier, an affinity between this kind of theater—with its emphasis of the visual picture formed onstage—and painting. Often, stage movement in performance art was also closely related to dance.

In an article in *Artsweek* in 1990, Jacki Apple explained how the emphasis in performance art shifted in the 1970s and 1980s:

> In the 1970s performance art was primarily a time-based visual art form in which text was at the service of image; by the early 80s performance art had shifted to movement-based work, with the performance artist as choreographer. Interdisciplinary collaboration and "spectacle," influenced by TV and other popular modes . . . set the tone for the new decade.[1]

PERFORMANCE ART
Anna Deavere Smith creates one-woman shows dealing with social issues and unrest. In her best-known works, she portrays real people whom she has interviewed and who have been involved with current politically charged events. Twilight: Los Angeles, 1992 dealt with the violence in that city following the trial of the police officers who had beaten Rodney King. In the scene here Smith portrays a character known as "Big Al." (Jay Thompson/ Mark Taper Forum)

In recent years the connotation of the term *performance art* has changed yet again. It is now often associated with individual artists who present autobiographical material onstage. Several such artists—Karen Finley (1956–) is one of the most visible—became a center of controversy when their work was seized on by ultraconservative religious groups and members of Congress as a reason to oppose funding the National Endowment for the Arts. These artists often espouse such causes as feminism and civil liberties for lesbians and homosexuals. Often nudity and other controversial representations of sexuality or sexual orientation are used to confront audiences. Such was the case in *Alice's Rape* (1989), in which Robbie McCauley performed nude as her great-great grandmother, a slave on the auction block. These performance artists are continuing a trend begun by early realistic and antirealistic dramatists, whose works challenged the social status quo and were often banned.

Off-off-Broadway has been the initial home of many performance artists. Two artists who began performing solo pieces in alternative spaces but have now received commercial productions are Spalding Gray (1941–) and Bill Irwin (1950–). Gray, a monologist who discusses issues that range from his own personal concerns to politics, is reminiscent of ancient storytellers who created a theatrical environment single-handedly. Irwin's performances are mime-like, and he uses popular slapstick techniques to reflect on the contemporary human condition.

Anna Deavere Smith (1952–), an African American performance artist, won considerable acclaim in the early 1990s for pieces dealing with racial unrest. In her works, she portrays numerous real people she has met and interviewed. Her *Twilight: Los Angeles 1992* presented people affected by the uprising that followed the acquittals in the first trial of police officers charged with brutalizing Rodney King. In 1997, Smith premiered a new work, *House Arrest: First Edition*, that was based on interviews recorded during the presidential campaign

---

[1]Jacki Apple, "Art at the Barricades," *Artsweek*, vol. 21, May 3, 1990, p. 21.

of 1996; in this work, however, Smith did not initially appear, but instead directed 14 performers in her performance style. She revised this work as a solo piece in 1999.

Other well-known performance artists are Eric Bogosian (1953–), Danny Hoch (1970–), John Leguizamo (1965–), and Ping Chong (1946–), an Asian American who mixed multimedia into his works.

A number of spaces have become recognized for their presentation of performance artists. These include two in New York City: PS 122, a converted public school in the east Village in Manhattan, and the Kitchen, also located downtown. In addition, many museums throughout the United States are known for presenting series of performance artists, including the Walker Museum in Minneapolis and the Museum of Contemporary Art in Chicago. The fact that performance art is most often presented in converted, found spaces or museums again reflects the diversity of the form and its relationship to earlier avant-garde movements and the visual arts.

Along with those in the United States, there are also significant performance artists in most major cities around the world, such as Issei Ogata (1952–) in Japan and the French-Canadian Robert Lepage (1957 –), who founded Ex Machina, a multimedia center in Quebec City.

Postmodernism

Contemporary theater, as can be seen from the examples of performance art above, is highly eclectic. Some works focus on political concerns; others focus on formal concerns. Many works mix techniques and styles. In contemporary theater many diverse and complex works are often described by critics as *postmodernist*. Postmodernism, which is difficult to define specifically, has several facets.

For one thing, postmodernism reflects issues of power in art. Postmodernists question the idea of an accepted "canon" of classics; they also ask why certain artists (such as playwrights) and certain groups (such as white males) should have held positions of power or "privilege" throughout theater history.

Accordingly, postmodernists rebel against traditional readings of texts, arguing that theater productions may have a variety of "authors," including directors and even individual audience members: they argue that each audience member creates his or her own unique reading. Postmodernist directors are noted for *deconstructing* classic dramas—that is, taking the original play apart, developing a new individual conceptualization, and trying to represent onstage the issues of power embedded in the text. When a classic is deconstructed in this way, it may serve simply as the scenario for a production.

One of the most famous groups known for deconstuction of texts is the Wooster Group, under the artistic direction of Elizabeth LeCompte (1944–). The Wooster Group's best-known productions are *Routes I & 9* (1981), which used sections of Thornton Wilder's classic *Our Town; L.S.D.* (1983); and *Brace Up* (1991), a performance adaptation of Chekhov's *The Three Sisters*. In 1997, the Wooster Group presented a highly theatricalized and physical version of Eugene O'Neill's *The Hairy Ape*, in a rundown theater in the Times Square area.

THE LION KING

Julie Taymor's production of The Lion King *for Disney employs postmodern staging techniques to create a commercially successful musical. Taymor mixes Asian puppetry, intense theatricality, spectacular stage machinery, and unique costumes, with pop music to create an entertainment for all generations. Here is an elaborate scene from the musical as staged at the New Amsterdam Theatre in New York City.* (© Joan Marcus/Walt Disney Theatrical Productions)

The group usually performs in a transformed garage in downtown Manhattan known as the Performing Garage. As with many of the Wooster Group's works, *The Hairy Ape* had been workshopped prior to this presentation, the performers adopted a highly presentational style, microphones and amplification were used to create unsettling vocal sounds, and video was also used. The production starred a film actor, Willem Dafoe (1955–   ), who began his acting career with this company and who has frequently returned to work with it.

The term *postmodernism* also suggests that the "modernist" interest in realism, antirealism, and form is no longer central to theater, that artists have now moved beyond being concerned with representing either reality or abstraction. Instead, postmodernists mix abstraction and realism, so that their works cannot be easily classified. Furthermore, the distinction between "high" art and popular art can no longer be clearly defined: postmodernists mix popular concerns and techniques with those of high art.

An intriguing example is the musical *The Lion King* (1997). Produced by Disney, a company whose presence has spurred on the economic revitalization of the Broadway theater district in New York City, this musical is based on a popular Disney animated film and has music by the rock composer Elton John. The director of *The Lion King*, as well as the designer of the masks and puppets, is Julie Taymor (1952–   ). Taymor, who is a designer, director, and adapter of literature for the stage, is known for her avant-garde use of puppet techniques borrowed from Asian theaters. For example, she used puppets in staging Shakespeare's *The Tempest* (1986) at New York's Theatre for a New Audience, in her frequently revived adaptation of a short story *Juan Darien* (1988), in a Tokyo production of the Igor Stravinsky's opera *Oedipus Rex* (1992) and in a production of *The Green Bird* (1996), an eighteenth-century comedy by Carlo Gozzi. The huge commercial success of *The Lion King*, however, clearly reflects the merging of popular and experimental theaters.

Disney continued this tradition when it produced the musical *Aida*, with music by Elton John (1947–   ), and directed by Robert Falls (1954–   ), a well-known director in Chicago who had won critical acclaim in 1999 for his revival of *Death of a Salesman*. Aida opened on Broadway in 2000, after being repeatedly reworked out of town.

Many alternative theaters, playwrights, and performance artists can be categorized as postmodernist.

International Trends

Although Chapters 15 and 16 have focused on contemporary theater in the United States, the theatrical fragmentation found here can also be seen throughout the world. A number of theater artists worldwide experimented with similar issues and concerns in the 1970s, 1980s, and 1990s.

Two African Playwrights

The concern for political and social equality in many African American dramas, which was noted in Chapter 15, is also at the heart of the work of the South African playwright Athol Fugard (1932–   ), who began writing in the 1960s and achieved international acclaim in the 1980s as apartheid, the separation of races in South Africa, came under increasing attack. Fugard, a white author who sometimes stages and acts in his own works, attacked apartheid in such plays as *The Blood Knot* (1964), *Sizwe Banzi Is Dead* (1973), *Master Harold . . . and the Boys* (1982), *Lesson from Aloes* (1987), and *Playland* (1992).

Another significant African playwright is the Nigerian Wole Soyinka (1934–   ), who is also a poet, essayist, and novelist. Soyinka began his career with the Royal Court Theatre in London in the

ATHOL FUGARD'S *VALLEY SONG*
Fugard is a South African playwright whose work has dealt with racial relationships and inequality in his own country. He has gained international recognition and acclaim. Fugard (right) is shown here with actress Lisa Gay Hamilton in a scene from his play Valley Song, *about an older man and a young woman in racially torn South Africa.* (© T. Charles Erickson/McCarter Theatre Center for the Performing Arts)

late 1950s. His politically charged works led to his arrest in Nigeria in 1967, and to 2 years' imprisonment. In 1973, he adapted Euripides' *The Bacchae* for the National Theatre in England. Soyinka gained international recognition in 1986, when he received the Nobel Prize in literature. Among his best-known dramas are *The Swamp Dwellers* (1957), *The Road* (1965), *Death and the King's Horsemen* (1975), and *Play of Giants* (1985).

Alternative Theater in Europe

Alternative theaters exist in most major cities worldwide. In London, there is an alternative to commercial theater known as *fringe theater,* and it is in fringe theater that many contemporary political playwrights began their careers. These British playwrights are in the postmodernist tradition, mixing reality with theatrical techniques and fusing concerns of high art with techniques of popular art. A good example is Caryl Churchill (1938–), in plays like *Cloud Nine* (1979), *Serious Money* (1987), *Mad Forest* (1990) and *Blue Heart* (1997).

Of course, there are many other significant playwrights in England. Tom Stoppard (1937–) continues to write dramas emphasizing wordplay and intellectual concerns. A significant number of "angry" playwrights continue to attack traditional political, social, and economic institutions; among the best-known are David Hare (1947–) and Howard Brenton (1942–). More contemporary socio-politically oriented British playwrights include Patrick Marber (1964–), author of *Dealer's Choice* (1995) and *Closer* (1997); Jez Butterworth (1969–), author of *Mojo* (1995), Sarah Kane (1971–1999), author of *Blasted* (1995), *Cleansed* (1998), and *Crave* (1998).

There is also a new generation of young Irish playwrights who dramatize social, political, and historical issues. One of the best known is Martin McDonagh (1970–), whose works include: *The Beauty Queen of Leenane* (1996), *The Cripple of Inishmaan* (1996), *A Skull in Connemara* (1997), and *The Lonesome West* (1997). Conor McPherson (1971–) has gained international attention for *St. Nicholas* (1996), *The Weir* (1997), and *Dublin Carol* (2000).

There have also been many directors on the European continent who have experimented with avant-garde theater techniques. Some of these directors have worked only in alternative environments, but others have brought their more experimental style of production into leading government-subsidized national theaters. Among the most renowned are Peter Stein (German, 1937–); Yuri Lyubimov (Russian, 1917–); Tadeusz Kantor (Polish, 1915–1990), and Ariane Mnouchkine (French, 1940–).

An English director who has used a more experimental style of production, along with reinterpretations of texts that focus on feminist, gender, and other sociopolitical issues, is Deborah Warner (1959–). Warner began her career with an alternative London troupe, the Kick Theatre Company, which she founded in 1980, when she was 21. She has since directed unique interpretations of the classics for the Royal Shakespeare Company and the National Theatre in London. She is best-known for the many productions she has directed that star the actress Fiona Shaw (1959–), including Shakespeare's *Richard II,* with Shaw in the title role;

Beckett's *Footfalls,* in which Beckett's precise stage directions were ignored and lines were transposed, leading to a lawsuit by the Beckett estate; and a site-specific staging of T. S. Eliot's *The Waste Land,* which used a variety of spaces, including a disco in Brussels, a fort in Dublin, an old movie theater in Montreal, a lecture hall in a Parisian medical school, and a dilapidated theater in New York's Times Square. In the summer of 2000 and again in the winter of 2001, Warner directed Shaw in an adaptation of *Medea.*

Today and Tomorrow: A Look Ahead

In the twentieth century, theater faced a series of unprecedented challenges. First came silent films, then radio, then sound films, then television. With each new challenge, it was assumed that theater would suffer an irreversible setback. After all, each of these new media offered drama in a form that was less expensive and much more accessible than the traditional theater setting. When sound film appeared, for example, it was argued that anyone who went out for entertainment would go to the movies rather than theater: film would be cheaper and would offer more glamorous stars. When television appeared, it was argued that people did not even need to leave their homes to see drama.

Inevitably, some changes in audiences' habits have resulted from new customs and from competition by films and television. For most of the eighteenth and nineteenth centuries, theater was the main source of escapist dramatic entertainment— both comedies and suspense melodramas. Today, television, with its situation comedies, provides much of the light entertainment formerly offered by theater, and film also provides much escapist entertainment. In addition, there is now concern that even newer technologies—such as interactive video and television—will further erode interest in theater.

But despite these shifts, theater has not suffered as predicted. Much to the surprise of the prophets of doom, there is probably more theatrical activity in the United States today—as the discussions in this chapter and Chapters 14 and 15 suggest—than at any time since the advent of movies.

Why is this so? First, in spite of their similarities, there is a basic difference between theater on the one hand and films and television on the other. As we pointed out in Chapter 1, the difference is the presence in theater of the live performer. Both film and television provide images or pictures of people, not the real thing. Human contact between audience and performers meets a profound, fundamental need that neither the large screens in movie theaters nor the small screens in our living rooms can ever satisfy. The human electricity that flows back and forth between performers and audience—the laughter at comic moments and the hushed silence at serious moments—cannot be created in these other media.

Second, there is the human impulse to create theater. Earlier, we said that this universal impulse leads every society to create its own theatrical activity, unless such activity is expressly forbidden. The need and desire for theater will continue into the future, throughout Europe and the Americas as well as other parts of the world.

Regional and alternative theaters are excellent examples of the powerful pull of live theater. The major American regional theaters have all been established during the very time when television was becoming firmly rooted in American life. And—as noted earlier—there are now many alternative theater companies which reflect specific concerns of ethnic and minority groups and which have helped shape American theater.

Influential playwrights and performers as well as important issues have been brought to the attention of the theatergoing public by African American theater companies and artists; by Hispanic groups such as INTAR, the Puerto Rican Traveling Company, and El Teatro Campesino; and by Asian American groups, including the Pan Asian Repertory Theatre. Similarly, gay and lesbian theater companies, such as the Ridiculous Theatre, and feminist groups have forced audiences to reexamine sexual and gender biases.

When we turn from the theater of today to the future, a question arises: Where will theater go from here? It is impossible, of course, to answer with any certainty. We can assume, though, that the trends described in this chapter and Chapters 14 and 15 will continue. Theater of the future will no doubt continue to present new works alongside a rich mixture of plays from the past. In both writing and production, theater will draw on many sources. We cannot know whether or not new plays will attain the greatness of the past, but playwrights show no sign of abandoning theater, despite the larger financial rewards offered by film and television.

We can be sure that theater will survive in a vigorous form, no matter what challenges it faces from electronic media. At the same time, modern technology will play an important role in theater: in lighting effects, with the use of computerized lighting boards; in the shifting of scenery; and in other ways. There will

Making Connections:

The Digital Arts

DIGITAL MEDIA
A question that confronts the theater is its relationship with the popular digital media. Will the theater lose audience members to interactive video or to live web broadcasts? How will the theater incorporate these new electronic arts? Seen here are two ten-year olds playing video games at Sony's PlayStation booth at the Los Angeles Convention Center. (AP/Wide World Photos)

Once again, in the twenty-first century, theater finds competition with other popular forms of entertainment. With the development of computer technology and various forms of digital entertainment, some cultural analysts wonder whether audiences will ever leave their homes to go and watch live performers.

The Internet has revolutionized audience's access to music (resulting, for example, in the legal battles over Napster), to video, and to live events. Do audiences really need to go to the theater when they can view people living their daily lives, in real time, on their computer screens?

And what about the live-action games that are available? Will audiences leave their homes when they can create their own dramatic scenarios and play those dramatizations out on their computers or on large-screen monitors?

And will DVD at home lead audiences to forsake film houses and theaters? Through DVD, the audience member can even alter the experience, view multiple endings, learn more about the artistic process, and take greater control of the material being viewed.

Yet theater continues to thrive and audience members do leave their homes. They seek out the live experience. Audiences want to be in the presence of live actors and in the community of other theatregoers. As the critic Michael Feingold of the *Village Voice* aptly reassures and warns the theater world:

> The theater has a future, in our geography as well as in our souls. . . . Millions of desk-locked, glazed-eyed Web workers will be flooding the streets, desperate for unplugged, un-downloaded human experience. We had better be ready for them. We had better know our history, our mission, our tradition, our means for reaching audiences, and our justification for addressing them (June 7–13, 2000).

What is also likely is that theater will, as always, find ways to appropriate elements from these digital media as it constructs a living art for the new century and for new audiences.

also, no doubt, continue to be multimedia experiments, fusing theater with film, television, and dance.

With all its innovations, however theater of the future will no doubt be an extension of theater of the past. Theater will continue to be enacted by women and men in person before an audience, and the plays they perform will deal primarily with the hopes, fears, agonies, and joys of the human race.

It is clear that the complexity of the modern world will result in a heterogeneous theater. Ongoing exploration of the diversity of contemporary society means that diverse theaters will continue to spring up. There is no question that as we enter the twenty-first century, theater will be as complex and fragmented as the world in which it exists. Yet from the start theater has always focused on human concerns, and they will remain the source of its appeal as far ahead as we can see.

SUMMARY

Contemporary theater is eclectic, combining styles and techniques from earlier periods as well as from other art forms. Today's playwrights and directors draw from a wide range of sources. The types of theater available include realism and departures from realism (similar to the movements covered in Chapters 14 and 15), and additional forms such as musical theater and many forms of ethnic and political theater: African American theater, Hispanic theater, feminist theater, gay and lesbian theater, and so forth. All these exist side by side in numerous production settings: the rich storehouse of theater available today includes regional, commercial, and noncommercial theater.

The vitality of today's theater in the face of challenges by film and television demonstrates the continuing appeal of live theater and the performer-audience relationship. If the present age is not one of great drama, it is a period of tremendous activity in writing and producing, in avant-garde experimental work, and in the revival of classics.

THEATER ON THE WEB

Use these sites to broaden your awareness of theater now being produced around the country and the world.

American Theater Web   http://www.americantheaterweb.com

A vast array of information about American theater in all its forms, from community theater to Broadway.

Internet Theatre Database   http://www.theatredb.com

ITDB is a searchable archive of theatrical shows past, present, and future.

Theatre Topics   http://calliope.jhu.edu/journals/theatre_ topics/index.html

This academic journal from Johns Hopkins University Press covers contemporary performance studies, dramaturgy, and theater pedagogy. (Full text available only to subscribing educational institutions.)

Arts on the Line   http://www.artslynx.org/aotl

Arts on the Line is a site advocating the role of the arts in our communities.

Theatre-link.com   http://www.theatre-link.com
An index to every genre of theater.

Using the above resources, make some predictions about future theater trends. Consider some or all of the following:

Will theater as we know it still be viable?
What will Broadway theater be like?
What about community and regional theater?
How will world theater be affected?
How will the Internet influence theater?
How will the economy affect the content and form of theater?
Will theater affect social change?

Be sure to support your predictions with examples and citations from the Web.

Glossary

Above Upstage or away from the audience.

Action According to the Greek philosopher Aristotle, a sequence of events linked by cause and effect, with a beginning, middle, and end. Said by Aristotle to be the best way to unify a play. More generally, the central, unifying conflict and movement through a drama.

Ad lib To improvise lines of a speech.

Aesthetic distance Physical or psychological separation or detachment of audience from dramatic action, usually considered necessary for artistic illusion.

Agon (AG-ohn) In classical Greek Old Comedy, a scene with a debate between the two opposing forces in a play.

Alienation Bertolt Brecht's theory that, in his epic theater, audiences' emotional involvement should be minimized to increase their intellectual involvement with the political message.

Allegory Symbolic representation of abstract themes through characters, action, and other concrete elements of a play.

Amphitheater Large oval, circular, or semicircular outdoor theater with rising tiers of seats around an open playing area; *also,* an exceptionally large indoor auditorium.

Antagonist Opponent of the protagonist in a drama.

Apprentice Young performer training in an Elizabethan acting company.

Apron Stage space in front of the curtain line or proscenium; also called the *forestage.*

Arena Stage entirely surrounded by the audience; also known as *theater-in-the-round.*

Artistic director Person responsible for all creative and artistic activities for resident and repertory companies.

Aside In a play, thoughts spoken aloud by one character (often, to the audience) without being noticed by others onstage.

At rise Expression used to describe what is happening onstage at the moment when the curtain first rises or the lights come up.

Auditions Tryouts held for performers who want to be considered for roles in a production.

Auteur director A director who believes that his or her role is to be the author of a production. An auteur director's point of view dominates that of the playwright, and the director may make textual changes and modifications.

Automated lights Generic term for a new type of lighting instrument that can tilt, pan, rotate, change colors, and change focus—all electronically by computerized remote control.

Avant-garde (ah-vahn GARD) Intellectual, literary, or artistic movement that breaks with tradition and seems ahead of its time.

Backdrop Large drapery or painted canvas which provides the rear or upstage masking of a set.

Backlighting Lighting that comes from behind.

Backstage Stage area behind the front curtain; also, the areas beyond the setting, including wings and dressing rooms.

Ballad opera Eighteenth-century English form which burlesqued opera.

Basic situation Specific problem or maladjustment from which a play arises.

Batten Pipe or long pole suspended horizontally above the stage, upon which scenery, drapery, or lights may be hung.

Beam projector Lighting instrument without a lens which uses a parabolic reflector to project a narrow, nonadjustable beam of light.

Beijing opera Popular theater of China which developed in the nineteenth century.

Below Opposite of *above;* toward the front of the stage.

Biomechanics Meyerhold's theory that a performer's body should be machinelike and that emotion could be represented externally.

Blackout Total darkening of the stage.

Blocking Pattern and arrangement of performers' movements onstage with respect to each other and to the stage space, usually set by the director.

Book (1) Spoken (as opposed to sung) portion of the text of a musical play. (2) To schedule engagements for artists or productions.

Border Strip of drapery or painted canvas hung from a batten to mask the area above the stage; *also,* a row of lights hung from a batten.

Bourgeois drama See *Domestic drama.*

Box Small private compartment for a group of spectators built into the walls of a traditional proscenium-arch theater.

Box set Interior setting using flats to form the back and side walls and often the ceiling of a room.

Build To create a costume from scratch in a costume shop.

Bunraku (buhn-RAH-koo) Japanese puppet theater.

Burlesque Satire of a serious form of literature.

Business Obvious and detailed physical movement of performers to reveal character, aid action, or establish mood.

Casting Assigning roles to performers in a production; this is usually done by the director.

Catharsis (kuh-THAR-sis) Greek word, usually translated as "purgation," which Aristotle used in his definition of tragedy, referring to the vicarious cleansing of emotions in the audience through their representation onstage.

Catwalk Narrow metal platform suspended above the stage to permit ready access to lights and scenery hung from the grid.

Cazuela (cah-zoo-EHL-ah) Gallery above the tavern in the back wall of the theaters of the Spanish golden age; the area where unescorted women sat.

Center stage Stage position in the middle acting area of the stage, or the middle section extended upstage and downstage.

Choregus (koh-REE-guhs) Wealthy person who financed a playwright's works at an ancient Greek dramatic festival.

Chorus In ancient Greek drama, a group of performers who sang and danced, sometimes participating in the action but usually simply commenting on it. In modern times, performers in a musical play who sing and dance as a group.

City Dionysia (SIT-ee digh-eh-NIGH-see-uh) The most important Greek festival in honor of the god Dionysus and the first to include drama.

Climactic structure Also referred to as *intensive structure.* Dramatic structure in which there are few scenes, a short time passes, there are few locales, and the action begins chronologically close to the climax.

Climax Often defined as the high point in the action or the final and most significant crisis in the action.

Comedia (koh-MAY-dee-ah) Full-length (three-act) nonreligious play of the Spanish golden age.

Comedy In general, a play that is light in tone, is concerned with issues that are not serious, has a happy ending, and is designed to amuse.

Comedy of manners Form of comic drama that became popular in seventeenth-century France and the English Restoration, emphasizing a cultivated or sophisticated atmosphere and witty dialogue.

Comic premise Idea or concept in a comedy that turns the accepted notion of things upside down.

Commedia dell'arte (koh-MAY-dee-ah dehl-AHR-teh) Form of comic theater, originating in sixteenth-century Italy, in which dialogue was improvised around a loose scenario calling for a set of stock characters.

Compañias de parte (cahm-pa-NYEE-ahs day PAHR-teh) Acting troupes in the Spanish golden age, organized according to a sharing system.

Complication Introduction, in a play, of a new force which creates a new balance of power and entails a delay in reaching the climax.

Composition How lighted areas are arranged onstage relative to each other.

Conflict Tension between two or more characters that leads to crisis or a climax; a fundamental struggle or imbalance—involving ideologies, actions, personalities, etc.—underlying a play.

Constructivism Post-World War I scene-design movement in which sets—frequently composed of ramps, platforms, and levels—were nonrealistic and intended to provide greater opportunities for physical action.

Corral Theater of the Spanish golden age, usually located in the courtyard of a series of adjoining buildings.

Counterweight Device for balancing the weight of scenery in a system which allows scenery to be raised above the stage by means of ropes and pulleys.

Created space. See *Found space.*

Crew Backstage team assisting in mounting a production.

Crisis Point within a play when the action reaches an important confrontation or takes a critical turn. In the tradition of the well-made play, a drama includes a series of crises that lead to the final crisis, known as the *climax.*

Cross Movement by a performer across the stage in a given direction.

Cue Any prearranged signal, such as the last words in a speech, a piece of business, or any action or lighting change, that indicates to a performer or stage manager that it is time to proceed to the next line or action.

Cue sheet Prompt book marked with cues, or a list of cues for the use of technicians, especially the stage manager.

Curtain (1) Rise or fall of the actual curtain, which separates a play into structural parts. (2) Last bit of action preceding the fall of the curtain.

Cycle plays See *Mystery plays.*

Cyclorama Permanent fixture or curved drop used to mask the rear and sides of the stage, representing sky or open space.

Dada Movement in art between the world wars, based on presenting the irrational and attacking traditional artistic values.

Denouement (deh-noo-MAHN) Point near the end of a play when suspense is satisfied and "the knot is untied."

Descriptive criticism Criticism that attempts to describe as clearly and accurately as possible what is happening in a performance.

Deus ex machina (DEH-oos eks MAH-kih-nah) Literally, "god from a machine," a resolution

device in classic Greek drama; hence, intervention of supernatural forces—usually at the last moment—to save the action from its logical conclusion. In modern drama, an arbitrary and coincidental solution.

Dialogue Conversation between characters in a play.

Dimmer Device for changing lighting intensity smoothly and at varying rates.

Dim out To turn out lights with a dimmer.

Director In American usage, the person responsible for the overall unity of a production and for coordinating the work of contributing artists. The American director is the equivalent of the British producer and the French *metteur-en-scène.*

Dithyramb (DITH-ih-ramb) Ancient Greek choral song describing the adventures of a god or hero.

Domestic drama Drama dealing with problems—particularly family problems—of middle- and lower-class characters; also called *bourgeois drama.* There are serious and comic domestic dramas.

Dominant trait Found in certain theatrical characters: one paramount trait or tendency that overshadows all others and appears to control the conduct of the character. Examples could include greed, jealousy, anger, and self-importance.

Dominus Leader of a Roman acting troupe.

Double entendre (DOO-bluh ahn-TAHN-druh) Word or phrase in comedy that has a double meaning, the second often sexual.

Doubling Term used when a performer takes more than one role in a play.

Downlighting Lighting that comes directly from overhead.

Downstage Front of the stage toward the audience.

Dramaturg Literary manager or dramatic adviser of a theater company.

Drame (DRAHM) Eighteenth-century French term usually denoting a serious drama that dealt with middle-class characters.

Dress rehearsal Rehearsal in which a play is performed as it will be for the public, including all the scenery, costumes, and technical effects.

Drop Large piece of fabric, generally painted canvas, hung from a batten to the stage floor, usually to serve as backing.

Emotional recall Stanislavski's exercise which helps the performer present realistic emotions. The performer feels a character's emotion by thinking of an event in his or her own life which led to a similar emotion.

Ensemble playing Acting that stresses the total artistic unity of a group performance rather than individual performances.

Entrance Manner and effectiveness with which a performer comes into a scene, as well as the actual coming onstage; *also,* the way this is prepared for by the playwright.

Environmental sounds Noises from everyday life that provide background sound in a production.

Environmental theater Branch of avant-garde theater stressing the environment in which a performance takes place.

Epic theater Form of episodic drama associated with Bertolt Brecht and aimed at the intellect rather than the emotions.

Epilogue A brief scene or speech by one of the performers to the audience after the conclusion of a play.

Episodic structure Also referred to as *extensive structure*. Dramatic structure in which there are many scenes, taking place over a considerable period of time in a number of locations. Many also employ such devices as subplots.

Existentialism Term applied to plays illustrating a philosophy whose principal modern advocate was Jean-Paul Sartre and which holds that there are no longer any fixed standards or values.

Exit A performer's leaving the stage, as well as the preparation for his or her leaving.

Exposition Imparting of information necessary for an understanding of the story but not covered by the action onstage; events or knowledge from the past, or occurring outside the play, which must be introduced for the audience to understand the characters or plot.

Expressionism Movement in Germany at about the time of World War I, characterized by the attempt to dramatize subjective states through distortion; striking, often grotesque images; and lyric, unrealistic dialogue.

Fade Slow dimming of lights, changing from brighter to darker, or vice versa.

Farce Dramatic genre usually regarded as a subclass of comedy, with emphasis on plot complications and few or no intellectual pretensions.

Flat Single piece of flat, rectangular scenery, used with other similar units to create a set.

Flood Lighting instrument without lenses which is used for general or large-area lighting.

Fly loft or flies Space above the stage where scenery may be lifted out of sight by means of ropes and pulleys.

Focus Aiming light on a particular area of the stage.

Follow spot Large, powerful spotlight with a sharp focus and narrow beam which is used to follow principal performers as they move about the stage.

Footlights Row of lights in the floor along the front edge of the stage or apron.

Forestage See *Apron.*

Found space Space not originally intended for theater use which is converted for productions. Avant-garde artists often produce in found spaces.

Fourth-wall convention Pretense that in a proscenium-arch theater the audience is looking into a room through an invisible fourth wall.

Freeze To remain motionless onstage, especially for laughs or in a tableau.

Fresnel (fruh-NEL) Type of spotlight used over relatively short distances with a soft beam edge which allows the light to blend easily with light from other sources; *also,* the type of lenses used in such spotlights.

Front of the house Portion of a theater reserved for the audience; includes both the auditorium and the lobby area. Sometimes called simply the *house.*

Futurism Art movement begun in Italy about 1905 which idealized mechanization and machinery.

Gallery In traditional proscenium-arch theaters, the undivided seating area cut into the walls of the building.

Gel Thin, flexible color medium used in lighting instruments to give color to a light beam.

Genre Category or type of play.

Gesamtkunstwerk Richard Wagner's theory of a unified work of theatrical art.

Gobo Template in a theater lighting instrument that determines the shape and arrangement of the beam or pool of light thrown by the instrument. For example, a pattern created by a gobo or template could result in stripes, leaves on trees, the outline of a windowpane, or the like.

Grid Metal framework above the stage, from which lights and scenery are suspended.

Groove system System in which tracks on the stage floor and above the stage allowed for the smooth movement of flat wings on and off the stage; usually there were a series of grooves at each stage position.

Ground plan Blueprint or floor plan of stage design that outlines the various levels on the stage and indicates the placement of scenery, furniture, doors, windows, and other necessary scenic elements.

Hamartia (hah-MARH-tee-ah) Ancient Greek term usually translated as "tragic flaw." The term literally translates as "missing the mark," which may suggest that hamartia is not so much a character flaw as an error in judgment.

Hanamichi (hah-nah-MEE-chee) In kabuki theater, a bridge running from behind the audience (toward the left side of the audience) to the stage. Performers can enter on the hanamichi; important scenes may also be played on it.

Hand props Small props carried on- or offstage by actors and actresses during a performance. See *Props.*

Happening Nonliterary or unscripted theatrical event using a scenario that allows for chance occurrences.

Hashigakari (ha-shee-gah-KAH-ree) Bridge in nō theater on which the performers make their entrance from the dressing area to the platform stage.

Heroic drama Serious but basically optimistic drama, written in verse or elevated prose, with noble or heroic characters in extreme situations or unusual adventures.

Hireling Member of an Elizabethan acting troupe who was paid a set salary and was not a shareholder.

Hubris (HEW-brihs) Ancient Greek term usually defined as "excessive pride" and cited as a common tragic flaw.

Inner stage Area at the rear of the stage which can be cut off from the rest by means of curtains or scenery and revealed for special scenes.

Iris Component of a lighting instrument that controls the size of the beam or pool of light thrown by the instrument.

Irony A condition the reverse of what we have expected or an expression whose intended implication is the opposite of its literal sense.

Kabuki Form of popular Japanese theater combining music, dance, and dramatic scenes.

Kathakali Traditional dance-drama of India.

Kill To eliminate or suppress; for example, to remove unwanted light or to ruin an effect through improper execution.

Lazzi (LAHT-zee) Comic pieces of business used repeatedly by characters in Italian commedia dell'arte.

Left stage Left side of the stage from the point of view of a performer facing the audience.

Light plot Detailed outline or diagram showing where each lighting instrument is placed in relationship to the stage.

Liturgical drama Early medieval drama, written in Latin and dealing with biblical stories.

Living newspapers In the United States, the Federal Theater Project's dramatizations of newsworthy events in the 1930s.

Long run Term used in commercial theater when a drama is performed for as long as it is popular.

Ludi Romani (LEW-dee roh-MAH-nee) Roman festival, in honor of Jupiter, into which drama was first introduced.

Magic if Stanislavski's acting exercise which requires the performer to ask, "How would I react *if* I were in this character's position?"

Mansions Individual scenic units used for the staging of religious dramas in the Middle Ages.

Mask (1) To cut backstage areas or technical equipment off from the view of the audience by means of scenery. (2) Face or head covering in the image of the character portrayed.

Masking Scenery or draperies used to hide or cover.

Masque Lavish and spectacular form of private theater in Renaissance Italy and the courts of France and England.

Melodrama Dramatic form made popular in the nineteenth century which emphasized action and spectacular effects and also used music; it had stock characters and clearly defined villains and heroes.

Mime Form of theatrical entertainment in ancient Greece and Rome which consisted of short dramatic sketches characterized by jesting and buffoonery.

Minor characters In a drama, those characters who have small, secondary, or supporting roles. These could include soldiers and servants.

Minstrelsy Type of nineteenth-century production featuring white performers made up in blackface.

Miracle play Medieval vernacular drama dealing with the lives of saints or the Virgin Mary.

Mise-en-scène (miz-on-SEHN) Arrangement of all the elements in a stage picture at a given moment or throughout a performance.

Morality play Medieval drama designed to teach a lesson. The characters were often allegorical and represented virtues or faults.

Motivated sounds Sounds called for in the script that usually come from recognizable sources.

Moving lights See *Automated lights.*

Multifocus theater Theater in which something is going on simultaneously in several playing areas.

Multimedia Use of electronic media, such as slides, film, and videotape, in live theatrical presentations.

Multiple setting Form of stage setting, common in the Middle Ages, in which several locations are represented at the same time; also called *simultaneous setting.* Used also in various forms of contemporary theater.

Musical theater Broad category which includes opera, operetta, musical comedy, and other musical plays (sometimes called *lyric theater*).

Mystery plays Also called *cycle plays.* Short dramas of the Middle Ages based on events of the Old and New Testaments and often organized into historical cycles.

Naturalism Special form of realism developed in Europe in the late nineteenth century, which was not carefully plotted or constructed but was meant to present a "slice of life."

Neoclassical ideals Rules developed by critics of the Italian Renaissance, supposedly based on the writings of Aristotle.

New Comedy Hellenistic Greek and Roman comedies which deal with romantic and domestic situations.

Nō Rigidly traditional form of Japanese drama combining music, dance, and lyrics.

Objective Stanislavski's term for that which is urgently desired and sought by a character, the desired goal which propels a character to action.

Obstacle That which delays or prevents the achieving of a goal by a character. An obstacle creates complication and conflict.

Offstage Areas of the stage, usually in the wings or backstage, which are not in view of the audience.

Old Comedy Classical Greek comedy which pokes fun at social, political, or cultural conditions and at particular figures.

Onstage Area of the stage which is in view of the audience.

Open To turn or face more toward the audience.

Orchestra Ground-floor seating in an auditorium; *also,* a circular playing space in ancient Greek theaters.

Pace Rate at which a performance is played; *also,* to play a scene or an entire event to determine its proper speed.

Pan Term used in theater lighting when a beam of light from a lighting instrument moves horizontally, from side to side.

Pantomime Originally a Roman entertainment in which a narrative was sung by a chorus while the story was acted out by dancers. Now used loosely to cover any form of presentation which relies on dance, gesture, and physical movement without dialogue or speech.

Parabasis (puh-RAB-uh-sihs) Scene in classical Greek Old Comedy in which the chorus directly addresses the audience members and makes fun of them.

Parodos (PAR-uh-dohs) In classical Greek drama, the scene in which the chorus enters. Also, the entranceway for the chorus in Greek theater.

Patio In the theater of the Spanish golden age, the pit area for the audience.

Peking opera *See* Beijing opera.

Performance art Experimental theater that initially incorporated elements of dance and the visual arts. Since performance art often is based on an individual performer or director's vision, rather than a playwright's, the autobiographical monologue has become a popular performance art form.

Period Term describing any representation onstage of a former age (e.g., *period costume, period play*).

Perspective Illusion of depth in painting, introduced into scene design during the Italian Renaissance.

Pit Floor of the house in a traditional proscenium-arch theater. It was originally a standing area; by the end of the eighteenth century, backless benches were added.

Platform Raised surface on the stage floor serving as an elevation for parts of the stage action and allowing for a multiplicity of stage levels.

Platform stage Elevated stage with no proscenium.

Plot As distinct from *story,* the patterned arrangement in a drama of events and characters, with incidents selected and arranged for maximum dramatic impact. *Also,* in Elizabethan theaters, an outline of the play which was posted backstage for the actors.

Point of attack The moment in the story when a play actually begins. The dramatist chooses a point which he or she judges will best start the action and propel it forward.

Pole and chariot Giacomo Torelli's mechanized means of changing sets made up of flat wings.

Poor theater Term coined by Jerzy Grotowski to describe his theater, which was stripped to the bare essentials.

Postmodernism A contemporary concept suggesting that artists and audiences have gone beyond the modernist movements of realism and the various departures from realism.

Preparation Previous arranging of circumstances, pointing of character, and placing of properties in a production so that the ensuing actions will seem reasonable; *also,* the actions taken by a performer in getting ready for a performance.

Prescriptive criticism Criticism that offers advice and sometimes suggests rules for what should be done in theater.

Private theaters Indoor theaters in Elizabethan England.

Producer In American usage, the person responsible for the business side of a production, including raising the necessary money. (In British usage, a producer is the equivalent of an American director.)

Prologue Introductory speech delivered to the audience by one of the actors or actresses before a play begins.

Prompt To furnish a performer with missed or forgotten lines or cues during a performance.

Prompt book Script of a play indicating performers' movements, light cues, sound cues, etc.

Props Properties; objects that are used by performers onstage or are necessary to complete a set.

Proscenium (pro-SIN-ee-um) Arch or frame surrounding the stage opening in a box or picture stage.

Protagonist Principal character in a play, the one whom the drama is about.

Public theaters Outdoor theaters in Elizabethan England.

Pull To choose a costume from an inventory owned by a theater company.

Rake To position scenery on a slant or at an angle other than parallel or perpendicular to the curtain line; *also,* an upward slope of the stage floor away from the audience.

Raked stage Stage which slopes upward away from the audience toward the back of the set.

Realism Broadly, an attempt to present onstage people and events corresponding to those in everyday life.

Regional theater (1) Theater whose subject matter is specific to a particular geographic region. (2) Theaters situated in theatrical centers across the country.

Régisseur (ray-zhee-SUHR) Continental European term for a theater director; it often denotes a dictatorial director.

Rehearsal Preparation by a cast for the performance of a play through repetition and practice.

Reinforcement Amplification of sounds in the theater.

Repertory or **repertoire** Acting company which at any given time can perform a number of plays alternately; *also,* the plays regularly performed by a company.

Representative characters Characters in a play who embody characteristics that represent an entire group.

Reproduction Use of mechanically re-created sounds in the theater.

Restoration drama English drama after the restoration of the monarchy, from 1660 to 1700.

Reversal Sudden switch of circumstances or knowledge which leads to a result contrary to expectations; called *peripeteia* or *peripety* in Greek drama.

Revolving stage Large circular turntable in a stage floor on which scenery is placed so that, as it moves, one set is brought into view while another one turns out of sight.

Right stage Right side of the stage from the point of view of a performer facing the audience.

Ritual Specifically ordered ceremonial event, often religious.

Romanticism Movement of the nineteenth century which sought to free the artist from rules and considered unfettered inspiration the source of all creativity.

Run Operation of a show; *also,* the length of time a production is performed.

Run-through Rehearsal in which the cast goes through the entire text of the play in the order that it will be performed.

Satire Dramatic form using techniques of comedy—such as wit, irony, and exaggeration—to attack and expose folly and vice.

Satyr play One of the three types of classical Greek drama, usually a ribald takeoff on Greek mythology and history that included a chorus of satyrs, mythological creatures who were half-man and half-goat.

Scaena (SKAY-nah) Stagehouse in a Roman theater.

Scene (1) Stage setting. (2) One of a series of structural units into which a play or acts of a play are divided. (3) Location of a play's action.

Scrim Thin, open-weave fabric which is nearly transparent when lit from behind and opaque when lit from the front.

Script Written or printed text—consisting of dialogue, stage directions, character descriptions, and the like.

Set Scenery, taken as whole, for a scene or an entire production.

Set piece Piece of scenery which stands independently in a scene.

Shareholders In Elizabethan acting troupes, members who received part of the profits as payment.

Sides Script containing only a single performer's lines and cues. Elizabethan actors learned their roles from sides.

Simultaneous setting Medieval tradition of presenting more than one locale onstage at the same time.

Skene (SKEE-nee) In ancient Greek theater, the scene house behind the orchestra.

Slapstick Type of comedy or comic business which relies on ridiculous physical activity—often violent in nature—for its humor.

Soliloquy Speech in which a character who is alone onstage speaks inner thoughts.

Spill Light from stage-lighting instruments which falls outside of the areas for which it is intended, such as light that falls on the audience.

Spine In the Stanislavski method, a character's dominant desire or motivation; usually thought of as an action and expressed as a verb.

Stage door Outside entrance to dressing rooms and stage areas which is used by performers and technicians.

Stage convention Understanding established through custom or usage that certain devices will be arbitrarily accepted or assigned a specific meaning.

Stage house Stage floor and all the space above it up to the grid.

Stage left Left side of the stage from the performer's point of view. From the audience's perspective, it would be the right side of the stage.

Stage manager Person who coordinates all the rehearsals for the director and runs the actual show during its performances.

Stage right Right side of the stage from the performer's point of view. From the view of the audience, it would be the left side of the stage.

Stage picture Visual composition of how an entire scene onstage will appear to the audience.

Standing room only (SRO) Notice that all seats for a performance have been sold but standees can be accommodated.

Stanislavski method Constantin Stanislavski's techniques and theories about acting, which promote a naturalistic style stressing (among other things) "inner truth" as opposed to conventional theatricality.

Stock character Character who has one outstanding characteristic of human behavior to the exclusion of virtually all other attributes. These characters often seem like stereotypes and are most often used in comedy and melodrama.

Stock set Standard setting for a locale used in every play which requires that environment.

Storm and stress Antineoclassical eighteenth-century German movement which was a forerunner of romanticism; in German, *Sturm und Drang.*

Strike To remove pieces of scenery or props from onstage or to take down an entire set after a final performance.

Subplot Secondary plot that reinforces or runs parallel to the major plot in an episodic play.

Subtext Meaning and movement of a play below its surface; that which is not stated but implied.

Summer stock Theater companies which operate outside of major theatrical centers during the summer, often producing a different play every week.

Surrealism Departure from realism that attempted to present dramatically the working of the subconscious.

Symbolism Movement of the late nineteenth and early twentieth centuries which sought to express inner truth rather than represent life realistically.

Teaser Short horizontal curtain just beyond the proscenium used to mask the fly loft and, in effect, to lower the height of the proscenium.

Technical Term referring to functions necessary to the production of a play other than those of the cast and the director, such as functions of the stage crew, carpenters, and lighting crew.

Technical director Person who oversees all technical aspects of a theater production, especially the building, painting, and installation of scenery and related elements.

Technical rehearsal Rehearsal at which all the design and technical elements are brought together.

Tetralogy In classical Greek theater, four plays—three tragedies and a satyr play—written by one author for a festival.

Theater of the absurd Plays expressing the dramatist's sense of the absurdity and futility of existence.

Theater of cruelty Antonin Artaud's visionary concept of a theater based on magic and ritual which would liberate deep, violent, and erotic impulses.

Theater-in-the-round *See* Arena.

Theatricalism Exposing the elements of theater so that the audience members are aware that they are watching theater.

Theme The central thought of a play; the idea or ideas with which a play deals and which it expounds.

Thespian Synonym for "performer"; from Thespis, who is said to have been the first actor in ancient Greek theater.

Thrust stage Theater space in which the audience sits on three sides of the stage.

Tilt Term in theater lighting used when a beam of light from an instrument moves vertically, up and down.

Tiring house Elizabethan stage house.

Tragedy Dramatic form involving serious actions of universal significance and with important moral and philosophical implications, usually with an unhappy ending.

Tragic flaw The factor which is a character's chief weakness and which makes him or her most vulnerable; it often intensifies in time of stress.

Tragicomedy During the Renaissance, a play having tragic themes and noble characters but a happy ending; today, a play in which serious and comic elements are integrated.

Trap Opening in the stage floor, normally covered, which can be used for special effects or allows for a staircase ostensibly leading to a lower floor.

Trilogy In classical Greece, three tragedies written by the same playwright and presented on a single day; they were connected by a story or thematic concerns.

Unities Term referring to the preference that a play occur within one day (unity of time), in one place (unity of place), and with no action irrelevant to the plot (unity of action).

Unit set Single setting which can represent a variety of locales with the simple addition of properties or scenic elements.

Unity A requirement of art; an element often setting art apart from life. In drama, the term refers to unity of action in structure and story and to the integrity and wholeness of a production.

Upstage At or toward the back of the stage, away from the front edge of the stage.

Wagon stage Low platform mounted on wheels or casters by means of which scenery is moved on- and offstage.

Well-made play Dramatic form popular in the nineteenth and early twentieth centuries which combined apparent plausibility of incident and surface realism with a tightly constructed plot.

Wings Left and right offstage areas; *also,* narrow standing pieces of scenery, or "legs," more or less parallel to the proscenium, which form the sides of a setting.

Work lights Lights arranged for the convenience of stage technicians, situated either in backstage areas and shaded or over the stage area for use while the curtain is down.

Yard Pit, or standing area, in Elizabethan public theaters.

Zanni (ZAH-nee) Comic male servants in Italian commedia dell'arte.

Bibliography

General Topics (Chapters 1 through 9)

Allen, John, *Theatre in Europe,* Offord, Eastbourne, England, 1981.

Aristotle, *Aristotle's Poetics,* S. H. Butcher (trans.), introduction by Francis Fergusson, Hill and Wang, New York, 1961.

Aronson, Arnold, *American Set Design,* New York, 1985.

Atkinson, Brooks, *Broadway,* rev. ed., Macmillan, New York, 1974.

Austen, Gayle, *Feminist Theories for Creative Criticism,* University of Michigan Press, Ann Arbor, 1990.

Bay, Howard, *Stage Design,* Drama Book Specialists, New York, 1974.

Beckerman, Bernard, *Dynamics of Drama: Theory and Method of Analysis,* Drama Book Specialists, New York, 1979.

Benedetti, Jean, *Stanislavski: An Introduction,* Theatre Arts, New York, 1982.

——, *Stanislavski and the Actor,* Routledge, New York, 1998.

Benedetti, Robert, *The Actor at Work,* Prentice-Hall, Englewood Cliffs, N.J., 1971.

Bentley, Eric, *The Life of the Drama,* Atheneum, New York, 1964.

—— (ed.), *The Theory of the Modern Stage,* Penguin, Baltimore, Md., 1968.

Betsko, Kathleen, and Rachel Koenig, *Interviews with Contemporary Women Playwrights,* Beech Tree, New York, 1987.

Bradby, David, and David Williams, *Director's Theater,* St. Martin's, New York, 1988.

Burns, Elizabeth, *Theatricality,* Harper and Row, New York, 1973.

Case, Sue-Ellen, *Feminism and Theatre,* Routledge, Chapillan, and Hall, New York, 1987.

Chinoy, Helen K., and Linda W. Jenkins, *Women in American Theatre,* rev. ed., Theatre Communications Group, New York, 1987.

Clark, Barrett H. (ed.), *European Theories of the Drama,* rev ed., Crown, New York, 1965.

Clurman, Harold, *On Directing,* Macmillan, New York, 1972.

Cohen, Robert, *Acting Power,* Mayfield, Palo Alto, Calif., 1978.

Corrigan, Robert (ed.), *Comedy: Meaning and Form,* Chandler, San Francisco, 1965.

—— (ed.), *Tragedy: Vision and Form,* Chandler, San Francisco, Calif., 1965.

Corson, Richard, *Stage Makeup,* 6th ed., Prentice-Hall, Englewood Cliffs, N.J., 1981.

Dolan, Jill, *The Feminist Spectator as Critic,* University of Michigan Press, Ann Arbor, 1988.

Dukore, Bernard, *Dramatic Theory and Criticism: Greeks to Grotowski,* Holt, New York, 1974.

Emery, Joseph S., *Stage Costume Technique,* Prentice-Hall, Englewood Cliffs, N.J., 1981.

Felner, Mira, *Free to Act,* Holt, Rinehart, and Winston, New York, 1990.

Fergusson, Francis, *The Idea of a Theater,* Princeton University Press, Princeton, N.J., 1949.

Finney, Gail, *Women in Modern Drama,* Cornell University Press, Ithaca, N.Y., 1989.

Gassner, John, *Masters of the Drama,* 3d ed., Dover, New York, 1954.

——, and Edward Quinn, *The Reader's Encyclopedia of World Drama,* Crowell, New York, 1969.

Goffman, Erving, *Presentation of Self in Everyday Life,* Overlook, New York, 1973.

Goldman, Michael, *The Actor's Freedom: Toward a Theory of Drama,* Viking, New York, 1975.

Heilman, Robert G., *Tragedy and Melodrama: Versions of Experience,* University of Washington Press, Seattle, 1968.

Izenour, George, *Theatre Design,* McGraw-Hill, New York, 1977.

Jones, Robert E., *The Dramatic Imagination,* Meredith, New York, 1941.

Kerr, Walter, *Tragedy and Comedy,* Simon and Schuster, New York, 1967.

Kirby, Michael, *Happenings,* Dutton, New York, 1965.

Lahr, John, and Jonathan Price, *Life-Show,* Viking, New York, 1973.

Langer, Susanne K., *Feeling and Form,* Scribner, New York, 1953.

Larson, Orville K., *Scene Design in the American Theatre from 1915 to 1960,* Fayettesville, Ark., 1989.

Miller, Arthur, *The Theatre Essays of Arthur Miller,* Robert Martin (ed.), Viking, New York, 1978.

Novick, Julius, *Beyond Broadway,* Hill and Wang, New York, 1968.

Oenslager, Donald, *Scenery Then and Now,* Norton, New York, 1936.

Parker, W. Oren, and Harvey K. Smith, *Scene Design and Stage Lighting,* 4th ed., Holt, New York, 1979.

Pilbrow, Richard, *Stage Lighting,* rev. ed., Van Nostrand and Reinhold, New York, 1979.

Pottlitzer, Joanne, *Hispanic Theatre in the United States and Puerto Rico,* Ford Foundation, New York, 1988.

Rodenburg, Patsy, *The Actor Speaks: Voice and the Performer,* St. Martin's Press, New York, 2000.

Roemer, Rick, *Charles Ludlam and the Ridiculous Theatrical Company,* McFarland, Jefferson, N.C., 1998.

Savran, David, *In Their Own Words: Contemporary American Play-wrights,* Theatre Communications Group, New York, 1988.

Schechner, Richard, *Environmental Theater,* Hawthorn, New York, 1973.

——, *Essays on Performance Theory,* Routledge, New York, 1988.

Schevill, James, *Breakout! In Search of New Theatrical Environments,* University of Chicago Press, Ill., 1972.

Shank, Theodore, *American Alternative Theatres,* St. Martin's, New York, 1988.

Stanislavski, Constantin, *An Actor Prepares,* Elizabeth Reynolds Hapgood (trans.), Theatre Arts, New York, 1936.

Wilson, Edwin, and Alvin Goldfarb, *Anthology of Living Theater,* 2nd ed., McGraw-Hill, New York, 2001.

Young, Stark, *The Theatre,* Hill and Wang, New York, 1963.

General Theater Histories (Chapters 10 through 16)

Berthold, Margot, *A History of World Theater,* Felicia Londre (trans.), Ungar, New York, 1972.

Banham, Martin, (ed.), *The Cambridge Guide to the Theatre,* updated version, Cambridge University Press, New York, 1992.

Brandon, James R. (ed.), *Cambridge Guide to Asian Theatre,* Cambridge University Press, New York, 1993.

Brockett, Oscar, and Frank Hildy, *History of the Theatre,* 8th ed., Allyn and Bacon, Boston, 1999.

Brockett, Oscar, and Robert Findlay, *Century of Innovation: A History of European and American Theatre and Drama since the Late Nineteenth Century,* 2d ed., Allyn and Bacon, Boston, 1991.

Carlson, Marvin, *Theories of the Theatre: A Historical and Critical Survey from the Greeks to the Present,* expanded ed., Cornell University Press, Ithaca, N.Y., 1993.

Cole, Toby, and Helen K. Chinoy (eds.), *Actors on Acting,* rev. ed., Crown, New York, 1980.

—— and —— (eds.), *Directors on Directing: A Source Book of the Modern Theatre,* Macmillan, New York, 1986.

Gillespie, Patti P., and Kenneth M. Cameron, *Western Theatre: Revolution and Revival,* Macmillan, New York, 1984.

Hartnoll, Phyllis, and Peter Found (eds.), *The Concise Oxford Companion to the Theatre,* New Edition, Oxford University Press, New York, 1993.

Londre, Felicia, *The History of World Theater: From the English Restoration to the Present,* Continuum, New York, 1991.

Londre, Felicia Hardison, and Daniel J. Watermeier, *The History of North American Theater: From Pre-Columbian Times to the Present,* Continuum, New York, 1998.

Nagler, Alois M., *Sources of Theatrical History,* Theatre Annual, New York, 1952.

Postlewait, Thomas, and Bruce McConachie (eds.), *Interpreting the Theatrical Past: Essays in the Historiography of Performance,* University of Iowa Press, Iowa City, 1989.

Roberts, Vera M., *On Stage: A History of the Theatre,* 2d ed., Harper and Row, New York, 1974.

Watson, Jack, and Grant F. McKernie, *A Cultural History of Theatre,* Longman, New York, 1993.

Wickham, Glynne, *A History of the Theatre,* Cambridge University Press, England, 1992.

Wilmeth, Don B., and Tice L. Miller (eds.), *Cambridge Guide to American Theatre,* Cambridge University Press, New York, 1993.

Wilson, Edwin, and Alvin Goldfarb, *Living Theater: A History,* 3rd ed., McGraw-Hill, New York, 2000.

Origins of Theater (Chapter 10)

Brown, Ivor, *The First Player: The Origin of Drama,* Morrow, New York, 1928.

Hunningher, Ben, *The Origin of the Theater,* Hill and Wang, New York, 1961.

Kirby, E. T., *Ur-Drama: The Origins of Theatre,* New York University Press, New York, 1975.

Ridgeway, William, *The Drama and Dramatic Dances of Non-European Races,* Cambridge University Press, England, 1915.

Turner, Victor, *From Ritual to Theatre,* Performing Arts Journal Publications, New York, 1982.

Greek Theater (Chapter 10)

Arnott, Peter D., *The Ancient Greek and Roman Theatre,* Random House, New York, 1971.

——, *Public and Performance in the Greek Theatre,* Routledge, New York, 1991.

Aylen, Leo, *The Greek Theater,* Associated University Presses, London, 1985.

Bieber, Margarete, *The History of Greek and Roman Theater,* 2d ed., Princeton University Press, Princeton, N.J., 1961.

Butler, James H., *The Theatre and Drama of Greece and Rome,* Chandler, San Francisco, Calif., 1972.

Dearden, C. W., *The Stage of Aristophanes,* Athlone, London, 1976.

Flickinger, Roy C., *The Greek Theatre and Its Drama,* 4th ed., University of Chicago Press, Ill., 1936.

Pickard-Cambridge, A. W., *The Dramatic Festivals of Athens,* 2d ed., rev. by John Gould and D. M. Lewis, Clarendon, Oxford, England, 1968.

Rehm, Rush, *Greek Tragic Theatre*, Routledge, New York, 1992.

Stone, Laura, *Costume in Aristophanic Comedy*, Arno, New York, 1981.

Vince, Ronald W., *Ancient and Medieval Theatre: A Historiographical Handbook*, Greenwood, Westport, Conn., 1984.

Walton, J. Michael, *Greek Theatre Practice*, Greenwood, Westport, Conn., 1980.

Walton, J. Michael, *Living Greek Theatre: A Handbook of Classical Performance and Modern Production*, Greenwood, Westport, Conn., 1987.

Webster, T. B. L., *Greek Theatre Production*, 2d ed., Methuen, London, 1970.

Wiles, David, *Tragedy in Athens: Performance Space and Theatrical Meaning*, Cambridge University Press, New York, 1997.

Roman Theater (Chapter 10)

Allen, James T., *Stage Antiquities of the Greeks and Romans and Their Influence*, McKay, New York, 1927.

Beare, William, *The Roman Stage: A Short History of Latin Drama in the Time of the Republic*, Methuen, London, 1968.

Duckworth, George E., *The Nature of Roman Comedy*, Princeton University Press, Princeton, N.J., 1952.

Forehand, Walter E., *Terence*, Twayne, Boston, Mass., 1985.

Wiles, David, *The Masks of Menander: Sign and Meaning in Greek and Roman Performance*, Cambridge University Press, New York, 1991.

Asian Theater (Chapter 11)

Arnott, Peter, *The Theatres of Japan*, Macmillan, New York, 1969.

Bowers, Faubion, *Theatre in the East: A Survey of Asian Dance and Drama*, Grove, New York, 1969.

Dolby, William, *A History of the Chinese Drama*, Harper and Row, New York, 1976.

Ernst, Earle, *The Kabuki Theatre*, Oxford University Press, New York, 1957.

Gargi, Balwant, *Theatre in India*, Theatre Arts, New York, 1962.

Jain, Nemi Chandra, *Indian Theatre: Tradition, Continuity, and Change*, Vikas, New Delhi, 1992.

Keene, Donald, and Kaneko Hiroshi, *Nō and Bunraku: Two Forms of Japanese Theatre*, Columbia University Press, New York, 1990.

Howard, Roger, *Contemporary Chinese Theatre*, Heinemann Educational, London, 1978.

Leiter, Samuel L., *The Art of Kabuki: Famous Plays in Performance*, University of California Press, Berkeley, Calif., 1979.

Ortolani, Benito, *The Japanese Theatre: From Shamanistic Ritual to Contemporary Pluralism*, rev. ed., Princeton University Press, Princeton, N.J., 1995.

Richmond, Farley, et al., *Indian Theatre: Traditions of Performance*, University of Hawaii Press, Honolulu, 1990.

Scott, A. C., *The Classical Theatre of China*, Allen and Unwin, London, 1957.

Waley, Arthur, *The No Plays of Japan*, Knopf, New York, 1922.

Medieval Theater (Chapter 11)

Case, Sue-Ellen, "Re-Viewing Hrosvit," *Theatre Journal*, vol. 35, December 1983, pp. 533–542.

Chambers, E. K., *The Medieval Stage*, 2 vols., Clarendon, Oxford, England, 1903.

Hanawalt, Barbara A., and Michal Kobialka (eds.), *Medieval Practices of Space*, University of Minnesota Press, Minneapolis, 2000.

Hardison, O. B., *Christian Rite and Christian Drama in the Middle Ages*, Johns Hopkins Press, Baltimore, Md., 1965.

Kobialka, Michal, *This Is My Body: Representational Practices in*

The Early Middle Ages, University of Michigan Press, Ann Arbor, 1999.

Nagler, Alois M., *Medieval Religious Stage: Shapes and Phantoms*, Yale University Press, New Haven, Conn., 1976.

Nelson, Alan H., *The Medieval English Stage: Corpus Christi Pageants and Plays*, University of Chicago Press, Ill., 1974.

Tyedeman, William, *English Medieval Theatre, 1400–1500*, Routledge, London, 1986.

Vince, Ronald W. (ed.), *A Companion to the Medieval Theatre*, Greenwood, Westport, Conn., 1989.

Wickham, Glynne, *The Medieval Theatre*, Weidenfeld and Nicolson, London, 1974.

Young, Karl, *The Drama of the Medieval Church*, 2 vols., Clarendon, Oxford, England, 1933.

Italian Renaissance Theater (Chapter 12)

Bjurstrom, Per, *Giacomo Torelli and Baroque Stage Design*, National Museum, Stockholm, Sweden, 1961.

Ducharte, Pierre, *The Italian Comedy*, R. T. Weaver (trans.), Dover, New York, 1966.

Gordon, Mel (ed. and trans.), *Lazzi: The Comic Routines of the Commedia dell'Arte*, Performing Arts Journal, New York, 1992.

Hewitt, Barnard (ed.), *The Renaissance Stage: Documents of Serlio, Sabbatini, and Furttenbach*, University of Miami Press, Coral Gables, Fla., 1958.

Mullin, Daniel C., *The Development of the Playhouse: A Survey of Architecture from the Renaissance to the Present*, University of California Press, Berkeley, 1970.

Oosting, J. Thomas, *Andrea Palladio's Teatro Olimpico*, UMI Research Press, Ann Arbor, Mich., 1981.

Richards, Kenneth, and Laura Richards, *The Commedia dell'Arte: A Documentary History*, Blackwell, New York, 1990.

Vince, Ronald W., *Renaissance Theatre: A Historiographical Handbook*, Greenwood, Westport, Conn., 1984.

English Renaissance Theater (Chapter 12)

Adams, John C., *The Globe Playhouse: Its Design and Equipment*, Barnes and Noble, New York, 1966.

Beckerman, Bernard, *Shakespeare at the Globe, 1599–1602*, Macmillan, New York, 1962.

Bentley, Gerald E., *The Profession of Player in Shakespeare's Time, 1590–1642*, Princeton University Press, Princeton, N.J., 1984.

Chambers, E. K., *The Elizabethan Stage*, 4 vols., Clarendon, Oxford, 1965.

Eccles, Christine, *The Rose Theatre*, Routledge, New York, 1990.

Gurr, Andrew, *Playgoing in Shakespeare's London*, 2nd ed., Cambridge University Press, New York, 1996.

———, *The Shakespearean Playing Companies*, Oxford University Press, New York, 1996.

———, *The Shakespearean Stage, 1574–1642*, Cambridge University Press, Cambridge, 1970.

———, and John Orrell, *Rebuilding Shakespeare's Globe*, Routledge, New York, 1989.

Hildy, Franklin J. (ed.), *New Issues in the Reconstruction of Shakespeare's Theatre: Proceedings of the Conference Held at the University of Georgia, February 16–18, 1990*, vol. 1, *Artists and Issues in the Theatre*, Lang, New York, 1990.

Hodges, C. W., *The Globe Restored: A Study of the Elizabethan Theatre*, Coward, McCann, and Geoghegan, New York, 1953.

Leggatt, Alexander, *Jacobean Public Theatre*, Routledge, New York, 1992.

Nagler, Alois M., *Shakespeare's Stage*, Yale University Press, New Haven, Conn., 1958.

Orrell, John, *The Human Stage: English Theatre Design, 1567–1640*, Cambridge University Press, New York, 1988.

Smith, Irwin, *Shakespeare's Blackfriar's Playhouse: Its History and Its Design*, New York University Press, New York, 1964.

Thomson, Peter, *Shakespeare's Theatre*, Routledge, New York, 1992.

Theater of the Spanish Golden Age (Chapter 12)

Allen, John J., *The Reconstruction of a Spanish Golden Age Playhouse: El Corral del Principe, 1583–1744*, University Presses of Florida, Gainesville, Fla., 1983.

Crawford, J. P. W., *Spanish Drama Before Lope de Vega*, Lippincott, Philadelphia, Pa., 1937.

McKendrick, Melveena, *Theatre in Spain, 1490–1700*, Cambridge University Press, Cambridge, England, 1989.

Shergold, N. D., *A History of the Spanish Stage from Medieval Times until the End of the 17th Century*, Clarendon, Oxford, England, 1967.

Stoll, Anita K., and Dawn L. Smith, *The Perception of Women in Spanish Theater of the Golden Age*, Associated University Presses, Cranbury, N.J., 1991.

French Neoclassical Theater (Chapter 12)

Arnott, Peter D., *An Introduction to the French Theatre*, Rowman and Littlefield, Totowa, N.J., 1977.

Lawrenson, T. E., *The French Stage in the 17th Century: A Study in the Advent of the Italian Order*, rev. ed., AMS, New York, 1986.

Lough, John, *Paris Theatre Audiences in the Seventeenth and Eighteenth Centuries*, Oxford University Press, Oxford, England, 1957.

Turnell, Martin, *The Classical Moment: Studies in Corneille, Molière, and Racine*, New Directions, New York, 1963.

Wiley, W. L., *The Early Public Theatre in France*, Harvard University Press, Cambridge, Mass., 1960.

Theater of the English Restoration (Chapter 13)

Hotson, Leslie, *The Commonwealth and Restoration Stage*, Russell and Russell, New York, 1962.

Hume, Robert D. (ed.), *The London Theatre World, 1660–1800*, Southern Illinois University Press, Carbondale, 1980.

Kenny, Shirley Strum (ed.), *British Theatre and the Other Arts, 1660–1800*, Folger, Washington, D.C., 1984.

The London Stage, 1660–1800, 11 vols., Southern Illinois University Press, Carbondale, 1960–1968.

McCollum, John I. (ed.), *The Restoration Stage*, Houghton Mifflin, Boston, Mass., 1961.

Milhous, Judith, and Robert D. Hume, *Producible Interpretation: Eight English Plays, 1675–1707*, Southern Illinois University Press, Carbondale, 1985.

Southern, Richard, *Changeable Scenery: Its Origin and Development in the British Theatre*, Faber and Faber, London, 1952.

Summers, Montague, *The Restoration Theatre*, Macmillan, New York, 1934.

Vince, Ronald W., *Neoclassical Theatre: A Historiographical Handbook*, Greenwood, Westport, Conn., 1988.

Eighteenth-Century Theater (Chapter 13)

Baur-Heinhold, Margarete, *The Baroque Theatre: A Cultural History of the 17th and 18th Centuries*, McGraw-Hill, New York, 1967.

Brown, Frederick, *Theater and Revolution: The Culture of the French Stage*, Viking, New York, 1980.

Bruford, W. H., *Theatre, Drama, and Audience in Goethe's Germany*, Greenwood, Westport, Conn., 1974.

Carlson, Marvin, *Goethe and the Weimar Theatre*, Cornell University Press, Ithaca, N.Y., 1978.

———, *The Italian Stage: From Goldoni to D'Annunzio*, McFarland and Company, Jefferson, N.C., 1981.

Hughes, Leo, *The Drama's Patrons: A Study of the 18th Century London*

Audience, University of Texas Press, Austin, 1971.

Nicoll, Allardyce, *The Garrick Stage,* University of Georgia Press, Athens, 1980.

Pedicord, Harry W., *The Theatrical Public in the Time of Garrick,* King's Crown, New York, 1954.

Price, Cecil, *Theatre in the Age of Garrick,* Rowman and Littlefield, Totowa, N.J., 1973.

Prudhoe, John, *The Theatre of Goethe and Schiller,* Blackwell, Oxford, England, 1973.

Stone, George Winchester, Jr. (ed.), *The Stage and the Page: London's "Whole Show" in the Eighteenth-Century Theatre,* University of California Press, Berkeley, 1981.

Theater from 1800 to 1875 (Chapter 13)

Booth, Michael, *English Melodrama,* Jenkins, London, 1965.

Carlson, Marvin, *The French Stage in the 19th Century,* Scarecrow, Metuchen, N.J., 1972.

———, *The German Stage in the 19th Century,* Scarecrow, Metuchen, N.J., 1972.

Durham, Weldon B. (ed.), *American Theatre Companies, 1749–1887,* Greenwood, Westport, Conn., 1986.

Engle, Ron, and Tice L. Miller (eds.), *The American Stage: Social and Economic Issues from the Colonial Period to the Present,* Cambridge University Press, New York, 1993.

Grimstead, David, *Melodrama Unveiled: American Theatre and Culture, 1800–1850,* University of Chicago Press, Ill., 1968.

Marshall, Herbert, and Mildred Stock, *Ira Aldridge, the Negro Tragedian,* Southern Illinois University Press, Carbondale, Ill., 1968.

McConachie, Bruce, *Melodramatic Formations: American Theatre and Society, 1820–1870,* University of Iowa Press, Iowa City, 1992.

Rowell, George, *The Victorian Theatre: A Survey,* Oxford University Press, London and New York, 1956.

Vardac, A. Nicholas, *Stage to Screen: Theatrical Methods from Garrick to Griffith,* Harvard University Press, Cambridge, Mass., 1949.

Theater from 1875 to 1915 (Chapter 14)

Appia, Adolphe, *Essays, Scenarios, and Designs,* Walther R. Volbach (trans.), Richard C. Beacham (ed.), UMI Research Press, Ann Arbor, Mich., 1989.

Bentley, Eric, *The Playwright as Thinker: A Study of Drama in Modern Times,* Reynal and Hitchcock, New York, 1946.

Garten, Hugh, *Modern German Drama,* Grove, New York, 1962.

Hatch, James V., and Ted Shine, *Black Theater, U.S.A.,* Free Press, New York, 1974.

Innes, Christopher, *Edward Gordon Craig,* Cambridge University Press, New York, 1983.

Isaacs, Edith J., *The Negro in the American Theatre,* Theatre Arts, New York, 1947.

Koller, Ann Marie, *The Theatre Duke: Georg II of Saxe-Meiningen and the German Stage,* Stanford University Press, Stanford, Calif., 1984.

Miller, Anna Irene, *The Independent Theatre in Europe 1887 to the Present,* Long and Smith, New York, 1931.

Mitchell, Loften, *Black Drama: The Story of the American Negro in the Theatre,* Hawthorn, New York, 1967.

Patterson, Michael, *The Revolution in the German Theatre, 1900–1933,* Routledge and Kegan Paul, London, 1981.

Roose-Evans, James, *Experimental Theatre: From Stanislavsky to Peter Brook,* Routledge and Kegan Paul, London, 1984.

Shattuck, Roger, *The Banquet Years: The Arts in France, 1885–1918,* Harcourt, Brace, New York, 1961.

Slonim, Marc, *Russian Theatre from the Empire to the Soviets,* Collier, Cleveland, Ohio, 1962.

Styan, J. L., *Max Reinhardt,* Cambridge University Press, New York, 1982.

Valency, Maurice, *The Flower and the Castle: An Introduction to Modern Drama,* Macmillan, New York, 1963.

Volbach, Walther R., *Adolphe Appia, Prophet of the Modern Theatre,* Wesleyan University Press, Middletown, Conn., 1968.

Whitton, David, *Stage Directors in Modern France: Antoine to Mnouchkine,* Manchester University Press, England, 1987.

Theater from 1915 to 1945 (Chapter 14)

Abramson, Doris, *Negro Playwrights in the American Theatre, 1925–1959,* Columbia University Press, New York, 1969.

Artaud, Antonin, *The Theatre and Its Double,* M. C. Richards (trans.), Grove, New York, 1958.

Brecht, Bertolt, *Brecht on Theatre,* John Willett (trans.), Hill and Wang, New York, 1964.

Carter, Huntly, *The New Spirit in the European Theatre, 1914–1924,* Doran, New York, 1926.

Clunes, Alec, *The British Theatre,* Cassell, London, 1964.

Goldberg, RoseLee, *Performance Art: From Futurism to the Present,* Abrams, New York, 1988.

Houghton, Norris, *Moscow Rehearsals,* Harcourt, Brace, New York, 1936.

Rabkin, Gerald, *Drama and Commitment: Politics in the American Theatre of the Thirties,* Indiana University Press, Bloomington, Ind., 1964.

Rovit, Rebecca, and Alvin Goldfarb, eds., *Theatrical Performance during the Holocaust: Texts, Memoirs and Documents,* Johns Hopkins University Press, Baltimore, Md., 1999.

Rudlin, John, *Jacques Copeau,* Cambridge University Press, New York, 1986.

Willett, John, *Expressionism,* McGraw-Hill, New York, 1970.

Theater from 1945 to the Present (Chapters 15 and 16)

Bigsby, C. W. E., *Contemporary American Playwrights,* Cambridge University Press, New York, 1999.

————, *Modern American Drama, 1945–1990,* Cambridge University Press, New York, 1992.

Brook, Peter, *The Empty Space,* Atheneum, New York, 1982.

Calandra, Denis, *New German Dramatists: A Study of Peter Handke, Rainer Werner Fassbinder, Heiner Müller, Thomas Bernhard,* Macmillan, Routledge, New York, 1983.

Carlson, Marvin, *Performance,* Routledge, New York, 1996.

Cohn, Ruby, *Currents in Contemporary Drama,* Indiana University Press, Bloomington, Ind., 1969.

Esslin, Martin, *The Theatre of the Absurd,* Anchor, Garden City, N.Y., 1969.

Grotowski, Jerzy, *Towards a Poor Theatre,* Simon and Schuster, New York, 1969.

Kantor, Tadeusz, *A Journey through Other Spaces: Essays and Manifestos, 1944–1990,* Michal Kobialka (trans.), University of California Press, Berkeley, 1993.

Kolin, Philip C. (ed.), *American Playwrights since 1945: A Guide to Scholarship, Criticism, and Performance,* Greenwood, Westport, Conn., 1989.

Marranca, Bonnie, *The Theatre of Images,* Drama Book Specialists, New York, 1977.

Mottram, Ron, *Inner Landscapes: The Theatre of Sam Shepard,* University of Missouri Press, Columbia, 1984.

Patterson, Michael, *Peter Stein: Germany's Leading Theatre Director,* Cambridge University Press, New York, 1981.

Perkins, Kathy, and Roberta Uno, *Contemporary Plays by Women of Color: An Anthology,* Routledge, New York, 1996.

Poggi, Jack, *Theater in America: The Impact of Economic Forces, 1870–1967,* Cornell University Press, Ithaca, N.Y., 1968.

Savran, David, *The Wooster Group, 1975–1985: Breaking the Rules,* UMI Research Press, Ann Arbor, Mich., 1986.

Schechner, Richard, *Public Domain: Essays on the Theatre,* Discus, New York, 1970.

Shyer, Laurence, *Robert Wilson and His Collaborators,* Theatre Communications Group, New York, 1989.

Svoboda, Josef, *The Secret of Theatrical Space: The Memoirs of Josef Svoboda,* Jarka Burian (trans.), Applause, New York, 1993.

Weales, Gerald, *American Drama since World War II,* Harcourt, Brace, and World, New York, 1962.

Williams, Mance, *Black Theatre in the 1960s and 1970s,* Greenwood, Westport, Conn., 1985.

Index

Note: If not stated in the text, dates for key individuals and works are given in the index.

Abbey Theater (Dublin), 332
Above, 390
Absurdism, 25, 348
Absurdist theater (*see* Theater of the absurd)
Abyssinia (musical), 353
Ace Ventura, Pet Detective (film), 183
Acosta, Iván, 373
Acrobatics, 3, 40, 53, 222, 224, 237, 240, 307
Act drop, 303
Acting, 1, 10–11, 13, 14, 37, 38–57, 203, 220, 221, 228, 235, 237, 238, 240, 244, 245, 252, 258–260, 271, 278–279, 284, 292, 303–304, 311
  believability in, 10, 40, 46–47
  body in, 42–43, 46, 52–53
  challenges of, 40–41
  classical, 38–40
  as craft, 42–46
ensemble, 47, 50
  exercises for, 43, 44
  Stanislavski system of, 47–48, 50–52
  synthesis and integration, 54, 56
  viewpoints theory of, 52
  voice in, 40, 43–46
  websites on, 57
  (*See also* Dramatic characters)
Acting Company, The, 114, 173
Action, 390
Acton, Wallace, 146
Actor(s), actress(es):
  audience effect on, 6–7, 11–12, 19, 20–23, 35, 56, 385
  as basic element of theater, 9, 10–11, 13, 14
  casting of, 64, 194
  direction of, 60, 64–68, 69
  role-playing, 1, 38, 57
  (*See also* Acting)
Actor-managers, 60, 280, 312
Actors Company (New York), 68
Actors Equity Association, 194, 221
Actors Studio (New York), 51
Actors Theater of Louisville, 145, 363
Actor's Workshop, 99

Actos, 373
Ad lib, 390
Adams Memorial Theater (Utah), 24
Adamson, Eve, 126
Adler, Stella, 51, 57
Aeschylus, 34, 60, 214, 231
Aesthetic distance, 22–23, 93, 390
African American theater, 25, 35, 147, 329, 352–355, 364, 366, 375, 379, 380, 385, 387
  background, 352
  nineteenth century, 352–353
  1900–1950, 353–354
  since 1950, 354–355
African Grove Theater, 352
African ritual, 210
Agitprop, 373
Agon, 220, 390
Aida (musical), 130, 361, 382
AIDS, 370, 378
Alam, Juan Shamsul, 373
Albee, Edward, 29, 123, 148, 168, 346, 348
Alchemist, The (Jonson, 1610), 168
Aldridge, Ira, 352, 353
Alice's Rape (McCauley), 379
Alienation, 336, 390
All My Sons (Miller), 344
All purpose and experimental space, 93, 94
Allegory, 390
Allen, John J., 277
Alley Theatre (Houston), 117, 179, 363
Alliance Theatre Company (Atlanta), 375
All's Well That Ends Well (Shakespeare), 189
Ally McBeal (television), 55
Alojero, 278
Alternative theater, 329, 352, 361–366, 370, 383–384
Amen Corner (Baldwin), 354
America Play, The (Parks), 375
American Ballet Theatre (New York), 9
American Buffalo (Mamet), 366
American Civil War, 13
An American Daughter (Wasserstein), 374

American Museum, 310
American Repertory Theatre (Boston), 181, 348
American Revolution, 297, 300
American Theatre Wing, 41
Amphitheater, 23, 44, 77, 79, 82, 83, 219, 220, 224, 283, 284, 390
Amusement parks, 3–4, 90
  (*See also* Popular entertainments)
Angelos, Maureen, 377
Angels in America: The Millennium Approaches (Kushner), 29, 99, 125, 355, 370, 378
Angels of Light (San Francisco), 378
"Angry young men," 346, 366
Animal acts, 307, 310
Animal battles, 227
Anna Christie (O'Neill), 329
Anna Lucasta, 354
Annals, Michael, 103
Annie Get Your Gun (musical), 359, 360
Anouilh, Jean (1910–1987), 157–158
Antagonist, 168–169, 390
Antigone (Anouilh, 1943), 157–158
Antigone (Sophocles), 165, 215
Antirealism (*see* Departures from realism)
Antoine, André, 325, 331
Antony and Cleopatra (Shakespeare, 1607–1608), 28, 97, 158
Apache war dance, 88
Apartheid, 382
Appia, Adolphe, 332, 333, 338
Apple, Jacki, 379
Apprentice, 271, 390
Apron, 294, 295, 300, 390
Arena stage, 12, 72, 78, 87–89, 90, 94, 390, 397
Arena Stage (Washington, D.C.), 68, 88–89, 363
Aristophanes, 168, 177, 180, 182, 183, 219, 231
Aristotle, 34, 220, 228, 231, 299
Arkin, Matthew, 100
Arms and the Man (Shaw), 185
Arsenic and Old Lace (Kesselring), 174, 182

Art, characteristics of, 7–10, 14
Art of Poetry, The (Horace), 228
Artaud, Antonin, 335–336, 349, 351, 378
Artistic director, 71, 194, 199, 390
Artists of Dionysus, 221
Artsweek (magazine), 379
As Is (Hoffman), 378
As You Like It (Shakespeare), 114, 266
Ashikaga Yoshimitsu, 242
Ashland Shakespeare Festival (Oregon),
    4, 5, 193
Asian American theater, 25, 35, 371–372
Asian American Theatre Workshop, (San
    Francisco), 371
Asian Exclusion Act (Seattle), 371
Asian theater, 87, 94, 118, 186, 233,
    234–245, 253, 335, 382
    acting in, 38, 52–53, 235, 237, 238,
        240, 244, 245, 252
    introduction to, 234
    time line, 236
    websites on, 253
    (*See also* Bunraku; Chinese theater;
        Japanese theater; Kabuki; Indian
        theater; Nô)
Aside, 390
Astor place riot, 307–308
Astor Place Theater (New York), 307
At the Foot of the Mountain
    (Minneapolis), 375
At rise, 390
Audience, 4, 6–7, 10, 11–12, 13, 14, 19,
    20–26, 27, 35, 351, 370–371, 385
Auditions, 64–65, 390
Auditorium, 79
Auschwitz, 337
Auteur director, 31, 61–62, 390
Authorship, 144, 380
Automated light, 132, 133, 390
Avant-garde theater, 25, 35, 40, 53–54,
    62, 163–164, 318, 334–336, 342,
    346–351, 370, 378, 383, 390
(*See also* Experimental theater)
Awake and Sing (Odets, 1935), 327, 329

Bacchae, The (Euripides), 213, 383
Backdrop, 295, 303, 390
Backlighting, 131, 390
Backstage, 89, 106, 390
Bad Boy Nietzsche! (Foreman), 364
Baird, Bill, 125
Baitz, Jon Robin, 65
Bakkhai, The, 213
Balanchine, George, 9
Balcony, 80, 313
Baldwin, James, 354
Ballad opera, 298, 390
Ballet, 9, 42, 52, 284, 359
Bankhead, Tallulah (1902–1968), 28
Baraka, Amiri, 154, 354
Barnum, P. T., 307, 310

Baroque, 297
Barton, John, 119
Basic situation, 390
Bates, Anna, 173
Batten, 134, 390
Bayreuth Festspielhaus, 312, 313, 314, 315
Beam projector, 390
Bear Garden, 272
Bearbaiting, 272
Beatles, The, 2, 3
Beats, 50
Beaumarchais (Pierre–Augustin Caron), 301
Beaumont, Francis, 273
Beauty Queen of Leenane, The
    (McDonagh), 383
Beckett, Samuel (1906–1990), 29, 53, 190,
    347, 348, 349, 350, 366, 369, 394
Beggar's Opera, The (Gay), 299
Behn, Aphra, 289
Beijing Opera (*see* Peking opera)
Belle Reprieve (Split Britches), 375
Below, 390
Benefit, 292
Bening, Annette, 65
Bennett, Michael, 113, 360, 370
Berlin, Irving, 357, 359
Berliner Ensemble, 336
Berlinsky, Harris, 160
Bernhardt, Sarah, 312
Bernstein, Leonard, 360
Beudert, Peter, 197
Bibiena family, 302
Bibiena, Giovanni, 302
Bibiena, Giuseppe, 302
Big Deal (musical), 125
Biomechanics, 333, 351, 391
Birdcage, The, 55
Birds, The (Aristophanes, 414 B.C.),
    168, 183
Black, Christopher, 160
Black and Blue (musical), 355
"Black Box" theater, 92
Black Crook, The (musical), 357
Black Elk, Nicholas, 374
Black Elk Speaks, 374
Black Horizons Theatre (Pittsburgh), 154
Black Power movement, 154
Black theater (*see* African American
    theater)
Black Theater (journal), 355
Black Theater Alliance, 355
Blackface, 353, 357
Blackout, 128, 132, 391
Blacks, The (Genêt), 41
Blake, Eubie, 353
Blasted (Kane), 383
Blocking, 66, 303, 304, 196, 391
Blood Knot, The (Fugard), 382
Blood Wedding (García Lorca), 99,
    114, 337
Bloolips, 375

Blue Heart (Churchill), 383
Bock, Jerry, 360
Body mike, 136
Body Politic (Chicago), 366
Bogart, Anne, 52
Bogosian, Eric, 380
Book, 357, 391
Book musical, 357, 359, 360
Booth, Edwin, 311, 312
Booth Theater (New York), 312–313, 315
Border, 295, 303, 391
Border lights, 132, 133
Bosco, Philip, 102
Bosnian-Serb war, 342
Boston Marriage (Mamet), 366
Boulevard du Temple, 298
"Boulevard" theaters, 298
Bourgeois drama, 187–188, 297–298, 391
    (*See also* Domestic drama)
Bowie, David, 2, 125
Box, 80, 263, 270, 277, 278, 294, 391
Box office manager, 203, 204
Box set, 80, 303, 313, 391
Boys in the Band, The (Crowley), 377
Brace Up (Wooster group), 380
Bradbury, Peter, 292
Brady, Sue, 292
Brahm, Otto, 325
Brand (Ibsen, 1866), 147
Brantley, Ben, 32–33
Brecht, Bertolt, 4, 5, 63, 158, 162, 165,
    335, 336
Brenton, Howard, 383
Breton, André, 335
Bring in 'da Noise, Bring in 'da Funk
    (musical), 125, 355, 356, 361
British musicals, 360
Broadhurst Theater (New York), 80
Broadway theater, 24, 81, 147, 353, 354,
    355, 361, 363, 381
Broderick, Matthew, 55, 362
Brook, Peter, 103, 351
Brooklyn Academy of Music, 145
Brown, Arvin, 363
Brown, Blair, 102
Brown, John Mason, 28
Brown, Roscoe Lee, 41
Brown, William, 352
Bubbling Brown Sugar (musical), 355
Buddhism, 234, 240, 242
Budget, 73
Build, 98, 199, 391
Building, 112
Bullins, Ed, 355
Bunraku, 244–245, 391
Buried Child (Shepard), 365
Burlesque, 183, 305, 356–357, 391
Burstyn, Ellen, 179
Burtka, David, 346
Butterworth, Jez, 383
Bush, Anita, 353

Bush, George W., 370
Business, stage, 66, 391
Business manager, 204

Cable Guy (film), 183
Caesar and Cleopatra (Shaw, 1899), 115
Café LaMama, 363
Calderón de la Barca, Pedro, 274, 277, 285
Cambridge, Godfrey, 41
Camino Real (Williams), 63
Campbell, Douglas, 218
Camus, Albert, 331, 348
Candles, lighting, 124, 271, 295, 303
Carmen (production by Peter Brook), 351
Carousel (musical), 359
Carrey, Jim (1962–), 183
Casting, 64, 194, 391
Cat on a Hot Tin Roof (Williams), 157, 344
Catharsis, 391
Cats (musical), 360
Catwalk, 391
Caucasian Chalk Circle, The (Brecht), 336
Cavea, 230
Cazuela, 278, 391
CD player, 6, 20
Cenci, The (Shelley), 126
Censorship, 23, 321, 325, 365
Center stage, 106, 391
Center Stage (Baltimore), 40
Centering, 45
Centola (New York), 378
Central image, 102, 103
Ceremonies in Dark Old Men (Elder), 354
Chain (Cleage), 375
Champion, Gower, 113, 360
Chang, Tisa, 371
Changling, The (Middleton and Rowley), 273
Chanter, 244, 245
Chaplin, Charlie, 362
Characteristics of art, 7–9
Characteristics of performing arts, 9–10
Characters *(see* Dramatic characters)
Chariot racing, 222, 227
Charles I, 273, 274, 288
Charles II, 288
Chausow, Lynn, 287
Chavez, César, 372
Chekhov, Anton, 7, 17, 29, 39, 46, 47, 48, 49, 161, 189, 318, 324, 326, 327, 329, 338, 344
Cherry Orchard, The (Chekhov), 48, 49, 324, 351
Chestnut Street Theater (Philadelphia), 313
Chevallier, Martine, 280
Chicano theater *(see* Hispanic theatre)
Chikamatsu Monzaemon (1653–1724), 144, 245
Children's Hour, The (Hellman), 377
Childress, Alice, 354

Chinese theater, 23, 118, 234, 237–240, 253
acting, 52, 237, 238, 240
early development of, 237
Ming dynasty, 238–239
Peking (Beijing) opera, 239–340, 390
Song dynasty, 237
Tang dynasty, 237, 240
theater space, 87, 94, 238, 240
Yuan dynasty, 237–238
Chong, Ping, 372, 380
Choral ode, 216, 217, 218
Choregus, 213, 391
Choreographer, 9, 67, 68, 69, 73, 359, 360
Choreography, 3
Chorus, 168, 224, 260, 357, 358, 391
Chorus in Greek Theater, 60, 168, 211, 214, 216, 218, 220, 391
Chorus Line, A (musical), 99, 360
Christianity, rise of, 230, 246
Christmas Carol, A, 125
Church, William, 323
Churchill, Caryl, 377, 383
Cicero, 44
Cid, The (Corneille), 185, 280
Circle of attention, 48
Circle theater *(see* Arena stage)
Circus, 89, 305, 307, 310, 332, 333, 351
Circus Maximus, 224, 227
Cirque du Soleil, 3, 4, 310
City Dionysia festival, 213, 219, 391
Civil rights, 342, 372
Classic Stage Company (New York), 325, 369
Claudel, Paul, 331
Clay, Caroline Stefanie, 44
Cleage, Pearl, 375
Cleansed (Kane), 383
Climactic plot structure, 156–158, 161, 169, 216–218, 283, 309, 391
Climax, 391
Clinton, Bill, 370
Close, Glenn, 55
Closer (Marber), 383
Cloud Nine (Churchill), 383
Clouds, The (Aristophanes, 423 B.C.), 182
Clurman, Harold, 63–64, 329
Cockettes (San Francisco), 378
Cockfighting, 272
Cockpit, The, 272
Cohan, George M., 357
Cold war, 342
Cole, Bob, 353
Coleridge, Samuel Taylor (1772–1834), 22
College theater *(see* University theater)
Colonial theater, 300
Colored Museum, The (Wolfe), 355
Colosseum, 224, 227
Columbus, Christopher, 176
Combination companies, 311
Comedia, 274, 276, 391

Comédie Française, 280, 283, 284, 299
Comédie Italienne, 299
Comedy, 147, 149, 174, 180–185, 191, 213, 219–220, 318, 391
Aristophanic, 182–183, 219–220
burlesque, 183, 305, 356–357, 391
comic premise, 182–183, 219, 391
commedia dell'arte, 4, 167, 256, 258–260, 280, 299, 333, 391
domestic, 185, 297
farce, 183, 250, 277, 393
forms of, 183–185
of humours, 289
of ideas, 185
of intrigue, 289
of manners, 185, 288–289, 298, 391
of menace, 190
natural laws, suspension of, 181–182, 183
satire, 149, 183, 219, 396
sentimental, 292, 298
slapstick, 181, 183, 260, 280, 379, 396
social order and individual, contrast between, 182
(*See also* Tragicomedy)
Comedy of Errors, The (Shakespeare), 266
Comic opera, 299
Commedia dell'arte, 4, 167, 256, 258–260, 280, 299, 333, 391
Commercial theater, 70, 71, 329, 361
Commonwealth, 288
Compañias de parte, 279, 391
Company (musical), 360
Complication, 154–155, 391
Composer, 9, 68, 357, 358, 359, 360
Composition, 128, 391
Computers, 4, 106, 386
Computer, design, 110, 132, 139, 140, 349
Concentration camp performances, 337
Concept musical, 360
Concert halls, 305
Conflict, 152, 391
Confraternity of the Passion, 283
Congreve, William (1670–1729), 60, 168, 185, 292
Constructivism, 333, 391
Contact (musical), 59
Contemporary theater *(see* Modern theater)
Contemporary Theatre, A (Seattle), 88
Continental seating, 313
Contrast, The (Tyler), 298
Cooper, Alice, 2
Cooper, Helmar Augustus, 44
Copenhagen (Frayn), 102
Corthron, Kia, 375
Corneille, Pierre, 185, 280, 285
Corral, 84, 277–278, 391
Corral de la Cruz, 277
Corral del Principe, 277

Costume, 2, 12–13, 14, 111–119, 210, 199, 220, 221, 240, 244, 245, 252, 260, 271, 295, 303, 312, 313
Costume design, 12–13, 14, 97, 111–119, 120, 198
   collaborators of designer, 119
   elements and related elements of, 115–119
   objectives of, 112–115
   responsibilities, 111–112
   websites on, 120
Costume designer, 65, 66–67, 68, 69, 73, 98, 112, 120, 198
   (*See also* Costume design)
Counterweight, 391
Country Wife, The (Wycherley), 288–289, 291, 292
Court entertainments, 237, 273–274, 284
Covent Garden (London), 294, 299, 314
Coward, Noël, 185
Crabtree, Howard, 118
Craft guilds, 252
Craig, Edward Gordon, 332, 338, 364
Crave (Kane), 383
Crawford, Cheryl, 329
Crazy for You (musical), 99
Created or found space, 78, 91–92, 94, 333, 393
Crew, 89, 392
Crimes of the Heart (Henley), 374
Cripple of Inishmaan (McDonagh), 383
Crises, 155
Crisis drama, 156
Criticism, 28–34, 35, 144
   audience and, 28
   criteria for, 30–34
   critic, 12, 28, 29, 30–34, 35, 144
   descriptive, 34, 392
   preparing for, 30
   prescriptive, 34, 260, 395
   reviewer, 28–30, 35
   websites on, 35
Cromwell, Oliver, 288
Cross, 392
Cross-dressing, 377
Cross-fade, 132
Crothers, Rachel, 377
Crowley, Mart, 377
Crucible, The (Miller, 1953), 152
Cryptogram, The (Mamet), 366
   Cuban American theater (*see* Hispanic theater)
Cue, 271, 392
Cue sheets, 392
Cumsty, Michael, 102
Cunningham, Merce, 52
Curtain, 392
Cutouts, 107, 303
Cycle plays, 248–250, 392
Cyclorama, 79, 392
Cymbeline (Shakespeare), 139
Cyrano de Bergerac (Rostand), 186

Dada, 334, 335, 378, 392
Dafoe, William, 381
Dance, 4, 9, 11, 14, 53, 62, 163, 210, 211, 220, 224, 234, 235, 237, 240, 244, 245, 273, 305, 330, 349, 356, 357, 359, 363, 378, 379, 387
Dance and the Railroad, The (Hwang), 371
Dance drama, 235
Dance rehearsal, 202
Daniels, Ron, 32
D'Aquila, Diane, 218
Dark ages, 246
Darwin, Charles (1809–1882), 60, 305, 318
Das Kapital (Marx), 305, 318
Davenant, William (1606–1668), 294
Davies, Howard, 32
Davison, Peter J., 102
Davy, Babs, 377
Day of Absence (Ward), 355
Days Before: Death, Destruction, and Detroit III, The (Wilson), 53
Dealer's Choice (Marber), 383
Death and the King's Horsemen (Soyinka), 383
Death of a Salesman (Miller), 103, 179, 166, 344, 345, 382
Death of the Last Black Man in the Whole Entire World, The (Parks), 375
Decker, Carmen, 167
Deconstruction, 380
Deer Hunter, The (film), 55
de Mille, Agnes, 359
Dench, Judi, 362
Denouement, 392
Denver Center Theatre, 119, 374
Departures from realism, 100, 101, 318, 320, 330–337, 338, 346–351, 366, 371, 380
Descriptive criticism, 34, 392
Design, elements of, 12–13, 14
Design concept, 101–103, 197
Designers, 65, 66–67, 68, 69, 73, 97, 98–120, 124–140, 194, 197–199
   (*See also* Costume design; Lighting design; Scene design; Sound design)
Desire Under the Elms (O'Neill), 329
Deus ex machina, 158, 280, 392
Dialogue, 392
Diary of Anne Frank, The, 29
Dibbell, Dominique, 377
Digital arts, 386
Dim out, 392
Dimmer, 128, 129, 392
Dimmer board, 313
Dinner theater, 4, 240
Dinner with Friends (Margulies), 100, 113
Dionysus, 211, 213

Director, 12, 13, 14, 31, 59, 60–70, 73, 109–110, 144, 194, 303–305, 312, 360, 364, 380, 383, 392
   auteur, 61–62
   as basic element of theater, 12, 13, 14
   casting by, 64
   collaborators of, 68–70
   designers and, 65, 66–67, 68, 69
   developments in directing, 303–305, 312
   elements of, 62–67
   emergence of, 60–61
   in rehearsals, 65–67
   technical rehearsals and, 67
   websites on, 74
Director-choreographer, 360
Directorial concept, 64, 73, 195
Disney, 361, 381, 382
Disneyworld, 3
Dithyramb, 392
Dithyrambic chorus, 211
Diversity, of audiences, 23–24, 25, 35, 370–371
Doctor Faustus (Marlowe), 44, 264, 351
Documentary drama, 346, 366
Dodson, Owen, 354
Dold, Mark H., 126
Doll's House, A (Ibsen), 166, 321, 322
Domestic comedy, 185
Domestic drama, 185, 187–188, 245, 297, 392
Dominant trait, 392
Dominus, 228, 392
Donmar Warehouse (London), 341
Don't Bother Me, I Can't Cope (musical), 355
Dorset Garden (London), 294
Double entendre, 392
Doubling, 271, 392
Downie, Penny, 331
Downlighting, 131, 392
Downstage, 105, 106, 392
Drama of catastrophe, 156
Drama Review (journal), 154
Dramatic action, 13, 14, 151–152
Dramatic characters, 13, 149, 150, 165–169
   dialogue of, 164
   dominant trait or humor, 167–168, 392
   extraordinary, 165
   juxtaposition of, 168–169
   minor, 168
   narrator or chorus, 168
   nonhuman, 168
   representative, 166, 396
   stock, 166–167, 187, 228, 258, 260, 289, 292, 397
   types, 165–168
Dramatic script (*see* Script)
Dramatic structure, 13, 62–64, 150–164, 169

climactic and episodic forms
  combined, 161
climactic and episodic forms
  compared, 156–161, 161
climactic plot construction, 156–158,
  161, 216–218, 283, 309, 391
creation of, 153–155
  crises and climaxes, 155
  obstacles and complications,
    154–155, 395
  opening scene, 153–154
episodic plot construction, 158–161,
  169, 250, 267, 276, 299, 336, 393
essentials of, 150–153
  action, 151–152
  balance of forces, 153
  conflict, 152, 391
  opposing forces, 152–153
  plot, 150–151, 158–159, 216–218,
    271, 349, 395
types of, 163–164
Dramatist (see Playwright)
Dramatist Guild, 148
Dramaturg, 70, 73, 194, 203, 392
Drame, 297, 392
Dream Play, A (Strindberg), 330, 331
Dress a set, 111
Dress rehearsal, 67, 110, 201, 202, 392
Dreyer, Carl, 362
Drop, 392
Drottningholm Theater (Stockholm), 300
Drury Lane Theater (London), 294, 299,
  304
Dublin Carol (McPherson), 383
duBois, Pene, 113
Duchess of Malfi, The (Webster), 273
Duet, 357
Dumb and Dumber (film), 183
Duse, Eleonora, 311, 312
Dutchman (Baraka), 354
Duttine, Joe, 248
DVD player, 1, 20, 386

East-West Players (Los Angeles), 371
Ebert, Joyce, 175
Eclectics, 334–336, 351
Edict of Nantes, 279
Edison, Thomas, 124, 314, 362
Editing, sound, 137
Edward II (Marlowe), 264
Egypt, ancient ceremonies in, 210
Eighteenth-century theater, 80, 288,
  292, 295–305, 315
  acting, 38, 303–304
  background, 295–297
  drama, 297–299
  director, 303–305
  living history:
    The Marriage of Figaro, 301
  neoclassicism, departure from, 297
  theater production, 299, 300–305

theater space, 300
time line, 296
websites on, 315
Einstein, Albert (1879–1955), 181, 318
Eisenhauer, Peggy, 125
Eisenstein, Sergei, 362
Ekkyklema, 220
El-Amin, Hassan, 355
El Teatro Campesino, 372, 373, 385
Elder, Lonne (1932–), 354
Electra (Euripides, 412 B.C.), 147
Electra (Sophocles, c. 410 B.C.), 129,
  147, 156, 185, 186
Electric light, 124–125
Elevator stage, 313
Eliot, T.S., 382
Elizabeth I, 264, 273
Elizabethan period, 264
Elizabethan theater (see English theater)
E-mail, 1
Emery, Lisa, 100
Emotional recall, 51, 392
Emperor Jones, The (O'Neill), 165, 335
Empty Space, The (Brook), 351
English theater, 23, 44, 60, 256,
  264–274, 276, 277, 278, 285,
  288–295, 315, 325
  acting, 38, 271, 292
  Elizabethan age, 264
  Elizabethan drama, 264–267
  Elizabethan playwrights, 264,
    266–267, 273
  Elizabethan theater production,
    267–271, 273
  English monarchy, return of, 288
  English Renaissance, end of, 273–274
  Jacobean theater, 273–274
  living history:
    Hamlet, 268
  popular entertainment, 272
  private theaters, 270–271
  public theaters, 267, 269–270
  Restoration drama, 288–292
  Restoration theater production, 292,
    294–295
  theater space, 84–86, 94, 267–271,
    294–295
  time line, 265, 290
  websites on, 285
Enlightenment, 176, 297
Ensemble acting, 47, 50, 392
Ensler, Eve, 55
Entrance, 392
Entrepreneur, theatrical, 292, 294
Environment (see Theater spaces)
Environmental sounds, 135, 196, 392
Environmental theater, 342, 349, 351,
  366, 378, 392
Epic theater, 336, 392
Epidaurus, theater at, 83
Epilogue, 393

Episode, 216, 217
Episodic plot structure, 158–161, 169,
  250, 267, 276, 299, 336, 393
Epstein, Alvin, 348
Equestrian performance, 222, 310
Esslin, Martin, 348
Ethnic theater, 352, 371
Euripides, 34, 147, 176, 177, 214,
  231, 280
Every Man in His Humour (Jonson,
  1616), 167
Every Man Out of His Humour (Jonson,
  1616), 167–168
Everybody Loves Raymond
  (television), 185
Everyman (morality play), 248
Evita (musical), 360
Ewing Manor, 193, 195
Ex Machina (Quebec), 380
Execution of Justice (Mann), 145
Existentialism, 348, 393
Exit, 393
Experimental theater, 25, 35, 40, 53–54,
  62, 163–164, 318, 327, 329,
  332–336, 342, 346–351,
  363–365, 370, 378, 383
Experimental theater groups,
  163–164, 363
Exposition, 157, 309, 393
Expressionism, 25, 334–335, 393

Fade, 132, 393
Falls, Robert, 361, 382
Famous Door Theater (Chicago), 195
Farce, 183, 250, 277, 393
Farr, Michele, 279
Father, The (Strindberg), 321, 323
Faust (Goethe), 102, 308
Fearon, Ray, 178
Federal Theater Project, 329, 354, 373
Fefu and Her Friends (Fornes), 374,
  375, 376
Feingold, Michael, 32, 33, 386
Feminist theater, 23, 25, 35, 150, 364,
  370, 371, 374–377, 385, 387
Fences (Wilson), 26, 41, 154, 354
Fencing consultant, 68
Festivals, 213, 214, 222, 228
Fichlander, Zelda, 68
Fiddler on the Roof (musical), 360
Fierstein, Harvey (1954–), 378
Fight choreography, 202
Fight consultant, 68, 194
Film, 1, 2, 3, 4, 5, 6, 7, 10, 11, 20, 55,
  61, 63, 109, 147, 148, 181, 219,
  221, 222, 276, 308, 324, 330, 349,
  362, 365, 384, 385, 386, 387
Film and Theater, 362
Finley, Karen, 379
Fiorello!, 145
Fire, 124

Firth, Colin, 362
Fischer, Linda, 117
Fisher, Jules, 125
Five Lesbian Brothers, 377
Flanagan Davis, Hallie, 329
Flats, 107, 125, 303, 313, 393
Fleshler, Glenn, 365
Fletcher, John, 273
Flies, The (Sartre), 348
Flockhart, Calista, 55
Floodlights, 132, 133, 393
Fly loft, 80
Fly space, 80, 107, 313, 393
Flyin' West (Cleage), 375
FOB (Hwang), 371
Focus, lighting, 127, 134, 201, 393
Folk drama, 235
Follies (musical), 360
Follow spot, 131, 134, 393
Fool for Love (Shepard), 365
Footfalls (Beckett), 384
Footlights, 129, 295, 393
Force Continuum (Corthron), 375
Foreman, Richard, 62, 63, 164, 364
Forestage, 393
Fornes, Maria Irene, 373, 374, 375, 376
Forrest, Edwin, 307
Fort, Paul, 331
Fortune Theater (London), 84–85, 270
Forty-Five Minutes from Broadway
    (musical), 357
42nd Street (musical), 99, 360
Fosse, Bob, 113, 125, 359, 360
Fotopoulos, Dionysis, 119
Found space *(see* Created or found space)
Fourth wall, 79, 393
    (See also Proscenium stage)
Franco, Francisco, 320, 337
Frayn, Michael, 102, 183
Freedman, Gerald, 213
Freeze, 393
Freie Bühne, 325
French revolution, 297, 299
French theater, 44, 80–81, 177, 256,
    279–284, 285, 288, 298, 299,
    315, 325, 331
    acting, 284
    background, 279
    living history: *Tartuffe*, 282
    neoclassical dramatists, 280, 283
    neoclassical era, 280
    theater production, 283–284
    theater space, 80–81, 283–284
    time line, 281
    websites on, 285
Fresnel, 131, 133, 393
Freud, Sigmund (1856–1939), 60, 318
Friends (television), 185
Fringe theater, 365, 383
Frogs, The (Aristophanes, 405 B.C.), 168
Front of the house, 73, 393

Fugard, Athol, 382
Fuller, Charles (1939–), 355
Fuller, Elizabeth, 107
*Funny Thing Happened on the Way to
    the Forum, A* (musical), 226
Futurism, 334, 335, 393
F/X (Tune), 4

Galileo, 256
Gallardo, Edward, 373
Gallery, 263, 270, 277, 278, 283, 284,
    294, 393
Gao Ming (ca. 1301–1370), 239
García Lorca, Federico, 99, 337
Garrick, David, 303, 304, 311, 315
Gas table, 313
Gaslight, 124, 313
Gass, Kristen, 173
Gay, John, 298
Gay and lesbian theater, 23, 25, 35, 364,
    370, 371, 385, 387
Gay rights movement, 377
Geidt, Jeremy, 348
Geiogamah, Hanay, 374
Gel, 129, 393
Gelbert, Larry, 226
Gems, Pam, 377
Gender, 374, 375, 377, 385
General manager, 194, 204
General mike, 136
Genêt, Jean, 41, 348
Genovèse, Eric, 280
Genre, 173, 174, 190, 297–299, 393
    (*See also* Comedy; Tragedy)
George, Libby, 267
Germany, 298–299, 312, 320, 325, 337,
    342, 346, 352
Gershwin, George, 357, 359
Gesamtkunstwerk, 312, 393
Getting Out (Norman), 39
Ghost Sonata, The (Strindberg), 330
Ghosts (Ibsen), 40, 157, 321
"Gibson girl," 119
Gilbert, W. S., 357
Gillett, Arden, 183
Gilpin, Charles, 353
Gilpin, Jack, 175
Giron, Arthur, 373
Gish, Lillian, 362
Given circumstances, 48
Gladitorial combats, 224, 227
Glass Menagerie, The (Williams), 39,
    55, 168, 344
Glengarry Glen Ross (Mamet), 366
Globe Theater (London), 18, 21, 84–85,
    267, 269
Glover, Savion, 356
Gobo, 132, 393
Goethe, Johann Wolfgang von, 102, 158,
    299, 304–305, 308, 311, 315
Goetz, Augustus, 309

Goetz, Ruth, 309
Goetz von Berlichingen (Goethe), 299
Goldberg, Whoopi, 226
Golden Boy (Odets), 329
Golden Child (Hwang), 371
Goldoni, Carlo, 287, 299
Goldsmith, Oliver, 185, 298
Goldstein, Jess, 100, 113
Gone with the Wind (film), 119
Good Natur'd Man, The (Goldsmith), 298
Good Person of New Haven, 67
Good Person of Setzuan, The (Brecht),
    4–5, 336
Goodman Theater (Chicago), 373
Gordone, Charles (1925–), 354
Gossett, Louis, 41
Gotanda, Philip Kan, 371
Gozzi, Carlo, 11, 287, 299, 382
Grammy awards, 90
Grand Canyon, 20
Grand Hotel (musical), 360
Gray, Spalding, 379
Great Lakes Theater, 151, 213
Great White Hope, The, 41, 99
Greek National Theatre, 209
Greek theater 4, 7, 13, 23, 43–44, 60,
    77, 149, 176, 177, 210,
    211–221, 226, 231
    acting, 38, 220, 221
    chorus, 60, 168, 211, 214, 216, 218,
        220, 391
    comedy, 213, 219–220
    criticism, 34, 220–221
    culture and, 211–214
    golden age, 176, 211
    hellenistic, 220, 221, 227, 231
    living history: *Antigone*, 215
    and myth, 214
    origin, 211
    popular entertainments, 227
    and religion, 211, 213
    theater production, 220
    theater space, 77, 79, 82, 83, 94,
        219, 220
    time line, 212
    tragedy, 214–219
        dramatists, 214–216
        structure, 216–218
    websites on, 231
    (*See also* Aeschylus; Euripides; Sophocles)
Green Bird, The (Gozzi), 11, 100, 382
Greenshow, 204
Greenwich Mews Theater, 354
Greenwood, Jane, 112
Grein, Jacob Thomas, 325
Grid, 393
Griffith, D. W., 362
Groove system, 263, 295, 313, 393
Grotowski, Jerzy, 52, 91, 351, 378
Ground plan, 104–105, 197, 393
Ground row, 303

Groundlings, 270
Group Theater, 327, 329
Grusin, Richard, 287
Guare, John, 148, 363
Gurney, A. R., 148
Gussow, Mel, 29
Guthrie Theater (see Tyrone Guthrie Theater)
Guys and Dolls (musical), 360

Haberle, Sean, 325
Hagen, Uta, 52, 57
Hair (musical), 99, 360
Hairstyles, 118–119, 120
Hairy Ape (O'Neill), 380, 381
Hall, Peter, 119
"Hall of Machines," 80–81, 284
Hamartia, 393
Hamilton, Lisa Gay, 382
Hamlet (Shakespeare), 1, 39, 60, 114, 131,
    153, 154, 155, 160, 161, 177,
    188, 228, 266, 268, 311, 362
Hammer, Mak, 365
Hammerstein, Oscar, II, 358, 359
Hanamichi, 246, 393
Hand props, 393
Hansberry, Lorraine, 188, 352, 354, 355
Happenings, 349, 366, 378, 394
Happy Days (Beckett), 53–54
Hard Day's Night, A (film), 2
Hard flat, 107
Hare, David, 383
"Harlequinade" (Balanchine), 9
Harnick, Sheldon, 360
Harris, Rebecca, 346
Hart, Lorenz, 357
Hartford Stage Company (Connecticut),
    62, 63, 159, 274, 363
Hashigakari, 242, 394
Hathaway, Anne, 266
Having Our Say (Mann), 145
Headley, Heather, 361
Healey, Peg, 377
Hedda Gabler (Ibsen), 65, 169, 317,
    321, 324
Heidi Chronicles, The (Wasserstein), 374
Heiress, The (Goetz), 309
Hellenistic Age, 220, 221, 227, 231
Hellman, Lillian, 329, 338, 377
Hello, Dolly! (musical), 99, 360
Help (film), 2
Henley, Beth, 374
Henry IV, 279
Henry IV, Part 1 (Shakespeare), 188, 266
Henry IV, Part 2 (Shakespeare), 266
Henry V (Shakespeare), 266
Hepburn, Katherine (1909–), 28
Herbert, Victor, 357
Hernani (Hugo), 308
Herodotus, 211
Heroic drama, 185–187, 394
Heroic tragedy, 186, 188

Hewlett, James, 352
Heyward, DuBose, 359
Hicks, Greg, 119
Hill, Abram, 354
Hingston, Sean Martin, 59
Hippocrates, 211
Hirelings, 271, 394
Hispanic theater, 25, 35, 147, 364,
    372–373, 385, 387
Historical accuracy in design, 303,
    311, 313
Historification, 337
Hitchcock, Alfred, 55
Hitler, Adolf, 320, 336, 337
Hoch, Danny, 380
Hoffman, Philip Seymour, 64
Hoffman, William M., 378
Holbrook, Hal, 165
Holder, Donald, 123, 130
Hollander, Tom, 37
Homer, 28, 214
Horace, 34, 228
Hot Peaches (New York), 378
Hôtel de Bourgogne (Paris), 283, 284
House, 79
House Arrest: First Edition (Smith), 379
House manager, 204
House of Bernarda Alba, The (García
    Lorca), 100–101, 337
Howard University, 354
Howe, Tina, 46
Hrosvitha of Gandersheim
    (ca. 935–973), 246
Hubris, 394
Hudson Valley Shakespeare Festival, 255
Hughes, Langston, 354
Hugo, Victor, 308
Humanism, 256
Humor (see Comedy)
Huntington Theatre Company (Boston),
    51, 139, 355
Huntley, Paul, 117
Hwang, David Henry, 371
Hyman, Earle, 346

Iambic pentameter, 264
Ibsen, Henrik, 7, 46, 144, 146, 147, 157,
    158, 166, 188, 317, 318, 321,
    322, 323, 324, 329, 330, 338, 344
Ice T, 3
Iceman Cometh, The (O'Neill), 29,
    32–33, 329
Iliad (Homer), 214
Illinois Shakespeare Festival, 193–204, 298
Illinois State University, 193, 201
Imaginary Invalid, The (Molière), 168,
    280
Imitation, 38
Impromptu of Versailles, The (Molière), 60
Improvisation, 164, 167, 256, 258–260,
    351, 363

In Dahomey (musical), 353
In the Jungle of the Cities (Brecht), 117
Incandescent lamp, 124, 314
Independent Theater (London), 325, 327
Independent theaters, 325, 327, 331–332
Indian theater, 234–237, 253
    acting, 52, 235
    dramatic criticism, 235
    later drama, 235, 237
    Sanskrit drama, 234–235, 237
    theater space, 235, 237
Industrial revolution, 176, 187, 297, 305
Ingalls, James, 17
Inner City Theatre (Los Angeles), 154
Inner stage, 270, 394
Inquisition, 274
Intar, 385
Integration, 54, 56
International Center for Theater
    Research (Paris), 351
International trends, 382–384
Internet technology, 386
Interpretation of Dreams (Freud), 318
Into the Woods (musical), 360
Investigation, The (Weiss), 346
Ionesco, Eugène, 168, 190, 348, 366
Iphigenia in Aulis (Euripides), 300, 333
Iris, 132, 394
Irony, 183, 394
Irwin, Bill, 369, 379
Israeli-Arab conflicts, 342
Italian Renaissance theater, 4, 80, 176,
    256–260, 279, 283, 284, 285,
    288, 300, 302–303
    acting, 258–260
    background, 256
    commedia dell'arte, 256, 258–260
    living history:
        commedia dell'arte, 259
        neoclassic ideals, 260
    theater production, 260–264
    theater space, 78, 94, 260–263
    time line, 257
    websites on, 285

Jacobean theater, 273–274
Jacobi, Derek, 189
Jacobs, Sally, 103
James, Henry, 309
James I, 273, 274
Japanese theater, 234, 240–246, 253
    acting, 52, 244, 245
    background, 240
    bunraku, 244–245, 392
    kabuki, 118, 245–246, 394
    living history: Sotoba Komachi, 241
    nô, 87, 233, 240–244, 245, 395
    theater space, 87, 94, 242, 244, 246
Jarry, Alfred, 332
Jean Cocteau Repertory Theater, 107,
    126, 160, 336

Jelly's Last Jam (musical), 355
Jesus Christ Superstar (musical), 360
jingju, 240
(*see also* Peking opera)
Jitney (Wilson), 51, 154
Joan of Arc, 165
Joe Turner's Come and Gone (Wilson), 44, 154, 354
John, Elton, 361, 381, 382
Johnson, William, 353
Jones, Cherry, 46
Jones, Christine, 100
Jones, Felicity, 114
Jones, Inigo, 274
Jones, James Earl, 41
Jonson, Ben, 165, 167–168, 273, 289
Jory, Jon, 363
Juan Darien, 382
Judas Kiss, The, 37
Julia (film), 55
Julius Caesar (Shakespeare), 114, 158, 159, 266, 332
Julliard School (New York), 52
Juno and the Paycock (O'Casey), 329, 330

Kabuki, 118, 245–246, 394
Kaiser, Georg, 335
Kalidasa, 234
Kan'ami, 240, 242, 243
Kane, Sarah, 383
Kantor, Tadeusz, 383
Kathakali, 235, 237, 394
Katz, Natasha, 130
Kazan, Elia, 63
Keaton, Buster, 362
Keil, Robert, 145
Kelly, David Patrick, 62
Kern, Jerome, 357, 358
Kerr, Walter (1919–), 21
Kesselring, Joseph, 174
Kessler, Karen, 194–195
Khan, Genghis, 237
Khan, Kublai, 237
Kick Theater Company (London), 383
Kierkegaard, Seren, 189
Kill, 394
Killigrew, Thomas, 294
Kilner, Kevin, 100
King, the Greatest Alcalde, The (Calderón), 276
King and I, The (musical), 359, 372
King John, 194
King Lear (Shakespeare), 29, 153, 158–159, 165, 177, 266
King Oedipus (Sophocles), 154, 156–157, 165, 209, 216–218, 332
King Shotaway, 352
King Stag, The (Gozzi), 287
Kinney, Terry, 152
Kinter, Richard, 279
Kiss, 2

Kiss Me, Kate (musical), 99, 359, 360
Kitano temple, 242
Kitchen (New York), 380
Klotz, Florence, 113
Knight, Laura, 323
Kopit, Arthur (1937–), 182
Kordian (Grotowski), 351
Korean war, 342
Kramer, Larry, 378
Kramer vs. Kramer (film), 55
Kron, Lisa, 377
Kuba initiation rites, 210
Kushner, Tony, 370, 378

La Bohème (opera), 361
La Jolla Playhouse (California), 363
La MaMa (New York), 372
Labor theater, 364
Lafayette Players, 353
Lake, The, 28
Lamos, Mark, 363
Landau, Tina, 108
Larsen, Johnathan, 361
Las Vegas, 3, 4, 90
Late Henry Moss, The (Shepard), 366
Laughing comedy, 298
Laughter, 180
Laurents, Arthur, 360
Lazzi, 258, 394
LeCompte, Elizabeth, 380
Lee, Derrick, 44
Lee, Shin Young, 372
Left stage, 105, 394
Leguizamo, John, 380
Lepage, Robert, 380
Lerner, Alan Jay, 359, 360
Les Misérables (musical), 81, 360
Lessing, Gotthold Ephraim, 298–299
Lesson From Aloes, A (Fugard), 382
Letter to Queen Victoria, A (Wilson), 54
Liar, Liar (film), 183
Libation Bearers, The (Aeschylus, 458 B.C.), 147
Libretto, 258, 357, 358
Licensing Act of 1737, 294, 299
Lie of the Mind, A (Shepard), 365–366
Life Is a Dream (Calderón), 128, 274, 277
Light plot, 134, 200, 202, 394
Lighting cues, 132
Lighting design, 12–13, 14, 123, 124–134, 138–139, 140, 313–314, 200
   collaborators of designer, 134
   history of, 124–125
   instruments, 125, 131–133
   objectives of, 125–128
   qualities of, 128–131
   resources, 131–133
Lighting designer, 65, 66–67, 68, 69, 73, 124, 125, 128, 134, 140, 199, 202
Lillo, George (1691–1739), 188

Lincoln, Abraham, 13, 44, 151
Lincoln Center Theater (New York), 309, 332
Lincoln's Inn Fields (London), 294
Lion King, The (musical), 130, 287, 361, 381–282
Literary arts, 8, 14
Little Johnny Jones (musical), 357
Little Richard, 2
"Little theater" movement, 327, 329
Liturgical drama, 248, 394
Live performance, 1–7, 14, 351, 385
Living newspapers, 394
Living Theater, 163, 363
Loesser, Frank, 360
Loewe, Frederick, 359, 360
London Merchant, The (Lillo), 188
Lonesome West, The (McDonagh), 383
Long, William Ivey, 116
Long Day's Journey into Night (O'Neill), 153, 179, 329
Long run, 311, 394
Long Wharf Theater (New Haven), 67, 86, 117, 175, 317, 363
Look Back in Anger (Osborne), 346
Looking Glass Theater (New York), 377
Lorca, Federico García (*see* García Lorca)
Lord Chamberlain, 294, 299
Lord Chamberlain's Men, 266
Lord's rooms, 270
Los Angeles Convention Center, 386
Lost Colony, The, 116
Louis XIV, 279, 284
Love! Valour! Compassion! (McNally), 113, 378
L.S.D. (Wooster group), 380
Luan, 107
Ludi Romani, 222, 394
Ludlam, Charles, 370, 378
Lugné-Poë, Aurélien-Marie, 331–332
Lumiére, Auguste, 362
Lumiére, Louis, 362
Lute Song (Gao Ming), 239
Lyric, 357, 358
Lyricist, 68, 357, 358, 360
Lysistrata (Aristophanes, 411 B.C.), 182, 219
Lyubimov, Yuri, 383

M. Butterfly (Hwang), 371, 372
Ma Rainey's Black Bottom (Wilson), 154, 354
Mabou Mines, 54, 363
Macbeth (Shakespeare), 48, 64, 101, 124, 151, 152, 160, 165, 177, 188, 266, 321, 329, 332
MacDonald, Antony, 17
Machines, 284
Macklin, Charles, 303
Macready, William Charles, 307, 308
Mad Forest (Churchill), 383

Madeira, Marcia, 139
Madison Square Garden (New York), 90
Madonna, 1–2
Madrigal, 204
Maeterlinck, Maurice, 331
"Magic if," 50, 394
Magnetic amplifiers, 125
Makeup, 2, 117–118, 235, 240, 245
  (See also Costume; Costume design)
Malkovich, John, 364
Mamet, David, 148, 365, 366
Man Who, The (Brook), 351
Manager (see Producer)
Managing director, 71, 194
Manhattan Theater Club (New York), 363
Mann, Emily (1952–), 145
Man's World, A (Crothers), 377
Mansions, 250, 252, 394
Manson, Marilyn, 2–3
Marat/Sade (Weiss), 351
Marber, Patrick, 383
Margulies, Donald, 100
Margulies, Julianna, 375
Marie Antoinette, 107
Marionettes (see Puppets)
Mark Taper Forum (Los Angeles), 86, 93
Marketing, 204
Marley, Donovan, 374
Marlowe, Christopher (1464–1593), 44,
  264, 266
Marriage of Figaro, The
  (Beaumarchais), 301
Martial arts, 52–53
Martín, Manuel, 373
Martin, Steve, 181
Marvel, Elizabeth, 325
Marx, Karl (1818–1883), 60, 305, 318
Marx Brothers, 183
Masking, 295, 303, 394
Masks, 119, 120, 174, 210, 220, 221,
  228, 244, 260, 382, 394
Masque, 273–274, 394
Master Builder, The (Ibsen), 330
Master Harold . . . and the Boys (Fugard),
  382
Mastro, Michael, 135
May, Corinna, 42
Mayer, Stefan, 102
Mazzie, Marin, 359
McAnuff, Des, 363
McCabe, Richard, 178
McCarter Theatre Center (New Jersey),
  129, 145, 156
McCauley, Robbie, 379
McDermot, Galt, 360
McDonagh, Martin, 383
McKenna, Seana, 48
McNally, Terrence, 148, 378
McPherson, Conor, 383
McTeer, Janet, 166
Measure for Measure (Shakespeare), 41,
  189, 255

Mechane, 220
Medea, (Euripides), 138, 165, 176, 384
Media, 1, 2, 349, 362, 384, 386
Medieval theater, 23, 88, 149, 168, 188,
  246–252, 253, 274
  acting, 252
  background, 246
  cycle plays, 248–250
  farce, 250
  liturgical drama, 248, 394
  living history: Noah's Ark, 249
  miracle plays, 248, 394
  morality plays, 248, 394
  mystery plays, 248–250, 394
  religious drama, decline of, 252
  secular theater, 250
  theater space, 84, 91, 248, 250–252
  time line, 247
  websites on, 253
Meiningen players, 312
Meisner, Sanford, 51–52, 57
Melodrama, 1, 149, 185, 187, 216, 276,
  297, 298, 308, 310, 318, 321,
  324, 356, 357, 384, 394
Menaechmi, The (Plautus), 225, 226
Merchant of Venice, The
  (Shakespeare), 124
Mercury Theater (New York), 354
Merry Wives of Windsor, The
  (Shakespeare), 5, 267, 272
Metaphor, 102, 103
Metcalf, Laurie, 364
Meyerhold, Vsevolod, 62, 332–333,
  338, 349, 351
Michelangelo, 8, 256
Michels, Stephanie, 59
Michigan Public Theater, 167
Microphones, 13, 134, 136–137, 380
Middle Ages (see Medieval theater)
Middleton, Thomas, 273
Midsummer Night's Dream, A
  (Shakespeare), 55, 103, 266, 351
Mielziner, Jo (1901–1976), 103
Mikado, The (Gilbert and Sullivan), 357
Miller, Arthur, 7, 42, 143, 188, 344,
  345, 366
Milwaukee Repertory Theatre, 44
Mime (see Pantomime)
Minor characters, 168, 394
Minstrel show, 305, 310, 353, 357
Minstrelsy, 310, 394
Miracle plays, 248, 394
Mirren, Helen, 341
Misanthrope, The (Molière), 168, 280
Mise-en-scène, 394
Miser, The (Molière), 167, 280
Miss Julie (Strindberg), 152, 165, 321,
  323, 324
Miss Saigon (musical), 81, 109,
  360, 372
Mixing, sound, 137
Mnouchkine, Ariane, 383

Modern theater, 318–338, 342–366,
  370–387
  African American theater, 25, 35,
    147, 329, 352–355, 364, 366,
    375, 380, 385, 387
  alternative theater, 329, 352,
    361–366, 370, 383–384
  background, 318–320
  contemporary trends, 370–382
  departures from realism, 318, 320,
    330–337, 338, 371
    after 1915, 334–336, 338
    1945–1980, 346–351, 366
  diversity and eclecticism of, 370–378,
    387
  experimental theater, 25, 35, 40, 54,
    62, 163–164, 318, 327, 329,
    332–336, 342, 346–351,
    363–365, 370, 378, 383
  feminist theater, 23, 25, 35, 150, 364,
    370, 371, 374–377, 385, 387
  future of, 384–387
  international trends, 382–384
  living history:
    A Doll's House, 322
    The Sea Gull, 326
    Waiting for Godot, 347
  musical theater, 53, 68, 137, 352,
    356–361, 366, 371, 394
  naturalism, 324
  performance art, 144, 349, 369, 370,
    378–380, 395
  postwar realistic theater, 342–346, 366
  postmodernism, 318, 370, 380–382
  producers of realism, 325, 327
  realism, 318–329, 337, 338,
    342–346, 366
    playwrights, 321–324
    playwrights between wars, 329
  realism after 1915, 327–329,
    338, 371
  selective realism, 344–346
  time line, 319, 328, 343
  totalitarianism and, 320, 337
  tragicomedy, 324
  websites on, 338, 367, 387–388
Mojo (Butterworth), 383
Molière (Jean-Baptiste Poquelin;
  1622–1673), 4, 7, 40, 52, 60,
  62, 149, 167, 168, 173, 177,
  180, 182, 183, 279, 280, 282,
  283, 285, 288, 315
Moon for the Misbegotten, A
  (O'Neill), 329
Morality plays, 248, 394
Morrison, James, 365
Moscow Art Theater, 47, 324, 327, 332
Most Happy Fella, The, 29, 113
Mother Courage and Her Children
  (Brecht), 162, 165, 336
Motivated sounds, 135, 394
Mount Everest, 20

Movie flat (*see* Hard flat)
Moving light (*see* Automated light)
Muhammad, Elijah, 145
Mulatto (Hughes), 354
Multiculturalism, 25
Multifocus theater, 92–93, 94, 394
Multimedia, 3, 333, 336, 349, 394
Multimedia theater, 25, 62, 93, 349, 366, 380, 387
Multiple setting, 394
Multipoint perspective, 302
Murasaki, Lady, 242
Museum of Contemporary Art (Chicago), 380
Music, 1, 4, 8–9, 11, 14, 187, 210, 224, 234, 235, 237, 240, 245, 273, 297, 298, 309, 330
Music hall, 310, 332
Music Man, The (musical), 81
Music of the Heart (film), 55
Musical, 356–357
Musical director, 68, 69
Musical revue, 163
Musical theater, 53, 68, 137, 352, 356–361, 366, 371, 394
Musicians' gallery, 270
Mussolini, Benito, 320
My Fair Lady (musical), 29, 360
Mystere (Cirque du Soleil), 4
Mystery (cycle) plays, 248–250, 394
Myth, 153, 210, 214, 234, 235

N' Sync, 2, 3
Naked Gun (film), 183
Napoleon, 297
Narrator, 168, 337
National Endowment for the Arts, 379
National Theatre (London), 383
Nationalism, 288, 305
Native American theater, 25, 35, 210, 374
Native American Theatre Ensemble (New York), 374
Native Son (Wright), 354
Naturalism, 324, 395
    (*See also* Realistic theater)
Natyasastra, 235
Naughton, Greg, 40
Naughty Marietta (Herbert), 357
Neeson, Liam, 37, 362
Negro Ensemble Company, 355
Neighborhood Playhouse, 329
Neilsen, Kristine, 100
Neilson, Leslie, 183
Nemirovich-Danchenko, Vladimir, 327
Neoclassical ideals, 260, 298, 395
Neoclassicism, 157, 280, 283, 285, 297, 308
New Amsterdam Theatre (New York), 381
"New Art of Writing Plays, The" (Vega), 276

New Comedy, 219, 220, 222, 224, 231, 395
New Jersey Shakespeare Festival, 292
New Lafayette Theater, 355
New York, New York (Hotel), 4
New York City Ballet, 9, 125
New York City Opera, 113
New York Shakespeare Festival, 24, 29, 41, 63, 113
New York Times, 29, 32
Newsweek, 29
Neyolova, Marina, 324
Night of the Iguana, The (Williams), 344
'night, Mother (Norman), 156, 374
Nine (musical), 360
Nineteenth-century theater, 23, 157, 288, 305–314, 315, 318, 352–353
    acting, 38, 311
    background, 305
    dramatic forms, 308–310
    nineteenth–century life, 305–308
    theater production, 311–314
    theater space, 312–314
    time line, 306
    websites on, 315
Nô, 87, 233, 240–244, 245, 395
No Exit (Sartre), 157, 348
No Place to Be Somebody (Gordone), 354–355
Noah's Ark (cycle play), 249
Noble Prize, 383
Noises Off! (Frayn), 183
Noncommercial (not-for-profit) theaters, 71–73, 361–366
Nonrealism (*see* Departures from realism)
Nonverbal theater, 164
Normal Heart, The (Kramer), 378
Norman, Marsha, 39, 148, 156, 363, 374
North Atlantic Treaty Organization (NATO), 342
Nuyorican Poets' Café, 373
Nuyorican theater (*see* Hispanic theater)
Nyberg, Pamela, 151
NYU/Tisch School of the Arts, 52

"O" (Cirque du Soleil), 3, 4
Objective, 395
Obligatory scene, 309
Obstacle, plot, 154–155, 395
O'Casey, Sean, 329, 330, 338
O'Connor, Joyce Lynn, 375
Odets, Clifford, 327, 329
Odyssey (Homer), 214
Oedipus Rex (*see* King Oedipus)
Oedipus Rex (Stravinsky), 382
Off-Broadway theater, 329, 354, 361, 363, 364, 365, 366
Off-Loop theater, 364
Off-off-Broadway theater, 329, 361, 363–364, 365, 366, 379

Offstage, 89, 106, 395
Ogata, Issei,380
Oh, Dad, Poor Dad, Mama's Hung You in the Closet and I'm Feelin' So Sad (Kopit), 182
Oil lamps, 124, 303
Oklahoma! (musical), 359
Okuni, 245
Old Comedy, 219–220, 231, 395
Old Globe Theater (San Diego), 4, 165
Old Globe Theatre (London), 97, 155
Old Neighborhood, The (Mamet), 366
Oleanna (Mamet), 366
Omaha Magic Theater, 375
On Directing, 64
110 in the Shade, 99
Ontological–Hysteric Theatre Company (New York), 63
O'Neill, Eugene, 7, 32, 153, 165, 179, 329, 335, 338
Onstage, 395
Open, 395
Open Theater, 363
Opening scene, importance of, 153–154
Opera, 4, 9, 14, 44, 256, 258, 263
Opéra (Paris), 299
Operetta, 357, 358
Opposing forces, plot and, 152–153
Orange, theater at, 229
Orchestra, 79, 82, 83, 219, 220, 228, 229, 230, 261, 312, 395
Oresteia (Aeschylus), 214, 348
Origin of Species, The (Darwin), 305, 318
Orpheus Descending (Williams), 341
Ortiz, John, 274
Osborne, John, 346
Othello (Shakespeare), 1, 41, 168, 178, 266, 352, 353, 354
Other People's Money, 113
Otway, Thomas, 304
Our Town (Wilder, 1938), 168, 380
Out of Africa (film), 55

Pace of play, 66, 395
Pageant wagon, 250, 251
Palais-Cardinal, 283
Palais-Royal, 283
Pan, 132
Pan Asian Repertory Theatre, 371, 385
Pantomime, 40, 52, 53, 224, 227, 228, 234, 237, 244, 310, 379, 394, 395
Papp, Joseph, 41, 355, 373
Parabasis, 220, 395
Parados, 219, 220, 395
Parallel plot (*see* Subplot)
Parasite, 226
Paraskenion, 220
Parker, Dorothy, 28
Parker, Sarah Jessica, 55
Parks, Suzan–Lori, 375

Parterre, 283
Parthenon, 176, 211
Passion (musical), 360
Passion, The (mystery play), 248
Patel, Neil, 100
Patio, 278, 395
Patterson, Louis, 354
Payton-Wright, Pamela, 40, 117
Peakes, John, 167
Pear Garden, 237
Pearls for Pigs (Foreman), 62
Peer Gynt (Ibsen, 1867), 146, 147
Peking opera, 239–240, 390
Peña, Mario, 373
People's Republic of China, 237
Performance art, 144, 349, 369, 370, 378–380, 395
Performance Group, 163, 363
Performers *(see* Acting; Actor)
Peforming arts, characteristics of, 8, 9–10, 14
Performing Garage, 381
Period, 395
Persian Gulf war, 342
Perspective, 263, 302, 395
Perspective scenery, 263, 284, 302–303
Peters, Bernadette, 360
Phaedra (Racine), 280, 283
Phantom of the Opera, The (musical), 81, 109, 360
Phoenix Theater (New York), 29
Phormio (Terence), 226
Piano Lesson, The (Wilson), 154, 354
Picasso, 181
Picasso at the Lapin Agile (Martin), 181
Picture-frame stage, 4, 78–82, 87, 94
    (See also Proscenium stage)
Piñero, Miguel (1947–1988), 373
Pinter, Harold, 29, 190, 348, 366
Pippin (musical), 125, 360
Pirandello, Luigi, 334
Pirates of Penzance, The (Gilbert and Sullivan), 357
Piscator, Erwin, 337
Pit, 263, 271, 294, 395
"Pit, box, and gallery" auditorium, 263, 294, 312, 313, 314
Platform, 395
Platform stage, 84, 196, 242, 252, 269, 271, 278, 283, 395
Plato (427–348 B.C.), 211, 220
Plautus, 147, 224–226, 228, 231
Play About the Baby, The (Miller), 346
Play of Giants, A (Soyinka), 383
Playing area *(see* Ground plan)
Playland (Fugard), 382
Playwright, 9, 13, 14, 31, 68, 73, 143, 144–169, 190
    dramatic focus, 146–147
    dramatic purpose, 147–149

point of view, 174
    tasks of, 145–149
    websites on, 170, 191
    (See also Comedy; Dramatic structure; Tragedy)
Playwrights Horizon, 363
Plimpton, Martha, 317
Plot, 150–151, 158–159, 216–218, 271, 349, 395
Plough and the Stars, The (O'Casey), 329, 330
Poetics (Aristotle), 220, 221
Pojagi (Chong), 372
Point of attack, 395
Point of view of dramatist, 174
Pole-and-chariot system, 262, 263, 264, 295, 300, 302, 303, 313, 395
Polish Laboratory Theater, 163, 351
Political theater, 23, 25, 35, 371
Political spectacle, 90
Polo, Marco, 237
Poor theater, 351, 366, 395
Popular culture, 2, 310, 365, 381, 383
Popular entertainments, 2, 3, 53, 90, 222, 224, 227, 240, 246, 250, 258, 272, 305, 307, 310
    website on, 90
    (See also Amusement parks; Popular theater; Rock and roll)
Popular performance spaces, 90, 224, 227
Popular theater, 237, 239–240, 244–246, 258–260, 298, 305, 307, 310, 356–357
Porgy and Bess (musical), 359
Porter, Cole, 357, 359
Postmodernism, 370, 380, 395
Postmodernist theater, 318, 380–382, 383
Postwar era, 342–344
Powerhouse Theater (Milwaukie), 44
Preparation, 395
Prescriptive criticism, 34, 260, 395
Presence, onstage, 56, 385
Presley, Elvis, 2, 181
Previews, 67
Prida, Dolores, 373
Pride's Crossing (Howe), 46
Prince, 3
Prince, Harold, 113, 358, 360
Private theaters, 270–271, 395
Prizefighting, 224, 227
Problem plays, 189
Proctor, Kristin, 323
Producer, 14, 70–73, 395
Production manager, 199
Projection, vocal, 43–46, 220
Prologue, 396
Prompt, 396
Prompt book, 396
Prompter, 273
Props, 2, 109, 396

Proscenium doors, 295
Proscenium stage, 4, 78–82, 85, 87, 94, 261–263, 283–284, 294, 300, 312, 371, 396
Prose, 179, 180
Protagonist, 168–169, 396
Protagoras, 177
Protestant Reformation, 252, 274
Provincetown Playhouse, 327, 329
PS 122, (New York), 380
Psychophysical actions, 50–51, 52
Public Theater (New York), 55, 108, 355, 356, 373
Public theaters, 267, 269–270, 277, 396
Publicity, 203, 204
Puerto Rican theater *(see* Hispanic theatre)
Puerto Rican Traveling Theater, 373, 385
Pulitzer Prize, 346, 355, 365
Pull, 198, 396
Pulling, 112
Punic Wars, 222
Puppet theater, 244–245
    (See also Bunraku)
Puppets, 2, 3, 237, 244–245, 382
Puritans, 23, 274, 288
Pyant, Paul, 129
Pygmalion (Shaw, 1913), 360
Pythagoras, 176, 211

Racine, Jean, 177, 280, 283, 285
Radio, 362, 384
Ragni, Gerome, 360
Ragtime, 353
Raisin in the Sun, A (Hansberry), 354, 355
Raistrick, George, 331
Rake, 79, 396
Raked stage, 105, 396
Ramírez, Yvette, 373
Rauch, Bill, 67
Rawle, Jeff, 183
Realism, 46–47, 51–52, 81, 100, 101, 318–338, 342–346, 366, 371, 396
    (See also Departures from realism)
Redbird Arena (Illinois), 90
Red Earth Theatre (Seattle), 374
Rees, Roger, 189
Regional theater, 361, 363, 366, 385, 396
Régisseur, 304, 312, 396
Rehearsal, 65–67, 202, 271, 273, 396
Reign of Terror, 297
Reilly, John C., 64
Reinforcement, 136, 396
Reinhardt, Max, 334, 337
Religion, 210, 211, 213, 222, 230, 246, 248, 249
Religious drama *(see* Medieval theater)
Renaissance, 78, 80, 157, 176, 177, 256–285, 313
Rendering, 110, 197, 198
Rent (musical), 136, 361

Repertory, 202, 271, 396
Repertory company, 64, 271, 311
Repertory theater, 271, 311
Representational theater (see Realistic theater)
Reproduction, 135–136, 396
Restoration drama, 288–292, 396
Restoration theater, 23, 168, 288–295, 315
    acting, 292
    background, 28
    comedy, 288–292
    living history: The Country Wife, 291
    theater production, 292, 294–295
    theater space, 294–295
    time line, 290
Revenge tragedy, 228
Reversal, 396
Reviewer, 28–30, 35
Revolution, 288, 297
Revolving stage, 246, 313, 396
Rhinoceros (Ionesco, 1959), 54, 168
Rohe, Kathryn, 198
Rice, Tim, 360, 361
Richard II (Shakespeare), 383
Richard III (Shakespeare), 266
Richards, Lloyd, 354
Richards, Matthew, 128
Richelieu, Cardinal, 283, 284
Ride Down Mt. Morgan, The (Miller), 344
Riders to the Sea (Synge), 329
Ridiculous Theater Company, 370, 378, 385
Rigg, Diana, 176
Right stage, 105, 396
Ringling Brothers and Barnum and Bailey Circus, 90, 125
Rita, Rui, 100
Ritual, 88, 91, 163, 164, 210, 211, 231, 374, 378, 396
Ritz, The (McNally), 378
Rivals, The (Sheridan), 298
Rivera, Josè, 274
Road, The (Soyinka), 383
Robards, Jason, 29
Robbers, The (Schiller), 299
Robbins, Jerome, 359, 360
Robertson, Dennis, 267
Robeson, Paul, 335, 352, 353, 354
Robins, Laila, 152, 365
Robinson, Heather, 114
Rock and roll, 1, 2, 3, 6, 7
    rock concerts, 1–3, 7, 90, 222, 224, 308, 336
    (See also Popular entertainments)
Rock musical, 360
Rodgers, Richard, 357, 359
Rodriguez, Marco, 373
Role-playing, 1, 38, 57
Rolle, Esther, 355
Roman theater, 4, 23, 147, 210, 221–230, 231

acting, 228
comedy, 222, 224–226
culture and, 221–224
decline of, 229–230
dramatic criticism, 34, 228
living history: The Menaechmi, 225
mime, 224, 227, 228
popular entertainment, 221, 222, 224, 227
theater production, 228–229
theater space, 84, 94, 228–229, 230
time line, 223
tragedy, 226, 228
websites on, 231
Roman Theater at Orange, 229
Romance of the Western Chamber, The (Wang Shifu), 238
Romanticism, 299, 308, 396
Romeo and Juliet (Shakespeare), 1, 20, 84, 114, 115, 124, 126, 154, 160, 266, 360, 362
Romeo Must Die (film), 362
Ronstadt, Linda, 125
Roosevelt, Franklin Delano, 329
Roosters (Sanchez–Scott), 373
Rose Bowl (Pasadena), 90
Ross, David, 29
Rostand, Edmond (1868–1918), 186
Roth, Stephanie, 17
Roundabout Theatre (New York), 55, 189, 330
Routes I & 9 (Wooster group), 380
Rover, The (Behn), 289
Rowley, William, 273
Royal Court Theater (London), 346, 382
Royal Hunt of the Sun, The (Shaffer), 103
Royal National Theatre (London), 183, 248
Royal Shakespeare Company (London), 178, 186, 331, 383
Run, 111, 134, 396
Run Little Chillun (musical), 354
Run through, 67, 396
Running, 89, 138
Russian Revolution of 1917, 318
Rwandan civil war, 342
Ryan, Mitchell, 41
Rylance, Mark, 97, 155

Saint Joan (Shaw, 1923), 115, 187
St. Nicholas (McPherson), 383
Salle des machines (see "Hall of Machines")
Saloons, 305
Sanchez-Scott, Milcha, 373
Sanskrit drama, 234–235
Sardou, Victorien, 309
Sartre, Jean-Paul, 157, 348
Satire, 149, 183, 219, 396
Saturday Night Fever (musical), 99
Saturday Night Live (television), 219
Satyr play, 213, 396

Savoy Theater (London), 314
Saxe-Meiningen, George II, duke of, 60, 312, 313, 315
Scaena, 228, 261, 396
Scaena frons, 229, 261
Scary Movie (film), 183
Scenarios, 258
Scene, 396
Scene design, 12–13, 14, 98–111, 119, 120, 197, 262, 263–264, 302–303, 332
    collaborators of designer, 110–111
    elements of, 104
    materials of, 105–109
    objectives of, 98–103
    physical aspects of, 104–105
    process of, 109–110
    special effects in, 107, 108, 109, 138–139
    websites on, 120
Scene designer, 65, 66–67, 68, 69, 73, 98, 120, 332, 197
Scene model, 110, 197
Scene painting, 110, 263, 302
Scenery, 80–81, 88, 98–111, 246, 263, 271, 278, 295, 302–303, 313–314
Schechner, Richard, 349, 351
Schiller, Johann Christoph Friedrich von, 158, 299
Schneider, Alan, 41
School for Scandal, The (Sheridan), 298
Scott, Sir Walter, 28
Screenplay, 148
Screen projection, 103
Scribe, Eugne, 311
Scrim, 107–108, 109, 396
Script, 13, 14, 144, 169, 190, 396
    (See also Dramatic structure; Playwright)
Sea Gull, The (Chekhov), 17, 39, 48, 324, 326, 327
Seascape (Albee, 1974), 168
Seaworld, 3
Second Shepherds' Play, The, 188, 250
Secondary characters, 169
Seeking the Genesis (Corthron), 375
Seldes, Marian, 346
Selective realism, 344–346
Selverstone, Katy, 342
Seneca, 224, 226, 228, 231, 266
Sentimental comedy, 292, 298
Serban, Andrei, 287
Serious Money (Churchill), 383
Set, 197, 396
Set design (see Scene design)
Set piece, 396
Seven Guitars (Wilson), 27, 154, 354
Shaffer, Peter (1926–), 103
Shakespeare, William (1564–1616), 1, 5, 7, 18, 20, 21, 24, 28, 39, 48, 52, 62, 64, 68, 84, 85, 86, 101, 103, 114, 144, 152, 153, 155, 158, 159, 160, 165, 177, 178, 188, 189, 193,

194, 226, 255, 266–267, 268, 272, 273, 277, 285, 288, 292, 299, 308, 320, 332, 352, 353, 362, 382
Shakespeare and Company, 42
Shakespeare Festival Theater (New York), 93
Shakespeare festivals, 4, 24, 193–204
    Ashland, Oregon, 4, 5, 193
    Hudson Valley, 255
    Illinois, 193–204, 298
    New Jersey, 292
    New York, 24, 29, 41, 63, 113
    San Diego, 4
    Stratford, Ontario, 48, 82, 113, 218
    Utah, 24, 267, 279
    websites on, 205
Shakespeare in Love (film), 362
Shakespeare Theater (Stratford Festival, Ontario), 86
Shakespeare Theatre (Washington, D.C.), 146
Shakuntala (Kalidasa), 234
Sharaff, Irene, 113
Shareholders, 271, 279, 396
Sharing plan, 271, 284, 292
Shaw, Fiona, 186, 383, 384
Shaw, George Bernard, 28, 180, 185, 312, 325, 360
She Stoops to Conquer (Goldsmith), 117, 298
Sheep Well, The (Vega), 158, 277
Shelley, Paul, 97
Shepard, Sam, 64, 365–366
Sheridan, Richard Brinsley, 298
Sherin, Mimi Jordan, 126
Shevelove, Burt, 226
Shinto, 240
Short Eyes (Piñero), 373
Shotgun mike, 136
Show Boat (musical), 358
Shuffle Along (musical), 353
Shutters, 263, 283, 284, 295, 302, 303, 313
Sides, 271, 396
Side Man (Warren Leight), 135
Signor, Toni, 126
Silicon-controlled rectifiers, 125
Silkwood (film), 55
Simon, Neil, 185
Simotes, Tony, 42
Simpatico (Shepard), 366
Simultaneous settings, 396
Sinatra, Frank, 90
Singing, 9, 53, 220, 237, 245, 305, 356
Sinise, Gary, 152, 364
Sissle, Noble, 353
Sisters Rosensweig, The (Wasserstein), 374
Six Characters in Search of an Author (Pirandello), 334
Sizwe Banzi Is Dead (Fugard), 382
Skene, 219, 396

Skin of Our Teeth, The (Wilder), 63
Skinner, Kate, 146
Skull in Connemara, A (McDonagh), 383
Slapstick, 181, 183, 260, 280, 379, 396
Slave, The (Baraka), 354
Slave Ship (Baraka), 354
"Slice-of-life" drama, 324
Smith, Anna Deavere, 379–380
Soap Opera (television), 1, 276
Socrates, 176, 182–183, 211, 219, 220
Soldier Field (Chicago), 90
Soldier's Play, A (Fuller), 355
Soliloquy, 39, 101, 260, 396
Solo, 357
Sondheim, Stephen, 226, 360
Song for a Nisea Fisherman (Gotanda), 371
Sony PlayStation, 386
Sophie's Choice (film), 55
Sophocles, 34, 40, 144, 147, 177, 185, 209, 214, 215, 216, 217, 220, 231
Sotoba Komachi (Kan'ami), 241, 242, 243
Sound design, 12–13, 14, 124, 134–139, 140
    objectives of, 134
    recordings, 137–138
    reproduction and reinforcement, 135–136, 396
    special effects in, 138–139
    technology of, 136–138
Sound designer, 65, 66–67, 68, 69, 73, 134, 138, 140, 199
Sound effects, 134, 135, 138–139
Sound of Music, The (musical), 359
South Pacific (musical), 359
Soviet Russia, 23, 318, 320, 337, 342
Sovremennik Theater (Moscow), 324
Soyinka, Wole, 383
Space (Landau), 108
Spacey, Kevin, 32, 55, 362
Spanish theater, 44, 85–86, 256, 274–279, 285, 337
    acting, 278–279
    dramatic forms, 274–277
    golden age, 86, 274
    living history: The King, The Greatest Alcade, 276
    theater production, 277–279
    theater space, 84, 94, 277–278
    time line, 275
    websites on, 285
Spears, Britney, 3
Special effects, 2, 107, 108, 109, 138–139
Spectacle, 3, 80–81, 90, 284, 318
Spectators (see Audience)
Spill, 396
Spine, 50, 63–64, 397
Split Britches, 375
Spore, Richard, 175
Sporting events, 90
Sports arenas, 224, 227

Spotlight, 131, 133
Spring's Awakening (Wedekind), 331
Springsteen, Bruce, 90
Spunk (Wolfe), 355
SRO (standing room only), 397
Stage carpenter, 110
Stage convention, 397
Stage door, 397
Stage house, 219, 220, 397
Stage left, 105, 397
Stage lighting, 124–134, 140
Stage manager, 68–70, 73, 89, 199, 397
Stage picture, 66, 397
Stage right, 105, 397
Stalin, Joseph, 320, 337
Standards, 357
Stanislavski, Constantin, 47–48, 50–52, 56, 57, 189, 327, 332
Stanislavski method, 327, 397
Stanislavski system, 47–48, 50–52, 329
Star Wars (film), 41
Stear, Rick, 179
Steelbound (Touchstone Theatre), 91
Stein, Joseph, 360
Stein, Peter, 102, 308, 383
Steppenwolf Theater Company (Chicago), 152, 364, 366
Stewart, Patrick, 344
Still Life (Mann), 145
Stock characters, 166–167, 187, 228, 258, 260, 289, 292, 397
Stock company, 353
Stock set, 295, 397
Stone, Elise, 336
Stoppard, Tom, 29, 362
"Storm and Stress," 299, 308, 397
Story, 13, 151
    (see also Plot)
Storytelling, 210, 211
Strasberg, Lee, 51–52, 57, 329
Stratford Festival (Ontario), 48, 82, 113, 218
Stratford-upon-Avon, 266
Stravinsky, Igor, 382
Streep, Meryl, 55
Street theater, 91
Streetcar Named Desire, A (Williams), 113, 152, 153, 164, 344, 375
Streisand, Barbara, 90
Strike, 397
Strindberg, August, 46, 152, 157, 165, 188, 318, 321, 323, 324, 329, 330, 331, 338, 344
Strobe light, 138
Stokes-Mitchell, Brian, 359
Stroman, Susan, 59
Structure of play (see Dramatic structure)
Style, design, 98–101
Subplot, 158–159, 397
Subscription company, 325
Subsidized theater, 299, 329, 383

Substance of Fire, The, 113
Subtext, 397
Sueño (Rivera), 274
Sullivan, Arthur, 357
Sullivan, Daniel, 65
Summer stock, 397
Sunday in the Park with George (musical), 360
Sunset Blvd. (musical), 360, 361
Superobjective, 50, 54
Surrealism, 25, 334, 335, 378, 397
Svoboda, Josef, 349
Swamp Dwellers, The (Soyinka), 383
Swan Theater (London), 271
Sweet Charity (musical), 360
Symbolism, 240, 330, 331–332, 397
Synge, John Millington, 329, 338
Synthesis, 54, 56, 189

Tableaux, 54, 62, 164
Tai chi, 52–53
Taihei Shojo, 233
Take a Giant Step (Patterson), 354
Tale of Genji, The (Murasaki), 242
Tamburlaine (Marlowe), 264
Taming of the Shrew, The (Shakespeare, 1593–1594), 193–204, 359
Tantalus (Barton), 119
Tape recording, 6
Tartuffe (Molière), 149, 173, 182, 183, 184, 279, 280, 282
Taylor, Joseph Lyle, 135
Taymor, Julie, 11, 287, 380, 381
Teale, Owen, 166
Teaser, 397
Teatro de la Esperanza (California), 373
Teatro de la Gente (California), 373
Teatro Farnese (Parma), 261, 262
Teatro Olimpico (Vicenza), 261
Teatro Repertorio Español (New York), 373
Teatro Vista (Chicago), 373
Technical, 397
Technical director, 110, 197, 199, 397
Technical rehearsal, 67, 110, 201, 202, 397
Technical staff, 194, 199
Telegraphic language, 334, 348
Television, 1, 3, 4, 5, 6, 7, 10, 11, 13, 20, 29, 55, 109, 147, 148, 187, 219, 221, 222, 276, 308, 324, 330, 346, 349, 362, 384, 385, 386, 387
Tempest, The (Shakespeare), 18, 382
Terence, 147, 224, 226, 228, 231, 246
Tetralogy, 397
Text, 13, 14, 144, 169, 174, 190 (*see also* Dramatic action; Script; Playwright)
Texts for Nothing (Beckett), 369

Theater:
  as art form, 7–10, 14
  basic elements of, defined, 10–14
  as collaborative art, 14, 19
  defined, 4
  and mass media, 362, 384, 386
  origins of, 210–211
  visual aspects, 12–13
Theater, government regulation, 294, 299
Theater administration, 14
Theater for a New Audience (New York), 273, 382
Theater-in-the-round (*see* Arena stage)
Theater of the absurd, 190, 342, 346–349, 366, 397
Theater of cruelty, 25, 335–336, 397
Theater of the Ridiculous (*see* Ridiculous Theater Company)
Theater riots, 307–308
Theater spaces, 12, 13, 14, 24, 77, 78–94
  all purpose and experimental space, 93, 94
  arena stage, 12, 78, 87–89, 90, 94, 390
  created or found space, 78, 91–92, 94, 333, 393
  multifocus, 92–93, 94
  popular performance, 90, 224, 227
  proscenium stage, 4, 78–82, 85, 87, 94, 261–263, 283–284, 294, 300, 312, 371, 396
  thrust stage, 78, 82–87, 93, 94, 196, 220, 371, 397
  websites on, 94–95
Théâtre d'Art, 331
Théâtre de l'Oeuvre, 331
Théâtre du Marais, 283, 284
Théâtre Libre, 325, 331
Theatricalism, 332–333, 397
Theme, 397
Theme parks (*see* Amusement parks)
Thérèse Raquin (Zola), 325
Theresienstadt, 337
Thespian, 211, 397
Thespis, 211
Thomas, Richard, 123
Three Musketeers, The, 194
Three Sisters, The (Chekhov), 55, 324, 380
Three Tall Women (Albee), 346
Thrust stage, 78, 82–87, 93, 94, 196, 220, 371, 397
Thumbnail sketch, 109
Thymele, 219
Tibet, festivals, 88
Ticket sales, 203
Tilt, 132, 397
Tiny Alice (Albee), 123
Tirado, Cándido, 373
Tiramani, Jenny, 97
Tiring house, 270, 278, 397
Toilet, The (Baraka), 354

Tokugawa Ieyasu, 244
Tokugawa period, 244
Toller, Ernst, 335, 337
Tom Patterson Theatre (Canada), 82
Tommy Tune Tonight, 125
Torch Song Trilogy (Fierstein), 378
Torelli, Giacomo, 262, 264, 302
Torres, Omar, 373
Total theater, 312
Totalitarianism, 320, 337, 370
Touchstone Theatre, 91
Town Hall, New York, 143
Trade, 297
Tragedy, 174–180, 185, 188, 190–191, 318, 397
  Greek, 174, 176, 177, 211–221, 231
  modern, 177, 179–180, 189–190
  Renaissance, 176, 177, 260, 264–266, 280, 283
  and society's point of view, 176–177
  traditional, 177–179
  (*See also* Tragicomedy)
"Tragedy and the Common Man" (Miller), 179
Tragic circumstances, 178
Tragic flaw, 178, 397
Tragic heroes and heroines, 178, 179, 185
Tragic responsibility, 178
Tragic verse, 178, 180
Tragicomedy, 182, 185, 188–189, 324, 349, 398
Trap, 270, 398
Treadmill, 106
Treasure Island (Hotel), 4
Trestle stage, 84
Trilogy, 214, 398
Trinity Repertory Theatre (Providence, R.I.), 126
Trip to Coontown, A (musical), 353
Trouble in Mind (Childress), 354
True West (Shepard), 64, 365
Truth or Dare (film), 2
Tune, Tommy, 4, 360
Tupac Shakur, 3
Turntable, 106
Twelfth Night (Shakespeare), 24, 266
Twilight: Los Angeles, 1992 (Smith), 125, 379
Two Gentlemen of Verona (Shakespeare), 21
Two Trains Running (Wilson), 154
Tyler, Royall, 298
Tyrone Guthrie Theater (Minneapolis), 86, 93, 145
Tyson, Cicely, 41

Ubu Roi (Jarry), 332
Uncle Vanya (Chekhov), 189–190, 324
Unit set, 332, 398
Unities, 260, 398

Unity, 398
Universal studios, 3
University theater, 24
Upstage, 105, 106, 398
Usher, 204
Utah Shakespeare Festival, 24, 267, 279

Vaccaro, John, 378
Vagina Monologues, The (Ensler), 55
Vakhtangov, Yevgeny, 334
Valdéz, Luis, 372, 373
Valenciennes, passion play at, 252
Valley Song (Fugard), 382
Valtinos, Grigoris, 209
Variety theater, 183, 237, 305, 307
Vaudeville, 307, 310, 333, 356–357
VCR, 1
Vega, Lope de, 158, 159, 276, 277, 285
Venetian Opera house, 263
Venice Preserved (Otway), 304
Venus (Parks), 375
Verisimilitude, 260
Vernacular drama, 248
   (*See also* Medieval theater)
Verse, 44, 179, 180, 185, 264, 267, 271
VH1 awards, 90
Victory Gardens (Chicago), 366
Video projections, 108–109, 381
Video tape, 20, 62
Vietnam war, 342
View from the Bridge, A (Miller), 29,
   42, 344
Viewpoint, 174
Viewpoints theory, 52
Village People, The, 2
Village Voice, 32, 386
Visual arts, 8–9, 14, 62
Visual composition, 66
Vocal coach, 68, 194
Vogel, Paula, 148
Voice training, 43–46
Volpone (Jonson), 165, 273

Wagner, Richard, 312, 313
Wagner, Robin, 99
Wagon, 106, 250, 251
Wagon stage, 84, 250, 251, 398
Waiting for Godot (Beckett), 29, 99,
   163, 190, 347, 348, 349, 350
Walker, George, 353
Walker Museum (Minneapolis), 380
Walpole, Horace, 174
Wanamaker, Zoë, 156
Wang Shifu, 238
War of the Worlds (radio drama), 362

Warchus, Matthew, 64
Ward, Douglas Turner, 355
Warner, Deborah, 383–384
Warsaw Pact, 342
Washington, George, 272
Washington Square Players, 329
Wasserstein, Wendy, 148, 363, 374
Waste Land, The (Eliot), 384
Waterman, Mark, 160
Waters, Ethel, 354
Way of the World, The (Congreve), 168,
   292, 293
Websites:
   acting, 57
   criticism and theater reviews, 35
   design, 120
   directing, 74
   history:
      Asia, 253
      Eighteenth and Nineteenth
         century, 315
      Greece and Rome, 231
      Medieval, 253
      Renaissance, 285
      modern and contemporary
         theater, 338, 367, 387–388
      playwriting, 170, 191
      popular entertainments, 90
   Shakespeare festivals, 205
      theater spaces, 94–95
Webber, Andrew Lloyd, 360, 361
Webster, John, 273
Wedekind, Frank Benjamin, 331
Weeden, Derrick, 151
Weimar court theater, 304
Weir, The (McPherson), 383
Weiss, Peter, 346
Welles, Orson, 29, 329, 354, 362
Well-made play, 309, 398
Wendland, Mark, 126
Wenning, T. H., 29
Wertenbaker, Timberlake, 377
West End (London), 365
West Side Story (musical), 115, 360
When We Dead Awaken (Ibsen), 330
When Pigs Fly (musical), 118
Whistle Down the Wind (musical), 361
White, Julie, 100
Whitney Houston Bodyguard Tour
   (concert), 125
Who's Afraid of Virginia Woolf? (Albee),
   29, 346
Widower's Houses (Shaw), 325
Wild west shows, 310
Wilde, Oscar, 185

Wilder, Thornton (1897–1975), 168
Will Rogers Follies, The (musical),
   125, 360
Williams, Bert, 353
Williams, Shelly, 117
Williams, Tennessee (1911–1983), 7, 39,
   68, 152, 168, 188, 341, 344, 366
"Willing suspension of disbelief," 22
Wilson, August, 26, 27, 41, 51, 154, 354
Wilson, Lanford, 148, 363
Wilson, Robert (1944–), 53, 54, 62,
   164, 364
Wings, 263, 283, 284, 295, 302, 313, 398
Winter's Tale, The (Shakespeare), 41
Wisdom Bridge Theater (Chicago), 366
Wiz, The (musical), 355
Wogerbauer, Ferdinand, 102
Wolfe, George C., 355, 356, 361
Women's Experimental Theatre, 375
Wong, B.D., 371
Wood, Frank, 135
Woodruff, Robert, 273
Woodward, Joanne, 175
Woodward, Tim, 155
Wooster Group, 63, 163, 363, 380–381
Work lights, 398
Works Progress Administration
   (WPA), 329
World War I, 318, 329, 334, 335, 342,
   344, 357
World War II, 329, 334, 337, 342, 348,
   352, 370
Would-Be Gentleman, The (Molière,
   1670), 168
Wrestling, 224
Wright, Richard, 354
Wycherley, William, 60, 185, 288, 291

Xiqu, 240
(*see also* Peking opera)

Yale Repertory Theatre (New Haven), 375
Yale School of Drama, 55, 128, 354
Yard, 270, 278, 398
Yeats, William Butler, 218, 332
Yerma (García Lorca), 337
Yoo, Mia, 119

Zanni, 258, 398
Zeami Motokiyo, 240, 242
Zipprodt, Patricia, 113
Zola, Émile, 324
Zoom spotlight, 133
Zoot Suit (Valdéz), 373
Zuber, Catherine, 17